SAP FI/

Demystified

Questions & Answers

SAP FI/CO
Demystified
Questions & Answers

By
V. Narayanan

BPB PUBLICATIONS
B-14, CONNAUGHT PLACE, NEW DELHI-1

FIRST EDITION 2008

Copyright © 2008 BPB PUBLICATIONS, INDIA.

ISBN 10 : 81-8333-231-5
ISBN 13 : 978-81-8333-231-6

Distributors:

COMPUTER BOOK CENTRE
12, Shrungar Shopping Centre, M.G. Road,
BANGALORE-560001 Ph: 25587923,
25584641

MICRO BOOKS
Shanti Niketan Building, 8, Camac Street,
KOLKATTA-700017 Ph: 22826518/9

BUSINESS PROMOTION BUREAU
8/1, Ritchie Street, Mount Road,
CHENNAI-600002 Ph: 28410796, 28550491

BPB PUBLICATIONS
B-14, Connaught Place, NEW DELHI-110001
Ph: 23325760, 23723393, 23737742

BPB BOOK CENTRE
376, Old Lajpat Rai Market, DELHI-110006
PH: 23861747

MICRO MEDIA
Shop No. 5, Mahendra Chambers,150 D.N. Rd,
Next to Capital Cinema V.T. (C.S.T.) Station,
MUMBAI-400001 Ph.: 22078296, 22078297

DECCAN AGENCIES
4-3-329, Bank Street,
HYDERABAD-500195 Ph: 24756400, 24756967

INFO TECH
G-2, Sidhartha Building, 96 Nehru Place,
NEW DELHI-110019
Ph: 26438245, 26415092, 26234208

INFO TECH
Shop No. 2, F-38, South Extension Part-1
NEW DELHI-110049
Ph: 24691288

Published by Manish Jain for BPB Publications, B-14, Connaught Place, New Delhi-110 001 and Printed by him at Akash Press, New Delhi.

Dedication

To my dear wife: Meena

Trademark Acknowledgement

'**SAP**' is the registered trademark of SAP, AG. **SAP's trademarks and copyrights are duly acknowledged**. SAP AG is not the publisher of this book, and is not responsible for the views mentioned in this book.

Disclaimer

The contents of this book are the views of the author, together with inputs from his friends' experiences in consulting in SAP. The views expressed in this book should not be construed as that SAP. Omissions and factual inaccuracies, if any, to correctly depict SAP in the book, are purely incidental without any maleficent intention.

About the Author

A Post Graduate in Science, a Chartered Financial Analyst (CFA) and a Project Management Professional (PMP), V. Narayanan has more than two decades of work experience in accounting, banking, finance and Information Technology. Trained in SAP FI/CO, he is a practicing SAP FI/CO Consultant-cum-Project Manager. He has been instrumental in managing SAP implementations (new, roll-outs, upgrades etc) for a number of international Clients. Experienced in various versions of R/3 as well as SAP ERP and New Dimension Products of SAP, he currently works in 'SAP Consulting', in one of the Multinational IT Consulting Companies in India. Trained by Thames Valley University of UK, he is also a Professional Trainer and a Visiting Faculty in the areas of ERP, SAP, Banking etc.

Armed with an excellent understanding of SAP Financial Accounting and Controlling, and with good cross-module expertise, he has authored a best-selling book on SAP FI Transactions, a one of its kind!

Acknowledgment

A book like this requires a lot of inputs from experts so that the end-product is authentic. I have been fortunate enough to have a number of SAP experts, cutting across various functional and technical modules, as my friends and well wishers who were more than willing to provide me with helpful tips, clarifications and reviews in shaping up the several questions presented in this book. I have consciously avoided listing them here for the simple reason that it may be possible that inadvertently I leave one or more names, and that may look inappropriate in spite them helping me. Instead, I extend a loud 'thanks' to all of them.

As you will see inside the book, very uncommon to a book like this, I have peppered the entire volume with a large number of screen-shots taken from SAP application for easy understanding. Thanks to Mr. Hariharan of Maagnus Infotech, Chennai, India for allowing me to make use of their SAP system for generating these screen-shots.

I certainly need to thank Mr. Manish Jain of BPB Publishers for suggesting bringing out a book like this, which I was not even contemplating earlier.

Preface

Like my earlier book (*SAP FI: Transactions Made EASY*), this book is also different from the rest of the lot in the market: this one aims at providing an *all-round enrichment* of knowledge in SAP though the title mentions only FI/CO of SAP. The reason: unless you know the related components in SAP, it will be very difficult to comprehend SAP FI/CO. Yes, the focus is on FI/CO; but there are numerous other areas covered here to provide you with a bird's eye view of the related modules, sub-modules and components.

The book unravels the complexity of SAP FI/CO application and some of the related modules, through numerous '**Q**uestions & **A**nswers' in each of the crucial areas. The questions are collected, grouped and explained in a logical way so that you progress seamlessly from the basic to the advanced topics. Still, should you find it difficult to visualize what is dealt in a particular question / answer: there is help by way of numerous illustrations in the form of screen-shots, diagrams, flow charts et throughout the book. The screen-shots (taken out of SAP R/3 4.70 Enterprise and SAP ERP ECC6.0), in particular, will help you to comprehend as if you are in-front of a computer running the application!

The contents of the book are arranged in 10 sections:

1. SAP basics
2. ABAP & Basis
3. Project Implementation
4. Financial Accounting
5. Controlling
6. Logistics
7. Miscellaneous
8. SAP Tables
9. SAP Transaction Codes
10. SAP Terminology

The section, '**SAP basics** focuses on the evolution of SAP from a small accounting software to its current stature as the most preferred enterprise computing and management application. All you nee to know about the current offerings from SAP are outlined here.

The 2nd section, '**ABAP & Basis**', is on the technical side of the application. It is true that a functional consultant *may* not need to know the technical side of the application, in deep. But, it is necessary and often helpful that you have some idea on this area to appreciate how the application works and to comprehend some of the technical jargons you will come across.

Why there is a section on '**Project Implementation**' in a book like this? SAP implementation is a complex piece of work and you need to know every 'tip' and 'trick' to contribute to the successful completion of a project. You will find answers, in this section, for many of the questions which were unanswered earlier.

The 4ᵗʰ section, '**Financial Accounting**', has the most number of questions (213 to be exact), compared to other sections of this book. This section is sub-divided into:

- General
- Global & Enterprise Settings
- General Ledger Accounting
- Accounts Receivable
- Accounts Payable
- Asset Accounting

Though it is very difficult to cover the *entire* '**Controlling**' in a book like this, an attempt has been made to provide as much information as possible in this section. The following areas within CO are covered here:

- General Controlling
- Cost Element Accounting
- Cost Centre Accounting
- Internal Orders

It would really become difficult to understand FI/CO, without understating how other modules are *integrated* with this. Hence, a section titled '**Logistics**' is also included to provide an overview of the most important components viz., *Sales & Distribution (SD), Materials Management (MM) and Production Planning (PP)*, their organization and integration with SAP FI/CO.

There is a '**Miscellaneous**' section covering some of the interesting questions which may not strictly fall into any one of the other sections. You will find some very useful clarifications here.

Besides the questions, you will also see two sections dedicated for '**SAP Tables**' and '**SAP Transaction Codes**', grouped application component-wise / functionality-wise which will certainly act as a reference. Unlike an alphabetical listing of Transaction Codes / Tables which is the convention, this book attempts something functional and useful: these information are arranged the way you need, as most of the time you may not know the transaction code or Table to look at, but you know the functionality or task for which you are trying to find the table or transaction code.

Another useful add-on is the last section, '**SAP Terminology**', which comes at the end of the book, just before the Index. An alphabetical list of concepts, terminology and usage specific, mostly to SAP, this nearly-100 page section will prove to be your 'ready-reckoner' and 'one-point-reference' should you need a clarification. Yes, it may not be the *complete* listing, but you will appreciate that it covers the most important ones within the scope of this book.

How to use this book?

The answer is simple. Read in any way you want. Pick-up a section and read or simply pick-up a question, go to the relevant page and see the answer. Use the book as a reference or a study-guide or a just a reading material, but make sure you understand a particular question or concept before moving on to the next.

The answers to all the 472 questions enumerated in this book, will certainly improve your understanding of the subject, whether it is for job interviews in SAP, especially in FI/CO, or just to use the application in a better manner in your current job or the one you are aspiring for.

Table of contents

SAP Basics

1

SAP Basics

1. What is 'SAP'?

SAP is an acronym for '*Systeme, Anwendungen, Produkte der Dataenverarbeitung*' in German language, meaning '**Systems, Applications and Products in Data Processing**'. Founded in 1972, SAP - with its headquarters in Walldorf, Germany - is the global market leader in collaborative, inter-enterprise business solutions (shortly, 'business software'). SAP employs close to 40,000 employees worldwide, with more than 100,000 installations in about 40,000 companies in 120 countries. More than 12 million users make use of SAP on a day-to-day basis. There are more than 20 industry- specific 'Industry Solutions', popularly called as 'IS' (IS-Oil, IS-Retail, IS-IS-Bank etc).

2. Tell me more about (the history of) SAP.

- SAP was founded by five former IBM employees, in *1972*, to develop a standard business application software, with an idea of processing business information in real-time. The company, *SAP GmbH,* was started at *Mannheim, Germany.*
- During *1973*, the company brought out the first financial accounting software called, '*R1*' with the letter 'R' standing for '*Real-Time Processing*'.
- Close to the end of Seventies, SAP '*R/2*' was rolled out with IBM's database and a dialog-oriented business application.
- R/2 was further stabilized during the early years of Eighties; and the company came out with the version capable of processing business transactions in *multi-language,* and *multi-currency* to meet its international clientele.
- SAP GmbH became *SAP AG* in 1988. Later on, the company established subsidiaries in countries like US, Sweden, Denmark and Italy.
- Nineties saw the introduction of SAP '*R/3*', with the *Client-server architecture* and *GUI* which would run on almost any of the databases, and on most of the operating systems. SAP R/3 heralded a new era in enterprise computing, moving from '*main frame*' to *3-tier architecture* (Database-> Application -> User interface), and this had become the industry-standard from then on.
- By *1996*, the company had more than 9,000 installations world-wide. By close of Nineties, SAP brought out the *e-commerce* enabled *mySAP* suit of products for leveraging the *ever* expanding web technology.

- Twenty first century, for SAP, started with the ***Enterprise Portal*** and role-based access to business information.
- SAP continues to evolve and innovate, bringing cutting edge technologies for business information processing. SAP has already brought in SAP ***NetWeaver*** based on *Enterprise Services Architecture (ESS)* with application integration across diverse platforms for providing a one-stop end-to-end business processing. With NetWeaver, companies can now really integrate people, information and processes.

3.   What are all the 'Solutions' currently available from SAP?

As of now, the **SAP Solutions** include the following:
- SAP ERP
- SAP Business Suite
- SAP R/3 & R/3 Enterprise
- SAP for Industries
- SAP xApps
- SAP Solution Manager

4.   What are all the components of 'SAP ERP' Solution?

- SAP ERP Central Component (ECC 6.0)
- SAP SEM (Strategic Enterprise Management) (SEM 6.0)
- SAP cProject Suite (Project and Portfolio Management 4.0)
- SAP SRM for ERP (SRM 5.0)
- SAP Catalog Content Management (CCM 2.0 for ERP 2004)
- SAP Internet Sales for ERP

5.   What is the significance of 'SAP NetWeaver' platform?

SAP **NetWeaver** platform allows organizations to build new business solutions rapidly while realizing more business value from existing IT investments. SAP NetWeaver supports new cross-functional business processes and helps to lower the ***Total Cost of Ownership (TCO)*** by reducing the need for custom integration. It offers complete life-cycle management for all of your applications. It is also the foundation for ***Enterprise Services Architecture (EAS)*** and helps align people, information, and business processes across organizational and technological boundaries.

6.   What are all the components of 'NetWeaver'?

Providing an open integration and application platform thereby permitting the integration of the *Enterprise Services Architecture*, **SAP NetWeaver** helps in unifying business processes across technological boundaries, integrating applications for your employees as needed, and accessing / editing simple information easily and in a structured manner.

The following are the components:
- ***Security***
- ***People Integration***
  - o   Multi-channel access

     o   Portal

     o   Collaboration

- ***Information Integration***
  - o   Business Intelligence
- ***BI (Business Intelligence) Content***
  - o   Knowledge Management
  - o   Master Data Management
- ***Process Integration***
  - o   Integration Broker
  - o   Business Process Management
- ***Application Platform***
  - o   Java
  - o   ABAP
  - o   Business Services
  - o   Connectivity
  - o   DB and OS abstraction
  - o   SAP Knowledge Warehouse
- ***Life Cycle Management***
  - o   Customizing
  - o   Software Change Management
  - o   System Management

7.   What are all the components of 'SAP Business Suite'?

- SAP Customer Relationship Management (CRM 5.0)
- SAP Supply Chain Management (SCM 5.0)
- SAP Supplier Relationship Management (SRM)
  - o   SAP SRM 2007
  - o   SAP Catalog Content Management (SRM-MDM 1.0)
- SAP Product Life Cycle Management
  - o   SAP Product Life Cycle Management 4.00
  - o   SAP Environment. Health & Safety 2.7B
  - o   SAP PLM Recipe Management 2.1
  - o   Audit Management
- SAP Compliance Management for SOA
  - o   Management of Internal controls 1.0
- SAP Learning Solution 2,00
- SAP Strategic Enterprise Management (SEM)

8.   What are all the recent Releases in 'SAP R/3' Solution?

- SAP R/3 Enterprise Release 4.70
- SAP R/3 Release 4.6C / 4.6B / 4.5B / 4.0B

9. What are all the 'Industry Solutions' (IS) from SAP?

There are 22 **Industry Solutions** available from SAP. They are:
- SAP for Aerospace & Defence
- SAP for Automotive
- SAP for Banking
- SAP for Consumer Products
- SAP Contract Accounts Receivable & Payable
- SAP for Defence and Security
- SAP for Engineering. Construction & Operations
- SAP for Financial Service Provider
- SAP for Healthcare
- SAP for Higher Education and Research
- SAP for High Tech
- SAP for Insurance
- SAP for Media
- SAP for Mill Products
- SAP for Mining
- SAP for Oil & Gas
- SAP for Professional Services
- SAP for Public Sector
- SAP for Retail
- SAP for Telecommunications
- SAP for Utilities
- SAP for Wholesale Distribution

10. What is 'SAP xApps'?

The **SAP xApps** family of composite applications enables continuous business innovation and provides the flexibility necessary to respond quickly and profitably to business change. They extend the value of your core business investments and maximize the return on your strategic assets: employees, knowledge, products, business relationships, and IT.

SAP and SAP certified partners deliver these composite applications that drive specialized business processes, provide comprehensive business insights, and focus on the needs of a variety of industries.

All these applications combine Web services and data from multiple systems, in an application design made possible by the *SAP Composite Application Framework* within the *SAP NetWeaver* technology platform. This framework includes the methodology, tools, and run-time environment to develop composite applications. It provides a consistent object model and a rich user experience, and gives developers a productive way to create composite applications on top of a set of heterogeneous applications.

11. What are all the components of 'SAP xApps'?

- Duet

- SAP Document Builder
- SAP Global Trade Services
- SAP xApp Manufacturing Integration and Intelligence
- SAP xApp Resource and Portfolio Management
- SAP xApp Product Definition
- SAP xApp Cost and Quotation Management
- SAP xApp Integrated Exploration and Production
- SAP xApp Sales and Operations Planning

12.   What is known as 'Duet'?

A component under SAP xApps, '**Duet**' is a first-of-its-kind software solution from SAP and Microsoft that enables users to easily and quickly interact with SAP business processes and data via their familiar Microsoft Office environment. The result of a groundbreaking collaboration between SAP and Microsoft, it is the first joint product created by these two industry leaders and is designed to revolutionize how Information Workers interact with enterprise applications.

Duet enables:

- **Budget Monitoring**: Schedule time-critical alerts and notifications to monitor cost centers or internal orders, delivered directly to your Microsoft Outlook.
- **Demand Planning**: Create and use planning sheets, as well as analyze and manage demand planning data from the SAP System using your Microsoft Excel.
- **Duet Reporting**: Schedule reports to be delivered regularly to your Microsoft Outlook, receive individual reports on an as-needed basis and view reports in your Microsoft Excel.
- **Leave Management**: Add leave requests as Microsoft Outlook calendar items that integrate approval guidelines in the SAP System and enterprise-defined processes.
- **Sales Management:** Manage CRM accounts and contacts, create business activities and access sales analytics information using your Microsoft Outlook.
- **Team Management**: Access up-to-date information about yourself and employees, open positions, and organizational structures that are integrated from the SAP System into your Microsoft Outlook contacts area.
- **Time Management:** Record time in your Microsoft Outlook calendar, streamlining time entry while ensuring time-reporting compliance in the SAP System.
- **Travel Management**: Create a travel request and a travel expense report in the SAP System using your Microsoft Outlook.

13.   Explain 'SAP Document Builder'.

SAP Document Builder (CA-GTF-DOB) is a content-driven and cross-application solution for building and authoring complex documents. As a generic tool, it can be deployed within international organizations and large corporations to generate contract and bid invitation documents, banking-related documents, auto insurance policies, real estate contracts, and corporate employment policies.

You can deploy SAP Document Builder as a standalone application or integrate it with other SAP or non SAP components. For example, you can generate business documents required in a procurement system and store them in an electronic data storage system.

The SAP Document Builder supports you in several ways:

- Automating and streamlining the document creation process
- Enforcing best practices
- Building documents reflecting your company-specific styles and formats from one or more regulation sets.
- Determining inclusion or exclusion of clauses based on legal regulations by means of rules.

14.   Explain 'SAP Solution Manager'.

Providing a central access to *Tools, Methods and Pre-Configured Content*, **SAP Solution Manager** supports throughout the life-cycle of solutions from Business Blueprint to Configuration to Support.

The features include:

- *Implementation / Upgrade of SAP Solutions*
  - o   Central access to Project Tools (Project Administration, Business Blueprint, Configuration, Test Workbench, Group Rollout Templates)
  - o   Central management of Project Information (Roadmap, System Landscape, Documentation etc)
  - o   Enables comparing / synchronizing customizing in several SAP components
- *Solution Monitoring*
  - o   Central System Administration
  - o   System Landscape Analysis with System Level Reporting
  - o   Real-time System Monitoring
  - o   Business Process Monitoring
- *Services and Support*
  - o   Access to programs / services for monitoring and optimizing system performance and availability so as to minimize risks.
- *Service Desk*
  - o   Solution Support through Work Flow to create and manage Process / Problem Messages.
- *Change Management*
  - o   Trace and audit system changes and transports through Change Request Management.

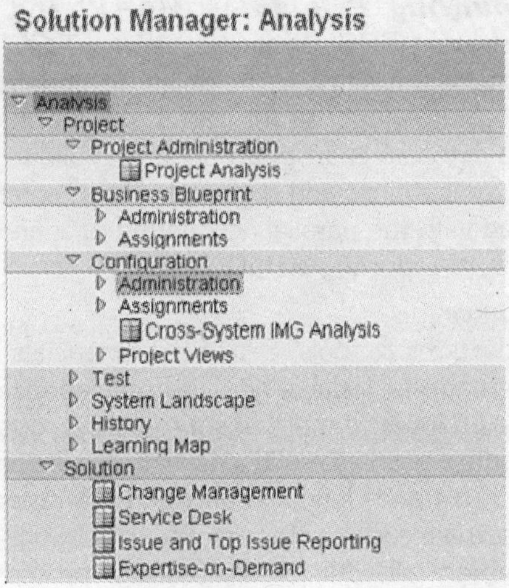

Figure 1: SAP Solution Manager

15. Explain how 'SAP ERP Financial 'Accounting' is better / different than 'R/3 Financial Accounting'.

SAP ERP Financials Accounting is built on ***NetWeaver*** platform which is the foundation for service-oriented business solutions, for deploying financial processes at a faster phase. Irrespective of the type business you are in, this is designed to support your financial accounting requirements with an idea of giving you a single complete platform to achieve excellence in accounting, performance management, financial supply chain, and corporate governance:

- *Industry Specific Financial Management*
  It provides a comprehensive and robust analytical framework to consolidate and/or dissect business information generated in your industry solutions or your core enterprise processes: all managers in all operations of your business will now have an improved visibility with a single integrated solution.

- *Performance Management*
  It provides a single solution for the entire life cycle of 'Corporate Performance Management' by delivering real-time, personalized measurements and metrics to improve business insight and productivity of non-technical users. You executives, managers, and business workers will now have access to information like business statistics and ***Key Performance Indicators*** (KPI) presented in the context of business tasks for better insight and faster decision making. It encompasses:
  - o Consolidated financial and statutory reporting
  - o Planning, budgeting, and forecasting
  - o Strategy management and scorecards
  - o Risk management
  - o Financial analytics

- *Financial and Management Accounting*
  It helps companies to comply with global accounting standards (like the US ***Generally***

Accepted Accounting Principles (GAAP) and *International Financial Reporting Standards* (IFRS). With the '*New FI-GL*' functionality (Refer to Q.181 for more details) you will now have the ability to generate financial statements of any dimension of the business (unit, profit center, geographical location etc). This offers a greater flexibility to extend a chart of accounts and allows an easier method of reporting by individual management units and segments. Helps companies reducing the complexity and costs associated with the parallel accounting or managing a set of books by region, industry, or regulatory reporting statute.

● *Corporate Governance*
  With a set of applications & tools, SAP ERP Financials Accounting assists in meeting the specific requirements of today's financial regulations such as the *Sarbanes-Oxley Act.* You now have an intuitive mechanism to collect, document, assess, remediate, and attest to internal control processes and safeguards to ensure transparent business activity. By configuring controls and defining rules and tolerances for your business, you can easily customize internal processes for security, reporting, and error prevention. Besides, you can now document all your internal control processes and make them visible to corporate executives, auditors, and regulators.

● *Financial Supply Chain Management*
  Provides the tools to help you manage your financial supply chain and cash-flow cycle more effectively, through end-to-end process support of:
  o   Credit Management
  o   Electronic Bill Presentment and Payment
  o   Collections Management
  o   Dispute Management
  o   In-house Cash Management,
  o   Cash and Liquidity Management
  o   Bank Relationship
  o   Treasury & Risk Management Processes

16.   What is a 'SAP Solution Map'?

SAP ERP besides supporting your most important business processes, also provides tools to help you to understand how these processes work. One such tool is the '**SAP Solution Map**' which is a multilevel blueprint of processes. It helps you to visualize, plan, and implement a coherent, integrated, and comprehensive IT solution; it also shows how various processes are covered, including the processes that SAP and its partners support. With solution maps, you quickly understand business solutions and the business value they can bring.

17.   What is a 'SAP Business One'?

'**SAP Business One**' is the low-cost, easy-to-implement business management solution from SAP, for Small and Medium Enterprises (SME). Unlike the regular ERP software from SAP, this solution gives managers on-demand access to critical real-time information through 'one single system' containing financial, customer relationship management, manufacturing, and management control capabilities. As a result, the solution enables rapid employee productivity, while empowering managers to make better business decisions to stay ahead of the competition. Equipped with a user-friendly interface, SAP Business One serves as your central ERP hub with standard interfaces to internal and external data sources, handheld computers, CRM applications, and other leading analysis tools.

SAP Business One is based on Microsoft Windows standard for making it easier to comprehend and use. The application comes with the 'demo company' which can be used by the implementing company to familiarize the functionalities.

The modules of SAP Business One include:

- Administration
- Financials
- Sales Opportunities
- Sales – A/R
- Purchasing – A/P
- Business Partners
- Banking
- Inventory
- Production
- MRP
- Service
- Human Resources
- Reporting

ABAP & Basis

2

ABAP & Basis

1.   What is 'Basis'?

Basis is a collection of R/3 programs, providing the run-time environment for ABAP/4. Imagine Basis as something 'sitting' in between the ABAP/4 program code and the computer's operating system. Basis reads ABAP/4 program code and interprets the same into operating system instructions; without Basis you will not be able execute any of your ABAP/4 programs.

SAP provides a plethora of tools to administer Basis, which ultimately helps to monitor system configuration, system performance & system maintenance. The Basis administrator is usually called as the 'Basis Consultant'.

2.   Explain the SAP R/3 'System Architecture'.

SAP R/3 is based on a 3-tier **Client-Server** model, represented by:
- Database Layer
- Application Layer
- Presentation Layer

In a 3-tier Client-server model, all the above three layers will be running on three different machines.

The **Database Layer** consists of a RDBMS (Relational Data Base Management System), which accepts the database requests from the *Application Layer*, and sends the data back to the *Application Layer*, which in turn passes on the same to the *Presentation Layer*.

The **Application Layer** or the server interprets the ABAP/4 programs, getting the inputs from them and providing the processed output to them.

The **Presentation Server** or *'Presentation Layer'* is what is installed on a typical workstation of a user. This is nothing but the *SAPGUI*, which when started provides the user with the interface of *SAP R/3* menus. This interface accepts the inputs from the user, passes the same on to the *Application Server*, processes the inputs and sends back the output. If database processing is required, the *Application Server* sends the details to the *Database Layer*, receives the data and then processes the same at the *Application Layer* level and sends back the output to the *Presentation Layer*, wherein the *SAPGUI* may format the data before displaying the same on the screen.

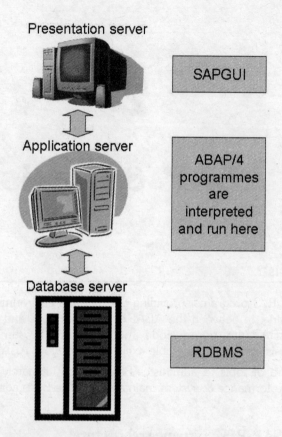

Figure 2: SAP R/3 System Architecture

3.   What is an 'Instance'?

Instance is an administrative unit that groups together components of an SAP R/3 system or simply an *Application Server*, which has its own set of work process. A *Client* can contain many instances. Loosely defined, an instance refers to a server.

Sometimes, the database is also referred to as an 'instance': in this case it is called as the '***Central Instance***'.

4.   What do you mean by 'SAP R/3 System Landscape'?

The **System Landscape**, in SAP, refers to a number of systems and their deployment within an SAP installation. The various systems could be designated as *Development*, *Test* and *Production Clients*.

5.   What is 'R/3 Data Dictionary'?

The **Data Dictionary** is a collection of logical structures of various objects (*Tables*, *Views* or *Structures*) used in application development in SAP, and shows how they are mapped to the underlying *RDBMS* in *Tables/Views*.

6. What is called as 'SAP Business Object'?

SAP Business Object is similar to the real world business objects like a *Sales Order, Invoice, Employee* etc, consisting of various Tables / programs which are related to each other in a business context. All the business objects are maintained in **BOR (Business Object Repository)**.

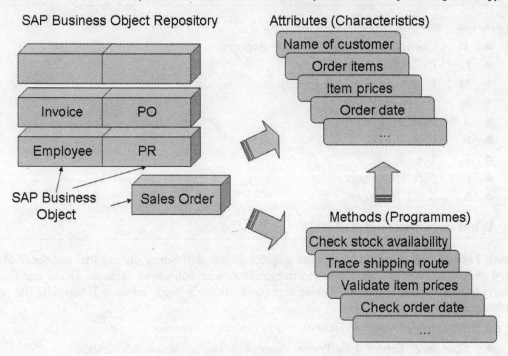

Figure 3: SAP Business Object

The various characteristics of an object are called as the '**Attributes**'. For example, the business object '*Sales Order*' is characterized by the following attributes:

- Date of the order
- Items of the order
- Prices of various items of the order
- Name of the customer to whom the order belongs to

The application program or programs used by the system to change or manipulate a business object is / are known as the '**Method(s)**', in SAP. For example, a program could be used to (a) check the availability of stock to deliver, (b) trace the shipment route, (c) check the item prices, (d) validate the order date etc.

So, attributes & methods are collectively representing the business object in SAP.

7. Explain 'Client-Dependent' and 'Client-Independent' Tables.

There are certain Tables, in SAP, which when changed will not affect a similar Table in other Clients. These are known as '**Client-Dependent**' Tables. All the Client-dependent Tables will have their first field as '**Mandt**'. Example: LFA1.

On the other hand, if a change made in one Table is reflected in a similar Table across various

Clients, then such a Table will be called as '**Client-Independent**'. In this case, the first field of the Table will not be '*Mandt*'. You need to be extra careful when changing the settings or content of these Tables as this will affect all the Clients.

8.   What are all the different 'Types' of 'ABAP/4 Programs'?

There are nine types of ABAP/4 programs in SAP:

- **1**   Executable Programs (ABAP Reports)
- **I**   INCLUDE Program
- **M**   Module Pool / Dialog programs
- **S**   Sub-Routine Pool
- **J**   Interface Pool
- **K**   Class Pool
- **T**   Type Pool
- **F**   Function Group
- **X**   XSLT Program

9.   What are 'Internal Tables'?

Internal Tables are standard data type objects which exist only during the 'runtime' of an ABAP/4 program. They are used to perform calculations on subsets of database Tables and for re-organizing the contents of database Tables according to user's need. Internal Tables fulfil the need for arrays in ABAP/4.

There are three *types* of internal Tables:

- *Standard Tables* with 'linear' index. The key is always 'non-unique'.
- *Sorted Tables* with either 'unique' or' non-unique' key.
- *Hashed Tables* (they do not have linear index) with key defined always as 'unique'.

10.   What is a 'Logical Database'?

A **Logical Database** is a special data retrieval program delivered by SAP, with its own dynamic *Selection Screens*. You need to code only the processing logic (*GET, CHECK* etc). The logical database consists of a 'read' program, in which the structure of the local database is reproduced with a selection screen.

Advantages:

- 'Check' functions to validate that user input is complete and correct
- Meaningful data selection.
- Central authorization checks for database accesses.
- Excellent read access performance while retaining the hierarchical data view determined by the application logic.

11.   What are the two methods of modifying SAP 'Standard Tables'?

You can modify the **SAP Standard Tables** using:

- Append Structures

- Customizing INCLUDES

12. What is 'BDC' Programming in SAP?

BDC (Batch Data Conversion) is an automated procedure for transferring large volume of external or legacy data into SAP system using ***batch input programming***. There are 3 ways of achieving this:

- Call Transaction Method
- Session Method
- Direct Input Method

Irrespective of the method, the techniques uses the following steps:

- Identify the screens of the transaction that the program will process.
- Write a program to build the BDC Table that will be used to submit the data (say, text file) to SAP.
- Submit the BDC Table to the system in the 'batch mode' or as a 'single transaction' by the CALL TRANSACTION command.

The 'Call Transaction' method cannot be used when you want to process multiple transactions. Instead, use 'BDC-insert function' to achieve this.

13. What is 'BAPI'?

BAPI (Business Application Programming Interface) is SAP's standardized application interface for integrating 3rd party applications with SAP's business processes and data thereby providing an entry into the R/3 system. A BAPI may be used to create a 'business object' or to change the attributes of a 'business object'. Note that the assignment of a BAPI to a 'business object' is always 1-to-1.

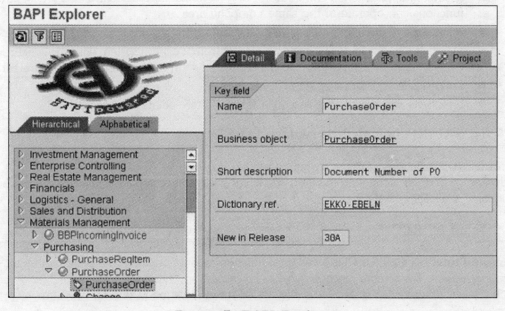

Figure 5: BAPI Explorer

A ***BAPI Explorer*** helps you to move around the collection of BAPIs in the system, which is grouped both hierarchically and alphabetically. For each BPAI in the explorer, you are provided with the several tabs for details, documentation, tools and project (to create new BAPIs).

Example of BAPI:

- Create a Purchase Order
- Change a Purchase Requisition
- Create a Customer
- Display an Invoice

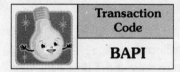

	Transaction Code
	BAPI

14.   What is 'ALE'?

ALE (Application Link Enabling) is used to support the construction and operation of distributed applications, through exchange of data messages ensuring data consistency across loosely coupled SAP applications, using both 'synchronous' and 'asynchronous' communications without a need for central database.

ALE comprises of three layers:

- Application services
- Distribution services
- Communication services

ALE helps to:

- Distribute applications across several SAP systems, so that centralized / decentralized functions can operate in the same company area
- Maintain and distribute master data elements from a central system
- Maintain and distribute control data objects from a central system with the synchronized configuration data (important to decentralize functions yet keep them integrated) ·
- Link R/2 & R/3 systems
- Link SAP and external systems, via **IDocs** (Intermediate Documents)

15.   Is 'SAP XI' intended to replace 'ALE'?

Most of the ALE solutions are custom built with very low degree of re-usability & scalability. The introduction of **SAP XI** along with the *NetWeaver* technology is to replace the ALE with out-of-box functionality available in SAP XI.

16.   What is 'RFC'?

A **Remote Function Call (RFC)** is a call to a 'function module' running in a system different from the 'calling-system'. The remote function can also be called from within the same system (as a 'remote call'), but usually the 'calling-system' and the 'called-system' will be in different systems.

RFC is helps to take care of the following communication:

- Communications between two independent SAP systems

- Client-server communications between an external Client and an SAP system acting as the server
- Client-server communications between an SAP System acting as the Client and an external server

17.   What is 'OLE'?

For Windows front-end, SAP provides interfaces based on Microsoft's **Object Linking and Embedding** Technology **(OLE Automation)** for embedding objects like MS-Excel file.

18.   What is a 'Match Code' in SAP?

Match Codes (now known as **Search Help** effective release 4.6), help to search and retrieve data when key of a record is not known. The technique involves (a) creating a **Match Code Object** (now known as '**Search Help Object**') and (b) specifying a **Match Code ID**. The system helps you to access the match codes (search help) by the following options:

- Keeping the cursor in the field, and then pressing '**F4**'
- Keeping the cursor in the field, clicking the 'right' button on the mouse and then selecting 'possible entries'
- Keeping the cursor in the field and then clicking on the 'magnifying glass'.

19.   What is a 'Drill-down' Report?

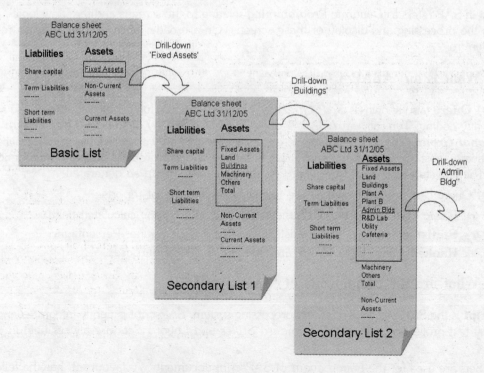

Figure 6: Drill-down report

A **Drill-Down Report**, also called as an ***Interactive Report***, helps to dig into the report to have more details. Imagine that you are looking at a *Balance Sheet*, which is presented as a 'drill-down' report.

The top-most list, also known as the '***Basic List***' contains the top-level information like current assets, fixed assets etc under the grouping 'assets' on one side of the *Balance Sheet*. The 'drill-down' functionality helps you select a line item form the Basic List, for example 'fixed assets', and 'drill–down' further to have a detailed list (***secondary list***) displaying various components of the fixed assets like land, buildings, machinery etc. You may again 'drill-down' further by double-clicking on the 'building' line, which will bring up the next detailed list, and so on.

You will be able to create a 'drill-down' report with maximum 'drill' levels of 20. That is, including the Basic List you will have a total of 21 levels in a single 'drill-down' report.

20.   What is 'ALV' programming in ABAP?

SAP provides a set of **ABAP List viewer** (**ALV**) Function Modules, which can be used to enhance the readability and functionality of any report output. This is particularly useful in a situation wherein the output of a report contains columns extending 255 characters in length. In such cases, this set of ALV functions can help the user to choose and arrange columns from a report output and also save different variants for report display. This is very efficient for dynamically sorting and arranging the columns providing a wide array of display options.

21.   What is 'DynPro'?

DynPro in SAP refers to *Dynamic Programming* relating to the screens and the 'flow logic', which controls the processing and display of these screens. On a broader term, a screen is also referred to as 'DynPro'.

22.   What is an 'ABAP/4 Query'?

ABAP/4 Query (also known as ***SAP Query*** or ***Query***) is a powerful tool to generate simple reports without any coding. Typically an ABAP/4 query is created first by defining a ***User Group*** and a ***Functional Group***. The functional group can either be created with reference to a 'logical' Table or a database Table. Once the functional group is defined, the user group is assigned to the functional group. The last step is to create the query on the functional group so generated.

ABAP/4 Query can be used to create the following three types of reports:

* **Basic List**: A report with basic formatting without any calculated fields.
* **Statistics**: Reports with statistical functions like Average, Percentages.
* **Ranked Lists**: Ranked lists are used for analytical purposes.

23.   What are the components of 'SAPscript'?

SAPscript is the SAP System's own text-processing system. SAPscript is tightly integrated and used for many text-processing tasks. SAP *Standard Styles* and *Layout Sets* are always held in *Client 000*.

Layout Sets are used for the *Page Layout* of SAPscript documents. A 'layout set' has the following elements:

- **Header Data** - Data related to development (created by, development class, etc.) and the layout set information (which elements are used) are both stored in the header data. A start page must be entered here.
- **Paragraph Formats** - Paragraph formats are required in layout sets. However, they are also used for word processing in layout sets, for example, to format text elements.
- **Character Formats** - You can also use character formats to format texts or paragraphs. Unlike paragraph formats, however, they are used to format text within a paragraph.
- **Windows** - Windows are names and window types, which are not physically positioned until they are allocated to pages and units of measurement, are specified.
- **Pages** - Pages are defined to provide the system with a start and end point in text formatting.
- **Page Windows** - Page windows are the combination of windows and pages, where the dimensions of a window and its position on a page are specified.

24.   Why do we need 'Enhancements'?

The standard R/3 application may not offer some of the functionality you need, for a particular customer or for a particular situation. The R/3 **Enhancement** functionality allows adding your own functionality to SAP's standard business applications or modifying the standard one to suit the business need.

The enhancement may be done through:

- *Customer exits*
  Customers' potential requirements, which do not form a part of standard software, are incorporated in the standard R/3 as empty modification 'shells'. Customers can then fill these with their own coding. SAP guarantees that all such exists will remain valid across all future releases. The customer exits include:
  - o   Menu Exits
  - o   Screen Exits
  - o   Function Module Exit
  - o   Keyword Exits
- *ABAP/4 Dictionary Elements*
  These are *ABAP/4 Dictionary Enhancements* (creation of Table Appends), *Text Enhancements* (customer-specific key words and documentation for data elements) and *Field Exits* (creation of additional coding for data elements).

25.   Differentiate 'Screen Painter' from 'Menu Painter'.

Screen Painter is an ABAP Workbench tool to create or modify the screens for your transactions. The screen painter allows you to make modifications to screen attributes, the flow control logic or the layout.

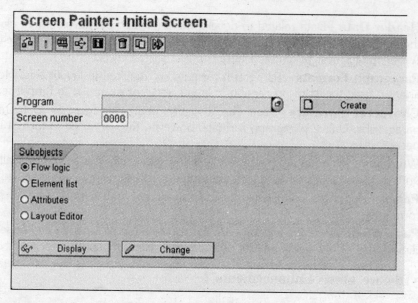

Figure 7: Screen Painter

Transaction Code
SE51

Menu Painter is a tool to design the interface components. Status, Menu Bars, Menu Lists, F-key settings, Functions and Titles are the components of menu painter.

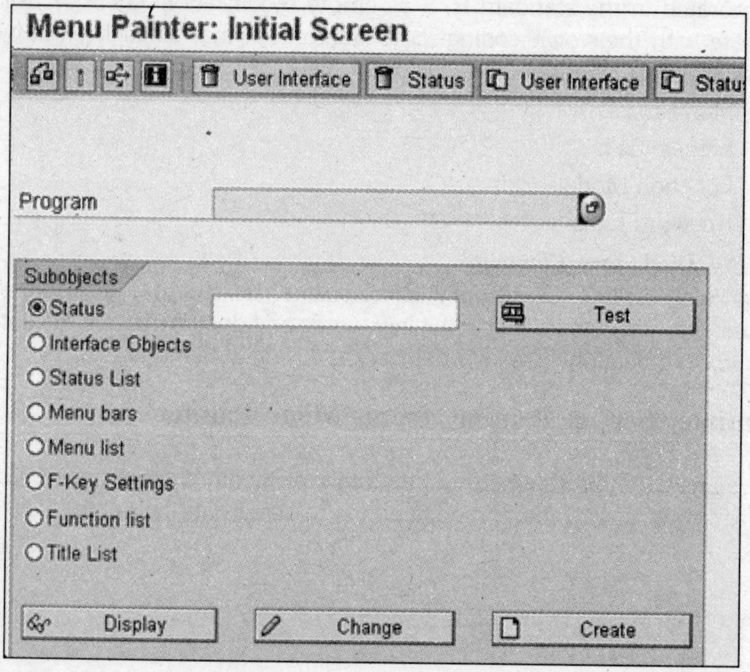

Figure 8: Menu Painter

Transaction Code
SE41

Both the screen painter and menu painter are graphical interface of ABAP/4 applications.

26. What is a 'Modification Assistant'?

The **Modification Assistant** is the tool that offers you support when making modifications to the standard, by branching to a 'special modification mode' whenever you are modifying objects from the standard in an ABAP workbench editor. Originals are initially protected in this mode and can only be changed with the help of the additional 'pushbuttons' that are placed at your disposal.

All changes that you make to the system are logged with the help of the modification assistant. This provides you with a detailed overview of modifications that is easy to read and that dramatically reduces the amount of effort needed to upgrade your system.

The modification assistant offers support in the following areas:
- ABAP Editor
- Class Builder
- Screen Painter
- Menu Painter
- Text Element maintenance
- Function Builder
- ABAP Dictionary

If an object can be edited using the modification assistant, a dialog box appears the first time when you attempt to edit that object informing you that editing functions are limited in modification mode. This dialog box appears exactly once per user for each of the various different kinds of transport objects.

27. What is a 'Spool Request'?

Spool Requests are generated during 'dialog' or 'background' processing and placed in the spool database with information about the printer and print format. The actual data is placed in the *Tem Se (Temporary Sequential objects)*.

28. What is 'CTS'?

Change and Transport System (CTS) is a tool that helps to organize development projects (in the ABAP workbench) and customized data (in customizing), and then move / transport these changes between the SAP Systems / Clients in your system landscape. A typical usage is something like moving the configuration settings from 'development' to 'test' and finally to 'production' Client. The changes (like creation of new Company Code, changing a document type etc) are assigned to a *'transport request'* and transported by the Basis or System Administrator.

29. What is a 'Transport'?

Transport in SAP is nothing but the transfer of R/3 System components from one system to

another. The components to be transported are specified in the object list of a **transport request**.
Each 'transport' consists of an 'export process' and an 'import process':

- The **export process** reads objects from the source system and stores them in a data file at operating system level
- The **import process** reads objects from the data file and writes them to the database of the target system

The system maintains a 'transport log 'of all actions during export and import. '**Transport organizer'** helps in managing the transports in SAP.

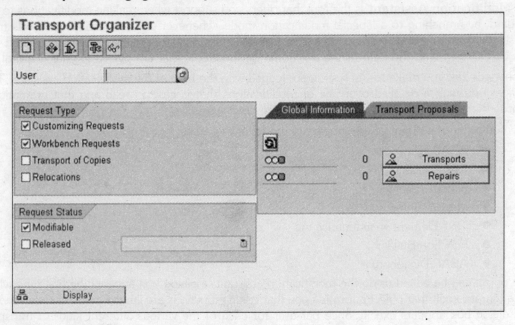

Figure 9: Transport Organizer

Transaction Code
SE10

30.   How do you find out who has 'Transported' a 'Transport Request'?

Look at Table **TPLOG** (go there using the Transaction Code **SE16**) and input the CMDSTRING field the transport name with '*'. **Example: *PZDK980001***

31.   What is an 'Authorization' in SAP?

Authorization is the process of giving someone permission to do or have something. In multi-user SAP systems, a SAP Basis Administrator defines which users are allowed access to the system and what privileges of use (such as access to which transactions etc).

32. Explain the 'Client' concept of SAP.

A **Client** is the top most organizational structure, which has its own set of master records. A Client is denoted by a 3-character alphanumeric code in SAP, and is a mandatory element. The settings made at the Client level, data maintained etc are available across all the Company Codes. A Client should have at least one Company Code defined.

SAP comes delivered with *Clients 001* and *002*, which contain all the default settings. Usually, copying from the default Clients creates additional and new Clients.

Also be aware that in SAP, typically you will have different '*types*' of Clients namely:

1. Development Client
2. Test Client
3. Production Client

In any implementation, it is necessary that you have at least 3 types of Clients as mentioned above. There are some companies where you will have more than three:

- Development Client
- Test Client
- Quality Assurance Client
- Training Client
- Production Client

A '***Development Client***' is also called as 'sand box' Client. Some times this is also termed as 'play' Client. This is the logical place in the SAP system where you will be trying out your new configurations, writing new programs etc. This is the place, as the name goes, wherein you can 'play' around before finalizing a scenario for customization.

Once you are Ok with the configuration or a new program, you will then move the same manually (transport) to the '***Test Client***' where you will carryout all the tests (both modular and integration). The end-users are provided with the training using the 'training' Client. Sometimes both the 'test' and 'training' Client could be in a single 'instance'. The 'quality assurance' Client is the one, which helps to undertake necessary quality checks before some thing is ready to be passed on to the 'production' Client.

After satisfactory results, the same will be transported (automatic) to the '***Production Client***'. You will not be able to make any modifications, manually, to the 'production' Client and the authorization is very limited because of the simple reason that this Client is the one where day-to-day business transactions are happening and any issues here will jeopardize the entire business operations. That is why this is also called as '***live***' Client.

Do not confuse this term with the 'client', which denotes a customer in normal business parlance.

33. How you can find the field / data underlying a 'Transaction'?

The common way of finding out the technical data underlying a transaction is placing the cursor on the field and pressing the key '***F1***', then click on the button '***Technical Data***' to see the details. This is OK as long as you are looking at the 'transparent' Table. In case the information is populated from a 'structure', then this is of no help. Because, the 'structure 'may be populated from a number of sources including some 'includes', and may also contain some calculated fields. If the 'include' is a Table, then the chances are your data comes from that Table. See if there is a 'logical' database in the business area you are looking at. Looking at the 'structure' of the 'logical' database often reveals the Tables used to drive that business area. See if the field name you are looking for is in any of the Tables. Logical databases can also be useful in determining how Tables are linked together.

You may also use other methods (listed below) to zero-in on the field. It is not that you should use these in the order it is listed here. Do any of these, in isolation or in combination till you are able to find out what you are looking for:

- Debugging
- SQL Trace
- Runtime Analysis

Start the 'transaction' in **Debug** mode. Set a 'watch-point' for the structure-field you are interested in. When the debugger 'breaks', look at the lines just above the 'break-point'. This will show where the field was populated. This may be a 'structure', in which case restart the process using that 'structure' for a 'watch-point'.

Switch **SQL Trace** on, and run your transaction. Switch the 'trace' off, and examine the log. This will detail the Tables hit, and the order in which they were hit. Not all Tables hit will be displayed - for example, configuration Tables will not show up, as they are buffered.

The **Runtime Analysis** will show all Tables accessed by the transaction.

ABAP Runtime Analysis: Initial Screen

🔡 Tips & Tricks

Measurement
◉○○   Reliability of Time Values

Short Descriptn

In Dialog		In Parallel Session	
◉ Transaction		⊕ Switch On/Off	
○ Program			
○ Function module		Schedule	
⊕ Execute		⊕ For User/Service	

Measurement Restrictions

Variant   🔲 📖 DEFAULT   From user

🗋 ✂ ✏ 🗑 🗔

Figure 10: ABAP Runtime Analysis

Transaction Code
SE30

34.   Explain 'LSMW'.

The **LSMW (Legacy System Migration Workbench)** is a free SAP-based tool that supports the one-time or periodic transfers of data from non-SAP systems to SAP. The LSMW can be used in conjunction with the **Data Transfer Workbench**. The LSMW assists in organizing your data migration project and guides you through the process by using a clear sequence of steps. The most common conversion rules are predefined. Reusable conversion rules assure consistent data conversion for different data objects.

The LSMW covers the following steps:

- Read the *legacy data* from one or several files (such as spreadsheets or sequential files)
- Convert the data from source format to target format
- Import the data using standard interfaces (***Batch Input, Direct Input, BAPI, IDoc etc***)

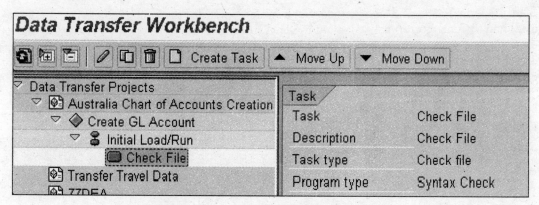

Figure 11: Data Transfer Workbench

35. How to transport 'LSMW' data from one system to another?

There are two ways of doing this:

1. ·***Export / Import method***: you have the flexibility·of subprojects or objects that need to be transported. Use the Menu Path '*LSMW > Extras > Export project*'.
2. ***Transport request***: if you transport this way, you will not be able to select the objects, and the project as a whole is transported. Use the Menu Path '*LSMW > Extras >Create change request*'.

36. Can you transport 'Variants' of multiple programs in one go?

Yes. Use program ***RSTRANSP*** using Transaction Code: SE38.

37. What do you understand by 'SAPNet'?

The **SAPNet** provides a remote connection to SAP's service and support group to provide assistance in the event of an implementation project system or production system problem. Additionally, the SAPNet provides information on the latest high priority SAP system information, including error alarm messages that help you to prevent problems before they occur. You can also find release, installation, upgrade and migration information. This functionality is included in standard SAP Basis System. Connection is made using ISDN or leased line through the project's telecommunications service provider.

Project
Implementation

3
Project Implementation

1. What is 'ASAP'?

ASAP (Accelerated SAP) is a methodology used in SAP for faster and cost-effective implementation of SAP projects. ASAP helps to (a) reduce the implementation time, (b) achieve quality implementations and (c) make effective & efficient use of the project resources.

ASAP integrates the following three components:

1. ASAP Roadmap
2. Tools (Questionnaires, templates etc.)
3. SAP services & training (Hotline, Early Watch, Remote Upgrade, Archiving etc)

ASAP Roadmap is aimed at providing a step-by-step direction & guidance through out the project implementation by providing a process oriented, clear and concise project plan. The roadmap meanders through the following milestones or phases in the project implementation life cycle:

1. Project preparation
2. Business blueprint
3. Realization
4. Final preparation
5. Go-live, support & continuous improvement

2. Explain 'ASAP Roadmap' phases.

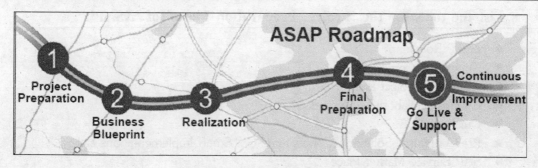

Figure 12: ASAP Roadmap

Project preparation is the <u>first</u> and initial phase of the ASAP roadmap where you are just starting the project. You will do activities like preparation of the initial scope, high level timeline and plan, project charter, identification of project team members, project kick-off etc.

Business blueprint is the <u>phase 2</u> in the implementation wherein you will try, identify and document the business requirements and goals with an idea to prepare the foundation for the future stages of the project. Ideally, you will organize 'business requirement gathering' workshops with the various business / functional users of the company, lead them through the discussion with structured business functionality questionnaires, understand their existing business processes, and identify & document their requirements in the wake of this new implementation. A 'sign-off' at the end of the phase ensures an agreement to move forward outlining the scope of the project. It is understood that whatever is explicitly stated in the business blueprint document is the only scope; no implied scope will be considered for system configuration in the next phase.

Realization is the <u>3rd phase</u> wherein the implementing team breaks-down the business processes identified in phase 2, and fits the same into the SAP system by means of configuration settings. Initially, you will do a ***Baseline Configuration***, test the system functionality and if necessary make changes to the baseline configuration and close the phase with ***Final Configuration*** signalling that all the business processes have been captured and configured into the system.

Final Preparation is the penultimate phase in the project. This phase also serves to resolve all crucial open issues. A 'go-live check' is also conducted to analyze whether the system has been properly configured. This phase is marked by the following activities:

- End-to-testing of the configured system (User Acceptance Test - UAT)
- Training of the end users (Usually follow the concept of 'Train-the-Trainer')
- System management activities (Creation of users, user profiles, allocation of roles to profiles etc)
- Cut-over (data migration activities)

An '*internal help desk*' should be staffed and supported mainly by employees of the enterprise. Setting up a help desk involves, among other things, installing office and technical equipment and defining OSS users. Problems which cannot be solved by this internal help desk are forwarded to SAP via the ***SAPNet / OSS*** system.

On successful completion of this phase, you are ready to run your business in your production system.

Go-Live & Support is the final and <u>5th phase</u> of the project wherein the configured system is declared '*live*' for day-to-day business usage. Users make productive (live) business transactions in the system and all the issues cropping up in the wake of going-live are supported and resolved by a support team immediately after going 'live'.

---

3.   List the tools for the 'Project Preparation Phase' of 'ASAP'.

- ASAP Roadmap
- Knowledge Corner
- ASAP MS-Project Plan
- C-Maps (Collaborative Business Maps)
- Quicksizer
- Pre-Configured Solutions (Connect-and-Go, Smart Implementations etc)
- SAP Service Market Place

4.   List the tools for 'Business Case Development' in 'ASAP'.

- E-Business Case Builder
- C-Maps

5.   List the tools for 'Project Management and Methodology' in 'ASAP'.

- Solution Manager
- SAP Service Market Place
- ASAP MS- Project Plan
- ASAP Roadmap
- ASAP Question & Answer Database
- ASAP Business Blueprint
- ASAP BPP (Business Process and Procedures Document)
- ASAP BPML (Business Process Master List)
- ASAP Issue Database
- ASAP Implementation Assistant / Knowledge Corner

6.   When you will use the 'ASAP BPML' tool?

ASAP **Business Process Master List (BPML)** is used during the *Realization* (3rd Phase) of ASAP Roadmap.

7.   Explain 'Hardware' sizing for a SAP implementation.

ASAP provides a tool called, **Quicksizer**, to analyze the hardware requirements and to arrive at the hardware sizing for the project based on your inputs to a list of questions. The tool is a Web-based tool to make the sizing faster and easier. The Quick Sizer has been developed by SAP in close cooperation with all platform partners and is free. The Quick Sizer calculates CPU, disk and memory resource categories based on throughput numbers and the number of users working with the different SAP components in a hardware and database independent format. The tool gives customers (and prospects) an idea about the system size necessary to run the proposed workload, and is also useful for initial budget planning. Initially used during the Project Preparation and Blueprinting Phases, and anytime after these phases when there is a change the system requirements, the tool helps in arriving at the recommendations for hardware deployment.

8.   Explain 'ASAP BPML'.

ASAP BPMLs (Business Process Master Lists) are MS-Excel Sheets generated by the *ASAP Q&A Database* for facilitating configuration and testing of the system, and development of end-user documentation. These lists become the central repository from which you build the individual master lists to manage the initial configuration, final configuration, final end-user integration testing and any other end-user procedures including the documentation.

9.   What is 'BPP' in ASAP?

ASAP BPP (Business Process and Procedures) are templates that typically walk you through a transaction in SAP and helps you to document the same. The templates are replete with *Best Practices* or *Standard Procedures* for completing a particular transaction which you can customize for end-user training. You will assign ASAP BPPS to the ASAP BPML.

10.   Explain 'C-Maps'.

C-Maps or **C-Business Maps (Collaborative Business Maps)** represent a comprehensive portfolio of industry-specific and cross-industry process blueprints that show you how the SAP's e-business platform can help your business. These maps define the activities, roles, system interfaces, and business documents required for inter-enterprise collaboration. They also show which SAP Solutions and Services you need to make your organization a truly collaborative e-business.

C-Business Maps explain what happens when you deploy e-business solutions to integrate existing resources and transcend the borders of individual enterprises. They give you a complete picture of the benefits and advantages of collaborative business processes.

11.   What is the advantage of SAP's 'Smart Implementations'?

Smart Implementations contain pre-configuration, documentation, installation and configuration accelerators for the specific SAP ERP components. Smart Implementations provide tools to assist with technical infrastructure planning, installation of necessary components, system configuration and integration into an existing SAP system landscape, and infrastructure management in a production system.

The Smart Implementation for the SAP ERP Workplace includes the following installation and configuration steps:

- Easy system infrastructure configuration with the ***Configuration Assistant***
- Automatic ***SAP ERP Workplace*** component installation
- Easy integration of multiple component systems
- Pre-configuration of all software components, including the Web server and Internet Transaction Server (ITS)
- Basis customization of the SAP R/3 System (Workplace Server)
- The ***System Administration Assistant***, an easy-to-use tool providing a comprehensive administration concept to support the system administrator in important tasks.

12.   What is 'SAP Solution Architect'?

The **SAP Solution Architect** is the portal that integrates all content, tools, and methodologies necessary for the solution-oriented evaluation, implementation, quick adaptation and continuous improvement of the ***SAP ERP e-Business platform***. It is fully integrated into the *Customer Engagement Life Cycle (CEL),* open to partner content, and an integral part of the SAP Service Infrastructure.

The SAP Solution Architect integrates in one portal:

- ***Best Practices*** for SAP ERP to evaluate, implement and extend e-Business solutions
- Tried and tested implementation tools such as the ***Implementation Guide (IMG)*** and the ***Test Workbench***

- Access to **C-Business Maps** for in-depth information on collaborative business scenarios
- The **ASAP** method for running SAP ERP projects
- An authoring environment with which customers and partners can create their own pre-configured implementation solutions
- Access to evaluation products such as the **E-Business Case Builder** and the **Solution Composer**

The benefits of using SAP Solution Architect include:

- Consistent access to all contents, tools, and methods for evaluating, implementing, adapting and continuously improving your SAP ERP e-business solution.
- Rapid evaluation and implementation with Best Practices for SAP ERP
- Tried and tested evaluation and implementation tools that have been enhanced specifically for use with SAP ERP
- Improved project communication and efficiency through a central portal
- A consistent and integrated approach that passes the business-oriented project definition from one phase to the next.
- Complete alignment with the ASAP Roadmap
- Information about updates, training, and changes via the SAP Service Marketplace

13. What is 'Configuration' in SAP?

Configuration is the process of maintaining settings (parameters) in the system to support specific / customized business requirements. Remember SAP is an 'all-encompassing' application which needs to be 'configured' to meet your specific requirements.

14. What is 'IMG'?

IMG (Implementation Guide) in SAP provides you with the various configuration steps in a tree-like structure for easy access with the nodes at bottom representing the configuration objects. This is the central repository for customizing, providing step-by-step guide for carrying out the various activities. Besides the steps / activities, this also contains the explanation including in which order you need to make the customization. When you execute an activity from the IMG, you are indirectly changing the values (parameters) in the underlying Table.

The IMG is structured and arranged into <u>four</u> major logical groups:

1. **General Settings** (Country settings, currencies, calendar maintenance, time zones, field display characteristics etc)
2. **Enterprise Structure** (Definition, assignment, consistency check etc)
3. **Cross-Application Components** (ALE, Time sheet, CATT, CAD integration, DM-Document Management, EDI, Engineering Change Management- ECM, etc)
4. **Functional Area Settings** (FI, CO, Logistics, PP, PM, QM etc)

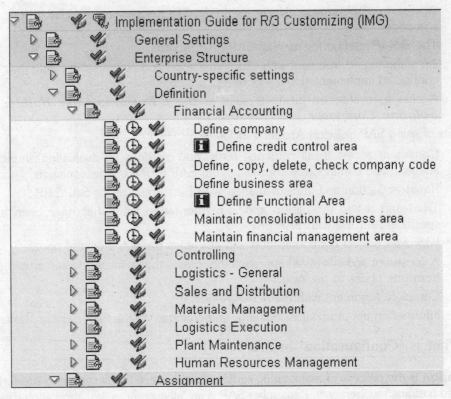

Figure 13: SAP R/3 IMG

Transaction Code
SPRO

15.   Explain various 'Types' of IMGs.

SAP Reference IMG provides all the customizing steps for all the functional areas. This, as the name suggests, is the *'reference IMG'* from which you may create your own IMG to meet the exact requirements of the (1) enterprise and (2) project.

The **Enterprise IMG** is, usually, an exact copy of the 'SAP Reference IMG', but limited to the countries wherein the implementation is carried out. From the *Enterprise IMG*, you may create your *Project IMG* which will contain the application components / business processes that is required in the current project.

It is also possible that you create the **Project IMG** by directly generating from the SAP Reference IMG. In this case, the country selection is done when the Project IMGs are created

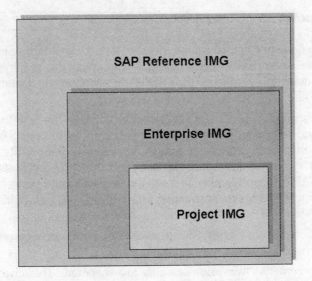

Figure 14: IMG (Reference, Enterprise & Project)

16. What are all the various ways of 'Customizing'?

You can customize SAP using:

- **IMG**: Just follow the IMG tree, step-by-step. No technical knowledge (about Tables, views etc) is required.

  Example: Configure 'Country Code'. Just follow the IMG Menu Path '*General settings > Set countries > Define countries*'

- **Tables**: Need to know the name and structure of Tables where in the parameters are directly entered. Technical knowledge of customizable objects required.

  Example: Configure 'Country Code'. Use transaction code: **OY01**. Enter the details in the Table **V_T005**.

17. Why 'IMG' route of customizing is easier than the 'Tables' route?

- IMG is a logical way to access data from multiple physical Tables without even knowing from where the data are flowing. This is because there are many transactions, which affect more than one Table.

- There is no need to know about the names of Tables and fields, though it always helps to know about the major Tables.

- IMG is gives you the step-by-step way of progressing from one activity to the other. Also, you could classify the activities into various views like 'mandatory / critical / optional', 'Client-dependent / Client-independent' etc so that you can proceed as per your requirements and time.

- Since IMG provides you with the functional view, it becomes easier to 'configure' and test the same immediately as in most of the standard configurations like, account group, chart of accounts etc.

18.   What is known as 'Going-Live Check'?

Going-live Check is done just before you cut over to 'live' (production) operation in a project. This is to test whether the system is properly configured to meet the requirements of the business. The check includes detecting problems in (a) SAP Application, (b) Database and (c) Operating System.

First, this involves an analysis of the major system components of the SAP installation with regard to system consistency and reliability. For this, SAP experts log on to your SAP system via a remote connection, inspect the configuration of individual system components, and provide valuable recommendations for system optimization. By analyzing the individual system components before production start-up, SAP can considerably improve the availability and performance of the customer's live system. In addition, the technical application analysis provides information on how to speed up the core processes within SAP.

Secondly, the transactions with high resource consumption are searched for and necessary adjustments made.

Thirdly, the changes from the two prior sessions are validated. This check is performed in the productive operation system.

After a system goes live, some fine tuning and eliminating of potential bottlenecks is still necessary. This is carried out four weeks after 'going live' with the System.

19.   When to conduct 'Business Process Re-engineering' (BPR)?

Typically the **Business Process Re-engineering (BPR)** needs to be completed well before the SAP implementation starts. This will help to identify any improvements that can be made prior to implementation and begin the process of change within the organization. Improvements that will be system-enabled will form part of implementation and also help the project team identify areas of change.

However, it is also possible (but not recommended, if there are large areas requiring total process re-engineering) to do BPR as you go by during the business blueprint phase provided the project team is not carried away but works within the boundary of the initial scope defined.

20.   What is 'User Parameter'?

SAP provides a way of lessening your day-to-day data entry operations by facilitating default entries for fields, and bringing out the most suitable **Display Variant** for document display, document entry, open / line item processing etc. The user parameter, also known as '**Editing Options**' is a boon as it (a) saves time and (b) results in more accuracy as data entry errors are eliminated with the default values.

You can, among many alternatives, set that:

1. System to default the '*exchange rate*' from the first line item
2. User does not process any '*special GL transactions*' or '*foreign currency transactions*'
3. The document needs to be complete before it is '*parked*'
4. System always calculates the tax component on '*net*' invoice and not on '*gross*'
5. Your document currency either as the '*local currency*' as the one used in the last document

6. System needs to make a currency conversion if documents are to be fetched from '*archives*'
7. Documents needs to be displayed using '*reference number*'
8. '*Payment reference*' is used as a selection item in open item processing
9. Activate branch/head office '*dialog*' while processing line items

Transaction Code
FB00

Financial Accounting (FI)

4

Financial Accounting (FI)

General

1. Explain 'Financial Accounting (FI)', in SAP.

The **FI (Financial Accounting)** module of SAP is the back-bone which records, collects or processes the financial transactions or information on a real-time basis to provide the necessary inputs for external (statutory) reporting. The module is integrated with other modules (like Material Management-MM, Sales & Distribution-SD, Human Resources-HR, Production Planning-PP, Controlling-CO etc). The module FI has several sub-modules which are tightly integrated.

2. What are all the 'Sub-Modules' within FI?

- **FI-AA**   *Asset Accounting*
  Integrated with FI-GL, FI-AR, FI-AP, CO, MM, PP & PM, this module manages the financial side (depreciation, insurance etc) of the assets throughout their entire life cycle starting with procurement of assets and ending with scrapping or sales.

- **FI-AP**   *Accounts Payable*
  Integrated with FI-GL, FI-AA, FI-TR & MM, this sub-module manages vendor transactions by linking with material management, asset accounting, travel management etc. Notable is the 'payment program' for making payment to the vendors.

- **FI-AR**   *Accounts Receivable*
  Integrated with FI-GL, FI-AA, FI-TR, MM & SD, this sub-module manages customers and receivables, in integration with SD. Well known for credit management functionalities and 'dunning' program.

- **FI-BL**   *Bank Accounting*
- **FI-FM**   *Funds Management*
- **FI-GL**   *General Ledger Accounting*

This sub-module is integrated with all other sub-modules within FI and outside FI.

- **FI-SL**   ***Special Purpose Ledger***
  This sub-module is used to provide the summary information from multiple applications at a level of detail that the user defines.
- **FI-LC**   ***Legal Consolidations***
  This sub module helps in the central task of combining the financial operating results of the companies within a group to provide overall results for the group.
- **FI-TM**   ***Travel Management***

3. Name the sub-modules within FI, from where FI-GL gets simultaneous postings.

- Accounts Receivable (FI-AR)
- Accounts Payable (FI-AP)
- Asset Accounting (FI-AA)

4. Mention three distinct characteristics of FI-GL.

- Multi-Currency capability
- Flexible real-time reporting
- Real-time transaction entries

Global & Enterprise Settings

Before getting into the questions, please look into the FI organization structure depicted below and understand how the structure is. When moving through the questions, at any point of time if you have a clarification on the arrangement of the various organizational elements, do visit this page again. To be successful as a FI /CO consultant you need to have a thorough grasp on this basic fundamental block in SAP FI / CO.

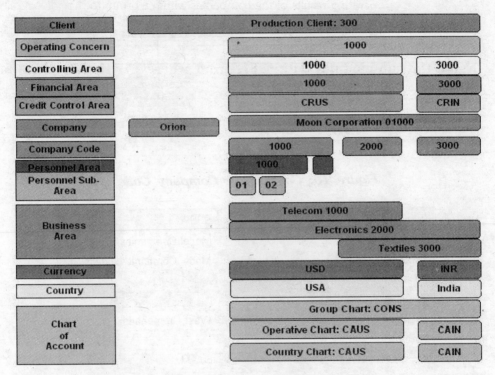

Figure 15: FI Organization Structure

5.   What do you mean by 'Organizational Units' in SAP?

The '**Organizational Units**' in SAP, are the elements or structures representing the business functions, and are used in reporting. For example, Client (across the various modules), Company Code (FI), Controlling Area (CO), Plant (logistics), Sales Organization (SD), Purchasing Organization (MM), Employee Group (HR) etc.

6.   What are the important 'Organizational Units' in FI, in SAP?

1. Company
2. Company Code
3. Business area

7.   What is a 'Company'?

A **Company** in SAP is represented by 5-character alphanumeric code and usually represents the enterprise or the group company. A Company can include one or more Company Code. The creation of Company, in SAP, is optional.

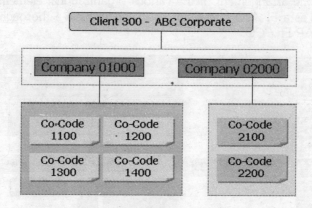

Figure 16: Company & Company Code

Company	9999M
Company name	Model Companies Worldwide
Name of company 2	Model Companies Worldwide

Detailed information	
Street	West Promenade
P.O.Box	
Postal code	60000
City	Frankfurt
Country	DE
Language key	DE
Currency	EUR

Figure 17: Define a Company

8.   What is a 'Company Code', and how this is different from 'Company'?

A **Company Code** in SAP is the smallest organizational unit for which you can draw individual Financial Statements (Balance Sheet and Profit & Loss Account) for your external statutory reporting. It is denoted by a 4-character alphanumeric code. The creation of Company Code is mandatory; you need to have at least one Company Code defined in the system, for implementing FI.

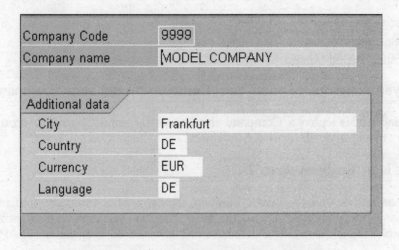

Figure 18: Define a Company Code

You may define a Company Code by copying from an existing one (*Copy, Delete, Check Company Code Option*).

	Transaction Code
	EC01

You may also define the Company Code afresh (the second option in the following figure), from scratch.

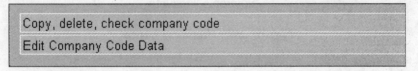

Figure 19: Options to define a Company Code

9.   What are the important 'Global Settings' for a Company Code?

General data:
- Company Code
- Company Name
- City
- Address
- Currency
- Country
- Language

Global data:
- Chart of Accounts
- Credit Control Area

- Fiscal Year Variant
- Field Status Variant
- Posting Period Variant

10.   Can you assign more than one 'Company Code' to a 'Company'?

All the Company Codes within a Company should use the same *Chart of Accounts* and same *Financial Year*, though they all can have different *Local Currencies*.

11.   What is a 'Business Area'?

Business Areas correspond to specific business segments of a company, and may cut across different Company Codes (for example product lines). They can also represent different responsibility areas (for example, branch units). The definition of business area is optional in SAP.

2000	Plant engineering & construct.
3000	Automotive
3400	Metal, Wood and Paper
3500	Aerospace & Defence
4000	Chemicals
4500	Engineering & Construction
5000	Consumer Products: Non-Food
6000	Pharmaceuticals
7000	Electronic Products

Figure 20: Business Area

The financial statements drawn per business area are for internal reporting purposes. You need to put a 'tick' mark in the check box in the configuration, against the company for which you want to enable business area financial statements.

Co	Company Name	City	Business area FS
SL01	Services Logistics SP	New York	☐
TR00	Company 00	Frankfurt	☑
TR01	Company 01	Hamburg	☑
TR02	Company 02	München	☑

Figure 21: Enable Business Area Financial Statements

Transaction Code
OB37

When transactions are posted in FI, you have the option of assigning the same to a Business Area so that the values are properly captured business area-wise for internal financial statements.

12. Can you attach 'Business Area' to a Transaction, by not assigning the same in a posting?

Yes. The business area can also be derived from other account assignments: for example, cost centre. But to do this, you need to define the business area in the master record of that cost centre.

13. How to post Cross-company Code Business Area postings?

By using a cross Company Code transaction, one should be able to post to different 'Business Areas' cutting across various Company Codes. Any number of 'Business Area –Company Code' combinations are possible.

14. What is a 'Credit Control Area'?

The **Credit Control Area**, in SAP, helps in administering the credit management functions relating to the customers. This organizational unit is used both in SD and FI-AR modules. By definition, you can have more than one credit control area in a Client and each Company Code is assigned exactly to one credit control area. However, it is true that you can attach many Company Codes to a the same credit control area.

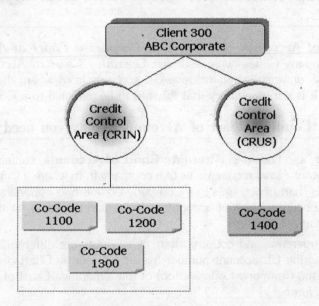

Figure 22: Credit Control Area

15. What is a 'Chart of Accounts'?

A **Chart of Accounts** is the list of GL accounts used in one or more Company Codes. All the GL accounts in a chart of accounts will have an account number, account name and some control information. The control information decides how the GL account can be created.

16.   What are all the major components of a 'Chart of Accounts'?

A **Chart of Accounts** is defined with the following items:
- Chart of account key
- Name
- Maintenance language
- Length of the GL Account Number
- Controlling Integration
- Group chart of accounts (Consolidation)
- Block Indicator

17.   What is an 'Operating Chart of Accounts'?

This is the chart of account, which is used for the day-to-day postings. Both FI and CO use this chart of account. It is mandatory that this chart of account be assigned to the Company Code. This is also known as '**Operative**' or '**Standard**' chart of account.

18.   How 'Group Chart of Accounts' differs from 'Operating Chart of Accounts'?

The **Group Chart of Accounts**, also known as *Corporate Chart of Accounts*, is used for consolidating all Company Codes (with dissimilar *Operative Chart of Accounts*) falling under a Company. This is the 'universe' of all-inclusive GL accounts from where the *Operative Chart of Accounts* is derived. It is not mandatory that this has to be assigned to a Company Code.

19.   What is a 'Country Chart of Accounts'? Why you need this?

This chart of accounts, also known as **Alternate Chart of Accounts**, contains the GL accounts to meet the specific statutory / legal requirements of a company from where a Company Code operates. The assignment of this chart of accounts to a Company Code is also optional. It is possible that both the operative and the country chart of accounts are one and the same. In that case, you will not need two different charts of accounts.

In cases, where the operative and country chart of accounts are different, the link needs to be established by entering the GL account number from the 'Country Chart of Accounts', in the GL master record (under the Company Code section) of the 'Operative Chart of Accounts' in the field '*Alternate Account Number*'.

20.   Can one 'Chart of Accounts' be assigned to several Company Codes?

Yes. One chart of accounts can be assigned to several Company Codes. However, the reverse is not possible i.e., you will not be able to assign more than one chart of accounts to a single Company Code.

21.   What is a 'Fiscal Year' and 'Fiscal Year Variant'?

A 'fiscal year' is the accounting period, which normally spreads over 12 months. The financial statements are drawn for a fiscal year. The fiscal year, in SAP, is defined as a '**Fiscal Year Variant**'. All *Calendar Year Fiscal Year Variants*, in standard SAP are denoted usually as K1, K2 etc.

FV	Description	Year-depend...	Calendar yr	Number of posti...	No. of special pe
F1	366 periods	☐	☐	366	
I4	Calendar year, 4 spec. periods	☐	☑	12	4
K0	Calendar year, 1 spec. period	☐	☑	12	
K1	Calendar year, 1 spec. period	☐	☑	12	1
K2	Calendar year, 2 spec. periods	☐	☑	12	2
K3	Calendar year, 3 spec. periods	☐	☑	12	3
K4	Calendar year, 4 spec. periods	☐	☑	12	4
Q1	Quarters	☐	☐	4	
R1	Short.fiscal year Jan-Sept.94	☑	☐	12	4
UL	Special Purpose Ledger	☑	☐	100	

Figure 23: Fiscal Year Variant

The fiscal year may or may not correspond to the calendar year. In the standard SAP system, the **Non-Calendar Fiscal Year Variants** are denoted by V1, V2 etc.

V3	Apr.- March, 4 special periods	☐	☐	12	4
V6	July - June, 4 special periods	☐	☐	12	4
V9	Oct.- Sept., 4 special periods	☐	☐	12	4

Figure 24: Fiscal Year Variant (non-calendar year)

It is also possible that the fiscal year may be shorter than 12 months, and this is called as '**Shortened Fiscal Year**' (R1, in Figure-23).

Transaction Code
OB29

22. How do you assign a 'Fiscal Year Variant' to Company Code?

One **Fiscal Year Variant** can be assigned to one or more Company Codes.

9990	India Inc.	K4	Calendar year, 4 spec. periods
9999	MODEL COMPANY	K4	Calendar year, 4 spec. periods

Figure 25: Assign Fiscal Year Variant to a Company Code

Transaction Code
OB37

23. What is a 'Posting Period'?

A fiscal year, in SAP, is divided into various **Posting Periods**, with a start and end date defined for each of these periods. Any document posting is possible only when the 'posting periods' are in place in the system. Normally there will be 12 posting periods. A posting period consists of a month and year.

24.   How the system identifies a 'Posting Period'?

Based on the posting date entered into the system while posting a document, the system automatically determines the period, by looking at the document date and the year. However, for this to occur you should have properly defined the fiscal year variant.

25.   What happens when you post to year 2006, when you are in 2007?

First of all, to post a document relating to a previous year, say, 2006 when you are in 2007, the relevant posting period should be 'open' in the system. When such a posting is done, the system makes some adjustments on the background:

One: the carry forward balances of the current year, already done, are updated in case the posting is affecting balance sheet items.

Two: if the posting is going to affect the Profit & Loss accounts, then the system adjusts the carried forward profit or loss balances to the Retained Earnings account(s).

26.   What do you mean by 'Opening /Closing' of Posting Periods?

Postings in SAP are controlled by 'opening' or 'closing' of posting periods. Normally, the current posting period is open for document posting and all other periods are closed. At the end of the period (month), this posting period is closed and the new one opened for postings. This way it provides better control.

It is, however, possible to keep all the periods or select periods open.

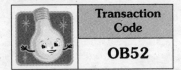

Transaction Code
OB52

27.   What is a 'Posting Period Variant'?

A **Posting Period Variant** is useful in 'opening / closing' posting periods across many Company Codes, at one go. Define a posting period variant and assign the same to various Company Codes. Since the posting period variant is cross-Company Code, opening and closing of posting period is made simple. Instead of doing individually for different Company Codes, you just need to open or close the posting period variant.

28.   Can you selectively 'Open' and 'Close' accounts?

Yes. It is possible to selectively control the 'opening' and' closing' for various types of accounts. Usually, a '+' is mentioned in the top most entry indicating that all the accounts types are allowed for posting. Now, against the GL(S) accounts specify the period which needs to be open. This ensures that all the account types are open for the current period, indicated by' +', and only the GL accounts are open for the previous period.

Not only that select account types can be opened or closed for a specific period, select accounts within an account type can also be opened or closed.

29. Why it is not able to post to a customer a/c in a previously closed 'Period'?

When you want to selectively 'close' or 'open' posting period of some accounts (account range), there will be no problem with that if you are doing it for GL accounts. But, if it is a sub-ledger account (like the customer), the same has to be achieved via opening or closing the account interval of the *reconciliation account* of that account type.

30. Can you open a 'Posting Period' only for a particular user?

Yes. SAP allows you to open or close the posting period only for specific users. This can be achieved by maintaining an *authorization group* at the document header level.

31. What is a 'Special Period'? When you will use that?

Besides the normal posting periods, SAP allows for defining a maximum of four more posting periods, known as **Special Periods** as these are used for year-end closing activities. This is achieved by dividing the last posting period into more than one (maximum 4) period. However, all the postings into these special periods should fall within the last posting period.

The special periods cannot be determined automatically by the system based on the posting date of the document: the special period need to be manually entered into the 'posting period' field in the document header.

32. What can be the maximum number of 'Posting Periods' in SAP?

Under GL accounting, you can have a maximum of 16 posting periods (12 regular + 4 Special Periods). However, you can have up to a maximum of 366 posting periods in case of '*special purpose ledgers*'.

33. What is a 'Special Purpose Ledger'?

Special Purpose Ledgers (FI-SL) are used in reporting. These are all basically user-defined ledgers, which can be maintained either as GL or subsidiary ones with various account assignment objects (with SAP-dimensions like cost centre, business area, profit centre etc or customer-defined dimensions like region, area etc)

Once defined, this functionality helps you to report at various levels. Ideally you collect the information, combine them and create the totals. This is something like an additional reporting feature, and usage of this feature will have no effect on the regular functionalities of SAP.

34. What variations are possible in defining a 'Fiscal Year'?

- *Fiscal Year is the same as that of the Calendar Year*
  The fiscal year starts on Jan-1, there are 12 posting periods; the posting periods correspond to the calendar months; there is no need to define each of the posting periods.

Posting Period	StartDate	EndDate
1	1-Jan	31-Jan
2	1-Feb	28/29 Feb
3	1-Mar	31-Mar
4	1-Apr	30-Apr
5	1-May	31-May
6	1-Jun	30-Jun
7	1-Jul	31-Jul
8	1-Aug	31-Aug
9	1-Sep	30-Sep
10	1-Oct	31-Oct
11	1-Nov	30-Nov
12	1-Dec	31-Dec

- *Fiscal Year is NOT the same as that of the Calendar Year*
  In this case, you need to specify (1) how many posting periods you want and (2) how the system should derive the posting period. Since the posting period does not correspond to the calendar month, the start and end date of each of the posting period need to be maintained.

35. What is known as 'Year Shift' / 'Displacement' in a Fiscal Year?

Fi.year variant	V3	Apr.- March, 4 special periods
		No. posting periods 12

☐ Year-dependent   ☐ Calendar year

Periods

Month	Day	Period	Year shift
1	31	10	-1
2	29	11	-1
3	31	12	-1
4	30	1	0
5	31	2	0
6	30	3	0
7	31	4	0
8	31	5	0
9	30	6	0
10	31	7	0
11	30	8	0
12	31	9	0

Figure 26: Year shift / displacement in Fiscal Year Variant

When the fiscal year is not the same as that the calendar year, we need to define a 'displacement factor' for each of the posting period so as to correctly identify the number of the posting period.

For example, consider the fiscal year variant V3 (Figure-26). The fiscal year starts on 1st April, ending on 31st March of the next calendar year, the displacement factor or year shift from April to December is '0, and for January to March, it will be '–1'. By defining this way, the system is able to recognize the correct posting period. A posting made on 25th Jan 2006, will then be interpreted as 10th posting period in fiscal year 2005.

36.   Can you have 'non-Calendar' months as 'Periods' in a 'non-Calendar' Fiscal Year?

Yes. The 'non-calendar fiscal year' can either correspond to (1) calendar months or (2) non-calendar months.

In case of non-calendar months as the posting periods, you need to specify the start and end date of these posting periods. Consider a fiscal year starting on 16th April 2005 and ending on 15th April 2006. Here, the posting period-1 starts on 16th April and ends on 15th May and so on. Note that the posting period-9 will have 2 displacements (0 & -1) as indicated below in the Table:

Posting Period	StartDate	EndDate	Year	Year Displacement
1	16-Apr	15-May	2005	0
2	16-May	15-Jun	2005	0
3	16-Jun	15-Jul	2005	0
4	16-Jul	15-Aug	2005	0
5	16-Aug	15-Sep	2005	0
6	16-Sep	15-Oct	2005	0
7	16-Oct	15-Nov	2005	0
8	16-Nov	15-Dec	2005	0
9	16-Dec	31-Dec	2005	0
9	1-Jan	15-Jan	2006	-1
10	16-Jan	15-Feb	2006	-1
11	16-Feb	15-Mar	2006	-1
12	16-Mar	15-Apr	2006	-1

As a result, a posting made on 27th Dec 2005, as well as the posting made on 14th Jan 2006 are correctly identified as the postings corresponding to the period-9.

37.   What is a 'Year-dependent' Fiscal Year?

A calendar year fiscal variant, when defined as 'year-dependent', is relevant and valid only for that year.

38.   What precautions you need to take while defining 'Shortened Fiscal Year'?

Note that the **Shortened Fiscal Year** is always year-dependent. This has to be followed or preceded by a full fiscal year (12 months). Both the shortened and the full fiscal year, in this case, have to be defined using a single fiscal year variant.

39. Tell me more about 'Shortened Fiscal Year'.

As mentioned already, a **Shortened Fiscal Year** is one containing less than 12 months. This kind of fiscal year is required when you are in the process of setting up of a company, or when you switch over from one fiscal year (say, calendar year) to another type of fiscal year (non-calendar).

40. How do you open a new 'Fiscal Year' in the system?

You do not need to 'open' the new fiscal year as a separate activity: once you make a posting into the new fiscal year, the new fiscal year is automatically opened. Or, the new fiscal year is automatically opened when you run the '*balance carry forward'* program.

However, you need to have (1) the relevant posting period already opened in the new fiscal year, (2) completed the document number range assignment if you are following year-dependent number range assignment and (3) defined a new fiscal year variant if you follow year-dependent fiscal year variant.

41. How do you 'Carry-Forward' the account balances?

If you have already posted into the new fiscal year, you do not need to 'carry-forward' the balances manually. Else, use the various 'carry-forward' programs supplied by SAP for this task.

42. Can you explain how 'Carry-Forward' happens SAP?

For all the Balance Sheet items, the balances of these accounts are just carried forward to the new fiscal year, along with account assignments if any. This also true for customer and vendor accounts.

In case of Profit & Loss accounts, the system carries forward the profit or loss (in the local currency) to the Retained Earnings account, and the balances of these accounts are set to '0'. No additional account assignments are transferred.

43. Is there a pre-requisite for 'Carry-Forward' activity?

Yes, for Profit & Loss accounts, you should have defined the Retained Earnings account in the system. Additionally, you should have also specified the '*Profit & Loss Account Type'*, in the master record of each of these for Profit & Loss accounts.

There are no such requirements for GL accounts, customer and vendor accounts.

44. How many 'Retained Earnings' a/c can be defined?

You can define as many **Retained Earnings Accounts** as you need. But normally, companies use only **one** retained earnings account. Remember, to define more than one, you should use the profit and loss account type.

45.   Can you have multiple 'Retained Earnings' a/cs?

Normally it is sufficient if you use one '**retained earnings' account**. However, if you are configuring for a multinational company where the legal requirements require treating some of the tax provisions differently from that of other countries, then you will require more than one retained earnings accounts to take care of the situation.

46.   How do you maintain 'Currency' in SAP?

A **Currency** (the legal means of payment in a country) in SAP is denoted by a 3-character **Currency Code**, maintained as per the ISO standards. Example: USD (US Dollars), INR (Indian Rupee), GBP (Great Britain Pound) etc. Each currency code in the system will have a validity defined.

A currency is defined in SAP using the IMG path: *General settings > Currencies > Check exchange rate types.*

47.   What is a 'Local Currency'?

When you define a Company Code, you also need to mention in which currency you will be maintaining the accounts / ledgers in financial accounting. This currency is called as the '**Local Currency'**. This is also known as '*Company Code Currency'.*

48.   What is a 'Parallel Currency'?

When defining the currencies for a Company Code, it is possible to maintain, for each of these company Codes, two more currencies in addition to the 'Local Currency'. These two currencies are called as the '**Parallel Currencies'** which can be the:

- Group Currency
- Hard Currency
- Global Company Currency
- Index-based Currency

To translate the values from one currency to the other, you will need to maintain *exchange rate* for each pair of the defined currencies in the system. When parallel currencies are defined, the system maintains the accounting ledgers in these currencies as well, in addition to the local currency.

49.   What is a 'Group Currency'?

This is the currency defined at the Client level.

50.   What is the 'Global Company Code Currency'?

The currency defined for the Company (or the Consolidated Company) is called as the **Global Company Code Currency**.

51.   What is an 'Account Currency'?

When defining the GL accounts in the system, you are required to define a currency in which an account will be maintained, and this is called as the **Account Currency**. This is defined in the

'Company Code' area of the GL master record, and is used for (a) postings and (b) account balance display.

52.   What are all the pre-requisites for posting in a 'Foreign Currency'?

The following are the pre-requisites, you need to take care, before posting in a foreign currency:
- Local currency already defined for the Company Code (in the global parameters)
- Foreign currency defined in the currency code Table
- Exchange rate defined for the foreign currency and the local currency
- Translation Ratio maintained for the local and foreign currency

53.   How 'Exchange Rates' are maintained in SAP?

An **'Exchange Rate'** is defined for each pair of currencies, and for each 'exchange rate type' defined in the system. The exchange rate is defined at the document header level.

54.   What is an 'Exchange Rate Type'? List some of them.

The **Exchange Rate Type** is defined according to various purposes like valuation, translation, planning, conversion etc. The commonly used exchange rate types include:

B	Standard translation at bk.selling rate
G	Standard translation at bank buying rate
I	Intrastat exchange rate type
INT	Internal clearing exchange rate
M	Standard translation at average rate
P	Standard translation for cost planning

Figure 27: Exchange Rate Types

55.   What is known as 'Translation Factor'?

The relation between a pair of currencies per 'exchange rate type' is known as **'Translation Factor'**. For example, the translation factor is 1 when you define the exchange rate for the currencies USD & INR:

$$\frac{USD}{INR} = \frac{1}{1}$$

56.   Is there an easy way to maintain Exchange Rates, in SAP?

SAP offers a variety of tools to maintain the exchange rates, on an on-going basis. The tools include:
- Exchange Rate Spreads
- Base Currency
- Inversion

Use the SAP supplied program ***RFTBFF00***, for populating the exchange rate Table automatically form an input file, in a multi-cash format from a commercially available input file.

57. What is known as 'Exchange Rate Spread'?

The difference between the 'bank-buying rate' & the 'bank selling rate' is known as the **Exchange Rate Spread**, which remains almost constant. When you maintain the exchange rate spread, it is sufficient if you maintain the '***average rate***' for that currency in question in the system as you will be able to deduce the buying / selling rate by adding / subtracting the spread to / from the average rate.

58. Explain usage of 'Direct' or 'Indirect Quotation'.

It is possible to maintain the exchange rates, in SAP, by either of these two methods. What decides the usage of a particular type of quotation is the business transaction or the market standard (of that country).

SAP adopts two prefixes to differentiate the direct and indirect quotes during entering / displaying a transaction:

- ''– Blank, no prefix. Used in Direct Quotation
- '/' – Used in Indirect Quotation

When there is no prefix entered, (blank), the quotation is construed as the 'direct quote' by the system. The possible scenarios:

- The company in question is mainly using the 'Indirect Quotation'. Use ''(blank) as the prefix for default notation for indirect quotation. Use '*' as the prefix for the rarely used direct quotation. If some one tries entering a transaction using direct quotation, but without the '*' in the exchange rate input field, the system will issue a warning.
- The company in question is mainly using the 'Direct Quotation'. You do not need to make any specific settings as the default is the ''(blank) prefix for the direct quotation, and '/' for the indirect quotation. So, unless you make a transaction entry with '/' prefix, the system takes all the entries as that of direct quotation.
- There could be instances of requirements where in you are required to configure in such a way that a prefix is mandatory irrespective of the type of quotation. In this case, define the direct quotation prefix as '*', and the indirect one as the system default '/' prefix. This necessitates to prefix each of the entries either by '*' or '/'. Else, the user will get a warning to correct the entry.

59. Explain how 'Taxes' are handled in SAP.

SAP takes care of tax calculation, tax postings, tax adjustments and tax reporting, through the three FI components namely GL, AP and AR. The processing of the following kinds of taxes is possible:

1. Tax on Sales and Purchases
    a. Input Taxes (Purchase Tax)
    b. Output Taxes (Sales Tax)
2. Additional Taxes (these are country specific and in addition to the tax on sales and purchases)

    3. Sales Tax (Sales and Use tax as in USA)
    4. Withholding Tax (Income Tax in India)
        a. Classic Withholding Tax
        b. Extended Withholding Tax

SAP allows taxation at three levels:

    1. National level or federal level (Europe, South Africa, Australia etc)
    2. Regional or jurisdiction level (USA)
    3. National and Regional level (India, Canada, Brazil etc)

60.   How Tax is calculated in SAP?

SAP uses a technique called '***Condition Method*** to calculate taxes (except Withholding Tax) in the system. The system makes use of '***Tax (Calculation) Procedures***' defined in the system together with the ***Tax Codes*** for calculating the quantity of tax.

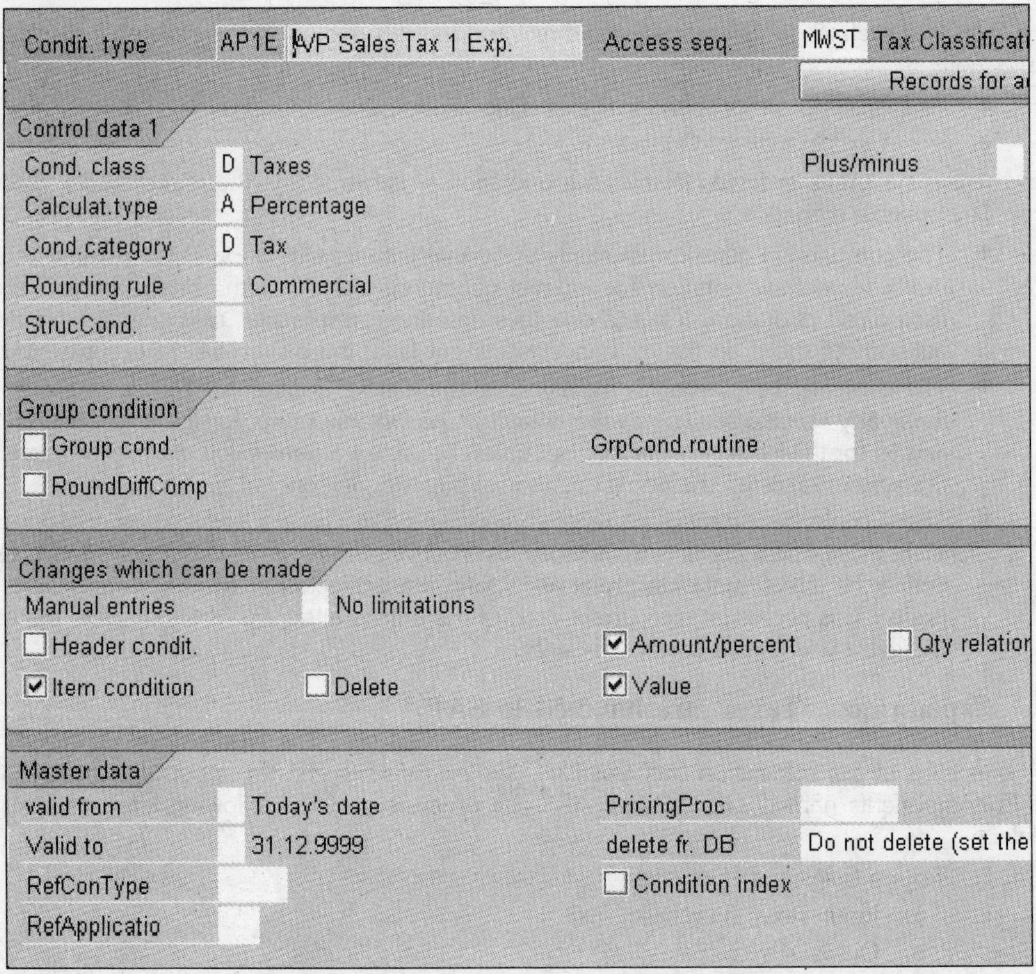

Condit. type	AP1E	AVP Sales Tax 1 Exp.	Access seq.	MWST Tax Classificati
				Records for a

Control data 1

Cond. class	D	Taxes	Plus/minus
Calculat.type	A	Percentage	
Cond.category	D	Tax	
Rounding rule		Commercial	
StrucCond.			

Group condition

☐ Group cond.   GrpCond.routine
☐ RoundDiffComp

Changes which can be made

Manual entries   No limitations
☐ Header condit.   ☑ Amount/percent   ☐ Qty relation
☑ Item condition   ☐ Delete   ☑ Value

Master data

valid from	Today's date	PricingProc	
Valid to	31.12.9999	delete fr. DB	Do not delete (set the
RefConType		☐ Condition index	
RefApplicatio			

Figure 28: Condition Type (Tax Processing)

1. The **Tax Code** is the starting point in the tax calculation. The tax code is *country specific*, with every country having a country specific *Tax Procedure* defined in the standard system, which is used as the template for defining various tax codes. The system uses the tax code to verify the following:

   a. Tax type
   b. Amount of tax calculated/entered
   c. GL account for tax posting
   d. Calculation of additional tax portion, if any

2. **Tax Rates** are defined for each of the tax codes. The tax rates are then associated with **Tax Types** which are included in the tax procedures. (Because of this relationship, it is technically possible that a single tax code may have multiple tax rates for various tax types)

3. The tax code is assigned to a **Tax Procedure** which is tagged to a GL master record. A particular tax procedure is accessed whenever that GL account is used in a document processing.

Procedure			TAXB Sales Tax - Belgium							

Control Data

Reference Step Overview

Step	Cou..	CTyp	Description	Fro	To	Man	Re	Stat	P	SuTo
100	0	BASB	se Amount			☐	☐	☐		
110	0	MWAS	Output Tax	100		☐	☐	☐		
120	0	MWVS	Input Tax	100		☐	☐	☐		
130	0	MWVN	Non-deduct.Input Tax	100		☐	☐	☐		
140	0	MWVZ	Non-deduct.Input Tax	100		☐	☐	☐		
150	0	MWAL	Sumptuary Tax	100		☐	☐	☐		
160	0	MWAA	Clearing Tax	110		☐	☐	☐		
170	0	NLXA	Acqu.Tax Outgoing	100		☐	☐	☐		
180	0	NLXV	Acquisition Tax Deb.	100		☐	☐	☐		
190	0	NLXN	Non-deduct.Input Tax	170		☐	☐	☐		
200	0	NLNA	Non-deduct.Input Tax	170		☐	☐	☐		

Figure 29: Steps in Tax processing

A **Tax Procedure** contains the following:

- **Steps** - To determine the sequence of lines within the procedure
- **Condition Types** - Indicates how the tax calculation model will work (whether the records are for fixed amount or percentages? Whether the records can be processed automatically? etc)
- **Reference Steps** - Where from the system obtains the amount/value it uses in its calculation (for example, the base amount)
- **Account / Process Keys** - Provide the link between the tax procedure and the GL accounts to which tax data is posted. This helps in automatic tax account assignments. To enable that these keys have necessary information for automatic assignment, you need to define the following:

o **Posting keys** (unless you have a specific requirement, it will be sufficient to use the GL posting keys: Debit: 40, Credit 50)

o **Rules** to determine on which fields the account determination is to be based upon (like the tax code or country key)

o **Tax accounts** to which the postings need to be made

SAP comes with a number of predefined account / process keys, and it is recommended that the standard keys be used.

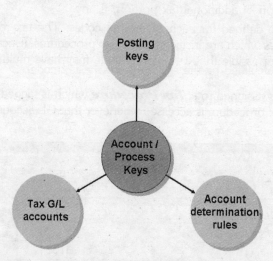

Figure 30: Account / Process Key for tax processing

4. The **Access Sequence** helps in identifying the sequence of Condition Tables to be used and identifying which field contents are the 'criteria' for reading the **Condition Tables** (a group of Condition Types).

5. The tax amount so calculated is normally posted to the same side as the GL posting that contains the tax code. When exchange rate differences occur (due to tax adjustments in foreign currencies) these differences are generally posted to the specific account(s) for exchange rate differences. However, it is possible to specify (per Company Code) that the exchange rates for tax items can also be entered manually or determined by the posting or the document date, and the resulting differences posted to a special account.

6. SAP has a number of predefined account keys, and it is recommended that the standard keys be used.

61.   Explain the Configurations required for Taxes in SAP.

You need to define the following in the customizing:

1.   Base Amount for Tax Calculation

For each Company Code you need to define whether the **Base Amount** includes the cash discount as well. If the base amount includes the discount, then the tax base is termed as '**Gross**', else it is '**Net**'. You may also define a similar base amount for calculating the '**Cash Discount**'. This is also to be maintained for each of the Company Codes.

2. **Tax Codes**

   Tax Code is 2-digit code specifying the percentage of tax to be calculated on the base amount. While defining the tax code, you will also specify the *'Tax Type'* to classify a tax code relating to either *'Input Tax'* or *'Output Tax'*. The tax types are country specific and determine how a tax is calculated and posted.

3. **Tax Rate**

   Tax Rate is the percentage of tax to be calculated on a base amount. You will be able to define tax rates for one or more tax types when you define a single tax code.

4. **Check Indicators**

   By making use of the check indicators, you configure the system to issue **Error / Warning Messages** when the tax amount entered manually is incorrect vis-à-vis the tax amount calculated by the system using the tax code.

62. What is a (Tax) 'Jurisdiction Code'?

A **Jurisdiction Code**, used in countries like US, is a combination of the codes defined by tax authorities. It is possible to define up to four tax levels below federal level. The four levels can be:

- Sub-city level
- City level
- Country level
- State level

Before you can use the jurisdiction codes for tax calculation, you need to define the following:

1. Create Access Sequence (to include the country /tax code/ jurisdiction fields)
2. Create Condition Types (which references the access sequence as defined above)
3. Create the Jurisdiction Codes

The tax rates are defined in the tax code on a jurisdiction basis. When posting taxes with a jurisdiction code, note that the taxes may be entered per jurisdiction code or per tax level.

63. Tell me about the 'Tax Reports' in SAP.

SAP comes delivered with country-specific default **Tax Reports** to meet your tax reporting requirements. However, it is not uncommon to use third-party software for the same purpose. As a process, it is recommended that the 'closing operations' are completed before running the tax reports. This will ensure that the system makes relevant adjustment entries (between payables and receivables, exchange rate differences etc) so that the correct tax amounts are reported.

64. How 'Master Data' is different from 'Transaction Data'?

There are three kinds of data residing in any SAP system:

1. Table Data
2. Transaction Data
3. Master Data

Table Data refer to the customized information for a particular Client. This includes data like payment terms, discounts, pricing, tolerance limits etc which you do not normally change on a day-to-day basis.

Transaction Data is the day-to-day recording of business information like purchase orders, sales returns, invoices, payments, collections etc. This includes both the system-generated (tax, discount etc automatically calculated by the system during document posting) as well as user-generated.

Master Data are the control information required to decide how transaction data gets posted to various accounts (like customers, vendors, GL etc). The master data are usually shared across modules (example: customer master records are common both to FI and SD in SAP) obviating the need for defining the same in various application areas. The master data remain in the system for fairly a long period.

In case **GL Master Records**, the data is created in two areas:

1. **Chart of Accounts Area** (common to all Company Codes: Chart of accounts, GL account number, account name-short & long text, B/S or P&L indicator, account group etc)

2. **Company Code Area** (specific to that particular Company Code: Company Code, tax code, currency, open item management, line item display, sort key etc)

In case of **Customer / Vendor Master Record**, the data is created in two areas:

1. **Client Specific** (general data like account number, name, telephone, bank information etc which are common to all the Company Codes using this master)

2. **Company Code Specific** (valid only for the Company Code, this include: terms of payment, dunning procedure, reconciliation account, sort key, sales area, purchasing information etc)

65.   Can you post an a/c document if 'Credit' is not equal to 'Debit'?

In general, unless the 'debits' are equal the 'credits' in a document; you will not be able to post the document. However, system allows you to post some of the documents, even if this not true:

- **Noted items**: this will contain only a debit or credit. Since there is no updating of accounting entries, system will allow you to go ahead with the posting of these items.

General Ledger Accounting

66. What is a 'Document' in SAP?

SAP is based on the '*document principle*' meaning that a document is created out of every business transaction in the system. The **Document** is the result of a posting in accounting in SAP, and is the connecting link between various business operations. There are two types of documents:

1. **Original Documents**: these documents relate to origin of business transactions. Example: invoices, receipts, statement of accounts from bank etc.
2. **Processing Documents**: These include '*accounting documents*' generated out of postings in the system, '*reference documents*', '*sample documents*' etc. The processing documents, other than the accounting ones, are also known as '*special documents*' and they aid in simplification of document entry in the system.

Each document consists of:

- A *Document Header*
- Two or more *Line Items*

Before attempting to enter a document, note to call up the relevant **document entry function** as the system provides a variety of ready made document entry templates suited to different transactions like regular GL entry, customer invoice posting etc. The details entered in a document can be simulated and displayed before it is actually posted in the system. You may also choose to '*park*' the document and post it later.

67. What is a 'Document Header'?

The **Document Header** contains information that is valid for the <u>whole document</u> such as:

- Document Date
- Document Type (Control Information)
- Document Number
- Posting Date
- Posting Period
- Company Code

Besides the above, the document header also has information (editable, later on) like (a) trading partner, (b) document header text, (c) reference, (d) cross Company Code number etc.

68. What is a 'Document Type'?

SAP comes delivered with a number of **Document Type**s, which are used in various postings. The document type helps to classify an accounting transaction within the system, and is used to control the entire transaction determining account types a particular document type can post to. For example, the document type '**AB**' allows you to post to all the accounts, where as type '**DZ**' allows you to post only the customer payments. Every document type is assigned to a number range.

The common document types include:

Doc.Type	Description	Doc.Type	Description
AA	Asset posting	**KG**	Vendor credit memo
AB	Accounting document	**KN**	Net vendors
AF	Depreciation postings	**KR**	Vendor invoice
DG	Customer credit memo	**KZ**	Vendor payment
DR	Customer invoice	**KG**	Vendor credit memo
DZ	Customer payment	**SA**	GL accourt document
X1	Recurring entry doc.	**X2**	Sample document

Transaction Code
OBA7 (Define)
OBAB (Change)

69. How 'Account Type' is connected to 'Document Type'?

The '**Document Type**' is characterized by 2-character codes like AA, DG etc whereas an '**Account Type**' is denoted by a 1-character code like A, D etc specifying as to which are all the accounts a particular document can be posted to. The common account types include:

- **A** Assets
- **D** Customer (Debtor)
- **K** Vendor (Creditor)
- **M** Materials
- **S** GL

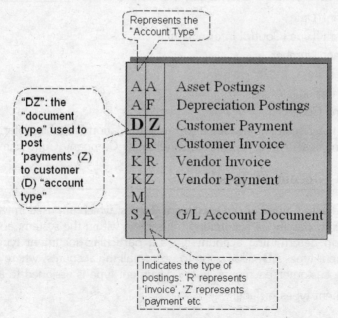

Represents the "Account Type"

"DZ": the "document type" used to post 'payments' (Z) to customer (D) "account type"

A	A	Asset Postings
A	F	Depreciation Postings
D	**Z**	Customer Payment
D	R	Customer Invoice
K	R	Vendor Invoice
K	Z	Vendor Payment
M		
S	A	G/L Account Document

Indicates the type of postings. 'R' represents 'invoice', 'Z' represents 'payment' etc

Figure 31: Document & Account Types

70. What do you mean by 'Net' Postings'?

Usually, when a transaction is posted, say vendor invoice (document type: KR), the system posts the 'Gross' amount with the 'tax' and 'discount' included. However, SAP provides you the option of posting these items as 'Net'. In this case, the posting excludes 'tax' or 'discounts'. Remember to use the special document type **KN**. (Similarly you will use the document type **DN** for 'customer invoice – Net' against the normal invoice postings for the customer using the document type **DR**). For using this 'net method' of posting you should have activated the required settings in the customization.

71. Explain various 'Reference Methods'.

SAP recommends, '**Reference Methods**' as a *'document entry tool'* to facilitate faster and easier document entry into the system, when it is required to enter the same data time and again. Besides making the document entry process less time consuming, this also helps in error-free document entry.

The various Reference Methods used in SAP include:

1. Reference Documents
2. Account Assignment Models
3. Sample Documents

72. What is 'Document Change Rule'?

The functionality '**Document Change Rules**' configured in the system, maintains the information relating to 'what fields can be changed?' and 'under what circumstances?'. As you are already aware, SAP's **document principle** does not allow changing the 'relevant' fields once a document is posted; any changes can only be achieved through 'Reversal' or additional postings. The fields like: company code, business area, account number, posting key, amount, currency etc., can never be changed once the document is posted. However, SAP allows changing some of the fields, in the line items, like: payment method, payment block, house bank, dunning level, dunning block etc. Either these can be changed document by document or using '**mass Change**' for a number a documents in a single step.

The changes to 'master data' are tracked and stored per user for an 'audit trail'.

73. Differentiate 'Account Assignment Model', 'Recurring Entries' & 'Sample Document'.

Account Assignment Model is a *'reference method'* used in document entry when the same distribution of amounts to several Company Codes, cost centers, accounts etc is frequently used. Instead of manually distributing the amount among accounts or Company Codes, you may use **equivalence numbers** for distributing both the credit and debit amounts. A cross Company Code account assignment model can also be created.

The account assignment model may contain any number of GL accounts. The GL account items need not be complete. The model can be used across several Company Codes, and can even include Company Codes from non-SAP systems.

- You can use the account assignment model while 'parking' a document (but you cannot use 'reference document' for 'parking').

- Use of account assignment model is limited to GL accounts.

Acct assgnmt modelUTILITY22							
Utility Payments model				Company code		1000	
Currency		EUR					
Debit distribution		5,000.00		Credit distribution		5,000.00	

Account assignment model items									
PK	CoCd	G/L acct	Tx	Jurisdictn code	BA	Cost ctr	Amount	Equiv	
40	1000	416100	V0		9900	1000	1,000.00	20	
40	1000	416100	V0		9900	2100	1,500.00	30	
40	1000	416100	V0		9900	2100	2,500.00	50	
50	1000	113105			9900		5,000.00	100	

Figure 32: Account Assignment Model

Unlike a '**Sample Document**', an account assignment model may be incomplete which can be completed during document entry, by adding or deleting or changing the data already saved in the model.

	Transaction Code
	FKMT

Recurring Entry original document is used by the system as a 'reference document' for enabling posting of periodically recurring postings such as loan repayments, insurance premium payments, rent etc. Since this document is not an accounting document, the account balances are not affected. In a recurring entry original document, you will not be able to change (a) posting key, (b) account and (c) amount. The ***recurring entry documents*** are defined with a special number range (**X1**). Unlike an account assignment model, this cannot be used for cross Company Code postings.

The ***recurring entry document*** *per se* does not update transaction figures but acts only as a reference and as the basis for creating accounting documents. The SAP program **SAPF120** creates the accounting documents from the recurring entry original document. There are two ways of setting the exact date when this document should be posted to:

- ***Posting frequency***: enter the day of the month and the period (in months) between two postings.
- ***Scheduled run***: configure the 'run schedule' specifying the calendar days on which the program should post these documents.

A **Sample Document** is like a template, which is created and stored so that the information contained therein, can be easily copied into new documents and posted in the system. But, once a sample document is created note that you will not be able to change the 'line items' already contained in that document; all you can do is to change the amounts in that sample document. But you can over come this either (a) by defining a new sample document which can contain other line items or (b) you may add new line items to the FI document which is created by copying from the original sample document.

Sample documents have separate number ranges (**X2**).

74. What is a 'Line Item'?

The **Line Items** contain information relating to account number, amount, debit/credit, tax code, amount etc. SAP allows a maximum of 999 line items in a single document. Besides the one entered by you during an document entry, the system may also create its own line items called '*system generated line items*', like tax deductions etc. Irrespective of number of line items entered, it needs to be ensured that the total of these are always zero (that is total debits should equal total credits). Else, the system will not allow you to post the document.

75. What is a 'Posting Key'?

A **Posting Key** in SAP is a 2-digit alphanumeric key, which controls the entry of line items. SAP comes with many posting keys for meeting the different business transaction requirements: **40** (GL debit), **50** (GL credit), **01** (customer invoice), **11** (customer credit memo), **21** (vendor credit memo), **31** (vendor payment) etc.

The posting key determines:

1. What account can be posted to
2. Which side of the account (debit or credit) to be posted to
3. What is the 'layout' screen needs to be used for that particular transaction

Transaction Code
OB41

It is a normal practice not to change any of the default posting keys in the system, as very rarely you would require additional posting keys.

76. Differentiate 'Parking' of documents from 'Holding'.

Parking of Document, in SAP, is one of the two *preliminary postings* (the other being 'Holding' of documents) in the system referring to storing of incomplete documents in the system. These documents can later on be called upon for completion and posting. While 'parking' a document, the system does not carry out the mandatory 'validity checking'. The system does not also carry out any automatic postings (like creating tax line items) or 'balance checks'. As a result, the transaction figures (account balances) are not updated. This is true in case of all financial transactions except in the area of *TR-CM (Cash management)* where 'parked' documents will update the transactions.

Parking of documents can be used to 'park' data relating to customers, vendors or assets (acquisition only). When a cross Company Code document is 'parked', only one document is created in the initial Company Code; when this 'parked' document is posted all other document relevant for all other Company Codes will also be created. However, it is to be noted that *substitution* functionality cannot be used with document 'parking', as substitution is activated only upon transaction processing.

The added advantage is that a document 'parked' by an accounting clerk can be called upon for completion by some one else. The 'parked' documents can be displayed individually or as a list from where the required document can be selected for completion and posting. The number of the 'parked' document is transferred to the posted document. The original 'parked' document, if necessary, can be displayed even after the same has been posted to.

During a transaction when the user finds that she/he is not having a piece of information required to be entered, he/she can 'Hold Document' and complete the same later. As in the case of 'parked' documents, here also the document does not update the transaction figures.

The essential difference between these two types of preliminary postings can be summarized as under:

Attribute	'Park' document	'Hold' document
View the document in 'Account Display'?	Yes	No
Changes to the document?	Any user can access, view and/change the document	No other user, except the creator, will be able to access, view and/change the document
Document number?	System assigned	Manually entered by the user
Use of data in the document for evaluation purposes?	Possible	Not possible

77. What is an 'Automatic Posting'?

When you post documents in SAP, there are instances where the system also adds some more line items (like: tax, cash discount, gain / loss from foreign exchange transactions etc) besides the ones you have entered in the document. This helps to reduce your work as the system calculates these automatically. However, you need to define accounts you want the system to automatically post to; this will bring in a control whereby no manual posting is allowed to any of these accounts.

78. What is 'Clearing'?

A 'Clearing' in SAP refers to squaring-off open debit entries with that of open credit entries. Clearing is allowed in GL accounts maintained on 'open item' basis, and in all customer / vendor accounts. The clearing can either be manual or automatic. In case of **manual clearing**, you will view the open items and select the matching items for clearing. In case of **automatic clearing**, a program determines what items need to be cleared based upon certain pre-determined open item selection criteria and proposes assignments before clearing these assigned items. Whatever be the type of clearing, system creates a **clearing document** with the details and enters the 'clearing number' against each the cleared open items. The **clearing number** is derived from the document number of the clearing document.

You will also be able to do a '**partial clearing**' when you are unable to match open items exactly; in this case, the balance amount not cleared is posted as a new open item. You may also configure **clearing tolerance** and also define rules on how to tackle the situation when the net amount after clearing is not zero (like, writing off, posting the difference to a separate 'clearing difference' account etc)

In case of customers who are also vendors, you will be able to clear between these two provided the same is duly configured in the relevant master data (by entering the customer number in the vendor master record, and vendor number in the customer master record).

79. How you can manually 'clear' the 'Open Items'? When?

Under **Manual Clearing**, you will select the open items, based on the incoming payment so that the selected 'open items' are 'cleared' (knocked-off). In cases like refunds from a vendor or transactions involving bank sub-accounts and clearing accounts etc you will resort to manual clearing. When cleared, the system flags these line items as 'cleared', creates a ***clearing document*** and enters the clearing document number and clearing date in these open items. Besides the clearing document, the system may also generate 'additional documents' in cases like ***partial*** or ***residual processing***, and for posting the loss / gain to the assigned GL account.

While doing this, if there is a ***payment difference***, the same can be treated the way it is configured in the system:

- If the difference is with in the ***tolerance limit***, defined in the system using the ***tolerance groups*** (defined at the company code level), the ***cash discount*** is adjusted or the system automatically posts the difference to a gain/loss GL account.
- When the payment difference exceeds the limits of defined tolerance, then the incoming amount may be processed as a ***partial payment*** (the original open item is not cleared, but the incoming payment is posted with a reference to that invoice) or the difference is posted as the ***residual item*** (the original open item is cleared and a new open item created by the system for the difference amount) in the system.

	Transaction Code
	F-18 (FI-AR)
	F-06 (FI-GL)

You may also use the Menu Path: *Accounting > Financial Accounting > Account Receivable > Document entry > Incoming payment > Post* or *Accounting > Financial Accounting > GL > Document entry > Incoming payment > Post*

80. Explain 'Reversal of Documents' in SAP.

In case you need to change some of the accounting information relating to an already posted document, you can only achieve the same by '**Reversing**' the original document and posting a new one with correct information. However, reversal is possible only when:

- The origin of the document is in FI (not through SD or MM etc)
- The information like business area or cost centre etc are still valid (that you have not deleted these business objects)
- The original document has no cleared items
- The document relates only to the line items of customer / vendor / GL

While reversing, the system automatically selects the appropriate document type for the reversal, besides defaulting the relevant posting keys. (Remember that the document type for ***reversal documents*** would have already been configured when document types were defined in the configuration) Also note that, if you do not specify the posting date for the reversal document, system defaults to the posting date of the original document.

81.   Explain 'True Reversal'. How it differs from regular 'Reversal'?

As you are aware, any reversal results in opposite postings to the credit/debit sides of the original posting, leading to an increase in the account balances and the 'trial balance' is automatically inflated, on both the sides. This is against the legal requirement in some of the countries like France wherein it is required that even after reversal, it should not result in increased account balances. As a result, SAP came out with '**True Reversal**' which overcomes this problem by '***negative postings***' to the same line item(s) during reversal. The account balance which was originally increased was restored to the actual balance during the reversal:

Type of Reversal	Type ofposting	Account 100000		Account 200000	
		Debit	Credit	Debit	Credit
Traditional Reversal	Original Posting	$ 2500			$ 2500
	Reversal		$ 2500	$ 2500	
'True'Reversal	Original Posting	$ 2500			$ 2500
	Reversal	-$ 2500			-$ 2500

82.   What is 'Fast Entry'?

Instead of the regular document entry screens, SAP provides '**Fast Entry**' screens for facilitating a quick way of entering repetitive line items in a transaction. For achieving this, you need to define a ***Fast Entry Screen Layout*** which will specify what fields you will require for data entry, and in what order. You may configure these fast entry screen layouts for GL account line items, credit memos and customer / vendor invoices. Each of these fast entry screen layouts will be denoted by a 5-character screen variant in the system. Fast entry screens are used in ***complex (general) postings***.

SAP's ***enjoy postings*** also meant for similar data entry screen; but the difference is that in case of 'fast entry' you will start from scratch in identifying the fields, positioning them in the line item etc. Where as in Enjoy Postings, system comes with all the fields activated and you will de-select the fields which you do not want to be made available for data entry.

83.   How to create a 'GL Account Master Data'?

The **GL Account Master Data** can be created by any one of the following methods:

1. Manually
2. Creating with reference
3. Through Data Transfer Workbench
4. Copying from existing GL accounts

The **Manual Creation** of GL account master records is both laborious and time consuming. You will resort to do this only when you can't create master records using any of the other methods listed above.

You will follow the second method, **Creating with Reference**, when you are already in SAP and have an existing Company Code (*Reference Company Code*) from which you can copy these records to a new Company Code (*Target Company Code*). You will be able to do this by accessing the Menu: '*General Ledger Accounting > GL Accounts > Master Data > GL Account Creation > Create GL Accounts with Reference*'. While doing this, you can copy the '***account assignments***' as well ensuring that the integration of GL with other applications is intact. SAP facilitates that you can (i) limit the number of GL records thus copied to the target Company Code, (ii) create new records if necessary, (iii) change the account number / name.

When you have GL accounts in a non-SAP system and you feel that these accounts will meet your requirement you will then use '**Data Transfer Workbench**' of SAP to transfer these records into SAP, and change the same to suit SAP environment. Since this will not have 'Account Assignment' logic as defined in SAP, you need to be careful in defining these assignments.

You will resort to the last option of **Copying from Existing GL Accounts** only when you feel that there is a *Chart of Accounts* in the system which 100% meets your requirement. Else, follow the second method described above.

84. What is 'Collective Processing' of GL accounts?

The **Collective Processing** helps you to make systematic changes to a number of GL accounts in a single step. For example, you have used '*creating with reference*' method to create GL accounts in a new Company Code and you want to change the account names as well as the 'GL account type' (P&L or B/S). Then you will use this *mass processing method* to achieve the same. You can make changes to:

1. Chart of accounts data
2. Company Code data

Use Menu Path: '*Accounting > Financial accounting > General ledger accounting >Master records > Collective processing*'. The same can be achieved in IMG through: "*Financial Accounting > General Ledger Accounting > GL Accounts > Master Data > GL Account Creation > Change GL Accounts Collectively*".

Remember that the 'collective processing' helps only to edit and you can not use this method if need to create new master records.

85. What is 'Individual Processing' of GL accounts?

Against the 'collective processing' of GL accounts where you edit a number of accounts in a single step, **Individual Processing** helps to edit or create GL account master records one at a time. Here you can edit (including display, change, block, unblock and delete) or create a new GL account in three different ways:

1. *Centrally*: You will be editing or creating a GL account master record in both chart of accounts area and Company Code area in one go. This is also known as '**one-Step**' **GL creation**.

Transaction Code
FS00

2. *In Chart of accounts area*: you first edit or create the record here before doing the same in the Company Code area.

Transaction Code
FSP0

3. **In Company Code area**: you edit or create the record here after the same has been done in the chart of accounts area.

Transaction Code
FSSO

Put together, steps-2 & 3 relate to 'step-by-step' creation of GL account master records.

86.   Is it possible to change an existing B/S GL a/c to P&L type?

Technically, you will be able to change all the fields, except the account number, of a GL account in the Chart of Accounts area. However, in this particular instance when you change the 'GL account type' from 'B/S' to 'P&L', make sure that you again run the 'balance carry forward' program after saving the changes so that the system corrects the account balances suitably.

87.   Why system does not allow changing 'Tax Category' in a GL a/c master?

You will be able to change the '**Company Code**' related fields like tax category, currency etc provided that there has not been any posting to these accounts. Pay attention to the following:

1. If you need to denote an existing GL account to henceforth be managed on 'open item basis' or vice versa, then make sure that the account balance is zero in either case.

2. If you are trying to change an existing 'reconciliation account' (to a regular GL), then make sure that the account has not been posted to.

3. If you are attempting to denote an existing ordinary GL account into a 'reconciliation account', ensure that the account has zero balance.

88.   What is an 'Account Group'?

The **Account Group** (or **GL Account Group**), a 4-character alphanumeric key, controls how the GL account master records are created in the system. This helps to 'group' GL accounts according to the 'functional areas' to which they must belong. Account group is mandatory for creating a master record. The same account groups can be used by more than one more Company Code if they all use the same chart of accounts. Each GL account is assigned to only one account group.

The Account Group determines:

1. What **number interval** is to be used while creating the master record?

2. What **screen layout** is to be used while creating the master record in the Company Code area?

While defining the account groups in the system, you also need to define the corresponding **field status** for each of these groups. Else, you will not be able to see any fields as all these would be hidden by default.

SAP comes delivered with a number of 'account groups' like:

● **SAKO** (GL accounts general)

● **MAT.** (Materials Management accounts)

● **FIN.** (Liquid Funds accounts)

INT	MA60	AR60/Materials manag.accounts	10000000	10999999
INT	MAT	Materials management accounts		999999999
INT	MAT.	Materials management accounts		999999999
INT	PL	P&L accounts		999999999
INT	PL60	AR60/Income statement accounts	15000000	15999999
INT	RECN	Recon.account ready for input		999999999
INT	SA60	AR60/General G/L accounts	10000000	15999999
INT	SAKO	General G/L accounts		999999999

Figure 33: GL Account Group

In most of the situations, you will not require additional groups other than the ones already available in the standard system. However, if you need to create a new one, it is easier to copy an existing one and make modifications to the same instead of creating from scratch.

Transaction Code
OBD4

89.   Describe 'Number Range Interval'.

A **Number Range** refers to a number interval defined in the system so that when documents are posted, the system assigns a number form this range. You will define different number ranges for different document types. Each document in SAP is uniquely identified by the combination of (a) document number, (b) company code and (c) fiscal year.

NR Object	Accounting document
Subobject	0001

Intervals

	No	Year	From number	To number	Current number	Ext
	01	1993	0100000000	0199999999	0	☐
	01	1999	0100000000	0199999999	100000001	☐
	01	2007	0100000000	0199999999	0	☐
	01	9999	0100000000	0199999999	100000569	☐
	02	1992	0200000000	0299999999		☑
	02	1993	0200000000	0299999999		☑
	02	1999	0200000000	0299999999		☑
	02	2007	0020000000	0029999999	0	☐
	02	9999	0200000000	0299999999	0	☐

Figure 34: Document Number Range

The number range for a document type can be defined:

1. Per fiscal year or
2. Until a fiscal year in future.

If defined to last only one fiscal year, then this needs to be defined every year. When number ranges are defined every year, the system starts from the first number in the range for that particular year and this will help in not reaching the upper limit fast.

If you specify the fiscal year as '9999', then the document number range is valid for ever (well, almost!) and you do not have to do this exercise of maintaining number ranges every fiscal year. But, every year the system starts from the last number used up in the previous year and if a small number range is defined for a document type, you could easily run out of the number range fast.

The document numbers can either be:

1. **Internally** assigned by the system or
2. **Externally** input when the same is created

The number ranges can be defined in such a way that system generates the number automatically when a document is created. This is known as '**internal number assignment**'. Under this, the system stores the 'last number' used for a document in the *'Current Number'* field and will bring up the next number when another document is created.

If '**external numbering**' is used, the user needs to input a document number every time a document is created in the system. Since user supplies the number every time, the subsequent numbering may not be sequential. Unlike internal numbering, system does not store the 'last number' in the 'Current Number' field. All the external number ranges are automatically considered as 'year-specific' in the System.

The numbers in a number range can either be **numeric** or **alphanumeric**. If numbers are numeric, system will prefix the number with required zeros to make the number length uniform at 10 digits. If you are using alphanumeric numbering, then the number is padded with zeros from the right. For all number ranges defined as 'external', the best practice is to define them as alphanumeric.

The system creates a minimum of one document when a transaction is created / completed. SAP recommends 'filing' of original documents (under the number of the processing document (document generated in SAP)). The best practice is to enter the (external) number of the 'original document' in the *'Reference'* field of the document created in SAP system. For easy cross-reference, the SAP document number thus created needs to be noted down on the 'original document'.

The following are the activities you need to complete for configuring the number ranges properly in the system:

1. Defining the number ranges
2. Copying the number ranges to Company Code(s)
3. Copying the number ranges to fiscal year(s)

Transaction Code
FBN1 (Define number ranges)
OBH1 (Copy to Company Code)
OBH2 (Copy to fiscal year)

90. What is a 'Screen Layout'?

The 'account group' determines which **Screen Layout** should be used while creating a GL account master record. For each of the account groups, you can define different screen layouts, which essentially determines the *'Field Status'* of a field.

The field status refers whether the field is:

1. **Suppressed** (field is invisible, hidden from display)
2. **Required** (display on, entry mandatory)
3. **Optional** (display on, entry not mandatory)

	Suppress	Req. Entry	Opt. Entry
Due date	●	○	○
Value date	○	○	●
Payment terms	●	○	○
Cash discount deduction	●	○	○
Own Bank	○	○	●
Bank Business Partners	○	○	●

Figure 35: Field Status

All the above three are shown as 'radio buttons' against each of the fields in the screen layout, and you should select any one to set the status to that field; by default all the fields are 'suppressed'.

There are two levels of controls of field status, to decide which takes the priority, while deciding the screen layout:

1. Field status at the **account group** level
2. Field status at the activity (create / change/ display) level i.e. at the ***transaction level.***

You may also have field status defined for posting keys (40-debit & 50-credit for the GL account postings). Also remember to define the field status for 'reconciliation accounts' as you will not be able to define any such status in the sub-ledger accounts (for example: customer or vendor).

SAP has in-built rules to link, called ***link rules***, these two levels and to decide the final status of a field in the 'screen layout'. The link rules also help to over come the field-status settings differences arising out of different settings at (1) Client level (field status for posting keys), (2) Company Code level(field status settings at the account group level).

91. What is a 'Field Status Group'?

The 'field status' of an individual field or a group of fields is marked into a **Field Status Group**, which is then assigned to individual GL account master records. You may attach field status groups to a ***field status variant*** so that the same 'field status groups' are used in various Company Codes.

Field status variant	0001	Field status for 0001

	Field status group	Text
	G001	General (with text, allocation)
	G003	Material consumption accounts
	G004	Cost accounts
	G005	Bank accounts (obligatory value date)

Figure 36: Field Status Variant (FSV)

The **Field Status Variant** is named similar to the Company Code. For example, if your Company Code is 1000, the field status variant is also named as 1000, and the same is assigned to the Company Code.

Co...	Company Name	City	Fld stat.var.
BLUE	Blue Fish	New York	1000

Figure 37: Assign a FSV to Company Code

92. What do you mean by 'Balances in Local Currency' only?

When you create GL account master records, it is necessary to decide whether you want an account to have the transactions updated only in local currency. Then you will set this indicator accordingly in the 'Company Code area' of the master record. Pay attention to set this indicator for the ***clearing accounts*** like:

- Cash discount clearing accounts
- GR /IR clearing accounts

Note that you need to set this indicator 'on' for all the '*clearing accounts*' wherein you use the local currency to clear the line items in various currencies so that the transactions are posted without posting any exchange rate difference that other wise might arise.

Example: Consider an invoice for USD 1,000, which on that day translates into an amount of INR 45,000 with an exchange rate of I USD = INR 45. Imagine that when the goods are received, the exchange rate was 1 USD = INR 44.

- If the indicator is set, the system ignores the exchange rate as if the line items have been maintained only in the local currency (INR), and the items are cleared.
- If the indicator is NOT set, the system makes a posting for the 'exchange rate difference' (INR 1, 000) before clearing the two line items.

93. What is 'Line Item Display'?

To display line items of an account, you need to set the indicator '**Line Item Display**' to 'on' in that account's master record. This is mandatory for customer and vendor accounts. The line items can be displayed using (a) classical display or (b) SAP List Viewer (ALV). And, you can use several '*display variants*' to suit your need to display various fields when you feel that the *Standard Variant* is not meeting your requirements.

94.   What is 'Archiving'? How it differs from 'Deletion'?

Archiving refers to deleting data from the documents from the database and storing the same in a file, which can be transferred to an 'archiving system' later on. Archiving does not physically delete the documents. **Deletion** actually removes the documents from the database. To proceed with archiving and deletion you need to consider the following:

1. ***Block*** posting to these archived master records.
2. ***Mark*** (the master records) ***for deletion***: Mark for deletion at the 'Chart of Accounts area' to delete the records from all the Company Codes. However, if you do not want to delete from all the Company Codes, but only from one or more Company Codes then do the same in the 'Company Code area' of the master record(s).
3. ***Archive*** all the transaction figures from the relevant documents.
4. Call up a special program to '***delete***'the records: The program will check whether that particular document could be deleted. If yes, it will proceed to 'archive' and then to 'deletion'.

95.   Tell me the two usage of 'Blocking' an account.

You may use **'Blocking'** to:

1. Block an account from further postings
2. Block creation of account itself (at the Company Code level or chart of accounts area

96.   How to configure the GL a/c for the 'House Bank'?

A **House Bank** is defined using transaction code **FI12**. A '***bank key***' represents the bank. The house bank can contain several accounts; for each of these accounts you need to maintain a GL account. The bank determination, for automatic payment program, is configured using the Transaction Code **FBZP**.

Transaction Code
FI12 (Define House Bank) **FBZP** (Automatic Payment Program configuration)

97.   What is an 'Intermediate Bank'?

Intermediate Banks are used, in SAP, in addition to the 'house bank's and partners' banks, for making or receiving payments from business partners abroad. The payment processing, involving an intermediate bank, makes use of the '***bank chain***'which may consists of a house bank, a partner bank and intermediate banks.

98.   Explain 'Intercompany Postings'.

Intercompany Postings arise when a Company Code, for example, in a centralized procurement, pays for itself and on behalf of other Company Codes. When posted, the transaction results in three documents: (1) for the paying Company Code (say, 1111) in its books, (2) for the other Company Codes (say, 2222 & 4444) and (3) for the intercompany transaction itself.

Before making intercompany transactions, you need to configure both 'intercompany payables' and 'intercompany receivables'. For each combination of these Company Codes, you will be required to maintain a 'clearing account' which must be referenced to in each of these Company Codes. You will also be able to configure whether you manually input the transaction number or allow the system to automatically assign the numbers. In case of system generated transaction numbers, this 16 digit number consists of (1) 10 digit document number (1222222222) of the paying Company Code , followed by (2) 4 digits representing this paying Company Code(1111) and (3) 2 digits representing the last two digits of the financial year (07) (Example: 1222222222**1111**07).

99. How do you perform 'Period Closing' in SAP?

You do a **(Period) Closing** in SAP, in three steps:

- Completing the Pre-closing activities
- Financial Closing
- Managerial Closing

100. What is 'Pre-closing'?

You need to ensure the following as **Pre-closing** activities:

1. Post all the *Recurring Entries* for expenses and accruals.
2. Ensure that all the interfaced programs have been run so that the required data have been transferred to system.
3. Post all the depreciation, material receipts, invoices, salaries etc.

In short, ensure that all the transactions for the period in question have been duly recorded and posted into the system.

101. Explain 'Financial Closing'.

Financial Closing involves, completing the following activities and taking out the financial statements for the period concerned:

1. *Revaluate / Regroup:*
   - ***Revalue*** *Balance Sheet* items managed in foreign currencies – use the report ***RFSBEW00*** to valuate GL Balance Sheet Accounts managed in a foreign currency.(The report generates a *Batch Input* session to post the revenue or expense resulting from any exchange rate differences)
   - ***Clear*** *Receivable* or *Payable* with 'exchange rate difference'
   - ***Valuate*** all the *Open Items* using the report ***SAPF100***. This is used to valuate all the open receivables and payables, using the period-end exchange rates. Here also, the report generates a *Batch Input* session to post the entries resulting from any exchange rate differences.
   - ***Regroup*** GR/IR using the program ***RFWERE00*** to allocate the net balance (depending on whether the balance is a net debit or credit) in the GR/IR Account to GL Accounts (created to actually depict the net effect of the balance in the GR/IR Account)

2. **Ensure accounting accuracy:**
   Use the program **SAPF190**, to compare the totals created by the system in the (1) indexes (customers, vendors and GL) and documents(customers, vendors and GL) with that of the (2) account balances (customers, vendors and GL) to ensure the transaction accuracy.

3. **Run required reports:**
   Generate the **financial statements** (balance sheet and profit & loss account), using the **financial statement versions**. You may also generate the key figure/ratio reports (use the GL account information system).

102. What is a 'Financial Statement Version'?

Financial Statement Version helps to define the *Financial Statements* (both the **Balance Sheet** and **Profit & Loss statements**). When you copy the settings from an existing Company Code to a new one, you will also be copying the financial statement version defined for the 'source' Company Code.

Fin. Stmt.version	Financial Statement Version Name
BAIT	Commercial balance sheet (Italy)
BAJP	Financial statement (Japan)
BAKR	Financial Statement (Korea)
BANK	Bank financial statements
BANL	Commercial balance sheet (Netherlands)
BANO	Commercial balance sheet (Norway)
BAPT	Commercial balance sheet (Portugal)
BAR2	Commercial balance sheet for Russian Fed. (Form 2)
BARU	Commercial balance sheet (Russia)
BASE	Commercial balance sheet for Sweden (BAS90)
BASG	Commercial balance sheet (Singapore)
BATW	Financial Statement Version (Taiwan)
BAUC	Commercial balance sheet (CANA)
BAUS	Commercial balance sheet USA
BAZA	Commercial balance sheet (South Africa)
BICH	Commercial balance sheet (Switzerland)
BSUS	Commercial balance sheet USA

Figure 38: Financial Statement Versions

You may also define a new financial statement version and build the financial statements from scratch. You may create the financial statements both for (1) external reporting (Company Code financial statements) and (2) internal reporting (business area financial statements).

You may also create the balance sheets for a group of Company Codes using *FI-SL (Special Purpose Ledgers)*. The financial statements may be defined to provide information from (1) period accounting point of view (GL account groups wise) or (2) cost of sales point of view (functional area financial statements).

All the above statements can be configured and defined to provide different levels of details:

A financial statement version can have a maximum of 10 hierarchy levels, with each level assigned with an item (*account category*). As you go down the hierarchy, you define the account categories in more detail, with the lowest level being represented by the GL accounts. The system displays the relevant amount for each of these items.

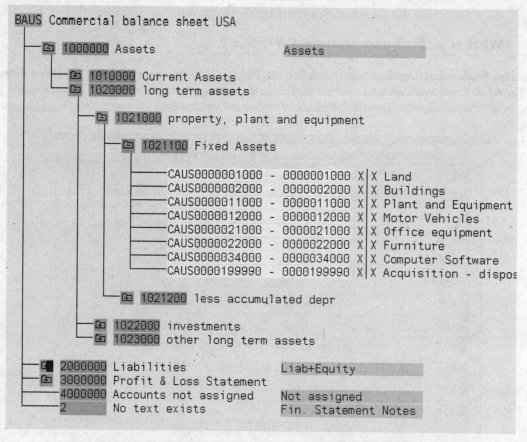

Figure 39: Financial Statement Version - BAUS

103. What are the minimum items in a 'Financial Statement Version'?

Irrespective of the details you require in a **Financial Statement Version**, it is mandatory that you have, at least, the following items defined:

1. ***Assets***
2. ***Liabilities***
   a. Net Result: Profit
   b. Net Result: Loss
3. ***P/L result*** (during annual closing, when you run the program **RFBILA00**, the system

calculates the profit or loss by subtracting the 'total liabilities' from 'total assets' and updates the relevant Net Result item - Profit or Loss)

4. ***Not assigned*** (posted amounts but not yet assigned to any of the account groups)

104. How to ensure 'correct' balances in 'Financial Statement Version'?

In order to have a balanced statement (*Profit & Loss* and *Balance Sheet*) you need to ensure that the accounts are correctly and completely assigned to the nodes of the ***Financial Statement Version***. You may do this by resorting to the necessary assignments at the (1) account balance level or (2) node balance level.

At the ***account balance level***, you need to ensure that the account is shown in two different nodes, but you will turn "ON" the 'debit indicator' of the account on one node and turn "ON" the 'credit indicator' on the other node. Imagine that you have a bank current account 10001000. When you turn "ON" the debit indicator, this account shows the only the debit balances and is construed as the asset. On the other hand, when the credit indicator is turned "ON", the balances on this node now indicates that you owe to the bank (overdraft).

You may also use the ***node level assignment***. In this case, the system uses the 'debit/credit shift' and shows only the 'effective' balance at the node and not at the individual account level.

105. How to perform 'Annual Closing' in SAP?

Annual Closing is also like any other 'period closing' and you will be performing all the activities which are required for a period-end-close. Besides, you will also be completing the following:

- Carry forward Vendor and Customer accounts
- Carry forward the GL account balances of all the Balance Sheet items. For GL account 'carry forward', use the program ***SAPF011***.
- Close the Profit & Loss Accounts and carry forward the balance (profit or loss) to the retained earnings account(s)

106. Explain 'Managerial Closing'.

The **Managerial Closing** involves completion of the following:

- Do a preliminary Controlling period closing
- Settle/re-allocate costs across Controlling organization
- Draw and review internal reports
- Re-open the Controlling period
- Correct and adjust the accounting data, if required
- Reconcile FI and CO by running the FICO *Reconciliation Ledger*
- Run re-adjustment programs to ensure that the *Business Areas* and the *Profit Centres* are balanced
- Draw reports and analyze

107. What is the 'New FI-GL' in FI in SAP ERP?

The traditional or '***Classic FI-GL accounting***' in FI has been focused towards providing a comprehensive external reporting, by recording all business transactions in the system. However, to meet the modern day requirements, this has now been enhanced, **New FI-GL'**, to include the following:

- *Parallel accounting*: Maintaining several parallel ledgers to meet different accounting principles.

- *Integrated legal and management reporting*: Unlike the traditional GL, the 'new FI-GL' enables you to perform internal management reporting along with the legal reporting. So, you are in a position to generate *Financial Statements* for any dimension (say, profit centre) in the business.

- *Segment reporting*: With the introduction of Segment dimension, SAP now enables you to produce Segment Reports based on **IFRS (International Financial Reporting Standards)** and the **US GAPP (Generally Accepted Accounting Principles)** accounting principles.

- *Cost of sales accounting*: Now it is possible to perform cost of sales accounting in the 'new FI-GL'.

However, the following functions have not yet been supported in this 'new FI-GL':

- Transfer Price
- SKF (Statistical Key Figure)
- Euro Translation
- AIS (Audit Information System)
- Archiving
- Data Retention Tool

The 'new FI-GL' needs to be activated in the system using *the IMG* Menu Path > *Financial Accounting (New) -> Financial Accounting Global Settings (New) / General Ledger Accounting (New)*.

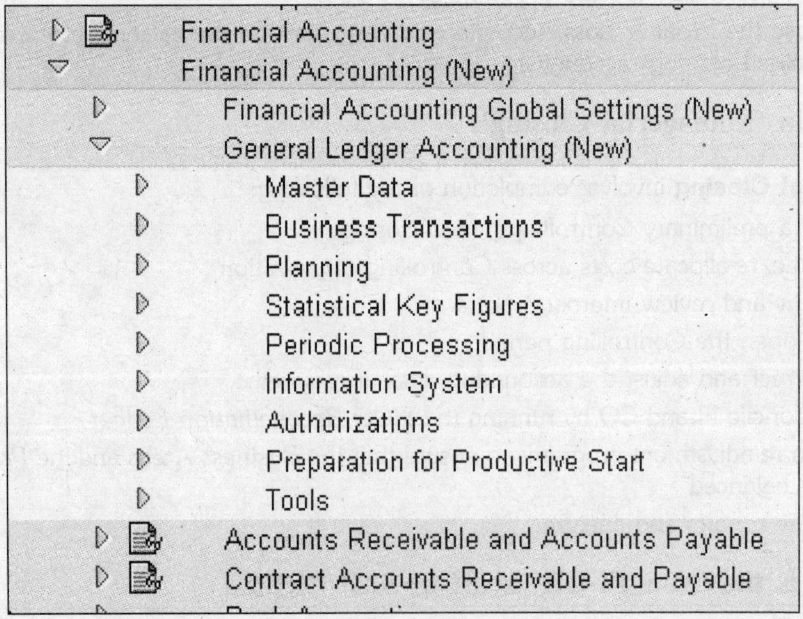

Figure 40: New FI-GL

In the standard system, the Tables from *'classic general ledger accounting'* (**GLT0**) are updated as well as the Tables in 'New FI-GL' during the activation. This enables you to perform a 'ledger comparison' during the implementation of 'New FI-GL'to ensure that your 'new GL accounting' has the correct settings and is working correctly. To compare ledgers, in Customizing choose *Financial Accounting Global Settings (New) -> Tools -> Compare Ledgers.*

It is recommended that you 'deactivate' the update of Tables for 'classic GL accounting' once you have established that 'new FI-GL' is working correctly. To do this, in Customizing, choose *Financial Accounting Global Settings (New) -> Tools -> Deactivate 'Update of Classic General Ledger'.*

Accounts Receivable

108. Explain 'Customer / Vendor Master Records'.

There are three categories of data maintained in a typical master record for a customer / vendor:
- General Data
- Company Code Data
- Sales Area Data (for customers) / Purchasing Organization Data(for vendors)

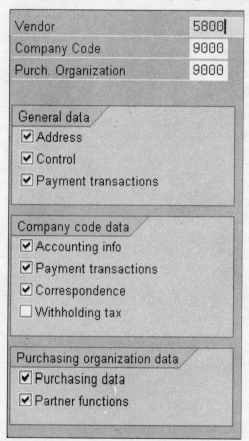

Figure 41: Vendor Master - Various Data

The **General Data** include general information like account number, name, telephone, bank information, trading partner, vendor (if the customer is also a vendor), group key, bank key, bank account, alternate payee etc that are common to all the Company Codes using this master.

The **Company Code Data** comprises of terms of payment, payment methods, tolerance group, clearing with vendor, dunning data (dunning procedure, dunning recipient, dunning block, dunning clerk etc), reconciliation account, sort key, sales area (purchasing organization in the case of vendor master), head office etc. Except the sales (purchasing) related information, all other details are usually maintained by the finance people who can also access the sales / purchase data when the master is maintained 'centrally'.

The **Sales Area Data** in the Company Code area of a Customer master record contains the following:

- Order related (sales district, sales office, sales group, customer group etc)
- Price related (pricing group, pricing procedure etc)
- Shipping data (shipping strategy, delivery priority etc)
- Billing data (payment terms (different from the payment terms maintained at the Company Code level), account assignment group etc)

The **Purchasing Organization Data** in the Company Code area of a Vendor master record contains the following:

- Conditions (order currency, payment terms, Incoterms, minimum order value etc)
- Sales data (A/c with Vendor)
- Control data (as in the screen shot below)

During creation of a master record, the system checks for 'duplicates' for the same customer / vendor which is achieved by the system through the 'Search-Id' (*Match Code*) configured on the address information.

As in the case of GL account master record, the creation of customer / vendor master record is also controlled by the '*Account Group*' which is called as '***Customer Account Group / Vendor Account Group***' (*CPD / CPDL / KREDI / LIEF*) which controls the numbering for customer / vendor master records, field status, whether an account is a regular one or '***One-Time' account*** etc.

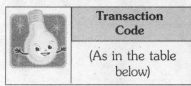

	Transaction Code
	(As in the table below)

Activity	In Accounting		Centrally	
	Customer	**Vendor**	**Customer**	**Vendor**
Create	**FD01**	**FK01**	**XD01**	**XK01**
Change	**FD02**	**FK02**	**XD02**	**XK02**
Display	**FD03**	**FK03**	**XD03**	**XK03**
Block / Unblock	**FD05**	**FK05**	**XD05**	**XK05**
Mark for Deletion	**FD06**	**FK06**	**XD06**	**XK06**

```
┌─────────────────────────────────────────────────────────────────┐
│ Conditions                                                        │
│   Order currency                USD      American Dollar          │
│   Terms of paymnt               ZB01                              │
│   Incoterms                     EXW                               │
│   Minimum order value                                             │
│   Schema Group, Vendor                   Standard procedure vendor│
│   Pricing Date Control                   No Control               │
│   Order optim.rest.                                               │
├─────────────────────────────────────────────────────────────────┤
│ Sales data                                                        │
│   Salesperson                   Mr. Miller                        │
│   Telephone                                                       │
│   Acc. with vendor                                                │
├─────────────────────────────────────────────────────────────────┤
│ Control data                                                      │
│   ☐ GR-Based Inv. Verif.        ABC indicator                A    │
│   ☐ AutoEvalGRSetmt Del.        ModeOfTrnsprt-Border              │
│                                 Office of entry                   │
│   ☐ Acknowledgment Reqd         Sort criterion                   │
│   ☑ Automatic purchase order                                      │
│   ☐ Subsequent settlement                                         │
│   ☐ Subseq. sett. index         ☐ Grant discount in kind         │
│   ☐ B.vol.comp./ag.nec.         ☐ Relevant for price determ. (del.│
│   ☐ Doc. index active                                             │
│   ☐ Returns vendor                                                │
│   ☐ Srv.-Based Inv. Ver.                                          │
└─────────────────────────────────────────────────────────────────┘
```

Figure 42: Purchasing Data

109.   Who is an 'Alternate Payee'?

A customer who pays on behalf of another customer is known as '**Alternate Payee**' (or **Alternate Payer**). Though the alternate payee pays on behalf of another, the system maintains all the transaction details in the account of the original customer. Designating 'alternate payee' does not absolve the customer of his / her obligation for payment.

The 'alternate payee' can be maintained in (a) Client specific data or (b) Company Code area. When maintained in Company Code area you can use that payer only in that Company Code; if defined at the Client level you can use the same across all Company Codes.

There are three ways of 'selecting 'the alternate payee when an invoice is processed:

1. The alternate payee (say, 1000) entered in the customer master record is the one selected by the system as default.

2. When there is more than one alternate payer (say, 1000, 1900, 2100 etc) defined for a single customer in the master record (you will do this by clicking on the '***allowed payer'*** button and create more than one payer), you may select a payer (say, 2100) (other than the default, 1000) while processing the invoice. Now the system will ignore the alternate payer (1000) coming from the master record.

3. If you have put a 'tick' mark in the *'individual entries'* check-box in *'alternate payer in document'* section in the customer master record, then this will allow you to propose a new alternate payer, say, 3000 (other than those already defined in the system). Now, after defining this alternate payer you can use the same in processing the invoice. In this case, this alternate payer (3000) takes precedence over the payers (1000 & 2100) in step 1 & 2 above.

110. What is the use of 'Trading Partner'?

The concept of **Trading Partner** is used to settle and reconcile 'inter-company transactions': both sales and purchases. This is generally achieved by entering the Company-ID (Not the Company Code) to which a customer belongs, in the 'trading partner' field under the tab *'Account Control'* in the customer master record. You can do a similar entry in the vendor master record.

111. Explain 'Tolerance' in transaction processing.

Tolerances are defined in the system to facilitate dealing with the differences arising out of accounting transactions and to instruct the system how to proceed further. Normally, you define tolerances (either in 'absolute terms' or in 'percentage') beyond which the system will not allow you to post a document should there be difference.

In SAP, tolerances are defined per Company Code and there are several types:

- Employee tolerance
- Customer / vendor tolerance
- GL account clearing tolerance

You will define an '***employee tolerance groups'*** in the system and assign the employees to these groups. While defining the tolerance group you will specify:

1. *Upper limits for various posting procedures*
   o Amount per document
   o Amount per open account item
   o Cash discount, in percentage

2. *Permitted payment differences*
   How much over or under payment an employee is allowed to process. This is defined both in absolute value and in percentage.

Besides defining the above two, at the Company Code level, you will also define similar tolerances for ***customer / vendor tolerance group***. Once defined, each of the customers (vendors) is assigned to one of these groups. Here also, you define the ***'permitted payment differences'***.

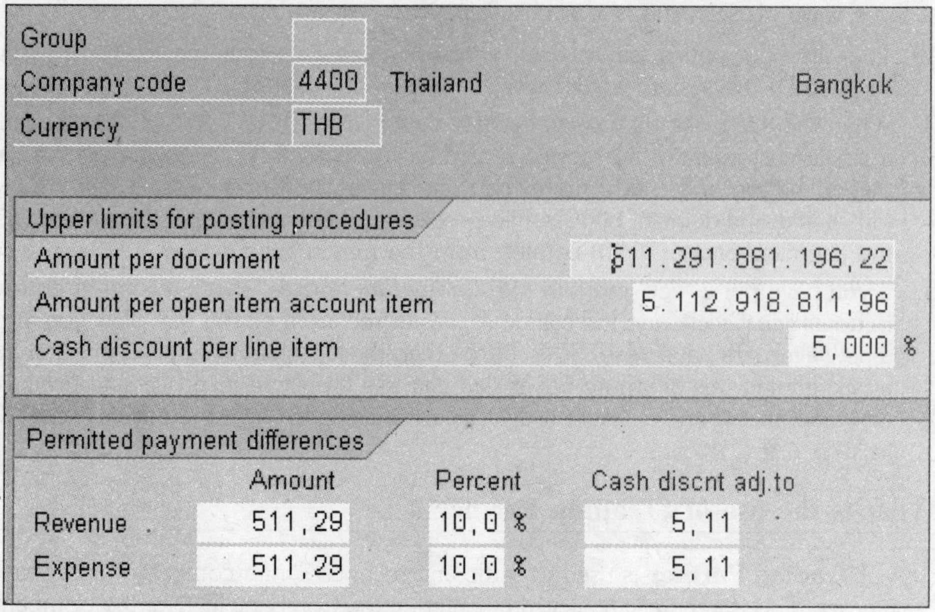

Group		
Company code	4400	Thailand	Bangkok
Currency	THB	

Upper limits for posting procedures

Amount per document	511.291.881.196,22
Amount per open item account item	5.112.918.811,96
Cash discount per line item	5,000 %

Permitted payment differences

	Amount	Percent	Cash discnt adj.to
Revenue	511,29	10,0 %	5,11
Expense	511,29	10,0 %	5,11

Figure 43: FI Tolerance Group for Users

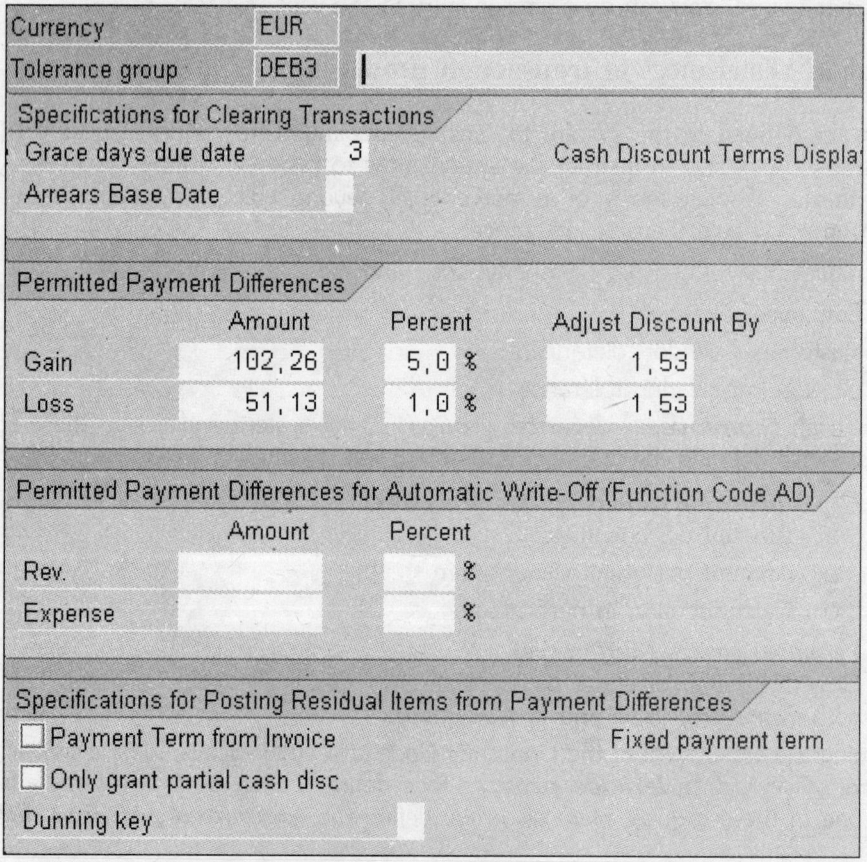

Currency	EUR	
Tolerance group	DEB3	

Specifications for Clearing Transactions

Grace days due date	3	Cash Discount Terms Displa
Arrears Base Date		

Permitted Payment Differences

	Amount	Percent	Adjust Discount By
Gain	102,26	5,0 %	1,53
Loss	51,13	1,0 %	1,53

Permitted Payment Differences for Automatic Write-Off (Function Code AD)

	Amount	Percent
Rev.		%
Expense		%

Specifications for Posting Residual Items from Payment Differences

☐ Payment Term from Invoice   Fixed payment term

☐ Only grant partial cash disc

Dunning key

Figure 44: Customer / Vendor Tolerances

While processing, the system compares the tolerance of an employee against the customer tolerance (or vendor tolerance or the GL) and applies the most restrictive of the two.

112. What is 'Dual Control' in master records?

Dual Control helps to prevent unauthorized changes, to the important and 'sensitive' fields, in the master records in the system. (All such sensitive fields are defined in the Table **T055F** during customizing the application. And, these fields are defined per Company Code and per Client) Consider, for example, a sensitive field like '*payment block*' in a vendor master record. When a user changes this field's content, the system requires another user (usually of higher authority) to approve this change and an *audit trail* is maintained of all such changes. Unless the change is approved, in this example, this particular master is blocked by the system for considering the same in the next '*payment run*'.

Transaction Code		
(As in the table below)		

Activity	Customer	Vendor
Display changes (accounting area)	**FD04**	**FK04**
Display changes (centrally)	**XD04**	**XK04**
Confirm changes, individually	**FD08**	**FK08**
Confirm changes, in a list	**FD09**	**FK09**

113. What is a 'Bank directory' in SAP?

SAP stores the master data (details like bank key, bank name, bank country, bank address and so on) relating to the banks in **Bank Directory** (Table: **BNKA**). Remember, the 'bank masters' are not created in the application but in the implementation side using the IMG. (Of course, you can also create the bank master in the application side in **FI-TR** and not in FI-GL or AP or AR). However, if you are in the process of creating of a master record for vendor or customer and you enter some bank details, which the system does not find in the 'Bank Directory', then the system automatically brings in the relevant screens for you to maintain and update the bank details in the bank directory.

You may create the bank directory in two ways:

1. *Manually* (IMG path: *Financial Accounting > Bank Accounting > Bank Accounts > Define 'House Banks'*)
2. *Automatically* (by importing the bank details using a special program)

Transaction Code
FI01 (Banks)
FI12 (House bank)

114. What is a 'House Bank'?

House Bank is the bank (or financial institution) in which the Company Code in question keeps its money and does the transactions from there on. A house bank in SAP is identified by a 5-character alphanumeric code. You can have any number of house banks for your Company Code, and the details of all these house banks are available in the '**bank directory**'.

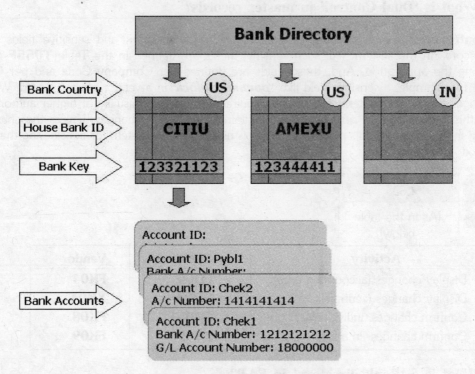

Figure 45: Bank directory

Each 'house bank', in the system, is associated with a **country key** (US, IN etc) representing the country where the bank is located, and a unique country specific code called '*bank key*'. The system makes use of both the 'country key' and the '*bank key*' to identify a '*house bank*'.

- For each of the '*house banks*', you can maintain more than one bank account; each such account is identified by an **account ID** viz., Chek1, Check2, Pybl1 etc. Here 'Chek1' may denote Checking account 1, 'Pybl1' may denote Payables account 1 and so on. You may name the accounts in such a way that it is comprehensible easily. The 'Account ID' is referenced in the *customer / vendor master record* and the same is used in the *payment program* by the system.

- For reach of this '*account ID*' you will also specify the **bank account number** (maximum length of this identifier is 18 characters). You may name this in such a way that it is also comprehensible easily.

- For each '*bank account number*' so defined in the '*house bank*', you need to create a GL account master record, and while doing so you will incorporate the '*house bank id*' and the '*account id*' in that GL master record.

115. Explain 'Sales Cycle' as in SAP.

The **Sales Cycle** comprises of all activities starting from quotation / inquiry, sales order, delivery, billing and collection. Following are the various Processes within SAP to complete a sales cycle:

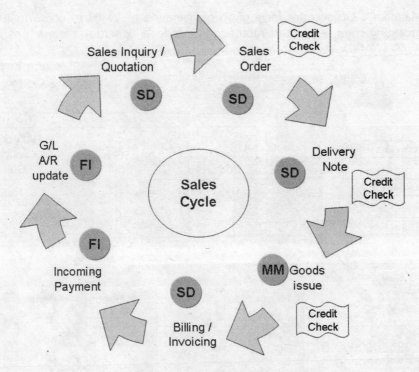

Figure 46: Sales Cycle

Typically the following are the documents created during a sales cycle:

- Inquiry
- Quotation
- Sales Order
- Delivery Note
- Goods Issue
- Order Invoice
- Credit / Debit Note

116. Explain 'Automatic Account Assignment' in SD.

During goods issue in the sales cycle, the system is usually configured to update the relevant GL accounts automatically and to create the relevant accounting documents. This customization in IMG is also called as *material account assignment* and is achieved through a number of steps as detailed below:

1. Determine '*valuation level*' (company code or plant).
2. Activate '*valuation grouping code*' and link the same with '*chart of accounts*' for each '*valuation area*'.
3. Link '*valuation class*' with '*material type*' (FERT, HAWA, HALB etc) with '*account category reference*' (combination of valuation classes).
4. Maintain '*account modification codes*' for '*movement types*'.
5. Link '*account modification codes*' with '*process keys*' (transaction / event keys)

6. Maintain a *GL account* for a given combination of *'chart of accounts'* + *'valuation grouping code '*+*'account modification code '*+*'valuation classes.*

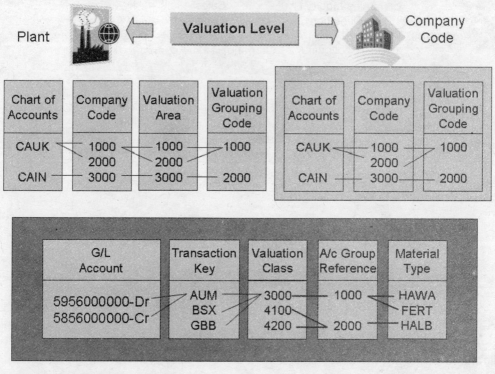

Figure 47: Automatic account determination in sales cycle

The process of **Automatic Account Determination** is as follows:

1. Depending upon the *'plant'*, entered during goods issue (GI), the *'Company Code'* is determined by the system which in turn determines the relevant *'chart of accounts'*.

2. The *plant* thus entered in goods issue, determines the *'valuation class'* and then the *'valuation grouping code'*.

3. The *'valuation class'* is determined from the *'material master'*.

4. Since the *'account modification code'* is assigned to a *'process key'* which is already linked to a *'movement type'*, the *'transaction key'* (DIF, GBB, AUM, BSX etc) determines the *'GL account'* as posting transactions are predefined for each *'movement type'* in *'inventory management'*.

117.   Explain 'Revenue Account Determination' in SD.

The billing documents created during the sales cycle results in automatic postings to GL accounts on the FI side. In general, **Account Determination** is based on the following five factors:

1. Chart of accounts
2. Sales organization
3. Account assignment group of the customer
4. Account assignment group of the material
5. Account key

The system determines the '***chart of accounts***' from the company code in the '***billing document***', and the '***sales organization***' is determined from the corresponding '***sales order***'. The '***account assignment group***' is taken from the respective masters of customer / material. The '***account key***' helps the user to define the various GL accounts, and this key is assigned to the '***condition type***' (KOFI) in the '***pricing procedure***'. These ***GL accounts*** are automatically determined when you make the following configuration in the system:

1. Assigning an '*account determination procedure*' to a '*billing document type*'
2. Assigning this '*account determination procedure*' to a '*condition type*'
3. Assigning this '*condition type*' to an '*access sequence*'
4. Configuring the '*condition tables*'

Table	Description
001	Customer grp/Material Grp./AccKey
002	Cust. Grp/AccKey
003	Material Grp/Acc Key
004	General
005	Acc Key

Application	Condtion Type	Chart of a/c	Sales Org	Acct Asg Grp	Acc Asgmnt	A/cKey	GL a/c
001	**Customer grp/Material Grp./AccKey: Details**						
V	KOFI	COMP	1000	01	10	ERL	5012100000
V	KOFI	COMP	1000	01	10	ERS	5012100000
V	KOFI	COMP	1000	02	10	ERL	5012200000
V	KOFI	COMP	1000	02	10	ERS	5012200000
V	KOFI	COMP	2000	01	20	ERL	5013100000
V	KOFI	COMP	2000	01	20	ERS	5013100000
V	KOFI	COMP	2000	02	20	ERL	5013200000
V	KOFI	COMP	2000	02	20	ERS	5013200000
005	**Acc Key: Details**						
V	KOFI	COMP	1000		MWS		2470000000
V	KOFI	COMP	2000			MWS	2470000000

Figure 48: Revenue account determination

118. Outline 'Credit Management' in SAP.

Credit Management helps in determining credit limits of customers, aids in creation of '***credit check***' policies besides helping the companies in monitoring and evaluation of their customers. This is a cross-functional responsibility in SAP, covering both the Sales & Distribution and Financial Accounting modules.

As in case of any automated process like dunning, payment etc, credit management in SAP requires certain pre-requisites to be defined before hand:

1. ***Customer master data*** is created both in SD & FI
2. ***Credit control area*** has been defined and assigned to Company Code

SAP makes use of the concept '***credit control area***' for credit management. As explained elsewhere, credit control area is an organizational element defined to which one or more Company Codes are attached. In case of customers defined under more than one Company Code, they may fall under different credit control areas. But, note that:

- o A Client can have more than one credit control area. But the converse is not true: one credit control area can not be assigned to more than one Client.
- o A credit control area can be assigned to more than one Company Code. But the converse is not true: one Company Code can not be assigned to more than one credit control area.

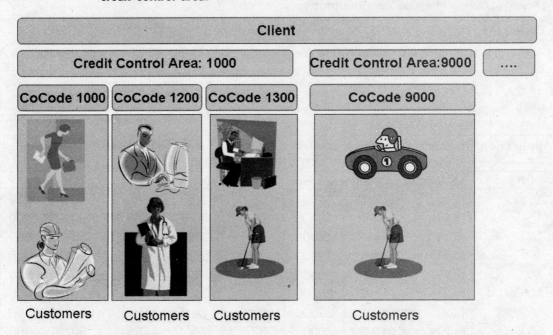

Figure 49: Client – Credit Control Area – Company Code - Customer

While defining the credit limit for a customer:

- o You will define a maximum limit per credit control area (Example: Credit Control Area AAAA -> USD 500, 000, Credit Control Area BBBB -> USD 200, 000)
- o You will define a global maximum limit for all credit control areas put together (USD 600, 0000)

3. ***Credit data*** (per credit control area 'maximum limit' as well as the 'total' for all areas, in the control data screen) for the customer has been created

4. ***Risk categories*** have been defined and assigned to customers

5. ***Credit groups*** (document credit group) for document types have been defined. Document credit groups combine order types and delivery types for credit control

6. Defined, in SD, at what of time (when order is received or when a delivery is made etc) the ***credit check*** should happen

The ***credit management process*** starts when a sales order is entered in SD. Imagine this results in exceeding the credit limit defined for the customer. Now:

a. System creates three ***comparison totals*** considering (1) open receivables, (2) sales order values, value of goods to be delivered, and billing document value from SD and (3) special GL transactions (e.g. 'down payments' and 'bills of exchange').

b. Based on (a) above the system throws an (1) error message, and prevents from saving the order or (2) warning message, and the system does not prevent saving, but order is 'blocked'.

c. ***Credit representative***, using the ***information functions*** (SD information system, FI information system, credit overview, credit master list, early warning list, oldest open item, last payment, customer master, account analysis etc), process this blocked order either (1) from the 'blocked SD documents list' or (2) the mail box, and releases the order, if necessary.

d. Delivery is created, billing document generated and posted, A/R updated

e. Customer pays the invoice, A/R is posted

119. How 'Credit Check' is defined?

Credit Check is defined for any valid combination of the following:

- Credit control area
- Risk category
- Document credit group

120. Differentiate 'Static Credit Check' from 'Dynamic Check'.

Under **Static Credit Check**, the system calculates the credit exposure of a particular customer as the total of:

- Open order (delivery not yet done)
- Open delivery (value of deliveries yet to be invoiced)
- Open billing documents (not transferred to accounting)
- Open items (AR item not yet settled by the customer)

Customer's credit exposure is not to exceed the established credit limit.

The **Dynamic Credit Check** is split into two parts:

- ***Static limit***: Total of open items, open billing, and open delivery values
- ***Dynamic limit*** (Open Order Value): The value of all un-delivered and partial delivered orders totalled and stored on a time-scale in future (10 days, 1 wk etc) known as ***'horizon date'***.

During the 'dynamic credit check', the system will ignore all orders beyond the 'horizon date'. The sum total of 'static' and 'dynamic limits' should not exceed the credit limit established for the customer.

121. List the Reports in 'Credit Management'.

SAP provides you with the following **Reports in Credit Management**:

- **RFDKLI10** Customers with missing Credit Data
- **RFDKLI20** Re-organization of Credit Limit for Customers
- **RFDKLI30** Short Overview of Credit Limit

- **RFDKLI40** Overview of Credit Limit
- **RFDKLI41** Credit Master Sheet
- **RFDKLI42** Early Warning List (of Critical Customers)
- **RFDKLI43** Master Data List
- **RFDKLI50** Mass change of Credit Limit Data
- **RVKRED06** Checking Blocked Credit Documents
- **RVKRED08** Checking Credit Documents which reach the Credit Horizon
- **RVKRED09** Checking the Credit Documents from Credit View
- **RVKRED77** Re-organization of SD Credit Data

122. How 'Partial Payment' differs from 'Residual Payment'?

When processing the '*incoming payment*' to apply to one or more of the 'open items' of a customer, there may be a situation wherein the incoming payment is more than the '*tolerances*' allowed. In this case, you can still go ahead and process the payment by resorting either to (1) Partial Payment or (2) Residual payment.

Partial payment results in posting a credit to the customer's 'open item', but leaves the original item intact. As a result, no open item is cleared. During partial payment, the system updates the '*invoice reference*' and '*allocation*' fields.

As against the partial payment, the **Residual payment** clears the particular 'open item' against which the payment is applied. However, since there are not enough amounts to clear the entire open item, the system creates a new open item being the difference between the original invoice item and the payment applied. Note that the new invoice/open item created by the system will have the new document date and new baseline date though you can change these dates.

123. What is a 'Payment Advice'?

A **Payment Advice** helps in automatic searching of 'open items' during the 'clearing' process to match an 'incoming payment'. This is possible because you can use the 'payment advice' number instead of specifying parameters in '*selection screen*'. A typical payment advice may contain details like: document number, amount, currency, reason for under payment etc. The payment advices are of various categories; the first 2 digits of the payment advice number helps to differentiate one payment advice from another:

- Bank advice
- EDI advice
- Lockbox advice (created during clearing process, available in the system whether clearing was successful or not)
- Manual advice
- Advice from a bank statement

Most of the payment advices are deleted as soon as the clearing is successful in the system.

124. Describe 'Lock Box' processing.

The **Lock Box** processing (configured in FI-TR module), of incoming payments, is used predominantly in the US. Here, the bank receives the checks from customers as incoming payment, creates payment advice for each of these customer check payments and informs the payee about the payment, in BAI file format. This lockbox file is sent to the payee who imports the details into the system using this electronic file. The system updates the payments into the GL by way of '*batch input*' processing.

125. How can 'Reason Codes' help in incoming payment processing?

Reason Codes configured in the system help to handle the 'payment differences' of individual open items in an invoice (either using payment or advice or in the normal course). To each of the reason codes, you will define the 'posting rules' and the GL accounts in the IMG.

Once done, when there is a payment difference against a particular open item, the system looks for the reason code:

- When '***charge-off indicator***' has been set for that reason code, then the system posts the payment difference to a GL account. When this indicator is <u>not</u> set, then a new open item is created for the payment difference.

- When '***disputed item indicator***' has been set, then the system ignores these line items from counting for customer's credit limit.

126. What is 'Dunning' in SAP?

The SAP System allows you to 'dun' (remind) business partners automatically. The system duns the open items from business partner accounts. The ***dunning program*** selects the overdue open items, determines the ***dunning level*** of the account in question, and creates ***dunning notices***. It then saves the ***dunning data*** determined for the items and accounts affected. You can use the dunning program to dun both customers and vendors. It may be necessary to dun a vendor in case of debit balance as a result of a credit memo.

Dunning is administered through a *Dunning Program*, which uses ***dunning key*** (to limit the dunning level per item), ***dunning procedure*** and ***dunning area*** (if dunning is not done at Company Code level).

Dunn.key	Max.level	Print sep	Text
1	1	☐	Triggers maximum dunning level 1
2	2	☐	Triggers maximum dunning level 2
3	3	☐	Triggers maximum dunning level 3
Z		☑	Payment has been made, separate item display

Figure 50: Dunning Key

Transaction Code
F150

127. What is a 'Dunning Procedure'?

SAP comes delivered with a number or **Dunning Procedures** which you can copy and create your own:

Procedure	Name
0001	Four-level dunning, every two weeks
0002	Four-level dunning, every month
0003	Payment reminder, every two weeks
FVVD	Four-level dunning, every two weeks (loans)
IMMO	Four-level dunning, every two weeks (real estate)

Figure 51: List of Dunning Procedures

A **dunning procedure** controls:

- ● *Dunning interval* / frequency
- ● *Grace days* / minimum days in arrear
- ● Number of d*unning levels* (at least one level)

Dunn.Procedure	0001			
Name	Four-level dunning, every two weeks			
Dunning level	1	2	3	4
Days in arrears/interest				
Days in arrears	2	16	30	44
Calculate interest?	☐	☐	☑	☑
Print parameters				
Always dun?	☐	☐	☐	☑
Print all items	☐	☐	☑	☑
Payment deadline			10	7
Legal dunning procedure				
☐ Always dun in legal dunning proc.				

Figure 52: Dunning Levels

- ● Transactions to be dunned
- ● Interest to be calculated on the overdue items
- ● Known or negotiated leave, if any, which needs to be considered in selecting the overdue items
- ● Company Code data like (a) Is dunning per 'dunning area'? (b) Is dunning per 'dunning level'? (c) Reference Company Code (d) Dunning Company Code etc
- ● *Dunning forms* / media to be selected for the *dunning run*

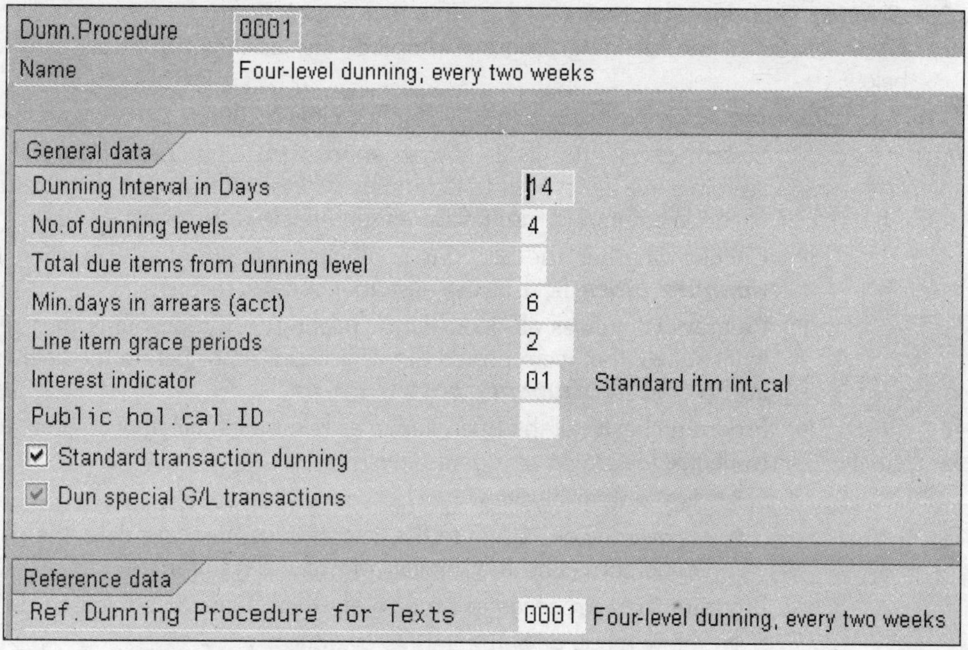

| Dunn.Procedure | 0001 |
| Name | Four-level dunning; every two weeks |

General data

Dunning Interval in Days	14
No. of dunning levels	4
Total due items from dunning level	
Min. days in arrears (acct)	6
Line item grace periods	2
Interest indicator	01 Standard itm int.cal
Public hol.cal.ID	
☑ Standard transaction dunning	
☑ Dun special G/L transactions	

Reference data

| Ref.Dunning Procedure for Texts | 0001 Four-level dunning, every two weeks |

Figure 53: Control Information in a Dunning Procedure

128. What is a 'Dunning Area'?

Dunning Area is optional, and is required only if dunning is not done at Company Code level. The Dunning area can correspond to a sales division, sales organization etc.

129. Describe the 'Dunning' process.

The **Dunning Process** involves three major steps:

1. Maintaining the **parameters** for the ***dunning run***
2. Creating / editing the ***dunning proposal*** generated by the system
3. Printing ***dunning notices***

1. *Maintaining Dunning Parameter*

   As the first step in dunning, you need to maintain certain parameters, which identify the current dunning run. Entering the date of execution and the dunning run identifier is the starting point, after which you will continue to maintain other parameters like:

   i. Dunning date to be printed on the notice
   ii. Document posted up to
   iii. Company Code
   iv. Account restrictions (optional)

   Now, you can save the parameters and display the log generated (to see if there were any errors), dunning list (list of accounts and items) and some dunning statistics (blocked accounts / items etc).

2. Creating Dunning Proposal

Once scheduled, the 'dunning program' prepares the 'dunning proposal' as described below:

  a. ***Dunning Program*** determines which accounts to dun:

  i. System checks the fields '***Dunn.procedure***' and '***Last dunned***' in the customer master record to determine whether the arrears date or the date of the last dunning run lies far enough back in the past.

  ii. Checks whether the account is blocked for dunning according to the ***dunning block*** field in the customer master record

  iii. Program processes all open items, relating to the accounts thus released in (ii) above, that were posted to this account on or before the date entered in the field '***Documents posted up to***'.

  iv. Program checks all the open items, as released in (iii) above, in an account to decide:

  - Is the item blocked?
  - Is overdue according to the date of issue, the base date, the payment conditions, and the number of grace days granted

  v. Program then proceeds to process all open items thus released, in (iv):

  - How many days the item is overdue
  - Which 'dunning level' for a particular open item

  vi. Program determines the highest 'dunning level' for the account based on (v) above. The highest 'dunning level' determined is stored in the master record of the account when you print the letters. This 'dunning level' determines the 'dunning text' and a 'special dunning form', if defined.

  vii. Program then proceeds to check each account:

  - Do the customer / vendor have a debit balance with regard to all open overdue items selected?
  - Are the total amount to be dunned and the percentage of all open items more than the minimum amount and percentage defined in the 'dunning procedure'?
  - Is the 'dunning level' for the account or the overdue items higher than it was for the last 'dunning run'? If not, are there new open items to be dunned (with a previous dunning level of 0)? If not, does the 'dunning procedure' for this level specify that dunning be repeated?

  b. Program creates the ***dunning proposal list***

  c. Edit ***dunning proposal list***

  i. You can edit the *Dunning Proposal* so as to:

  - Raise or lower the 'dunning level' of an item
  - Block an item from being dunned
  - Block an account for the current 'dunning run' or remove the block
  - Block an account in the master record for dunning or remove the block
  - Block a document for dunning or remove the block

ii. You can view the sample print out, to ascertain how the printed notice would look like. (Maximum 10 notices can be seen on the screen).

iii. You may also display 'logs' to see the changes made in the editing earlier, as a confirmation of what you wanted to change in the system generated proposal earlier. If necessary, you can go back and change the proposal.

3. *Print Dunning Notices*

You can use a 'single form' or 'multiple forms', which will have different text, based on the 'dunning levels'. There may also be a requirement to use a completely different form for **legal dunning**. Once the print option is activated, the program prints the notices, and the dunning related information like the 'dunning level', 'last dunned' etc are updated in the customer / vendor masters. SAP provides the option to optically 'archive' the notices as the system prints the dunning notices. There is also a provision to re-start the printing if the same is interrupted before complete printing.

130. Can you 'dun' customers across 'Clients' in a single 'Dunning Run'?

No. All the data processing is carried out *per Client*.

131. What differentiates one 'Dunning Level' from another?

This **Dunning Level** determines the 'dunning text' and (if one is required) a 'special dunning form'. The 'dunning program' determines what 'dunning level' should be used in the 'dunning run'. The dunning level so determined is stored in the master record of the account when the 'dunning letter' is printed. The dunning level may also determine whether there will be some 'dunning charges'.

132. How many 'Dunning Levels' can be defined?

You may define up to nine dunning levels. If there is only one dunning level, then it is called as the *'payment reminder'*.

Accounts Payables

133.   Explain 'Account Payables' sub-module.

Accounts Payables, a sub-module under Financial Accounting (FI) takes care of vendor related transactions as the module is tightly integrated with the purchasing transactions arising out of '**Procurement Cycle**'. The module helps in processing the outgoing payments either manually or automatically through '**Automatic Payment Program**'. Also helps in '**Vendor Evaluations**'.

134.   What documents result from 'Procurement Processes'?

In **Materials Management** (MM):

- **PR**: Purchase Requisition (manual or automatic using MRP)
- **PO**: Purchase Order

In **Financial Accounting** (FI):

- Invoice Verification
- Vendor Payment (manual or automatic)

Both MM and FI areas:

- Goods Receipt

You may also group these documents into (1) Order documents, (2) GR (Goods Receipt) documents and (3) IR (Invoice Receipt) documents. While GR/IR documents can be displayed both in MM and FI views, the order documents can be viewed in MM view only.

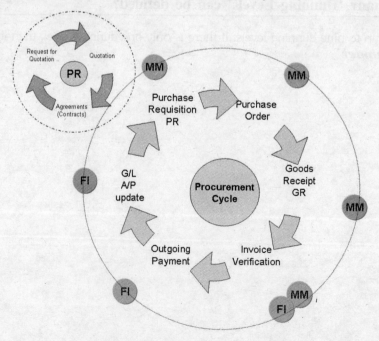

Figure 54: Procurement Cycle

135. Describe 'Purchase Cycle'.

The **Purchase Cycle or Procurement Cycle** encompasses all the activities starting from purchase requisition, purchase order, goods movement, goods receipt, invoicing, invoice verification, payment to vendors and ending with updating of vendor account balances.

136. What is 'Purchase Requisition'?

A **Purchase Requisition**, **PR**, is the document which outlines a company's purchasing needs of a material/service from vendor(s). A PR, typically an *internal document* that can be created automatically or manually, identifies the demand for a product and authorizes the purchasing department to procure the same. In automatic creation of PR, this is done as a result of **MRP** (*Material Requirements Planning*). The PR, after identifying the vendor, is processed further to result in a **RFQ** (*Request for Quotation*) or directly to a **Purchase Order** (**PO**).

137. What is 'Request for Quotation (RFQ)'?

A **RFQ (Request for Quotation)**, which can be created directly or with reference to another RFQ or a PR or an Outline Agreement, is actually an invitation to vendor (s) to submit a 'quotation' for supplying a material or service. The RFQ will contain the terms and condition for supply. You may send the RFQ to a single or multiple vendors, and you can monitor the same by sending reminders to those who have not responded to the RFQ.

138. What is an 'Outline Agreement'?

An **Outline Agreement**, a declaration binding both the buyer and seller, is the buyer's intention to purchase material/service with certain terms and conditions agreed to between both the parties. The essential difference between the 'outline agreement' and 'quotation' is that the outline agreements do not contain the details like delivery schedule or quantities. The outline agreements can be (1) *contracts* or (2) *scheduling agreements*.

139. What is a 'Contract'?

A **Contract**, also referred to as a '*Blanket Order*', is a long-term legal agreement between the buyer and the seller for procurement of materials or services over a period of time. The contract, created directly or with reference to a PR / RFQ or another contract, is valid for a certain period of time with start and end dates clearly mentioned. There are two types of contracts: (1) *Quantity Contracts* and (2) *Value Contracts*.

140. What is a 'Release Order'?

A **Release Order** is a 'purchase order' created against a Contract. The release orders usually do not contain information on quantities or delivery dates and are also called as '*Blanket Releases*' or *Contract Releases*' or '*Call-Offs*'.

141. What is a 'Scheduling Agreement'?

A **Scheduling Agreement** is also a long-term agreement with the buyer and seller for procurement of certain materials or services subject to certain terms and conditions. These agreements can be created directly or with reference to other documents like another scheduling agreement, or RFQ or PR. These agreements help in promoting *Just-In-Time (JIT)* deliveries, less paper work, reduce supply lead times and ensures low inventory for the buyer.

142. What is a 'Quotation'?

A **Quotation** contains information relating to the price and other conditions for supply of a material or a service by a vendor, and is termed as the vendor's willingness to supply the same based on those conditions. You will be able to compare the data from quotations using a *Price Comparison List* which will help in identifying the most reasonable vendor for supply of that item(s). After you receive the quotations, you will typically enter the quotation data (pricing/delivery) in RFQ. The SAP system can easily be configured to automatically print '*Rejections*' for vendors whose quotation are not selected.

143. What is a 'Purchase Order'?

A **Purchase Order (PO),** is a legal contract between a vendor and a buyer, mentioning the material/service to be purchased / procured on certain terms and conditions. The order mentions, among other things, the quantity to be purchased, price per unit, delivery related conditions, payment/pricing information etc.

A PO can be created:

1. Directly
2. With reference to a PR / RFQ / contract or another PO.

Remember, all items on a PO should relate to the same Company Code.

144. What is a 'PO History'?

The **Purchase Order History** (PO History) lists all the transactions for all the items in a PO like the GR/IR document numbers.

145. Will FI document be created during Purchase Order (PO)?

No. There will not be any document created on the FI side during creation of a PO. However, there can be a document for posting 'commitment' to a Cost Center in CO. (The offsetting entry is posted at the time of GR).

146. Explain FI-MM Integration.

The **FI-MM Integration** is based on the following:

- Movement Types
- Valuation Class
- Transaction Keys
- Material Type

MvT	Movement Type Text
101	GR goods receipt
102	Reversal of GR
103	GR into blocked stck
104	Rev. GR to blocked
105	GR from blocked stck
106	Rev.GR from blocked
107	GR to Val. Bl. Stock
108	GR to Val. Bl. Rev.
109	GR fr. Val. Bl. St.
110	GR fr. Val. Bl. Rev.

Figure 55: Movement Types

Movement Type is the 'classification key' indicating the type of material movement (for example, goods receipt, goods issue, physical stock transfer). The movement type enables the system to find pre-defined posting rules determining how the accounts in FI (stock and consumption accounts) are to be posted and how the stock fields in the material master record are to be updated.

Valuation Class refers to the assignment of a material to a group of GL accounts. Along with other factors, the valuation class determines the GL accounts that are updated as a result of a valuation-relevant transaction or event, such as a goods movement. The valuation class makes it possible to:

- Post the stock values of materials of the <u>same</u> material type to <u>different</u> GL accounts
- Post the stock values of materials of <u>different</u> material types to the <u>same</u> GL account

Transaction Key (also known as the '**Event Key** or **Process Key**') allows the users to differentiate between the various transactions and events (such as physical inventory transactions and goods movements) that occur within the area of inventory management. The transaction / event type controls the filing/storage of documents and the assignment of document numbers.

Material Type groups together materials with the same basic attributes, for example, raw materials, semi-finished products, or finished products. When creating a material master record, you must assign the material to a material type. The material type determines:

- Whether the material is intended for a specific purpose, for example, as a *Configurable Material or Process Material*
- Whether the material number can be assigned internally or externally
- The *Number Range* from which the material number is drawn
- Which screens appear and in what sequence
- Which user department data you may enter
- What *Procurement Type* the material has; that is, whether it is manufactured in-house or procured externally, or both

Together with the plant, the material type determines the material's inventory management requirement that is:

- Whether changes in quantity are updated in the material master record

- Whether changes in value are also updated in the stock accounts in financial accounting.

147. What happens, in SAP, when you post a 'Goods Receipt'?

When you post a **Goods Receipt** (**GR**), the stock account is debited (stock quantity increases) and the credit goes to **GR/IR Clearing Account** which is the intermediate processing account before you actually process the vendor invoice or payments to the vendor:

> Debit: Inventory Account
> Credit: GR/IR Clearing Account

During this (1) a material document is created, (2) an accounting document to update the relevant GL account is created, (3) PO order history is updated and finally (4) system enables you to print the GR slip.

148. Explain 'Invoice Verification (IV)' in SAP.

Invoice Verification involves:

1. Validating the accuracy of the invoices (quantity, value etc)
2. Checking for 'blocked' invoices (which varied to a greater extent from that of the PO)
3. Matching of invoices received from vendors with that of the Purchase Order/Goods Receipt. At this point of time PO History is updated for the corresponding PO Line Item(s) of the matched invoice.
4. Passing of matched invoices to FI module. The system posts the following entries:
   > Debit: GR/IR Clearing Account
   > Credit: Vendor A/c (Accounts Payable open line item)
   > Credit: GL Reconciliation Account

The different scenarios in invoice verification include:

1. *GR based Invoice Verification indicator is* not *set in the PO detail screen:*
   Although this setting enables you to post the invoice referenced to a PO prior to making a GR, the system will block the invoice for payment (as this kind of posting results in a **Quantity Variance** as there has not been a GR).

2. *GR based Invoice Verification indicator is set in the PO detail screen:*
   When the PO number is referenced the system brings up all the unmatched items of GR in the selection screen. You will not be able to post the invoice for its full value, unless the PO has been fully received.

149. How do you deal with the 'Tax' when you post an invoice?

When you enter an invoice, based on the configuration settings, the system checks the Tax Code, and calculates the applicable tax or validates the Tax Amount entered by you:

1. *Manual Entry:* Input the **Tax Code** and the **Tax Amount.** The system will validate and issue a message in case it does not find the tax code or if the amount is different.
2. *Automatic Entry:* Leave the Tax Code and Tax Amount fields blank. Tick the 'Calculate Tax' indicator. The system picks up the corresponding tax code and calculates the tax amount automatically.

150. What 'Variances' you will come across in Invoice Verification?

The system needs to be configured properly with *'Tolerances'* so that you are not hampered with variances when you try *Invoice Verification*. You need to define the lower and upper limits for each combination of the Company Code and the tolerance key defined for the various variances. The system, then, checks these tolerance limits and issues warnings or prevents you from proceeding further, when you process an invoice.

The **Variances** arise because of mismatch or discrepancies between the invoice and the PO against which the invoice has been issued. Normally you will encounter:

1. *Price Variance:* If there is a discrepancy in invoice price and PO item prices
2. *Schedule Variance:* If the planned delivery date is later than the invoice postings
3. *Quantity variance:* If the delivered quantity (or delivered quantity less previously invoiced quantity) is not the same as that of the invoiced quantity. When the invoiced quantity is more than the GR, the system requires more GRs to square off the situation.

151. Outline 'Vendor Payment' in SAP system.

The payments to a single or multiple vendors can either be handled in a manual process or through an *'Automatic Payment Program'*. The open liability item created for the vendor during the invoice verification will be squared off when you make the vendor payment or when you run the automatic payment program. The payment program in SAP is designed in such a way to allow you to enjoy the maximum discount allowed by that vendor.

152. Explain 'Automatic Payment Program'.

Automatic Payment Program in SAP helps to process payment transactions both with customers and vendors. AR/AP/TR/Bank Accounting uses payment program.

The 'automatic payment program' helps in determining:

- **What is to be paid?** To do this, you specify rules according to which the open items to be paid are selected and grouped for payment.
- **When payment is to be carried out?** The due date of the open items determines when payment is carried out. However, you can specify the payment deadline in more detail via configuration.
- **To whom the payment is made?** You specify the payee (the vendor or the alternate payee as the case may be).
- **How the payment is made?** You determine rules that are used to select a payment method.
- **From where the payment is made?** You determine rules that are used to select a bank and a bank account for the payment.

153. Explain 'Automatic Payment Program' Configuration.

Before you are ready to run the **Automatic Payment Program**, the following should have been defined / configured in the system:

- *House Bank* and the corresponding *bank accounts*
- *Payment Methods* to be used for the Company Code. SAP comes with pre-defined

payment methods, both for AR and AP. The following payment methods are available for you to select from depending upon the requirements:

a. Accounts Payable

    o   Check (S) / Transfer / Postal Giro transfer / Bill of exchange

b. Accounts Receivable

    o   Bank collection / Bank direct debit / Refund by check / Refund by bank transfer / BE payment request

- **Bank Chain** defined, if necessary. Bank chains are used to make payment via more than one bank, for example via the correspondent banks of the house bank, the recipient bank, or the intermediary banks. You can define up to three banks.

- **Payment Forms** defined. SAP delivers standard forms, which can be modified, or new forms can be created for use.

Transaction Code
FBZP

Customizing: Maintain Payment Program

> All company codes

> Paying company codes

> Pmnt methods in country

> Pmnt methods in company code

> Bank determination

> House banks

Figure 56: Customizing Automatic Payment program using FBZP

You may do most of the configurations by using the Transaction Code **FBZP** and branching to individual sections thereon. Or you may use the following Transaction Codes for individually doing the same:

1. (Sending) Company Code specifications

Transaction Code
OBVU

a. Sending Company Code – if Company Code 'A' is making payments on behalf of 'B', then 'B' is the *Sending Company Code*. Else, sending Company Code is considered as the paying Company Code (both are one and the same)

b. Tolerance days

c. Paying Company Code specifications
   - Minimum amounts for incoming and outgoing payments.
   - Forms for payment advice and EDI
   - Bill of Exchange parameters

2. Payment Methods /Country & Bank determination

Transaction Code
OBVCU

a. Payment Methods /country
   - Payment Method for outgoing/incoming
   - Payment Method classification
   - Master data requirements
   - Posting details – document types
   - Payment medium details - Print programs
   - Permitted currencies (leave blank to allow all currencies)

b. Bank Determination
   - Ranking Order
     - o Per Payment Method:
       - ➢ Which bank should be used first, second etc
       - ➢ Currency
       - ➢ Bill of Exchange
   - Bank accounts
   - Available amounts
     - o Per House Bank and Payment Method combination:
       - ➢ Offset a/c for sub-ledger posting
       - ➢ Available funds in each bank
       - ➢ Clearing accounts for Bill of Exchange
   - Value date
   - Charge

3. Payment methods per Company Code

Transaction Code
OBVU

a. For each Payment Method and Company Code you need to define:
- Minimum / maximum payment amounts
- Whether payment abroad or in foreign currency is allowed
- Payment Media
- Bank optimization

4. House Bank

Transaction Code
FI12

154. How do you execute 'Automatic Payment Program'?

The following are the series of events happening in the system when you try to execute an **Automatic Payment Program:**

1. Maintain Payment Parameters

To start with, you need to maintain the parameters required like date of execution of 'payment run', 'payment run identifier' etc. Once this is done, you need to specify what should be the 'posting date' of these payments, the 'document date' up to which the program should consider the items, the paying Company Code, payment methods to be considered, what will be the 'next posting date', is there certain accounts which need to be excluded from the run etc. The payment run, then needs to be scheduled either immediately or at a specified time/date

2. Payment Proposal

The system creates a 'payment proposal', based on the payment parameters maintained in (1) above. The system selects the eligible **Open Items** based on the following sequence:

a. **Due date** is determined via the **Base Line Date** and the **Terms of Payment** for each of the line item

b. Program calculates the **Cash Discount Period** and due date for the **Net Payment**

c. **Grace Period**s are then added to this due date

d. Which **Special GL** accounts are to be included, based on what you have already maintained as the parameters in (1) above

e. The system will determine whether to include an item during the current run or for the future one based on the specifications you made in (1)

f. **Blocking** an item

The payment proposal can be displayed for further processing; the 'log' can be checked to see the system messages, and the exception list generated for further evaluation.

3. **Payment Proposal**
   With the payment proposal available, you can now edit the proposal to:
   a. Change House Bank, from what was maintained earlier
   b. Change Payment Method, if necessary
   c. Change Payment Due Date so as to relax or restrict certain open items
   d. *Block / Unblock* line items

4. **Payment run**
   After the payment proposal has been edited, you can run the **Payment Program** that creates the payment documents and prepares the data for printing the forms or creating the tape or disk. Before printing the forms, check the logs to determine that the payment program run was successful.

5. **Print run**
   Payment Medium Programs use the data prepared by the payment program to create forms (payment advice, EDI accompanying sheet) or files for the data media. The data created payment program are stored in the following Tables:

   REGUH Payee or Payment Method data

   REGUP Individual Open Items data

   REGUD Bank Data and Payment Amounts data

   You need to define **Variants** for print programs:
   a. Per *Payment Method* per country : assign a *Print Program*
   b. To run the *Print Program* : at least one *Variant* per *Print Program* per *Payment Method*

Transaction Code
FI10

155.   Can you pay a vendor in a currency other than the invoice currency?

With the release 4.5A, it has been made possible that you can pay to a vendor in a currency which is different from that of the transaction / invoice currency. This is achieved by entering the required currency code directly in the open item. Prior to this release, to pay in a different currency, you have to manually process the payment.

156.   What is a 'Payment Block'?

A **Payment Block** prevents you from paying an open item of a vendor. The payment block is entered in the '**Payment Block**' field in (1) a vendor master record or directly in the (2) open line item.

Use the payment **'Block Indicators'** to define the '**Payment Block Reasons'**. You may use the SAP delivered payment block indicators (**A, B, I, R** etc) or create your own. An indicator like '*' is used when you want to skip the particular account, and a blank indicator indicates that the account / item is free for payment. However, for each of these 'block indicators', you need to configure whether changes would be allowed during processing the payment proposal. Then, it is also possible that you block a payment or release a blocked one while processing the '**Payment Proposal**'.

You may also propose a 'payment block indicator' while defining a Terms of Payment.

157.   How do you release 'Blocked invoices for payments'?

The system will **block an invoice** if it comes across with an item with a '**Blocking Reason**'. The blocking reason may be due to (1) variances, or (2) inspection related issues. When the system blocks an invoice for payment, 'payment block' field is checked by the system.

You will be using an '**Invoice Release Transaction**' to select the blocked invoices for processing further. The 'release' of blocked invoices for payments can be handled either manually or automatically.

158.   What is 'Account Assignment Category'?

The **Automatic Account Assignment** logic takes care of posting to the correct GL accounts for a '**Stock Material**' with the '**Material Type**' permitting inventory management, and the material master contains this information as to which GL account needs to be updated. But, there are material line items ('**Non-Stock**' materials) created manually in Purchase Requisition / Purchase Order / Outline Agreement for which some one needs to decide the account assignment data, and manually enter the same in the Purchase Requisition. It is here, the **Account Assignment Category** determines where to allocate the costs relating to such materials. The account assignment category helps you to define (1) the type of account assignment (Sales Order-C, Project-P, Cost Centre-K etc) and (2) which accounts are to be posted to when GR/IR is posted to.

159.   What is a 'Credit Memo'?

The **Credit Memo** is issued by the vendor who has earlier supplied you some services or materials. The occasion is necessitated when the delivered goods are damaged or you have returned some of the goods back to the vendor. The system treats both the invoices and the credit memo in the same way, except that the postings are done with the opposite sign.

If the credit memo is for the entire invoiced quantity, the system generates the credit memo automatically. On the contrary, if credit memo relates to a portion of the invoiced quantity, you need to process the same manually in the system.

160.   What are 'Special GL Transactions'?

Special GL Transactions are not directly posted to the GL (*Reconciliation Accounts*) though these are related to sub-ledger accounts like AR/AP. The transactions to these accounts are shown separately in the balance sheet. There are specific posting keys/indicators defined in the system to regulate the postings to these items. You need to specify a **Special GL Indicator** (like, **F**-Down Payment Request, **A**-Down Payment) for processing such a transaction. And, the system will make use of the specially defined posting keys (09-customer debit, 19-customer credit, 29-vendor debit and 39-vendor credit) for posting these special GL transactions.

There are three types of Special GL transactions:

- Free Offsetting Entries (Down Payment)
- Statistical Postings (Guarantee)
- Noted Items (Down Payment Request)

A	Down payment on current assets
B	Financial assets down payment
D	Discount
E	Unchecked invoice
F	Down payment request
G	Guarantee received
H	Security deposit
I	Intangible asset down payment
M	Tangible asset down payment
O	Amortization down payment
P	Payment request
S	Check/bill of exchange
V	Stocks down payment
W	Bill of exch. (rediscountable)

Figure 57: Special GL Indicators

161. Differentiate 'Free Offsetting Entry' from a 'Statistical Posting'.

Free Offsetting Entries postings are part of the regular postings but with a freely definable offsetting entry, and relate to the ***On-Balance Sheet Items***. On the other hand, in a **Statistical Posting**, you will always be posting to the same offsetting entry, and these are all the ***Off-Balance Sheet Items***.

162. What is a 'Noted Item'?

The **Noted Items** are never displayed on the *Financial Statements* as they serve only as reminders of a financial obligation like outstanding payments to be made or due to us, like the '***Down Payment Request***'. This kind of posting does not update any GL account in the system but helps to keep track of such obligations for *easy follow-up*. This is also, sometimes, referred to as a '***Memo Entry***'.

It will be interesting to note that while the *Special GL Indicator* for *Down Payment Request* is '***F***', you need to enter the indicator '***A***' as the target Special GL indicator, in the ***Down Payment Request Entry Screen***. When you post this entry, the system creates a one-sided memo entry for the customer or vendor but does not update the GL.

Asset Accounting

163. Explain 'Asset Accounting' (FI-AA).

The **Asset Accounting (FI-AA)** sub-module, in SAP, manages a company's fixed assets, right from the acquisition to retirement/scrapping. All the accounting transactions relating to depreciation, insurance etc of assets are taken care through this module, and all the accounting information from this module flow to FI-GL on a real time basis.

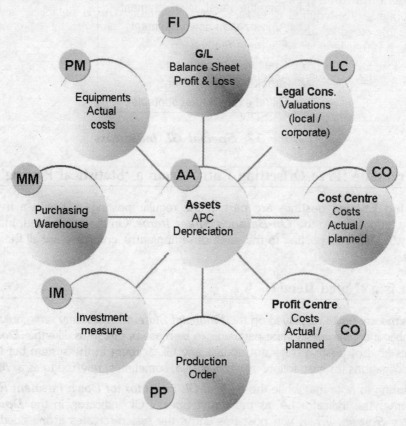

Figure 58: FI-AA integration with other modules

You will be able to directly post (the goods receipt (GR), invoice receipt (IR) or any withdrawal from a warehouse to fixed asset) from MM or PP to FI-AA. The integration with FI-AR helps in direct posting of sales to the customer account. Similarly, integration with FI-AP helps in posting an asset directly to FI-AA and the relevant vendor account, in cases where the purchase is not routed through MM module. You may capitalize the maintenance activities to an asset using settlements through PM module. FI-AA and FI-GL has a real-time integration wherein all the transactions like asset acquisition, retirement, transfer etc are recorded simultaneously in both the modules. However, batch processing is required to transfer the depreciation values, interest etc to the FI module.

The FI-AA and CO integration helps in:

- Assigning an asset to any of the **Controlling Objects** like cost centre, internal order

/ maintenance order, or an activity type. ***Internal Orders*** act as a two way link to the FI-AA: (i) they help to collect and pass on the capital expenditure to assets, and (ii) collect the depreciation / interest from FI-AA to controlling objects. (Note that when there is a situation where the asset master record contains an internal order and a cost centre, then the depreciation is <u>always</u> posted to the internal order and not to the cost centre.)

- The depreciation and the interest are passed on to the cost / profit centres

164. What is a 'Lean Implementation' in FI-AA?

The **Lean Implementation** is the scaled-down version of the regular FI-AA configuration in IMG, with minimal configuration required to enable asset accounting. This is suitable in cases of small companies using the standard functionalities of asset accounting, and also in situations where the *Asset Catalog* is not that large.

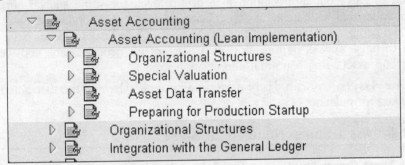

Figure 59: Lean implementation in FI-AA

You should not opt for lean implementation if:

- You need to *Depreciate In Foreign Currencies* as well
- You have *Group Assets*
- You need to define your own *Depreciation Keys / Transaction Types / Reports*
- You need a *Group Consolidation*

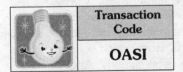

Transaction Code
OASI

165. What are all the kinds of 'Assets' in SAP?

An asset can be a ***Simple Asset*** or ***Complex Asset***. Depending upon the requirement, assets are maintained with ***Asset Main Number*** and ***Asset Sub-Numbers***. A complex asset consists of many ***Sub-Assets***; each of them identified using an asset sub-number. You may also use the concept of ***Group Asset***, in SAP.

166. Explain 'Complex Asset' and 'Asset Sub-Numbers'.

A **Complex Asset**, in SAP, is made up of many master records each of one which is denoted by an **Asset Sub-Number**. It is prudent to use asset sub-numbers, if:

- You need to manage the 'subsequent acquisitions' separately from the initial one (for example: your initial acquisition was a PC, and you are adding a printer later)
- You want to manage the various parts of an asset separately even at the time of 'initial acquisition' (for example: initial purchase of PC wherein you create separate asset master records for the monitor, CPU etc)
- You need to divide the assets based on certain technical qualities (keyboard, mouse etc)

When you manage a complex asset, the system enables you to evaluate the asset in all possible ways like (i) for a single sub-number, (ii) for all sub-number and (iii) for select sub-numbers.

167. What is a 'Group asset' in SAP? When you will use this?

A **Group Asset**, in SAP, is almost like a normal asset except that this can have (any number of) *sub-assets* denoted by *Asset Sub-Numbers.* The concept of group asset becomes necessary when you need to carry out depreciation at a group level, for some special purposes like tax reporting. Remember that SAP's way of depreciation is always at the individual asset level. Hence, to manage at the group level, you need the group asset. Once you decide to have group assets, you also need to have 'special depreciation areas' meant for group assets; you will not be able depreciate a group asset using a normal depreciation area.

Unlike **Complex Assets**, you can delete a group asset only when all the associated sub-numbers have been marked for deletion.

168. What is 'Asset Super Number' in SAP?

The concept of **Asset Super Number**, in FI-AA, is used only for reporting purposes. Here, you will assign a number of individual assets to a single asset number. By using this methodology, you will be able to see all the assets associated with the asset super number as a single asset (for example: brake assembly line) or as individual assets (for example: machinery, equipments in the brake assembly line).

169. What is 'Chart of Depreciation'? How it differs from 'Chart of Accounts'?

The **Chart of Depreciation** contains a list of country-specific depreciation areas. It provides the rules for the evaluation of assets that are valid in a given country or economic area. SAP comes supplied with default charts of depreciation that are based on the requirements of each country. These default charts of depreciation also serve as the 'reference charts' from which you can create a new chart of depreciation by copying one of the relevant charts of depreciation. After copying, you may delete the depreciation areas you do not need. However, note that the deletion must be done before any assets are created.

You are required to assign a chart of depreciation to your Company Code. Remember that one Company Code can have only one chart of depreciation assigned to, even though multiple Company Codes can use the same chart of depreciation.

The chart of accounts can be global, country specific and industry specifics based on the needs of the business. The chart of depreciation is only **country specific**. The charts of depreciation and charts of accounts are independent of each other.

Chart of Depreciation	Chart of Accounts
Established by FI-AA.	Established by FI.
A chart of depreciation is a collection of country specific depreciation areas.	The chart of accounts is a list of GL accounts used in a Company Code. The chart of accounts contain (1) chart of accounts area and (2) Company Code area.
The chart of depreciation is country specific. Usually you may not require more than one chart of depreciation. SAP comes delivered with many country specific charts of depreciation as 'reference charts' which can be copied to have your own chart of depreciation.	Depending upon the requirement you may have an 'operating chart of accounts', 'country specific chart of accounts', 'global chart of accounts' etc
One Company Code uses only one chart of depreciation.	One Company Code uses only one chart of accounts.
Many Company Codes, in the same country, can use the same chart of depreciation.	Several Company Codes within the same country can use the same chart of accounts.

170. How do you create an 'Asset Accounting Company Code'?

i.   Define the Company Code in FI configuration, and assign a chart of accounts to this Company Code

ii. Assign a chart of depreciation to this Company Code in FI-AA configuration

iii. Add necessary data for the Company Code for use in FI-AA, and your 'asset accounting Company Code' is now ready for use.

171. What is 'Depreciation'? Explain the various types.

Depreciation is the reduction in the ***book value*** of an asset due to its usage over time ('decline in economic usefulness') or due to legal framework for taxation reporting. The depreciation is usually calculated taking into account the ***economic life*** of the asset, ***expected value*** of the asset at the end of its economic life (***junk/scrap value***), ***method of depreciation calculation*** (straight line method, declining balance, sum of year digits, double declining etc) and the defined percentage decline in the value of the asset every year (20%, or 15%land so on).

The depreciation can either be (1) planned or (2) un-planned:

Planned depreciation is one which brings down the value of the asset after every planned period; say every month, till the asset value is fully depreciated over its life period. By this you will know what will be the value of the asset at any point of time in its active life.

On the contrary, ***unplanned depreciation*** is a sudden happening of an event or occurrence not foreseen (there could be a sudden break out of a fire damaging an asset, and forcing you to depreciate fully as it is no longer useful economically) resulting in a permanent reduction of the value of the asset.

In SAP, you will come across three types of depreciation:

1. ***Ordinary depreciation*** which is nothing but the 'planned depreciation'

2. ***Special depreciation*** which is over and above the 'ordinary depreciation', used normally for taxation purposes

3. Unplanned depreciation which is the result of reducing the asset value due to the sudden occurrence of certain events

172. Define 'Depreciation Area'.

The fixed assets are valued differently for different purpose (business, legal etc). SAP manages these different valuations by means of **Depreciation Areas**. There are various depreciation areas like book depreciation, tax depreciation, depreciation for cost-accounting purposes etc).

Chart of dep.	1IN	Sample chart of depreciation: India			

Define Depreciation Areas					
Ar.	Name of depreciation area		Real	G/L	Trg
1	Book depreciation		☑	1	
15	Depreciation as per Income Tax Act 1961		☑	0	
20	Cost-accounting depreciation		☑	3	
30	Consolidated balance sheet in local currency		☑	0	
31	Consolidated balance sheet in group currency		☑	0	
32	Book depreciation in group currency		☑	0	
41	Investment support deducted from asset		☑	0	
51	Investment support posted to liabilities		☑	1	

Figure 60: Depreciation Area

A depreciation area decides how and for what purpose an asset is evaluated. The depreciation area can be 'real' or a 'derived one'. You may need to use several depreciation areas for a single asset depending upon the valuation and reporting requirements.

The depreciation areas are denoted by a 2-character code in the system. The depreciation areas contain the depreciation terms which are required to be entered into the **asset master** records or **asset classes**. SAP comes delivered with many depreciation areas; however, the depreciation area **01 – Book Depreciation** is the major one.

The other depreciation areas are:

- Book depreciation in group currency
- Consolidated versions in local/group currency
- Tax balance sheet depreciation
- Special tax depreciation
- Country-specific valuation (e.g., net-worth tax or state calculation)
- Values/depreciations that differ from depreciation area 01 (example: cost-accounting reasons)
- Derived depreciation area (difference between book depreciation and country-specific tax depreciation)

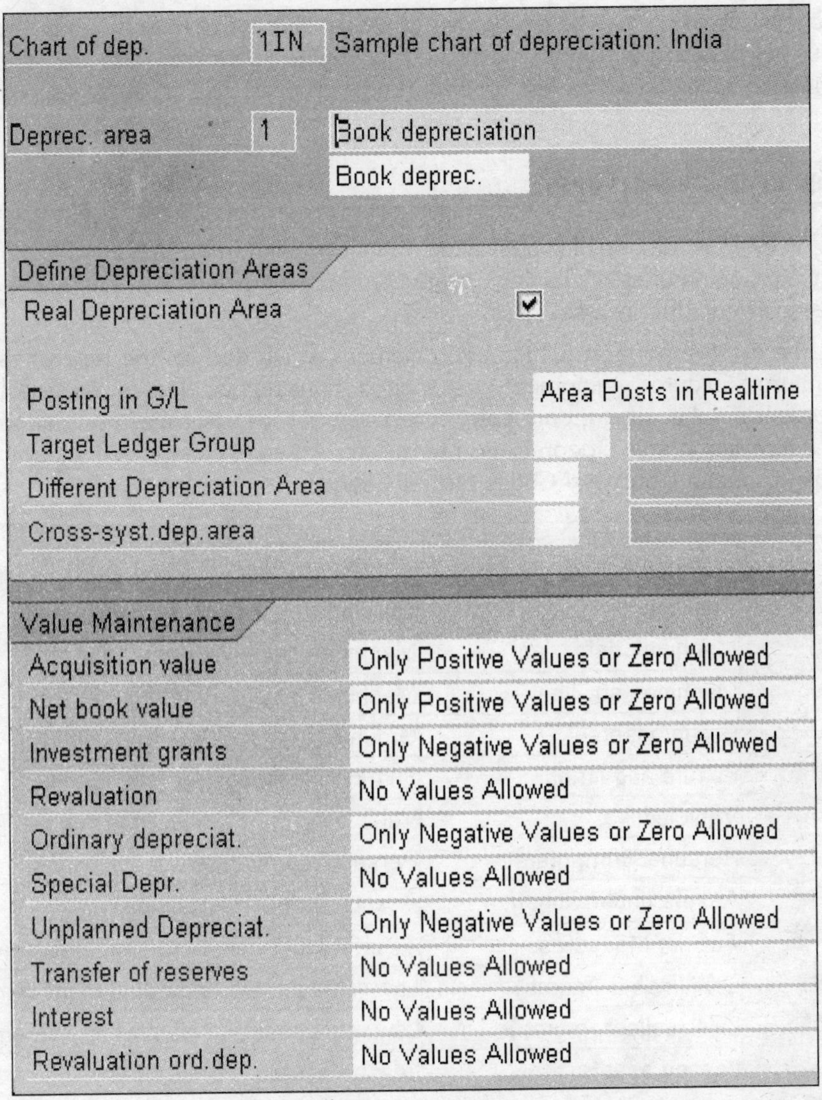

Chart of dep.	1IN	Sample chart of depreciation: India

Deprec. area	1	Book depreciation
		Book deprec.

Define Depreciation Areas

Real Depreciation Area   ☑

Posting in G/L	Area Posts in Realtime
Target Ledger Group	
Different Depreciation Area	
Cross-syst.dep.area	

Value Maintenance

Acquisition value	Only Positive Values or Zero Allowed
Net book value	Only Positive Values or Zero Allowed
Investment grants	Only Negative Values or Zero Allowed
Revaluation	No Values Allowed
Ordinary depreciat.	Only Negative Values or Zero Allowed
Special Depr.	No Values Allowed
Unplanned Depreciat.	Only Negative Values or Zero Allowed
Transfer of reserves	No Values Allowed
Interest	No Values Allowed
Revaluation ord.dep.	No Values Allowed

Figure 61: Details of 01-Book Depreciation

173. How to set-up 'Depreciation Areas postings' to FI from FI-AA?

You need to define how the various depreciation areas need to post to FI-GL. It can be any one of the following scenario:

- Post depreciation through 'periodic processing'
- Post both the APC (Acquisition and Production Costs) and depreciation through periodic processing
- Post the APC in 'real time' but depreciation through periodic processing
- No values are posted

However, you need to ensure that at least one depreciation area is configured to post values automatically to the FI-GL. Normally, this depreciation area will be 01 (book depreciation). For rest of the depreciation areas, it may be configured that they derive their values from this area and the difference thus calculated is automatically posted to FI-GL. There may also be situations wherein you may define depreciation areas just for reporting purposes, and these areas need not post to the GL.

174.   What is an 'Asset Class?

Asset Class, in SAP, is the basis for classifying an asset based on business and legal requirements. It is essentially a grouping of assets having certain common characteristics. Each asset in the system needs to be associated with an asset class.

Asset class is the most important configuration element which decides the type of asset (like land, buildings, furniture & fixtures, equipment, assets under construction, leased assets, low-value assets etc), the document number range, data entry screen lay out for asset master creation, GL account assignments, depreciation areas, depreciation terms etc. An asset class is defined at the Client level and is available to all the Company Codes of that Client.

Class	Short Text	Asset class description
1100	Buildings	Buildings
2000	Machines decl. depr.	Machines declining depr.
2100	Machines str.-line	Machines straight-line-depr.
2200	Group assets	Group assets (USA/Canada only)
3000	Fixture and fitting	Fixture and fittings
3100	Vehicles	Vehicles
3200	Personal computers	Personal computers
4000	Assets under Constr.	Assets under construction
4001	AuC for Measures	Assets under construction in investment me
5000	LVA (individ. mgmt.)	Low value assets (individual management)
5001	LVA (collect. mgmt.)	Low value assets (collective management)
6000	Leased assets	Leased assets
6001	Leased assets	Leased assets
9000	Leasing objects	Leasing objects
9360	Adm Purchasing	Administration Purchasing

Figure 62: Asset Class

The asset class consists of:

- A **header** section - control parameters for master data maintenance and account determination
- A **master data** section - default values for administrative data in the asset master record
- A **valuation** section - control parameters for valuation and depreciation terms

The asset class can be:

- Buildings

- Technical assets
- Financial assets
- Leased assets
- AuC (assets under construction)
- Low value assets

175. Why do you need 'Asset Classes'?

An **Asset Class** is the *link* between the asset master records and the relevant accounts in the GL. The ***account determination*** in the asset class enables you to post to the relevant GL accounts. Several asset classes can use the same account determination provided all these asset classes use the same chart of accounts and post to the same GL accounts.

176. What is an 'Asset Class Catalog'?

An **Asset Class Catalog** contains all the asset classes in an enterprise and hence valid across the Client. Since an asset class is valid across the Client, most of the characteristics of the asset class are defined at the Client level; however there are certain characteristics (like the depreciation key, for example), which can be defined at the chart of depreciation level.

177. Is it possible to create 'Asset Classes' automatically?

One of the benefits of lean implementation configuration is the ability to create asset classes automatically from the asset GL accounts. This tool selects the only necessary system settings so that the asset classes are created automatically in a very short time. During the process of creation, the system allows you to delete all the existing objects viz., asset classes, number ranges, account allocations, field selections etc. before creating the new ones.

The pre-requisites for automatic asset class creation include:

- Company Code is assigned to a chart of depreciation
- Depreciation areas have been defined
- GL account number is not more than 8 digits (else you need to assign the classes manually)

It is also to be noted that you may need to maintain the GL account for 'accumulated depreciation' manually. The system maintains the necessary account assignment only with regard to the depreciation area 01 (book depreciation): if you need more areas other than 01, you may need to do that manually in the IMG.

178. What is an 'Asset Value Date'?

The **Asset Value Date** will be the start date of depreciation for the asset. The 'planned depreciation' is calculated by the system based on this depreciation start date and the selected 'depreciation term' for that asset. Be careful with the posting date and asset value date: both these dates need to be in the same fiscal year.

179. What is an 'Asset Master'?

An **Asset Master** can be created by copying an existing asset in the same Company Code or another

Company Code; it can also be created from the scratch when it is done for the first time. Again, while creating the master, SAP allows to create multiple assets in one go, provided, all such assets are similar (having the same asset class and all belonging to the same Company Code).

From Release 4.5, the transaction codes for creating asset master has been changed to AS series instead of the earlier AT series (for example create asset is by **AS01** (**AT01** earlier), change asset is **AS02** (**AT02** earlier) and so on. If you are still comfortable with creation of assets using the conventional screen than with the 'tab' feature available now in AS transaction series, the news is that you are welcome to do so, but you can not find these transactions under 'ASMN'!

Each asset master contains the necessary information to calculate the depreciation:

- Capitalization date / acquisition period
- Depreciation areas relevant for the asset
- Depreciation key
- Useful life / Expired useful life
- Change over year, if any
- Scrap value, if any
- Start date of (ordinary depreciation)

180.   Explain the two ways of creating 'Asset Masters'.

- Copy an existing asset as a reference for creating the new one
- From an existing asset class create a new asset so that this asset class provides the default control parameters for the new asset.

181.   Is it possible to create multiple assets in a single transaction?

SAP enables you to create multiple (but *similar*) assets in one transaction. What you need to know is that all these assets should belong to the same asset class and same Company Code. Enter the number of assets you need to create in '**Number of similar assets**' field. After creating the assets, you will be able to change the individual descriptions / inventory numbers when you are about to save the master records. When you save the master records, the system assigns a range of asset numbers.

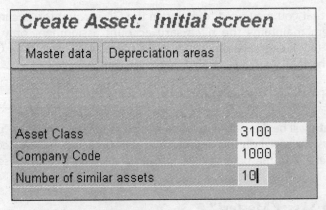

Figure 63: Create multiple assets

Transaction Code
AS01

The only drawback of using this method of creating assets in bulk is that you will not be able to create **long text** for any of these assets.

182. What are all the 'Time Dependent Data' in asset master?

All the cost accounting assignment related data like cost centre, internal orders or investment projects etc need to be maintained as **Time Dependent Data** in asset masters. Additionally, the information relating to *asset shut-down* and *shift operation* also needs to be maintained as time dependent. SAP maintains all the time-dependent data for the entire life span of the assets.

183. Explain 'Asset Acquisition'.

Asset Acquisition can be through any one of the following three routes:

1. **External Acquisition through Purchase**
   External acquisition of assets will be primarily from vendors, who are either your business partners or third parties. It can also be from your affiliated companies (use **Transaction Code: ABZP**). The external asset acquisition can be through different ways:
   i. The asset can be posted in MM module
   ii. The asset can be created in FI-AA with automatic clearing of the offsetting entry (Transaction Code: ABZON). This can be achieved either of the following ways:
       a. The posting is made initially in FI-AP and the clearing account cleared when the posting is made to the asset (FI-AA)
       b. Post the asset with the automatic offsetting entry(FI-AA), then clear the clearing account through a credit posting by an incoming invoice (FI-AP)
   iii. When <u>not</u> integrated with FI-AP, you may acquire the asset in FI-AA with an automatic offsetting entry without referencing to a Purchase Requisition (PR). This kind of acquisition is necessary when:
       a. You have not yet received the invoice or
       b. When the invoice has already been posted in FI-AP
   iv. When integrated with FI-AP, acquire the asset in FI-AA using an incoming invoice but without a reference to a Purchase Order PO)

2. **In-house Production / Acquisition**
   In-house Asset Acquisition is primarily the capitalization of goods/services produced by your company. The costs associated with the complete or partial production of the goods/services from within the company needs to be capitalized into separate asset(s). Usually, the capitalization is done as under:
   i. Create an order/project (in Investment Management) to capture the production costs associated with the goods/services produced in-house
   ii. Settle the order/project to an AuC (Asst under Construction)
   iii. Distribute/Settle the AuC so created in to new asset(s)

You will be using the **Transaction Type 110** for asset acquisition from in-house production

3. **Subsequent Acquisition**

When the asset /vendor accounts are posted, the system updates the corresponding GL accounts (FI-AP & FI-AA) through relevant account determinations. SAP uses various kinds of 'transaction types' to distinguish the different transactions. During acquisition the system makes the following entries in the asset master data:

- Date of initial acquisition / period & year of acquisition
- Capitalization date of the asset
- Start date for ordinary depreciation (start date is determined from the asset value date/period/year of acquisition)
- Vendor is automatically entered in the 'origin'

184. What values are automatically set in the asset masters during 'Initial Acquisition'?

- Date of capitalization
- Acquisition period
- Posting date of original acquisition
- Depreciation start date (per depreciation area)

185. Why it is necessary to 'Block' an asset master record?

In case you decide that you do not want to post any more acquisitions to an existing asset, then it is necessary that you set the **Block Indicator** in the asset master record. This is usually the case with AuC, where after the capitalization you no longer want any further additions to the asset. The block indicator prevents only further postings but not transfers or retirements or depreciation; even after an asset is blocked, you can continue to depreciate the same as in the case of other assets.

186. How do you 'Delete' an asset master?

You can **Delete an Asset Master** record from the system only when there are no transactions posted to it. The system will not allow you to delete the master record, if there are transactions against the asset: even if you reverse all the previous transactions pertaining to the asset and bring down the asset value to zero. However, unlike FI-AR, FI-AP or FI-GL where *archiving* is a pre requisite to delete the master records, you may delete the asset master records without archiving. When deleted, the system also deletes the asset number.

187. What is a '(Asset) Transaction Type' in FI-AA?

Transaction Types in FI-AA identify the nature of asset transaction (acquisition or transfer or retirement) so as to specify what is that updated, among (a) Depreciation area, (b) Value field and (c) Asset accounts (in B/S).

The following are some of the common transaction types used:

- **100** Asset Acquisition – Purchase
- **110** Asset Acquisition – In-house Production

- **200** Asset Retirement – without revenue
- **210** Asset Retirement – with revenue

The transaction type is extensively used in most of the asset reports, including the ***asset history sheet***, to display the various asset transactions differentiated by the transaction types. SAP comes with a numerous transaction types which will take care of almost all your requirement. However, should there be a specific case; you may also create your own transaction type.

Every transaction type is grouped into a ***Transaction Type Group*** (for example: 10 -> Acquisition) which characterizes the various transaction types (for example transaction types 100 & 110) with in that group. The system makes it possible to limit the transaction type groups be associated with certain asset classes.

TTy...	Transaction type name
020	Acquisition:Cost-accounting area only
030	Acquisition in the group area
040	Acquisition in the tax area only
060	Acq. areas 01, 02, 20
100	External asset acquisition
101	Acquisition for a negative asset
105	Credit memo in acquis. year
106	Credit memo in invoice year to affiliated
110	In-house acquisition
115	Acquisition from settlement from CO to
116	Acquisition from settlement of order / W
120	Goods receipt
121	Goods receipt for production order
122	Goods receipt from affiliated company (ı
130	Goods issue (External production)
131	Goods issue (In-house production)
140	Incidental costs without capitalization
145	Gross interco.transf.acq. curr-yr.acq. af
146	Gross interco.transf.acq. curr-yr.acq. af
147	Gross interco.transf. acquis. of prior-yr a
148	Gross interco.transf.acquis. of current-y
150	Acquisition from an affiliated company

Figure 64: (Asset) Transaction types

188.   Explain 'Assets under Construction (AuC)' in SAP.

The goods and/or services produced, in-house, can be capitalized into asset(s). But, there are two distinct phases during this process:

1. Construction phase (AuC)
2. Utilization phase (useful or economic life phase)

It, then becomes necessary, to show the assets under these two phases in two different balance sheet items:

The 'construction phase' is one in which you start producing or assembling the asset which is not yet ready for putting into economic utilization. SAP categorizes these kinds of assets into a special asset class called '**Assets under Construction**' (**AuC**).

The AuC is to be managed through a separate asset class with a separate asset GL account. SAP allows posting 'down payments' to AuC. It is also possible to enter credit memos for AuC even after its complete capitalization, provided you are managing this asset class allowing *negative* **APC** (**Acquisition and Production Costs**). The **IM** (**Investment Managemen**t) module helps to manage internal orders / projects for AuC. It is necessary that you use the **depreciation key** '0000' to ensure that you are not calculating any depreciation for AuC. But, you can continue to have s*pecial tax depreciation* and *investment support* even on these assets.

189.   How to capitalize AuC in SAP?

An '**Asset under Construction**' can be managed in two ways, as regard the asset master is concerned:

- As a 'normal' asset
- As an asset with 'line item management'

Later on, the AuC is capitalized and transferred to regular asset(s), by 'distribution' / 'settlement'. While doing so, the system with the help of different **transaction types** segregates the transactions relating to the current year with that of the previous years. The capitalization can be:

1. Lump sum capitalization
2. With line item settlement (when capitalized using line item settlement, it is not necessary that you need to settle (a) all the line items and (b) 100 % in a particular line item)

In case of integration with SAP-IM (Investment Management), capital investments can be managed as AuC by:

- Collecting the production costs associated to an order/project
- Settling the collected costs to an AuC
- Capitalizing the AuC into new assets by distribution/settlement

Transaction Code
AIAB
AIBU

190.   What do you mean my 'Low Value Assets'?

SAP uses the tem **Low Value Asset**s to denote assets which will be depreciated in the year of purchase or in the period of acquisition. This categorization usually follows the statutory requirements of the country of the Company Code, wherein you define a monetary limit and consider all those assets falling below the value, say $1,000, as low value assets. You have the flexibility of managing these assets either on an individual (*individual check*) basis or collective basis (*quantity check*).

SAP uses a special *depreciation key* called *LVA*, and the expected useful life of such an asset is considered to be one period (month).

191.   Explain 'Asset Transfer', in SAP.

Asset Transfer is of two types, namely:

1.   Inter-company asset transfer
2.   Intra-company asset transfer

Inter-company Asset Transfer is between the Company Codes, resulting in creation of the new asset in the target Company Code (the receiving one). The transaction posts the values as per the 'posting method' selected during the transfer. In doing so the system:

- Retires the asset in the source/sending Company Code by an ***asset retirement***
- Posts acquisition in the new/target Company Code by an ***asset acquisition***, and creates the new asset in the target Company Code
- Posts inter-company profit/loss arising out of the transfer
- Updates FI-GL automatically

An inter-company asset transfer is usually necessitated when (a) there is a need for physically changing the location from one company to the other or (b) there is an organization restructuring resulting that the new asset to be attached with the new Company Code. You may use the standard ***Transfer Variants*** supplied by SAP. The selection of a suitable transfer variant will be based on (1) the legal relationship among the Company Codes and (2) the methods chosen for transferring the asset values.

Inter-company asset transfer can be handled:

- Individually using the normal transaction for a single asset
- For a number of assets using the '***mass transfer***'

If you need to transfer assets cross-system, you need to use ALE functionality.

Intra-company Asset Transfer is the transfer of an asset within the same Company Code. This would have been necessitated by:

- Change in the asset class or business area etc.
- Settlement of an AuC to a new asset
- Transfer of stock materials into an asset (by posting a GI to an order through MM or settlement of a production order to an asset)
- Splitting an existing asset into one or more new assets.

Transaction Code
ABUMN

192.   What is a 'Transfer Variant'?

A **Transfer Variant** is dependent upon the whether the Company Codes involved are legally dependent or independent. Transfer variants specify (1) how the transferred asset will be valued at the receiving Company Code and (2) the type of transaction (acquisition or transfer) used for the transaction.

Vari...	Name
1	Gross method
2	Net method
3	Revaluation method
4	Transfer within a company code
5	Summary settlement from CO
6	Line item settlement from CO or from AuC
7	Gross variant (affiliated company)
8	Gross variant (non-affiliated company)
FIN	Finland - Transfer assets EVL depreciation

Figure 65: Transfer variant

193. Explain 'Asset Retirement' in FI-AA.

Asset Retirement is an integral part of asset management. You may retire an asset (1) by sale or (2) by scrapping. In case of sales, it can be (1) with revenue or (2) without revenue: again the asset sale can be (1) with customer or (2) with out customer.

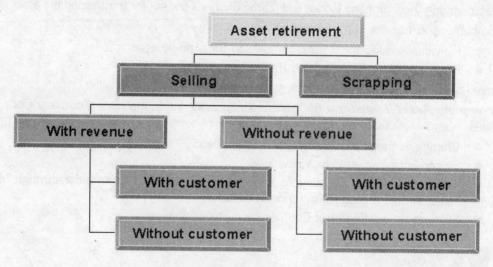

Figure 66: Asset Retirement

During asset sales transactions, the system removes the **APC (Acquisition and Production Costs)** and also the corresponding **accumulated depreciation**, then the **profit or loss** arising out of the sale is recorded in the system. Even, in case of 'partial retirement' or 'partial sales', the system records the proportionate gain/loss arising out of the transaction. Any tax posting arising out of the transaction is automatically created by the system.

SAP provides various ways of posting retirement in the system, which includes:

- Mass retirement
- Asset retirement with revenue
  - With customer (involving integration with FI-AR)
    - *Debit customer, credit assets*

- o Without customer
- Asset retirement without revenue
  - o With customer
    - Debit clearing account, credit asset
    - Debit customer in A/R, credit the clearing account
- Asset retirement using GL document posting

Transaction Code
ABOAN (Asset sale without customer)

194. Describe transfer of 'Legacy Asset Data' to SAP.

One of the challenges in the implementation of FI-AA is the transfer of **Legacy Asset Data** from your existing systems to SAP FI-AA. Though SAP provides multiple options and appropriate tools to carry out this task, you need a carefully planned strategy for completing this task. You may resort to transfer the old asset values through any one of the following ways:

- Batch data inputs (large number of old assets)
- Directly updating the SAP Tables (very large number of old assets)
- Manual entry (few old assets)

Normally, you will not be resorting to manual process as it is time consuming and laborious; however, you may do this if you have very limited number of assets. Else, you may use either of the other two options, though batch data input with error handling would be the preferred way of doing the same. You need to reconcile the data transferred, if you resort to any of the two automatic ways of transferring the data. You may also use, **BAPIs** (**Business Application Programming Interface**) to link and process the asset information in SAP FI-AA, from non-SAP systems.

The transfer can be (i) at the end of the last closed fiscal year, or (ii) during the current fiscal year following the last closed fiscal year. You will be able to transfer both (a) master data as well as (b) accumulated values of the last closed fiscal year. If required, you can also transfer the asset transactions, including depreciation, during the current fiscal year. It is important to note that the GL account balances of the old assets need to be transferred separately.

195. Outline 'Automatic Transfer of Old Assets'.

SAP provides you with the necessary interfaces for converting your' legacy asset data' into prescribed formats for upload into the SAP system. The **data transfer workbench** allows you to control the entire data transfer process.

i. These interface programs convert the data to be compatible with the SAP data dictionary Tables like **BALTD** for master data, and **BALTB** for transactions. If you have more than 10 depreciation areas, then you need to change the transfer structures for both **BALTD** and **BALTB**.

ii. The converted data are stored in sequential files.

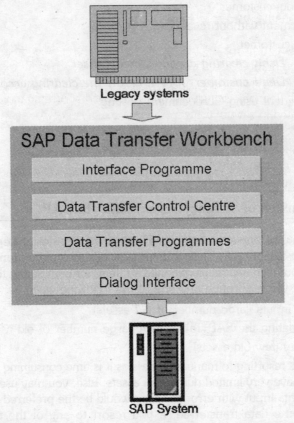

Figure 67: Legacy asset transfer to SAP FI-AA

iii. Use the data transfer program **RAALTD01** (for batch input) or **RAALTD11** (direct Table update) for transferring the data to SAP.

- Do a **test run**. This will help to correct errors if any.
- Do a **production run**, with a few asset records, to update the relevant Tables in FI-AA.
- Reset the values in the asset Company Code.
- Continue with the production run for all the assets

iv. All the asset records without errors will be updated immediately through background processing, in the relevant Tables like **ANLH, ANLA, ANLB, ANLC** etc.

v. The records with errors will be stored in a separate batch input session which can be processed separately.

196. What is 'Asset Transfer Date'?

The **Asset Transfer Date** refers to the 'cut-off' date for the transfer of old assets data from your existing system. Once established, you will not be able to create any old asset in SAP, before this reference date. Any transaction happening after the transfer date but before the actual date of asset transfer, needs to be created separately in SAP after you complete the old asset transfer.

197.   Describe 'Mass Change'. How to achieve this?

Mass Change enables you to make changes (like mass retirements, changes to incomplete assets etc) in FI-AA, to a large number asset master records at one go. The mass change functionality is achieved through **work lists** which are FI-AA standard tasks pre defined in the system. These tasks are assigned with 'work flow objects' which can be changed according to your specific requirements. The work lists are created in several ways from asset master records, asset value display, from asset information system etc.

For effecting a mass change you need to:

1. Create **substitution rule(s)** in which you will mention what are all the fields that are required to be changed. This rule will consist of an 'identifying condition' (for example: if the cost centre = 1345), and a 'rule to substitute' new values (for example: replace the 'field' cost centre with the value '1000')
2. Generate a list of such assets which needs to be changed
3. Create a 'work list' to carryout the changes
4. Select the appropriate 'substitution rule' (defined earlier in step-1 above)
5. Process the 'work list'. You may also release the same to some one else in the organization so that he/she can complete the task
6. Run a 'report' to verify the changes

198.   What is a 'Periodic Processing' in FI-AA? Explain.

Periodic Processing in FI-AA relates to the tasks you need to carry-out at periodic intervals to plan and post some of the transactions. The tasks include:

- Depreciation calculation and posting.

  As you are aware, SAP allows automatic posting of values from only one depreciation area (normally 01 – book depreciation). For all other depreciation areas, including the derived ones, you need to perform the tasks periodically so that FI is updated properly.

- Planned depreciation / interest for CO primary cost planning
- Claiming and posting of 'investment support' (either 'individually' or through 'mass change')

199.   What is a 'Depreciation Key'?

Depreciation is calculated using the **Depreciation Key** and **Internal Calculation Key**, in the system. Depreciation keys are defined at the chart of depreciation level, and are uniform across all Company Codes, which are attached to a particular chart of depreciation. The depreciation key contains all the control information defined, for the calculation of planned depreciation. The system contains a number of pre-defined depreciation keys (like **LINA, DWG, DG10** etc) with the controls already defined for calculation method and type. A depreciation key can contain multiple internal calculation keys.

	DepKy	Name for whole depreciation	Status	
	0000	No depreciation and no interest	Active	
	DG20	Declining balance 2 x	Active	
	DG25	Declining balance 2.5 x	Active	
	DG30	Declining balance 3 x	Active	
	DIG4	Sum-of-the-years-digits dep. 4 years	Active	
	GD10	Buildings decl.bal.10.0/ 5.0 / 2.5 %	Active	
	GD35	Buildings decl.bal.3.5/ 2.0 / 1.0 %	Active	
	GD50	Buildings decl.bal. 5.0 / 2.5 / 1.25 %	Active	
	GD70	Buildings decl.bal. 7.0 / 5.0 / 2.0 / 1.25 %	Active	
	GL20	Buildings straight-line 2%	Active	
	GL25	Buildings straight-line 2.5%	Active	
	GWG	LVA 100 % Complete depreciation	Active	
	IN1	Tax Depreciation - 5% - India	Active	

Chart of dep.   1IN   Sample chart of depreciation: India

Figure 68: Depreciation Key

200.   What is an 'Internal Calculation Key'?

Internal Calculation Keys are the control indicators with in a 'depreciation key'. Together with the depreciation key, these calculation keys help in determining the depreciation amounts. Each internal calculation key contains:

1. Depreciation type (ordinary or unplanned)
2. Depreciation method (straight-line or declining balance)
3. Base value
4. Rate of percentage for depreciation calculation
5. Period control for transactions (acquisition, retirement etc)
6. Change-over rules (in case of declining/double declining methods of calculation)
7. Treatment of depreciation after useful life period

201.   What is known as 'Depreciation Run' in SAP?

The **Depreciation Run**, an important periodic processing, takes care of calculating depreciation for the assets and posting the corresponding transactions in both FI-AA and FI-GL. The depreciation calculation is usually done in sessions, and the ***posting session*** posts the different depreciation types, interest/ revaluation, and also writing-off / allocating special reserves. The depreciation run is recommended to be started with a 'test run' before making it as the '***production run***' which will update the system. The system provides the facility to re-start a run session, should there be problems in the earlier run. The depreciation run needs to be completed per period. During every depreciation run, the system will create summarized posting documents per business area and per account determination; no individual posting documents are created.

202. Explain the various steps in a 'Depreciation Run'.

1. Maintain the parameters for the depreciation run on the initial screen of the Transaction **AFAB** (Company Code, fiscal year & posting period).

2. Select a 'reason' for the posting run (repeat run, planned posting run, restart run or unplanned run).

3. Select the appropriate check boxes in the 'further option' block if you need a list of assets, direct FI posting, test run etc. Please note that it is a good practice to select the 'test run' initially, see the outcome of the depreciation run, then remove this 'check box' and go for the 'productive run'.

4. Execute the test run (if the assets are less than 10, 000 in numbers, you may then do the processing in the foreground; else execute the run in the background).

5. Check the results displayed.

6. Once you are convinced that the test run has gone as expected, go back to the previous screen, uncheck the 'test run' check-box, and execute (in the background).

7. Complete the 'background print parameters', if prompted by the system. You may also decide to schedule the job immediately or later. The system uses the 'depreciation-posting program' **RABUCH00**, for updating the asset's values and generating a batch input session for updating FI-GL. The 'posting session' posts values in various depreciation areas, interest, revaluation besides updating special reserves allocations and writing-off, if any. If there are more than 100, 000 assets for depreciation calculation and posting, you need to use a special program **RAPOST00**.

8. Process the 'batch input session' created by the system in step-7 above. You may use the Transaction Code **SM35**. Again, you have the option of processing the session in the foreground or in the background.

9. System posts the depreciation in FI-GL.

203. How the system calculates the 'Depreciation'?

1. The system takes the 'depreciation terms' from the asset master record, and calculates the depreciation for the asset taking into account the 'useful life' and the 'depreciation key'. The start date for depreciation is assumed to be the first date of acquisition of the asset.

2. The system may also calculate other values like: interest, revaluation etc

3. The depreciation and / other values as in (2) are calculated for each of the depreciation areas.

204. Explain 'Derived Depreciation'.

The **Derived Depreciation** is a separate depreciation area which is 'derived' from two or more 'real depreciation' areas using a pre-determined rule. You may use this to calculate something like ***special reserves*** or to show the difference in valuation between local and group valuation etc. Since the values are derived, the system does not store any values in the database, but updates the derived values whenever there are changes in the real depreciation area or its depreciation terms.

You may also use the derived depreciation only for reporting purposes.

205. What is known as a 'Repeat Run' in depreciation process?

Repeat Run is normally used at the end of the fiscal year to carry out posting adjustments or corrections which may arise due to changes in depreciation terms or manual depreciation calculations. However, you can use this only within the same posting period. The 'repeat run' also provides the flexibility to restrict the calculations to specific assets.

206. What is 'Restart a Depreciation Run'?

Restart Depreciation Run is used only when there has been a problem with the previous run resulting in termination of that run. To make sure that all the steps in a depreciation run is completed without errors, the system logs the status at every stage of the processing and provides 'error logs' so as to find out the problem. This option of 'restart' is not available during the 'test run' mode.

207. What is 'Depreciation Simulation'?

Depreciation Simulation refers to 'what if' valuation of assets. This is achieved by changing and experimenting with the 'parameters' required for depreciating the assets. The simulation helps you to 'foresee' what would be the depreciation should there be changes in various 'depreciation terms'. You may simulate to see the valuation for the future fiscal years. *Sort versions* and options for *totals report* are also available in simulation. The depreciation simulation can be applied to a single asset or your entire asset portfolio.

208. What is a 'Sort Version'?

The **Sort Version** defines the formation of groups and totals in an asset report. You can use all the fields of the asset master record as group and/or sort criteria for defining of a sort version. The sort version can not have more than five *sort levels*.

209. Can you select 'Direct FI Posting' for a 'Depreciation Run'?

If the 'check box' to enable '**Direct FI Posting**' is ticked then the system will not create the 'batch input session' for depreciation posting; instead the FI-GL is posted directly. Be careful when checking Direct FI Posting check box, because there will not be an opportunity to correct mistakes, if any, in accounts and account assignments like business area, cost objects etc when you execute the depreciation run. Also, there will be no possibility to check and correct postings. Note that if this option is selected during a depreciation run, and if the run is terminated for any reason and needs to be re-started, this has to be kept checked during that time as well.

The standard system comes with the document type '*AF*' (number range defined as '*external numbering*') configured to be used in '*batch input*'. Hence, with this default configuration, you will get an error when you try depreciation posting run by selecting the option 'direct FI posting'. You can, however, overcome this by not restricting the same FI-AA customization (Use Transaction Code **OBA7** and remove the tick mark form 'Btch input only' check-box).

210. Explain the 'Year Closing' in FI-AA.

The year-end is closed when you draw the final balance sheet. But, to reach this stage, you need to ensure that the depreciation is posted properly: you can achieve this by checking the 'depreciation list' and also the 'asset history sheets'. After this is done, draw test balance sheet and profit & loss statement and check for the correctness of the depreciation. Correct the discrepancies, if any, by adjustment postings. You need to re-run the depreciation posting program if you change any of the depreciation values.

When you, now, run the **Year-End Closing Program**, the system ensures that the fiscal year had been completed for all the assets, depreciation had been fully posted and there were no errors logged for any of the assets. If there were errors, you need to correct the errors before re-running the year-end program. When you reach a stage where there is no error, the system will update the last closed fiscal year, for each of the depreciation areas for each of the assets. The system will also block any further postings in FI-AA for the closed fiscal year, If you need to re-open the closed fiscal year for any adjustments postings or otherwise, ensure that you re-run the year-end program so that the system blocks further postings.

211. Explain 'Asset History Sheet'.

SAP comes delivered with country specific **Asset History Sheets** which will meet the legal reporting requirements of a country. The asset history sheet is one of the important reports which can be used either as the *year-end report* or intermediate report whenever you need it. Asset history sheets help you to freely define the report layout, headers, and most of the history sheet items.

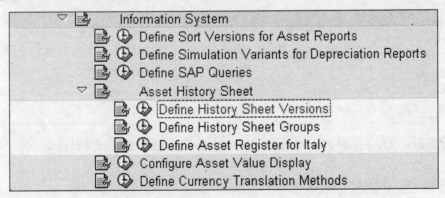

Figure 69: Configuring Asset History Sheet

You may create various version of Asset History Sheet:

	Language	Hist.sht.ver	Asset history sheet name
	EN	0001	In compl. w/EC directive 4 (13 col.,wide version)
	EN	0002	In compliance with EC diréctive 4 (13 col.)
	EN	0003	Depreciation by depreciation type
	EN	0004	Acquisition values
	EN	0005	Asset Register (Italy)
	EN	0006	Cost-accouting w/revaluation (derived from HGB2)
	EN	0007	Transferred reserves
	EN	0008	History of res.for spec.depr.

Asset hist. sheet versions

Figure 70: Asset History Sheet Versions

For each of the versions, you will be able to define various columns according to your requirement:

Ast.hist.sht.version	0006	Cost-accouting w/revaluation (derived from HGB2)
Language Key	EN	
☐ Hist.sheet complete		

Hist. sheet positions

		Column	00	Column	10	Column	20	Column
Line	02	APC FY start		Acquisition		Retirement		Transfer
Line	04	Dep. FY start		Dep. for year		Dep.retir.		Dep.transfer
Line	06	Bk.val.FY strt						

Figure 71: Field Positions in an Asset History Sheet Version

212. What is an 'Asset Explorer'?

Asset Explorer, is a handy and convenient single interface transaction helping you to display the asset values, depreciation details etc in a very user friendly way. Gone were the days, where you had to move to different pages, and re-enter the same transaction many a time for displaying the details of different assets.

Using asset explorer you have the convenience of:

- Moving from one asset number to the other effortlessly
- Displaying asset values, both planned and posted, for any number of depreciation areas from the same page but in various tab pages
- Jumping to the asset master or cost centre master or GL account master
- Calling up various asset reports
- Currency converted views

- Looking at the various transactions relating to an asset
- Looking up all the values for different fiscal years
- Distinguishing between real and derived depreciation areas with two differentiating symbols
- Displaying **depreciation calculation function**, and if necessary, recalculation of depreciation

Asset explorer is designed for easy navigation, with the following sections:

1. **Asset values window**

   The top-left area/window is the 'asset values' window which is in a tree-like structure expanding to various depreciation areas like 01, 03, 10 etc. By selecting any one of these depreciation areas, you will be able to view the value of an asset in the 'asset value details window'.

2. **Objects related to asset window**

   This is also on the left hand side of the display page, just below the 'asset values window'. With a drill-down tree-like structure you will be able to navigate between cost centres and GL accounts relating to the asset.

3. **Asset value detail window (with tab pages)**

   This is the main window on the right, usually occupying most of the page area. Here, you will see the information like Company Code, asset number selected, fiscal year etc. This window is made up of, completely re-sizeable, two components: the top area displaying the asset values and the bottom showing the asset transactions.

Transaction Code
AW01N

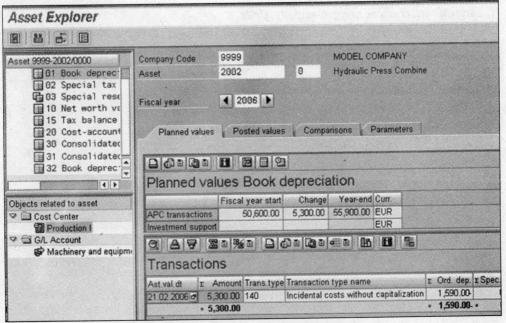

Figure 72: Asset explorer

213.   Explain 'Production Set-up' in FI-AA.

The **Production Set-up** is a collection of logical steps in FI-AA to ensure that all the required configuration and activities are in place for making the asset accounting Company Code 'productive'. This includes:

i.   *Consistency check*

This will enable to analyze errors, if any, in FI-AA configuration in the areas of charts of depreciation, assignment of Company Code to the chart of depreciation, definition of depreciation areas, asset classes, GL account assignments etc.

ii. *Reset Company Code*

As you will be having test data, before the Company Code becomes productive, resetting of company is necessary to delete all these data. Note that this is possible only when the Company Code in 'test' status. All the master records and values will be removed only from FI-AA. You need to remove all the FI and CO values separately as the resetting of asset account Company Code does not remove these. Resetting will not remove any configuration settings of FI-AA.

iii. *Reset posted depreciation*

This step is required to be performed when there had been errors during a previous depreciation run. This is also possible only when the asset Company Code is in a status of 'test'.

iv. *Set / reset reconciliation accounts*

Define GL accounts for FI-AA reconciliation, if not done already. You may also reset already defined reconciliation accounts in case of wrong account assignments earlier.

v.   *Transfer asset balances*

Transfer the asset balances to the GL accounts that have been defined as the *asset reconciliation accounts*.

vi. *Activate asset accounting Company Code*

This is the last step in the production set-up. All the previous status of the Company Code (test status / transfer status) becomes invalid now. No more transfer of old asset data is allowed when the asset Company Code becomes productive.

Controlling (CO)

5

Controlling (CO)

General Controlling

1. Explain 'Controlling (CO)' in SAP.

SAP calls **managerial accounting** as '**Controlling**' and the module is commonly known as '**CO**'. The CO module is, thus, primarily oriented towards managing and reporting cost/revenue and is mainly used in 'internal' decision making. As in with any other module, this module also has (a) configuration setup and (b) application functionality.

The controlling module focuses on the internal users, and helps the management by providing reports on cost centres, profit centres, contribution margins & profitability etc

2. What are the important 'Organizational Elements of CO'?

The important organizational structure of controlling includes:

- **Operating Concern** (the top most reporting level for profitability analysis and sales & marketing controlling)
- **Controlling Area** (central organization in 'controlling', structuring the internal accounting operations)
- **Cost Centres** (lower most organizational units where costs are incurred and transferred)

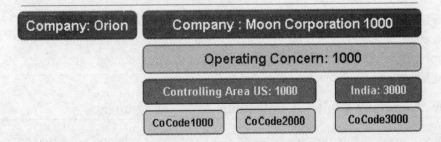

Figure 73: Operating Concern, Controlling Area and Company Code

3. What is a 'Controlling Area'? How it is related to Company Code?

A **Controlling Area** is the central organizational structure in '*controlling*' (CO), and is used in cost accounting. The controlling area, as in the case of Company Code, is a self contained cost accounting entity for internal reporting purposes. The controlling area is assigned to one or more Company Codes, so as to ensure that the necessary transactions, posted in FI, are transferred to controlling for *cost accounting* processing.

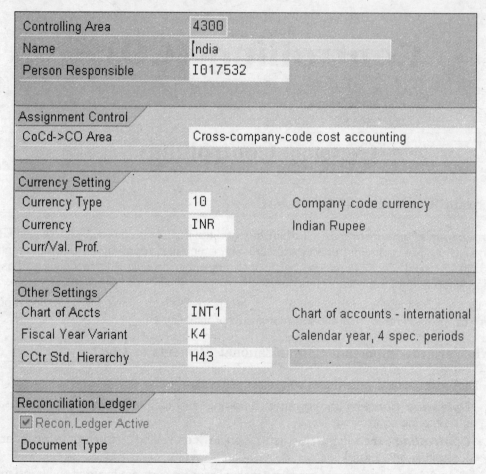

Figure 74: Controlling Area - Details

- One controlling area can be assigned one or more Company Codes
- One chart of accounts can be assigned to one or more controlling areas
- One or more controlling areas can be assigned to an operating concern
- One Client can have one or more controlling areas

4. Outline 'Company Code – Controlling Area' assignments.

There are 2 types of assignments possible between the Company Code and a controlling area:

- *One-to-one:* Here, one Company Code corresponds to one controlling area

- *Many-to-one:* More than one Company Codes are assigned to a single controlling area

5. Explain the types of 'Controlling Area / Company Code' assignments.

Controlling area-Company Code assignment	1:1 assignment	1: many assignment (cross Company Code cost accounting)
Chart of accounts	The chart of accounts should be the same between the controlling area and the Company Code	The 'operative chart of accounts' of the Company Codes, and the controlling area should be the same
Fiscal year variant (special and posting periods)	The number of special periods may be different, between the Company Code and the controlling area, but the number of posting periods should be the same. Also, the period limits of posting periods should be identical..	
Controlling area currency	Same as that of the Company Code currency	You may use the same currency as that of the Company Code You may also use another currency in controlling
Object currency	Additional currency, besides the controlling area currency, can be used for each account assignment objects in CO.	You can choose any object currency if all the assigned Company Codes have the same currency which is same as that of the controlling area currency. Else, the system automatically assigns the Company Code currency to the account assignment object as an object currency.
Transaction currency	Documents are posted in CO in the transaction currency.	
Allocations	Cross Company Code cost allocation in CO is not possible	Cross Company Code allocation in CO is possible

6. What are all the 'Components of Controlling'?

- Cost Element Accounting
- Cost Controlling
- Cost Center Accounting
- Internal Orders
- Activity-Based Costing
- Product Cost Controlling
- Profitability Analysis
- Profit Center Accounting

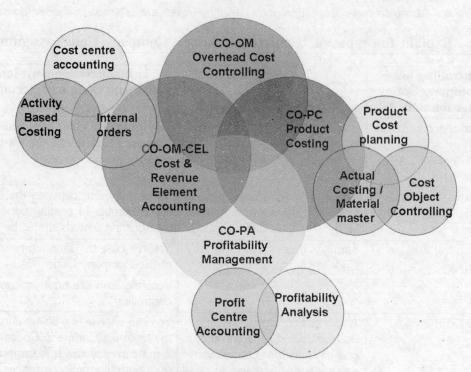

Figure 75: Controlling

Figure 76: Controlling Components

7.   Why you need 'Cost Element Accounting '?

Cost Element Accounting (*CO-OM-CEL*) helps you to classify costs / revenues posted to CO. It also provides you the capability to reconcile the costs between FI and CO. CO-OM-CEL provides the structure for assignment of CO data in the form of cost / revenue carriers called **cost element** or **revenue element.**

8.   Explain 'Cost Centre Accounting '?

Cost Centre Accounting deals with the difficult task of managing the 'overheads' within your organization. Since ***overhead costs*** are something which you can not directly associate with a product or service and which you find difficult to control, cost centre accounting provides you with the necessary tools to achieve this.

9. What is 'Activity Based Costing'?

Activity Based Costing, popularly called as **ABC**, helps you to view the overhead costs from the point of business processes. The result is, you will be able to optimize costs for the entire business process. As a single business process will cut across several cost centres, ABC will help you to have an enhanced view of the costs incurred.

10. What is 'Product Cost Controlling'?

Product Cost Controlling (**CO-PC**) deals with estimating of what will cost to produce a product / service. CO-PC is divided into two major areas:

    i.   Cost of materials

    ii. Cost of processing

With CO-PC, you will be able to calculate:

    a.   Cost of goods manufactured (COGM)

    b.   Cost of goods sold (COGS)

CO-PC is tightly integrated with ***Production Planning*** (PP) and ***Materials Management*** (MM), besides FI. The functionality helps to:

- Calculate *Standard Costs* of manufactured goods
- Calculate the *Work-In-Progress* (WIP)
- Calculate the *Variances*, at period-end
- Settlement of product costs

Note that CO-PC deals only with the production costs.

11. What is 'Profitability Analysis'?

Profitability Analysis (**CO-PA**) helps you to determine how profitable (denoted by the '***contribution margin***') your market segments are. The analysis is on the external side of the market. You will be able to define which segments, like customer, product, geography, sales organization etc., of the market which are required for analyzing the 'operating results /profits'. With multi-dimensional 'drill-down' capability, you have all the flexibility you require for the reporting.

12. How 'Profit Centre Accounting' (EC-PCA) is different from CO-PA?

Unlike CO-PA, wherein the focus is on external market segments' profitability, **Profit Centre Accounting** (EC-PCA) focuses on profitability of internal areas (***profit centres***) of the enterprise. Profit centre accounting is used to draw internal balance sheets and profit & loss statements. You may use EC-PCA in the place ***business area*** accounting.

Attribute	Profitability Analysis (CO-PA)	Profit Centre Accounting (EC-PCA)
Focus	External market segments	Internal responsibility centres
Reporting	Any point of time	During period-end
	Margin reporting	Profit & Loss statements
Accounting	Cost of Sales	Period based

Both CO-PA and EC-PCA serve different purposes, and are not mutually exclusive. It is possible that you might need them both in your organization.

13. Explain 'Integration of CO' with its components, and other SAP modules.

CO module is integrated with FI, AA, SD, MM, PP and HR:

- FI is the main source of data for CO. All expenses, posted in FI, flow to CO through the 'primary cost elements' to the appropriate 'cost centres'. Similarly, postings in Asset Accounting (like depreciations) are also passed on to CO.

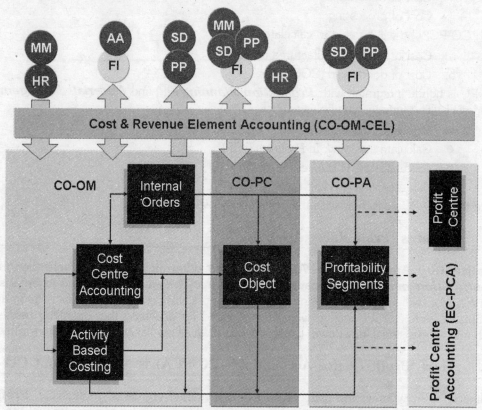

Figure 77: Integration of CO components within and outside CO

- Revenue postings in FI would result in postings in CO-PA and also in EC-PCA.
- SD, MM, and PP modules have many integration points in CO. Goods issue (GI) to a controlling object or goods receipt (GR) from 'production order' are some of the examples of integration. These modules are tightly integrated as consumption activities,

cost of goods issued, overhead charges, material costs etc are passed on to the production objects like PP production order or sales order. The *WIP* (Work-In-Progress) and the variances, at periods end, are settled to CO-PA, CO-PCA and also to FI. Revenues are directly posted when you generate billing documents in SD, if the sales order is a cost object item.

- HR module generates various types of costs to be posted in CO. Planned HR costs can also be passed on for CO planning.

The following Table illustrates how the various components of CO are integrated:

CO-OM	Overhead Cost Controlling
	External costs can be posted to cost centers / internal orders from other SAP modules
	Cost centers can then allocate costs to other cost centers, orders, and business processes in Activity Based Costing (ABC)
	Internal orders can settle costs to cost centers, other internal orders and to business processes in ABC
	ABC, in turn, can pass on costs to cost centers and orders
CO-PC	Product Cost Controlling
	Direct postings from FI, to the cost objects (like production orders)
	Cost from cost centres can be posted to the production orders, as overhead cost allocation
	Costs settled from internal orders can be passed on to the production orders
CO-PA	Statistical cost postings from all CO components
	Cost assessments from cost centres / ABC
	Costs settled from internal orders
	Production variances from CO-PC

14. What is a 'Cost Object'?

A **Cost Object**, also known as **CO Account Assignment Object**, in SAP denotes a unit to which you can assign objects. It is something like a repository in which you collect costs, and, if necessary, move the costs from one object to another. All the components of CO have their own cost objects like cost centres, internal orders etc.

The cost objects decide the nature of postings as to (a) *real postings* or (b) *statistical postings*. All the objects which are identified only with statistical postings are not termed as cost objects (example: profit centres).

15. Differentiate 'Real' and 'Statistical Postings' in CO.

The *CO account assignment objects* decide the type of postings allowed. This can be *real* or *statistical* posting.

The **Real Postings**, allow you to further allocate / settle those costs to any other cost object in CO, either as 'senders' or as 'receiver's. The objects which are allowed to have real postings include:

- Cost Centres

- Internal Orders (Real)
- Projects (Real)
- Networks
- Profitability Segments
- PP – Production Orders (make-to-order)

The *Statistical Posting*, on the other hand, are only for information purposes. You will not be able to further allocate / settle these statistical costs to other cost objects. The example of such objects includes:

- Statistical (Internal) Orders
- Statistical Projects
- Profit Centres

16.   How do you define 'Number Ranges' in CO?

You will be required to define, for each of the controlling area, **Number Ranges** for all transactions that will generate documents in CO. Once done for a controlling area, you may copy from one controlling area to other controlling areas when you have more than one such area.

To avoid too many documents, SAP recommends grouping of multiple but similar transactions, and then assigning number ranges to this group. Further, you may create different number ranges for *plan* and *actual* data. As in FI, the number ranges can be *internal* or *external*. The document number ranges in CO are independent of fiscal years.

17.   How 'Master Data' differs from 'Transaction Data' in CO?

The **Master Data** remain unchanged over a period of long time, where as the **Transaction Data** relate to the short-term. The transaction data are assigned to the master data.

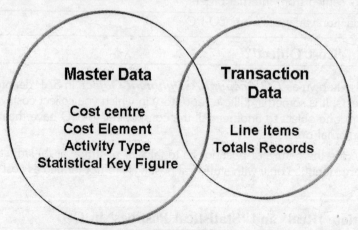

Master Data

Cost centre
Cost Element
Activity Type
Statistical Key Figure

Transaction Data

Line items
Totals Records

Figure 78: Master and Transaction Data in CO

Though you normally create the master data from transactions, note that you will be able to create these records from configuration side as well. When you need to create a large number of master data, you may use the '*collective processing*' option to create related master records in one-go. SAP deals master data in 'groups' for easy maintenance.

In case of master data of cost centre / cost elements / activity types, once they are created, you will not be able to change the date, and SAP calls this feature as the '*time dependency*' of master data. If necessary, you can extend the 'time', by creating a new one attaching the same to the existing objects. In case of **resources**, though the master data are time dependent the system will allow you to delete these objects. The **Statistical Key Figures (SKF)** are not time-dependent: once defined they are available in the system for ever.

Cost Element Accounting

18.   What is a 'Cost Element'?

The **Cost Elements** represent the origin of costs. There are two types of cost elements:
- Primary Cost Elements
- Secondary Cost Elements

19.   What is a 'Primary Cost Element'?

The **Primary Cost Elements** represent the consumption of production factors like raw materials, human resources, utilities etc. The primary cost elements have their corresponding GL accounts in FI. All the expense / revenue accounts in FI correspond to the primary cost elements in CO. Before you can create the primary cost elements in CO, you first need to create them in FI as GL accounts.

Note that SAP treats **revenue elements** also as primary cost elements in CO processing. The only difference is that all the revenue elements are identified with a *negative sign* while posting in CO. The revenue elements correspond to the revenue accounts in FI, and they fall under the Category 01 / 11 of **cost element category**.

20.   What is a 'Secondary Cost Element'?

The **Secondary Cost Elements** represent the consumption of production factors provided internally by the enterprise itself, and are present only in the CO. They are actually like cost carriers, and are used in **allocations and settlements** in CO. While creating these elements, you need to mention the cost element category which can be any of the following:
- *Category 21*, used in **internal settlements**
- *Category 42*, used in **assessments**
- *Category 43*, used in **internal activity allocation**

21.   What is a 'Cost Element Category'?

All the cost elements need to be assigned to a **Cost Element Category**, to determine the transactions for which you can use the cost elements.

Example:
- *Category 01*, known as the '***general primary cost elements***', is used in standard primary postings from FI or MM into CO.
- *Category 22* is used to settle order / project costs, or cost object costs to objects outside of CO (like assets, materials, GL accounts etc)

22.   How to, automatically, create 'Cost Elements'?

You will be able to create 'cost elements', automatically by specifying (i) the cost element, (ii) the cost element interval and (iii) cost element category for the cost elements. All these are achieved by making **default settings**. The creation of cost elements is done in the background.

The ***primary cost elements*** can be created only when you have the corresponding GL accounts in the chart of accounts of the Company Code. Even though the GL account names are used as the names of the primary cost elements thus created by the system, you have the option of changing these names in CO. All the ***secondary cost elements*** are created in CO; the naming of these cost elements comes from the ***cost element category***.

Cost Centre Accounting

23.   Define 'Cost Centre Accounting '.

Cost Centre Accounting (CO-OM-CCA) helps you to track where costs are incurred in your enterprise. All the costs, like salary and wages, rent, water charges etc., incurred are either assigned or posted to a *cost centre*.

24.   What is a 'Cost Centre '?

A **Cost Centre** is an organizational element within a *controlling area*.

You may define cost centres according to your specific needs; the most common approach being defining cost centre for each of the bottom most organizational units that are supposed to manage their costs. So, typical cost centres could be canteen, telephone, power, human resources, production etc.

There are other ways of designing cost centres: you may create cost centres representing geographical requirements or responsibility areas or activities / services produced etc.

After defining individual cost centres, you will assign each one of the cost centres to any the *cost centre categories*. All cost centres of a controlling area are assigned to a *standard hierarchy*.

25.   What is a 'Cost Centre Category '?

CCtC	Name	Qty	ActPri	ActSec	ActRev	PlnPri	PlnSec	PlnRev	Cm
1	Production	✔	☐	☐	✔	☐	☐	✔	
2	Service cost center	✔	☐	☐	✔	☐	☐	✔	
3	Sales	☐	☐	☐	✔	☐	☐	✔	
4	Administration	☐	☐	☐	✔	☐	☐	✔	
5	Management	✔	☐	☐	✔	☐	☐	✔	
6	Research & Develop.	✔	☐	☐	✔	☐	☐	✔	
7	Services	✔	☐	☐	✔	☐	☐	✔	
9	Allocation cost ctr	☐	☐	☐	✔	☐	☐	✔	
C	Consulting	☐	☐	☐	✔	☐	☐	✔	
E	Development	☐	☐	☐	✔	☐	☐	✔	
F	Production	✔	☐	☐	✔	☐	☐	✔	
G	Logistics	☐	☐	☐	✔	☐	☐	✔	
H	Service cost center	✔	☐	☐	✔	☐	☐	✔	
L	Management	☐	☐	☐	✔	☐	☐	✔	
M	Material	☐	☐	☐	✔	☐	☐	✔	

Figure 79: Cost Centre Category

A **Cost Centre Category** is an indicator in the cost centre master record to identify what kind of activities a particular cost centre will be performing. SAP comes delivered with default categories like administration, production, logistics, marketing, development, management etc. If necessary, as in other cases, you may create your own categories. The categorization is useful to assign certain standard characteristics to a group of cost centres performing similar activities.

SAP also allows you to store *special indicators* (like **lock indicators**) for each of the cost centre categories. These special indicators serve as defaults when you create a new cost centre.

26. What is a 'Standard Hierarchy'?

A tree-like hierarchy structure grouping all the cost centres, (of all the Company Codes belonging to a single controlling area) is known as the **Standard Hierarchy** in CO. This is SAP's way of grouping all the cost centres in a controlling area which helps in analyzing the cost summary at of the nodes of the hierarchy (cost centre or cost centre groups or at the top level). A cost centre can be attached to any number of cost centre groups, but you can not assign the same cost centre more than once within a cost centre group.

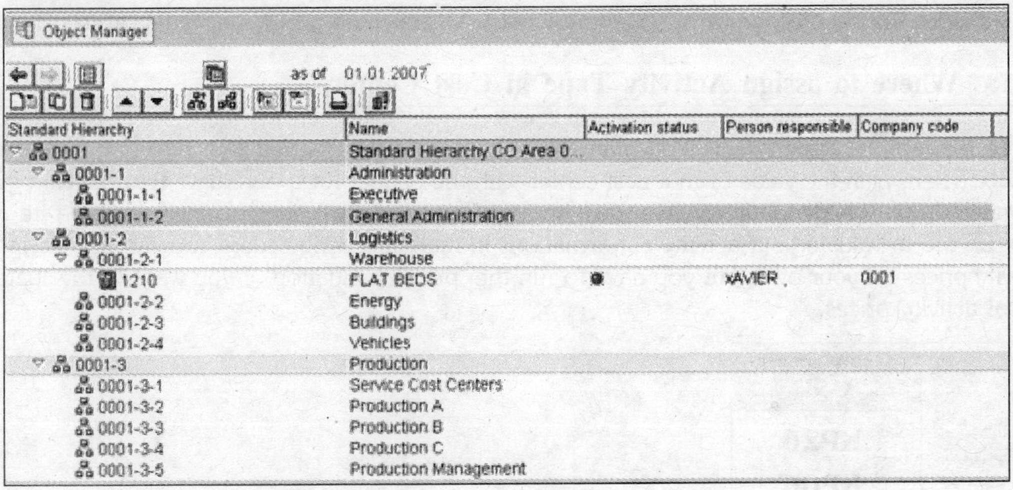

Figure 80: Standard Hierarchy- Sample

The standard hierarchy helps in easy maintenance of the cost centres / cost centre groups for creation of new ones or changing the existing ones. It supports the *drag-drop* functionality.

You may use **alternate hierarchies** to group cost centres according to your internal reporting requirements. You can have any number of alternate hierarchies but it is mandatory that you have one standard hierarchy. The alternate hierarchy is also known as **master data group**.

27. Explain posting of costs to 'Cost Centres'.

When you create accounting transitions in FI / FI-AA / MM, you typically post to one or more GL accounts. While doing so, provided you have already configured in such a way, you also require the user to input the cost centre for that transactions, so that when the transaction is posted the values (costs) flow not only to the GL but also to CO to the appropriate cost centre. The system will be creating two posting documents: one for FI and another for CO.

Besides, you will also be able to post non-financial information like direct labour hours from HR or PP modules to cost centres in CO.

28.   What is an 'Activity Type'?

Activity Type helps you do define the service / action (example: human labour, machine labour, repair hours etc) performed or provided by a cost centre. It forms the 'basis' for allocating costs to other cost centres or internal orders etc. You may assign an activity type to an operation so that they are reflected in PP: a CO document is created with the costs of the operation allocated from the cost center that produced the operation to a production order, when the operation is completed in PP.

You may group activity types into **activity type groups** for easy maintenance.

You need to arrive at the **activity price** which needs to be attached to that particular activity type for planning or recording the actual. The activity price is calculated by dividing the total costs by the total planned / actual activity quantity (hours, units etc).

It is not necessary that all the cost centres need to have activity types associated with them. If there is no output from a cost centre, then there will be no activity type for that cost centre.

29.   Where to assign Activity Type in Cost Centers?

There is no direct assignment. You plan the output for a cost center first by using **Transaction KP26**. Then, plan the value of that cost center with the budget for a period in **Transaction KP06**. 'Planned Activity expenditure' / 'Planned Activity Quantity' gives the 'planned activity rate' which you can use to valuate your activity confirmations in manufacturing orders. You can also define your activity prices on your own, but you have to run the 'price revaluation' if you want to revaluate your actual activity prices.

Transaction Code
KP26
KP06

30.   What is a 'Resource' in CO?

Resources are goods / services, consumed by CO objects like cost centre / internal order / WBS element, which are supplied (internally or externally) to an organization in order to produce business activities. The resources are used only in planning and not for tracking the actual.

There are three types of resources:

   ● Type **B** (used in base planning object)
   ● Type **M** (refers to a material)
   ● Type **R** (exists only in CO-OM)

31.   What is a 'Statistical Key Figure (SKF)'?

The **Statistical Key Figure (SKF)** is used as the basis (**tracing factor**) for making allocations (**assessments / distributions**). They are all the statistical data like number of employees, area in square meters etc. You will make use of SKF when you are faced with a situation wherein it is not possible to use any other conventional method or measure to arrive at the share of costs to be allocated to cost centres.

Suppose that you are incurring a monthly expense of USD 5, 000 in the cost centre cafeteria, the cost of which needs to be allocated to other cost centres. You can achieve this by SKF. Imagine that you want this to be allocated based on the 'number of employees' working in each of the other cost centres like administrative office (50 employees) and the factory (200 employees). You will now use the number of employees as the SKF for allocating the costs. The following illustration helps you to understand how SKF is used:

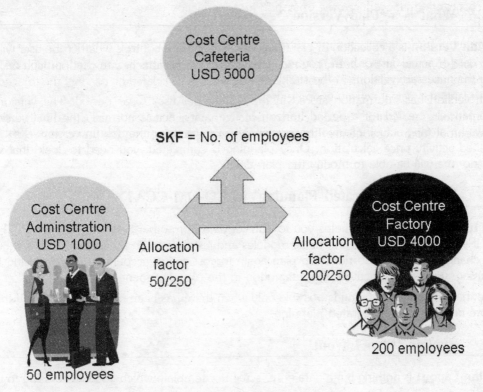

Figure 81: Statistical Key Figure

	Transaction Code
	KK01

In SKF allocation, you have the flexibility of using two different **SKF Categories** namely, (i) **Total value** or (ii) **Fixed value**. You will use fixed value in situations where the SKF does not change very often, as in the case of number of employees, area etc. You will use total value in case the value is expected to change every now and then, as in the case of power usage or water consumption and the like.

32. Explain the 'Planning' steps in CO-OM-CCA.

The three steps involved in planning in cost centre accounting include:

- Configuration required for planning
  - o Configure a **Plan Version**

o   Create or Copy **Plan Layout**s
o   Create **Plan Profile**
o   Insert Plan Layouts into Plan Profile
● Inputting the planned data
● Completing the planning activity

33.   What is a 'Plan Version'?

A **Plan Version** is a collection of planning data. The version controls whether the user will maintain plan data or actual data or both. You may create as many versions as you need, though SAP provides with the necessary versions in the standard system.

Each version has information stored in the system per fiscal year period. The version '000' is automatically created for a period horizon of five years, and is normally the final version as this allows for storing actual information as well. You will be using the data in version '000' for all the planned activity price calculation. Once planning is completed, you need to 'lock' that version so that no one will be able to modify the plan data.

34.   What is 'Integrated Planning' in CO-OM-CCA?

The **Integrated Planning** helps you to transfer data from other SAP modules like PP, HR, FI-AA etc. If you have planned data in these modules and just transferring these into CO, without making any changes, then you do not need plan again in cost centre accounting. Before using integrated planning, you need to activate the integration in the planning menu.

Note that integrated planning is possible only when there has been no data planned on that version before activating the integrated planning.

35.   Explain 'Plan Layout'.

A **Plan Layout** is nothing but a data entry screen or template which you will be using to input plan data.

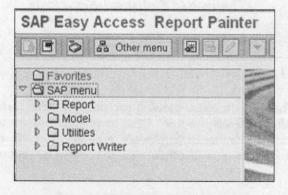

Figure 82: Report Painter

In most of the situations, it would be more than sufficient to use SAP supplied planning layouts; however, you may create your own by copying one of the existing layouts and altering the same with the help of **report painter**. While creating a custom layout, note that you have the flexibility to create up to nine **lead columns** (giving the details of the nature of the data associated with the value columns), and any number of **value columns** (plan data like amount, unit etc corresponding to the lead column).

You also have the option of using MS-Excel spread sheets as the data input screen in lieu of SAP's plan layouts; but to achieve this you need to activate 'integrating with Excel option' while assigning the layout(s) to a planner profile in IMG.

You need to define a plan layout for each of the three planning areas in CO namely:

    i.   Primary Cost and Activity Inputs

    ii.   Activity Output / Prices

    iii. Statistical Key Figures

36.   Explain 'Plan Profile'?

A **Plan Profile** (or **Planning Profile**) helps in controlling the whole process of planning by logically grouping the various plan layouts together. It determines the timeline for planning. You can have more than one planning layout per plan profile.

Before you actually start inputting the data, you need to set the plan profile, so that the system knows what layout needs to be used for the planning exercise.

37.   How to copy 'Plan Data' from one period to another?

SAP allows you to copy planning data, created manually earlier, from one fiscal year to the other or from one period to a different period within the same fiscal year. You have the options of (a) copying an existing plan data to a future period as a new plan data or (b) copying actual data from one period to another as the plan data.

38.   What is the recommended Planning Sequence, in CO?

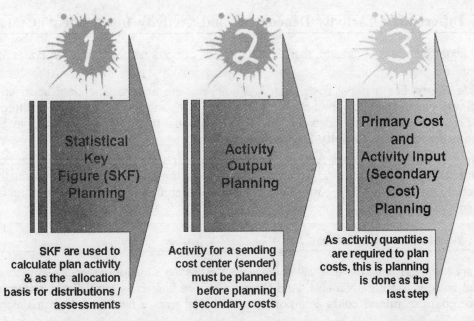

Figure 83: Planning Sequence for Cost Centre Accounting

SAP recommends three steps in the planning. In all the three steps, the planning can be carried out **manually** or **automatically**. You may use assessment, distribution, and indirect activity allocation or imputed costs for planning. You can also have **centralized planning** (cost element planning for all the cost centres) and **decentralized planning** (planning for individual cost centres) in your organization.

39.   What are the two options of entering Plan Data?

SAP provides you with a choice of two options to enter your plan data. You may use (i) **Form based entry** or **(ii) Free entry.**

In **form based entry**, all you need to do is to fill in the plan data in the rows corresponding to the characteristic values (cost centres, cost element etc) displayed on the screen. But, in **free entry**, you have the freedom of inputting even the characteristic values.

40.   What are 'Distribution Keys'?

The SAP system uses **Distribution Keys** to distribute planned values across various periods. With the standard distribution keys supplied by SAP, you will be able to achieve the type of distribution you will require:

- **DK1** (equal distribution)
- **DK2** (distribution as done earlier)
- **DK5** (copy values to period where there is no value)

For example, if you have planned annual value of 12000, by using **DK1** you will be able to distribute 1000 each as the monthly values. If you had plan values for last year which were something like 1000 for January to June, 500 for July, 1500 for August, and 1000 each for September to December, then by using **DK2**, you will be able to copy the same amounts to the next fiscal year. **DK5** will copy values to future periods only if there are no values already available for those periods.

41.   Differentiate 'Activity Dependent' and 'Activity Independent' Costs.

As you might be aware of already, there are two types of costs namely **variable costs** and **fixed costs**.

Variable Costs, like material costs, factory labour etc, are always dependent upon an activity, and will vary depending upon the activity. More the activity more will be the expenditure towards variable costs. In short, these costs are directly proportional to the level of activity. In SAP CO, these costs are known as **Activity Dependent Costs**.

In contrast to the variable costs, **Activity Independent Costs** or the **fixed costs** do not usually vary with the level of activity. And, you may need to incur these costs irrespective of whether there is an activity or otherwise. The costs like costs towards security, insurance premium etc fall under the category of fixed costs.

42.   What is a 'Mixed Cost'?

There are instances, wherein you will come across a costing situation when the Particular cost is classified both as fixed and variable. And, these costs are known as **semi-fixed costs** or **semi-variable costs** or **mixed costs** as a portion of the total costs is fixed and the remaining portion variable.

The classic example is the charges towards electricity in a production environment, where there is a basic minimum charge payable to the electricity provider (or towards heating requirements of the buildings) which remains fixed irrespective of the fact whether there is some production activity or not. When there is production, then you will use more electricity which varies with the level of production.

43.   Explain 'Manual Primary Cost Planning'.

Manual Primary Cost Planning is used to plan costs associated with the external procurement of goods and services. You will plan both the fixed and variable costs, and also mixed costs, if necessary. You will plan costs like salaries, wages etc as activity dependent costs; the costs towards security etc will be planned as activity independent costs.

You need to note that planning fixed primary costs is not vastly different from that of planning for variable primary costs. When you plan for the variable primary costs you need to mention the activity type associated with that. You may further break down this cost into fixed and variable proportions. The 'fixed primary costs' or 'activity independent primary costs' are planned using the primary cost elements on various cost centres, based on the activity performed on a particular cost centre.

You may use any of the following SAP supplied planning layouts:

- **1-101** - Activity independent or activity dependent primary costs
- **1-103** - Activity independent costs
- **1-152** - Activity independent costs (on a quarterly basis)
- **1-153** - Cost element planning (two versions simultaneously)
- **1-154** - Cost element planning (previous year's actual displayed in the lead column)
- **1-156** - Central planning (Cost element planning from Cost centre perspective)

44.   Explain 'Automatic Primary Cost Planning'.

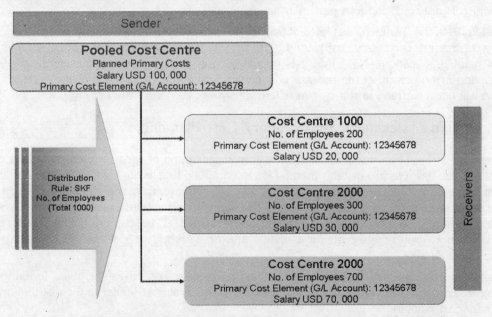

Figure 84: Distribution (Automatic Primary Costs Planning)

SAP provides you with two ways of handling **Primary Costs Planning** namely:

- Imputed Costs Calculation
- Distribution

Imputed Costs Calculation is used to smoothen the one-time costs (bonus, incentives etc) incurred by spreading the same over a period of time though the same is posted in FI side at the end of the year. You again have two methods of processing these costs (i) when there is no corresponding costs equivalent on FI side like the imputed family labour or imputed rent etc, and (ii) when there is a corresponding cost equivalent on the FI side like festival bonus etc.

Distribution helps in planning primary costs from one cost centre to the other. The cost centre from where the costs are distributed is known as the ***sender*** (or ***pooled cost centre*** or ***clearing cost centre***) and the other cost centres to which the costs are distributed or where the costs are received are known as ***receiver***.

Note that you will be able to distribute planned / actual primary costs only. Also note that the pooled cost centre does not incur any of these costs but acts as only as the 'clearing centre' for distribution to other cost centres. During the process, you will be using the SKF or the regular percentage method as the ***distribution rule*** for achieving the distribution. The ***distribution cycle*** helps to carry out the whole planning exercise.

45.   Explain 'Manual Secondary Cost Planning'.

Manual Secondary Cost Planning is required when you need to plan consumption quantities of a sender cost centre's planned activity from the view of receiving cost centre. The activity inputs may be planned either as the (i) activity dependent costs (variable) or as (ii) activity independent costs (fixed).

The 'activity dependent primary cost planning' is used only when you need the services like, for example, repair hours on a specified activity type. On the other hand, you will use 'activity independent primary cost planning' when you need the services like, for example, maintenance hours which is not restricted to a particular activity.

The system uses the 'planned calculated activity price' for posting the secondary cost. It is possible to carry out 'manual secondary cost planning' for activity types categorized as *Category -1* (manual entry / manual allocation). Note that it is important that you perform reconciliation of planned consumption of an activity at the receiver cost centre to the volume planned at the sender's level; else you will get a warning in the system when the system calculates the activity price.

46.   Explain 'Assessment' in Secondary Cost Planning.

Assessment is one of the methods used in 'automatic planning of secondary costs' in cost centre accounting. You will typically use this method when you need to allocate costs from one cost centre to other cost centres. The original costs, even if they are primary, from the cost centre are grouped and reclassified as secondary while allocating the same to other cost centres (imagine: you are collecting primary costs like postage, telephone, courier expenses, fax charges etc into a cost centre called 1000, now group these costs for assessment using a secondary cost element to receiver cost centres: 2000 & 3000).

You need to define an ***assessment rule*** (either 'percentage' or 'SKFs' or 'fixed amounts') for effecting assessment. You would have now noticed that this is almost similar to the distribution used in 'primary cost planning'.

So, why you need an assessment? Assessment is required when you need to allocate secondary costs, but you do not need the details which otherwise you get from distribution.

47. What is 'Allocation Structure'?

You need to define or use a secondary cost element, called 'assessment cost element', while you carry out the 'assessment' in 'automatic secondary cost planning'. Instead of defining individual assessment elements (for a group of primary cost elements) in individual segments, every now and then, you may define various assessment elements in an **Allocation Structure**, and use the same repeatedly.

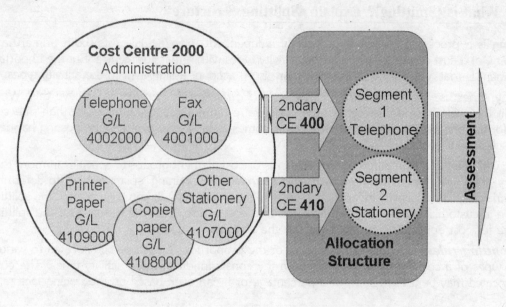

Figure 85: Assessment (Automatic Secondary Cost Planning)

48. Explain 'Segments' and 'Cycles'.

A **Segment** is one processing unit required to complete an automated allocation of distribution or assessment or reposting of planned/actual costs in controlling in SAP. A segment is made up of (a) allocation characteristics – to identify the sender / receiver, (b) values of the sender – plan / actual, type of costs to be allocated and (c) values of the receiver – basis for allocation i.e. the ***tracing factor*** like SKF, percentages etc.

When you combine multiple segments into a single process, then you call that as the **Cycle**. A Cycle helps you to process various segments in a chain-like fashion one, after another. A 'Cycle' consists of *header data* (valid for all Segments in a Cycle) and one or more *Segments*, with *summarized rules & settings* enabling allocation. The *Segments* within a 'cycle' can be processed *iteratively* (one segment waits for the results of another) or *non-iteratively* (all the segments are processed independently) or *cumulatively* (to take care of variations in receiver *Tracing Factors* or sender amounts).

Typically, while you start the cycles you will start them in a 'test' mode so as to see the allocations before actual postings. Technically, you can run the cycles in 'production' mode at any point of time, but the system will carry out the allocation postings only on the first day of a period. The utility of the cycle lies in the fact that you can run these, period after period.

49.   What is 'Iterative Processing' of Cycles?

Iterative Processing is nothing but the repetitive processing of sender / receiver relationships till the sender's entire cost is transferred to the receiver(s). Under this, you will not be able to use 'fixed amounts' as the 'sender rules'; you will also not be able to define a percentage to remain on the sender. You will be able to use both plan and actual data while using the iteration.

50.   What is 'Splitting'? Explain 'Splitting Structure'.

Splitting is a process used to assign 'activity independent' plan/actual costs, both primary and secondary, of a cost centre to the individual activity types within that cost centre. But the important requirement is that, you will use this when there is no account assignment to the activity types.

You may either use the (i) *Splitting rules* or (ii) *Equivalence number* to achieve this. When you split the costs from a cost centre, the cost centre temporarily *becomes* more than one cost centre for the purpose of allocation but, again becomes a single cost centre when posting happens in the subsequent period.

In case, you need to assign different cost elements or cost element groups to activities in more than one way, then you need to define a *splitting structure'* containing 'splitting rules' to determine the criteria of splitting 'activity independent' costs to an activity type. If you have created the splitting structure in customizing and assigned the same to a cost centre, then the system uses the splitting structure for cost apportioning; else it will use the equivalence number.

The '*splitting rules'* determines the amount or the proportion of costs to be allocated to various activity types of a cost centre; and is based on the consumption of these activity types. The costs thus allocated may be a fixed sum, or a percentage or it can even based on the tracing factors or SKFs.

The '*equivalence number'* is a basic method for splitting the costs when you manually plan for each of the activity types. By this, you will plan all activity independent costs according the equivalence numbers (default is 1).

51.   What is 'Activity Price Calculation?

You will be completing the planning process only when you perform the **Activity Price Calculation**, which is achieved based on planned activities and costs. By doing this you are valuating the planned secondary costs at receiving cost centres. If you do not want to use activity price thus calculated, you are free to use the *political price* for the activity type.

As you are aware of, the activity price is used for plan / actual allocation and is determined by using either (1) the political price or (2) the system calculated activity price.

52.   How system calculates 'Activity Price'?

The system calculates the **Activity Price**, for each activity type and cost centre, by following the underlying rule:

$$\text{Planned Activity Price} = \frac{\text{Planned Primary Costs} + \text{Planned Secondary Costs}}{\text{Planned Activity Type Volume}}$$

Note that the system will continue to calculate the activity price even if you have set the price indicator of an activity type to '*political price*'.

53. What is known as 'Political Price' for an activity type?

The **Political Price** is the price determined outside the SAP system, and used in manual input using the required planning layout in planning.

54. What is 'Allocation Price Variance'?

Allocation Price Variance is the difference between the 'political price' of an activity type and the 'system calculated activity price' of the same activity type.

55. What is 'Budgeting'?

Budgeting is used to augment the planning process at the cost centre level. While planning is considered as the '*bottom-up*' approach, budgeting is regarded as the '*top-down*' method to control costs.

Budget usually comes 'down' from the 'top (management)', and is used to guide the planning process at the cost centre level. Note that budgeting is <u>not</u> integrated with postings: you will get an error when the system comes across a posting which will result in the actual values exceeding the budget for that cost centre.

56. What are 'Direct Allocation' methods of postings in CO?

The **Direct Allocation** of postings in CO may be of (1) actual cost entry or (2) transaction based postings.

The *actual cost entry* is the transfer of primary costs from FI to CO, on real-time basis through the primary cost elements. You may also transfer transaction data by making the cost accounting assignment to cost objects from other modules like FI-AA, SD and MM:

- FI-AA: Assign assets to a cost centre (to post depreciation etc)
- MM: Assign GR to a cost centre / internal order
- SD: Assign or settle a sales order to a cost centre or internal order

Note that during actual cost entry, the system creates two documents, when you post the primary costs from FI to CO: (1) A document in FI and (2) a parallel document in CO, which is summarized from the point of cost object / element.

The *transaction based postings* are executed within the CO, again on real-time basis, enabling you to have up-dated cost information on the cost centres at any point of time. You will be able to carry out the following transaction based postings in CO:

- Reposting
  - o   Line items
  - o   Transactions
- Manual cost allocation

- Direct activity allocation
- Posting of Statistical Key Figures
- Posting of Sender activities

57. What is 'Indirect Allocation' method of postings in CO?

The **Indirect Allocation** of postings in CO may be used at the end of a period, as a periodic allocation. This is done after you have completed all the primary postings. You may post the following periodic allocations using indirect allocation;

- Periodic Reposting
- Distribution
- Assessment
- Accrual Cost Calculation (Imputed Cost Calculation)
- Indirect Activity Allocation

58. Explain 'CO Automatic Account Assignment'.

For transferring primary costs to CO, on real-time basis, you need to have **Automatic Account Assignments** defined in the system. By doing this, you will always be able to post a particular cost to a specified cost centre. You can also use this assignment for automatically posting the exchange rate differences (gain or loss), discount etc to CO.

You may also have additional account assignment at different levels like:

- Controlling area / account / Company Code in the customizing
- Controlling area / account / cost element in the master record
- Controlling area / account / Company Code / business area / valuation area in customizing.

The system always goes through the route of customizing first, then to the cost element master record while accessing the account assignment rules.

59. How 'Validation' differs from 'Substitution'?

SAP uses *validations* and *substitutions* to check the integrity of data entered before posting a document. When you have both substitutions and validations defined, the system first completes the substitution then goes on to validate the entries. Note that only one validation and one substitution can be activated at a time for a controlling area per '***call-up point***'.

A **Validation** uses a *Boolean logic* for ***checking*** any type of combination of specified criteria (like account type/cost centre combination) for ensuring the validity before allowing you to post a document. Example:

- ***Validation Rule:*** If cost element is '120000', then the cost centre is '1200'.
- ***Document:*** You try posting a document containing cost element as '120000' and the cost centre as '1400'.
- ***System Response:*** The system will throw an 'error message' after checking that the cost centre value does not match the cost centre value of the criteria for that given cost element value.

In contrast to validation which just checks for validity, **Substitution** ensures that the system replaces a value assigned to one or more fields based on pre-determined criteria, using, again, a '*Boolean logic'*.

Example:

- *Substitution Rule:* If cost element is '120000', then the cost centre is '1200'.
- *Document:* You try posting a document containing cost element as '120000' and the cost centre as '1400'.
- *System Response:* The system will replace the entered cost centre value of '1400' with that of the correct value '1200'.

60.   What is a 'Call-up Point'?

A **Call-up Point** is a particular point in transaction processing, triggering some action like substitution or validation.

61.   What is a 'Boolean Logic'?

Boolean Logic is based on the simple logic to determine true or false of a given statement. The logic works on the basic principle that a statement can either be true or false. In a complex statement (created by using operators '*and*' / '*or*' / '*nor*' etc) with many parts, the logic goes by assigning true or false from part to part, and then determines at the end whether the combination is true or false.

62.   Explain 'Reposting' in Cost Centre Accounting.

Reposting is one of the 'transaction based postings' in Cost Centre Accounting, used to re-allocate costs that were incorrectly posted to another cost centre earlier. Also called as *internal reposting,* there are two types:

- Line Item Reposting
- Transaction Reposting

Use **Line Item Reposting** when only a certain line items, from the original posting, needs to be reposted. Under this reposting, at the end of the transaction, the system creates a new a CO document, but keeps the original FI document unchanged. In the new CO document created, the original FI number is referenced to.

You will resort to the entire **Transaction Reposting**, when the original posting was incorrect. Here, the original FI documents is not referenced to in the new CO document created, though the original FI document remains unchanged.

63.   Is 'Periodic Reposting' different from 'Reposting'?

Periodic Reposting, a method under 'indirect allocation', is used to correct multiple postings made to cost centres, during a period. As such, this is similar to *multiple reposting* under 'transaction based postings'.

The periodic reposting is also similar to *distribution*, when you use this, at the period end, to transfer all the costs from a 'pooled cost centre' to other receivers. (Note that the 'distribution' is meant for primary cost allocation, but periodic reposting is meant for correction of the posting errors).

64.   Explain 'Manual Cost Allocation'.

Manual Cost Allocation – one of the 'transaction based postings' - is used to post both primary and secondary actual costs (<u>not</u> the planned costs), and also to transfer external data. You may also use this to correct secondary costs which were incorrectly posted earlier. In the process of manual cost allocation, remember that you can use any type of cost element except *43*, as this is meant exclusively for activity allocation.

You may use this among cost centres, internal orders, networks, network activities, sales orders, sales order items, WBS elements etc, identifying these cost objects as senders / receivers.

65.   What is 'Direct Activity Allocation'?

Direct Activity Allocation – one of the 'transaction based postings'- is used to record activities performed by a cost centre and allocating simultaneously to 'receiving cost centres'. You will be able to use this 'direct activity allocation' only when you know the activity volumes of the both the sender and the receiver. If it is not known, then use the ***indirect activity allocation*** at the period end.

You need to input the activity quantity, sender / receiver cost centre and date to enable the system to allocate the costs: the system will automatically determine the ***allocation cost element*** and the ***activity price*** (either the *planned price* or the *actual price*). The system multiplies the activity consumed with that of the activity price to arrive at the allocated cost.

66.   How do you calculate 'Accrued Costs'?

SAP provides two methods for calculating the **Imputed** or **Accrued Costs** in CO:

*   Target = Actual method
*   Cost Element Percent method

67.   Describe 'Reconciliation Ledger'.

The **Reconciliation Ledger** is used to keep track of all cross-Company Code transactions between FI and CO, as there is every chance that there may be some imbalance between the CO totals and FI totals when more than one Company Code is attached to a controlling area. This is because you may try to allocate costs from one cost centre to another assigned to a different Company Code.

The reconciliation ledger records the Company Code, business area, functional area, amount, cost objects, cost element, currency (Company Code and controlling area) etc. You can make reconciliation postings at the end of a period so as to synchronize FI and CO, with the configuration settings to automatically post the differences to FI.

While configuring the reconciliation ledger, you may use ***extended account assignments*** besides the normal account assignment for automatic transfer of reconciled postings. The extended account assignment helps in making more comprehensive assignments to the relevant reconciliation accounts, with the option and flexibility of specifying any field in the reconciliation ledger (Company Code, cost element, functional area etc) for checking in the 'substitution rules'.

To aid in determining possible reconciliation postings, you can opt for selecting individual cost flows from all the relevant cost flows. This is accomplished running the relevant report and looking for the relevant 'data block' (like total cost flows, basic overview list and detailed list).

68.   What is 'Variance Analysis' in CO-OM-CCA?

The **Variance Analysis** is the determination and interpretation of the difference(s) between the actual and planned (target) costs (within a cost centre / cost centre group) in cost centre accounting. The analysis is intended to provide important clues to the top management so as to plan better later.

69.   What are the 'Categories of Variances' CO-OM-CCA?

SAP helps to classify all the variances into two categories:
- Input Variance
- Output Variance

70.   Explain 'Input Variance'.

The **Input Variance** is the result from the mismatch of amounts / quantities of inputs planned and actually used. You will be able to identify the following ***input side variances***, in the system:

- ***Quantity variance*** – when there is a difference between planned and actual quantity of activity consumption. The inference is that there is some production inefficiency leading to more consumption or there is some loss / shrinkage in the quantities.

- ***Price variance*** – when there is a difference between plan and actual price of an activity. Inference will be that you may need to change the suppliers looking for lower prices or it is just a market condition.

- ***Resource (usage) variance*** – when there is a usage of unplanned cost element or there has not been a posting to a planned cost element. Inference is that there are some unidentified costs which may be planned in the next planning cycle, or just plain errors in postings.

- ***Remaining (input) variance*** – these are all miscellaneous variances where the system is not able to categorize a variance.

71.   What is 'Output Variance'?

The **Output Variance** results when the actual costs allocated from a cost centre differ from that of the planned (or target) cost allocation from that cost centre. The variances on the 'output side' may be of any one of the following categories:

- ***Volume variance*** – this occurs when actual and planned activities differ (in terms of activity quantity and or activity itself). It can arise in either or both the situations described below:
    - Volume variance = Plan Activity Cost – (Actual Activity Quantity * Planned Activity Price)
    - Volume variance = Plan Activity Price * (Planned Activity Quantity – Actual Activity Quantity)

- ***Output price variance*** – this variance occurs when the activity price used in the actual allocation is a *political activity price* (manually entered or plan price) differing from the *system calculated activity price (target price)*.

- ***Output quantity variance*** – this kind of variance occurs only on the actual side, when there is a difference between the actual activity quantity (manually) entered on the sender cost centre, and the actual activity quantity allocated from that sender cost centre.

- *Remaining variance* – this reflects the miscellaneous variance, at the cost centre level, identified by the system on the output side but remains not categorized into any of the above three types. The possible reason can be that you have deactivated the output variances in the *variance variant* configuration or the output variance is less than the 'minor difference' you have defined in the 'variance variant'.

72.   How you will deal with 'Variances'?

Though the system identifies and calculates the variances, they are not automatically dealt with by the system. Hence, these variances will remain at the cost centre as a *period-end balance* and you need to act on that:

- You may do actual activity price calculation so as to revalue all internal allocations with a newly calculated price (as against the initial planned activity price), and post the difference to all the cost centres which initially received the allocations. This will help you in clearing all or a portion of output price variances.
- You may 'transfer' the variance balance to other modules (like CO-PA) for further analysis.
- You may make additional automated allocations with in CO-OM-CCA to one or more cost centres.

73.   What are all the 'Standard Reports' in CO?

SAP comes delivered with a number of **Standard Reports** in CO module. The reports are grouped under:

- Planning reports
- Comparison reports
- Line item reports
- Report for activity prices
- Reports for variance analysis
- Master data reports
- Document display

All the reports are arranged in a '*report tree*' with the hierarchical arrangement of reports under various nodes. Note that you will not be able to change the standard report tree supplied by SAP; if you need you may copy the same, define your own reports and then attach these newly defined ones to the new report tree you just defined.

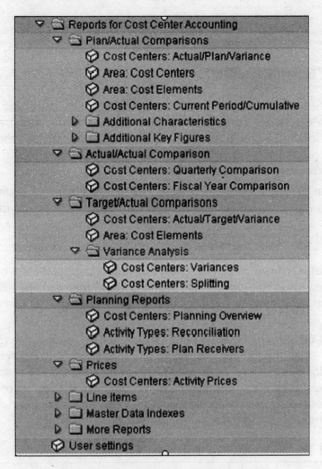

Figure 86: Report Tree in CO

74. What is 'Summarization' in CO?

The **Summarization** helps to condense and store the transaction data at the 'cost centre group' level. You may do the summarization for the highest node of the 'standard hierarchy' or any of the 'alternate hierarchies'. Once summarized, you will be able to create a vast number of reports with report run-time vastly reduced as all the data of the nodes are readily available from the summarized Table.

Internal Orders

75.   What is an 'Internal Order'?

An **Internal Order** is a cost object used mainly for recording costs associated with certain events taking place within the company. The events are unique like the marketing campaigns, repairs, trade exhibitions etc. Unlike the cost centres where you typically post only the costs, you will be able to post both the cost and revenue information to the internal orders. You can plan, monitor, collect and settle costs/revenue on internal orders.

The internal orders can be classified as (i) ***Single order / Individual order*** or (ii) ***Standing order***. The orders can also be (a) ***Real internal order*** or (b) ***Statistical internal order.***

76.   How 'Individual Order' differs from 'Standing Order'?

An **Individual (Internal) Order** is meant for collecting and settling costs of a one-time and unique business activity like new product launch. You will be settling the order in full at the end of the activity. Typically this type of orders are used for advertising campaigns, R & D costs, assets produced in-house etc.

A **Standing (Internal) Order**, on the other hand, is used in case of repetitive operations, the costs of which are generally smaller compared to the one-time orders. You will settle the costs, from these orders, on a 'periodic basis' (say, at the end of every month) and will keep the order open to receive future costs. You will be using this type of order for tracking costs on routine maintenance, telephone usage charges etc. These orders do away the need for creating a new order every time you need such a tracking: they are similar to the *standing instructions*.

77.   What are all the 'Groups' of Internal Orders?

The **Internal Orders** can be grouped into the following categories / groups:

- ***Overhead orders***
  Associated with monitoring of overhead costs incurred for a specific purpose like tracking a repair work, painting the factory, conducting an exhibition etc, the overhead cost orders are used only in the CO area.

- ***Investment orders***
  Tracking the costs incurred on fixed assets (*assets under construction*) like construction of a warehouse etc, these are also termed as ***capital investment orders***.

- ***Accrual orders***
  You will use accrual orders when it is required to make an offsetting posting of accrued costs to a cost centre in CO.

- ***Orders with Revenue***
  These orders help you to carry out cost accounting functionality of SAP SD (*customer orders*), when you have not implemented SD module. By doing this, you will be able to track costs and revenues.

78.   How 'Statistical Internal Orders' differs from 'Real Orders'?

A **Statistical Internal Order** is used to collect costs for the purpose of information and reporting, as the costs 'collected' on this order are never settled to a cost object. When you want to create such an order, you will be required to specify that the order is *'statistical'* in its master record. However, to make a posting to this kind of orders, you need to have 'real' or 'true' cost object specified during the transaction.

A **Real Internal Order** is always used to settle costs to other cost objects. So, even if you specify a real cost object while making a posting to a real order, the system will consider that cost object as a statistical one as the internal order itself is a real cost object.

Logistics

6

Logistics

Sales & Distribution (SD)

Depicted below is the broad organizational structure of logistics, which will help you to understand how the various units of SD, as well as MM modules are linked to FI:

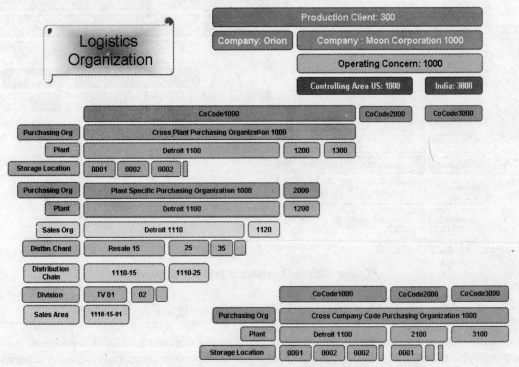

Figure 87: Logistics organizational structure in SAP

1. What are all the components of SAP's SD module?

The important **Components** in SAP Sales & Distribution module include:

- Master data
- Basic functions
- Sales (including foreign sales and sales support)
- Shipping & transportation
- Billing
- Sales support
- Information systems

2.   What are all the important organizational elements of SAP SD?

The important **Organizational Elements** in SAP Sales & Distribution include:

- Sales organization
- Distribution channel
- Division
- Sales area
- Sales group
- Sales person

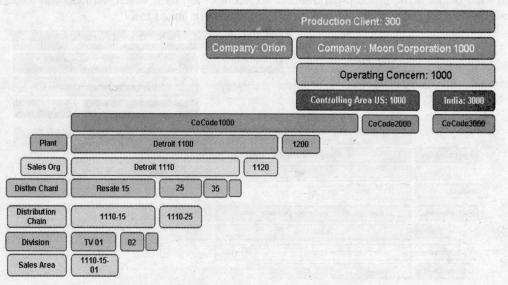

Figure 88: SD organizational structure

3.   Explain 'Sales Organization'. How it is assigned to a 'Plant'?

The **Sales Organization** is the top most organizational element in SD. It represents and takes care of all the transactions relating to selling and distribution of products or services. A ***distribution channel*** is assigned to one or more sales organization. The customer master can be maintained with different sales organization views.

The sales organization, identified by a 4-character code, is assigned to one or more *plants*. These *plants* are, in turn, assigned to a Company Code. So, it follows that any number of ***sales areas*** can be brought under a single Company Code.

Even though it is possible that you may have any number of sales organizations, it is recommended that you have minimum number of these units in your set-up. Ideal recommendation is for a single sales organization per Company Code. If you are selling the same product or service from more than one sales organization, then there is a clear indication that you are having more sales organizations defined than what is ideally required: in this case you should have only one sales organization.

4.   What is a 'Distribution Channel'?

A **Distribution Channel** depicts the channel through which the products or services reach the customers after it is sold (example: wholesale, retail, direct sales etc). Represented by a 2-digit identifier, the distribution channel is assigned to one or more **sales areas**. As a result, one customer may be serviced through more than one distribution channel. Like in **sales organization**, you may have the customer master data with different distribution channel views.

5.   What is a 'Distribution Chain'?

A **Distribution Chain** represents the possible combination of **sales organization**(s) and **distribution channel**(s). In the Figure-88, *Detroit 1110-Resale 15* forms a distribution channel and is normally denoted as '1110-15'.

6.   What is a 'Division'?

A **Division** depicts the product or service group for a range of products / services. For each of this division, you may define and maintain customer-specific parameters like terms of payment, pricing etc. The division may come under one or more distribution channels.

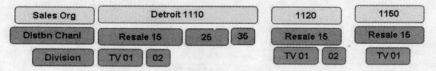

***Figure 89**: Sales Organization – Distribution Channel – Division assignment*

7.   Explain the assignments among Organizational Units in SD.

1 Company Code		>1 Plant
1 Sales Area		> 1 Plant
> 1 Sales Area	is assigned to	1 Company Code
1 Distribution Channel		> 1 Sales Area
1 Customer		>1 Distribution Channel
>1 Division		>1 Distribution Channel

8.   What is a 'Sales Area'?

A **Sales Area** is a combination of **sales organization, distribution channel** and **division**. From Figure-89 you can derive a sales area 1110-15-01 which in fact represents that the product

'*TV*' sold through '*resale*' distribution channel from sales organization '*Detroit*'. Usually, you will use sales areas for reporting purposes.

9.   Explain how 'Human Elements' are organized in SD.

There are three distinct organizational units in SD from the human angle:
- Sales Office
- Sales Group
- Sales Person

Sales Office represents the geographical dimension in sales and distribution. A sales office is assigned to a **sales area**. The staff of a sales office may be grouped into **Sales Groups**. This corresponds to sales divisions. A **Sales Person** is assigned to a sales group. This assignment is done at the personnel master record level.

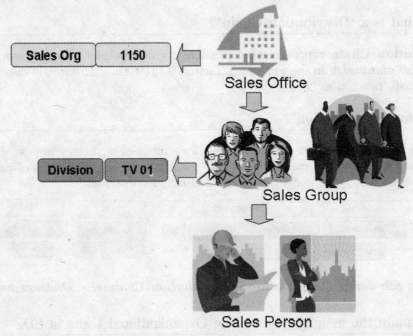

Figure 90: Sales office-Sales group-Sales person structure

10.   Where and how a 'Business Area Assignment' is done?

Business area assignment is done at two levels:
- Plant level
- Valuation area level

The 'business area' is assigned to the combination of 'plant'/'valuation area' and the 'division'.

11.   A 'Plant' is assigned to which of the entities in SD Organization?

A **Plant** is assigned to:

- Company Code
- Combination of Sales Organization & Distribution Channel
- Purchasing Organization

12. How the 'Shipping Point' is determined by the system?

Shipping Point is determined by the combination of ***shipping condition, loading group*** and ***plant*** assigned to a shipping point.

13. What are all the important basic 'Customer Master Records'?

Some of the important customer records are:
- Sold-to-Party record
- Ship-to-Party record
- Bill-to-Party record
- Payer record

14. What are the various sections of 'Customer Master Record'?

The different sections in a master record are:

- *General data*
  You will be able to create the *general data* like addresses, telephones, contact persons, unloading points etc either from the accounting side or from the sales side.

Transaction Code
VD01
XD01

- *Company Code data*
  You will be able to create data on account management (credit management, payment details, taxations, insurance etc) which pertains to the Company Code in which the customer is created. You will be doing this from the accounting side.

Transaction Code
XD01

- *Sales & Distribution data*
  The data on pricing, shipping etc comes under this category of information. You will be creating this from the SD area. You can have data on different sales area for a single customer.

Transaction Code
VD01

15.   What is a 'Customer-Material Information Record'?

The information relating to a material that applies only to a specific customer is known as **Customer-Material Information**. This is nothing but the description of your 'material by the customer', and you record this customer-specific information in the customer-material information record.

Transaction Code
VD51

16.   What is a 'Sales Order'?

A **Sales Order** is a contract between your *Sales Organization* and a *Customer,* for supply of specified goods and/services over a specified time frame and in agreed quantity or unit. All the relevant information from the customer master record and the material master record, for a specific sales area, are copied to the sales order. The sales order may be created with reference to a *'preceding document'* like quotation: then all the initial data from the preceding document is copied to the sales order.

The 'sales order' contains:

- *Organizational data* (sales organization, distribution channel, division, sales document type, pricing procedure etc).
- *Header data* (sold-to-party, sales office, sales group, pricing date, document date, order reason, document currency, price group, sales district, customer group, shipping condition, INCOTERMS, payment terms, billing schedule, PO number etc).
- *Item data* (item category, order quantity, material, batch number, product hierarchy, plant, material group, shipping point, route, delivery priority, customer material, item number etc).
- *Schedule line data* (schedule line, schedule line number, delivery date, order quantity, confirmed quantity, material availability date, loading date, proposed goods issue date, transportation date, movement type, shipping point etc).

17.   Explain the process flow for a 'Standard Sales Order'.

Starting with the quotation, a **Standard Sales Order** goes through the following process:

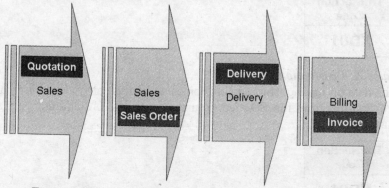

Figure 91: Standard Sales Order – Process Flow

18.   Outline the process flow for 'Sales Returns'.

Starting with the quotation, a **Sales Return** goes through the following process:

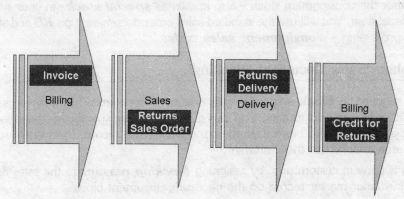

Figure 92: Sales Returns – Process Flow

19.   Describe the process flow for 'Credit Memo'.

The following diagram depicts a typical process flow for **Credit Memo**:

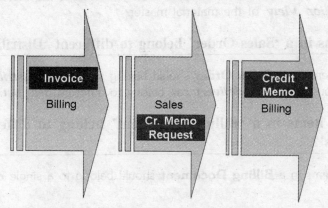

Figure 93: Credit Memo – Process Flow

20.   What are all the 'Special Sales Document Types'?

- **SO**   Rush Order
- **G2**   Credit
- **RE**   Return Order
- **KN**   FoC (Free-of-Charge) Subsequent Delivery Order
- **RK**   Invoice Correction Request

21.   What is 'Consignment Stock Process'?

In the **Consignment Stock Process**, you will allow your stock or material to be at the customer's site. You may also allow your stock or material to be made available at your site, but reserved for a particular customer. And, you will allow the customer to sell or consume as much stock as he wants from this. You will then bill the customer only for the quantities that he has consumed or sold.

You will monitor the consignment stock – also known as **special stock** - in your system customer-wise and material-wise. You will use the standard sales order document type **KB** and standard delivery type **LF** for processing a **consignment sales order**.

22.   Explain 'Sales Document Blocking'.

You may be required to **block** a specific sales document type from further processing, when you want to block undesirable customers. You can achieve this for specific customer or for a specific document type. You may also block it, in the customer master record, for a single *sales area* or for all the sales area attached to the customer.

The blocking is done in customizing, by assigning **blocking reasons** to the sales document types. Then in the customer master record do the necessary document block.

23.   Can you 'block' a transaction for a material which is 'Flagged for Deletion'?

When you set the '**deletion flag**' for a material at the *plant* level, still you will be able to enter an order even though the system will 'warn' you that the material has been flagged for deletion. If you require blocking any transaction for a material, then you need to use the '**Sales Status**' field in '**Sales Organization View**' of the material master.

24.   Can items in a 'Sales Order' belong to different 'Distribution Channels'?

No: The various items in a **Sales Order** should belong to a single **distribution channel** only. However, the various items in a **delivery** can belong to different *distribution channels*.

25.   Can the items in a 'Billing Document' belong to different 'Distribution Channels'?

No: The various items in a **Billing Document** should belong to a single **distribution channel** only.

26.   Differentiate between a 'Sales Area' and a 'Sales Line'.

A **Sales Area** comprises of sales organization, distribution channel and division whereas a **Sales Line** is the combination of sales organization and distribution channel.

27.   Can a 'Sales Area' belong to different Company Codes?

No: A **Sales Area** can belong to only one Company Code.

28.   What is the use of 'Storage Location Rule'?

The **Storage Location Rule** assigned in the *Delivery Document* type determines the *Storage Location*, even when storage location is entered during delivery creation. This is based on the following rules:

- **MALA** : Shipping Point/Plant/Storage condition
- **RETA** : Plant/Situation/Storage condition
- **MARE** : MALA then RETA

29.   How to configure 'Partner Determination Procedure' in SD?

The **Partner Determination Procedure** is configured as outlined in the following steps:

- Create *account group*
- Create and assign a *number range* to that account group
- Create and assign the *partner functions* to the account group
- Create a *partner determination procedure*
- Assign the partner functions to the partner determination procedure
- Finally assign the partner determination procedure to the account group

30.   Where to define 'Unloading Points' and 'Goods Receiving Hours'?

The **Unloading Points** and the **Goods Receiving Hours** are defined in the *Customer Master >
General Data > Unloading Points tab.*

31.   Where you will define 'Terms of Payment' for a customer?

The **Terms of Payment** for a specific customer is defined in the *Customer Master > Company
Code Data > Payment Transactions Tab*, and also in the *Billing Document Tab* in *Sales Area
Data* of the *Customer Master.*

Material Management (MM)

32.   What functions are supported in SAP's 'Material Management (MM)'?

The MM module of SAP supports the following functions:
- MRP (Material Requirements Planning)
- Procurement
- Inventory Management
- Inventory Valuation
- Invoice Verification

33.   What is 'MRP'?

MRP (Material Requirements Planning) is nothing but the determination of which materials are required, when and in what quantities, based on the current information and forecasts.

34.   Explain the basic 'Organization Structure' in MM.

The major **Organizational Elements** of MM include:
- Purchasing Organization
- Plant
- Storage Location

The **Purchasing Organization** is typically attached to one Company Code. But, a single Company Code can have one or more purchasing organizations. One or more **Plants** are attached to a purchasing organization. One or more **Storage Locations** are attached to a plant. One or more plants are assigned to a Company Code, but one plant is attached to only one Company Code.

Depending upon how the purchasing organization has been structured, you may come across with three types of structures as detailed below:

- ***Cross-plant purchasing organization***
  The purchasing organization caters to more than one plant of the same Company Code.

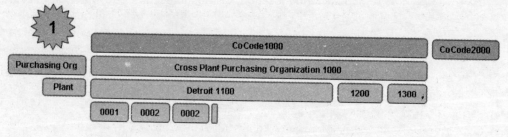

Figure 94: Cross-Plant Purchasing Organization

- ***Plant-specific purchasing organization***
  Each Plant has it is own purchasing organization.

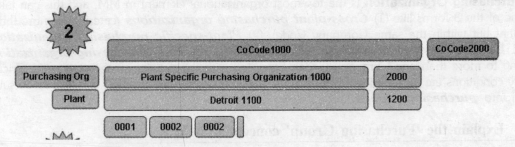

Figure 95: Plant-specific Purchasing Organization

- **Cross-company code purchasing organization**
  A single purchasing organization is responsible for the procurement activities of more than one Company Code. The plants attached to this purchasing organization are also Cross-Company Code. In this case, the purchasing organization is <u>not</u> attached to any of the Company Codes; instead the various plants are attached to the purchasing organization. This kind of purchasing organization is known as ***central purchasing organization***. This kind of organizational structure is essential in case of centralized procurement in an enterprise.

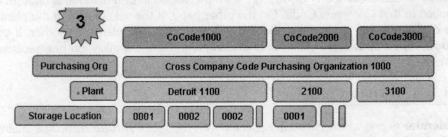

Figure 96: Cross-Company Code Purchasing Organization

35.   Define 'Plant' in SAP.

The '***Plant***' in SAP can denote a manufacturing location, distribution centre or a warehouse. With a unique numbers identifying each of the plants, though these are all not financial entities they can still be linked to a ***Business Area***. The Plant is the place where you normally valuate the inventory in SAP. The system, however, checks for the inventory either at the Plant or Plant/Storage Location during an Order entry.

36.   Explain 'Storage Location' in SAP.

A sun-division of a *plant*, the **Storage Location** defines a location for materials which can be a warehouse, bin, or a ***storage area*** of raw materials / WIP / finished product. You will manage the physical inventory, material movement, picking, cycle counting etc at the storage location level. In ***Warehouse Management,*** the storage location is further sub-divided.

37.   Explain 'Purchasing Organization' in SAP.

This refers to the organizational structure in SAP which is responsible for procurement of materials.

The **Purchasing Organization** is the top-most organizational element in MM, and this can take any one of the 3 forms like (1) *Cross-plant purchasing organizations (*catering to more than one plant but within the same Company Code), (2) *Plant-specific purchasing organization* (with 1:1 relationship with the plant) and (3) *Cross-company code purchasing organization* (catering to more than one Company Code). Entrusted with the activity of negotiating the price, delivery conditions etc of materials from vendors, the Purchasing Organization can further be sub-divided into *purchasing groups*.

38.   Explain the 'Purchasing Group' concept in MM.

The **Purchasing Group** carries out the actual activities of purchasing, and is assigned to a material in the material master. The activities of several purchasing organizations can be done by one purchasing group.

39.   Explain the 'Valuation Area' concept in MM.

The valuation of a material is done at the **Valuation Area** which can either be at (1) *Company Code* level or (2) *Plant* level. The level at which the valuation needs to happen is defined in the customizing. Note that once defined, you will not be able to change it later!

When the valuation is at the Company Code level, then the valuation of a material is uniform across the plants attached to that Company Code. On the other hand, if the valuation is at the plant level, then the value of the material is plant-specific and will vary from one plant to another. If you are using *PP (Production Planning) / MRP* in your company, then the valuation has necessarily to be at the plant level.

40.   What is a 'Factory Calendar'?

A **Factory Calendar** is one which is country-specific with the list of *public holidays* (maintained via *Holiday Calendar*) and *working days*, which is *Client-independent*. The factory calendar helps in controlling goods issues / receipts. Each *plant* is assigned with a factory calendar, and the calendar must be activated (through 'CTS functionality') before using the same.

41.   Explain how SD and MM are connected in SAP.

The goods/ services form a *plant* can be sold by one or more *sales organizations*. It is also possible a single sales organizations sells goods/services for several plants. When the sales organization sells for more than one plant belonging to one or more Company Codes, then this becomes the *inter-company sales*, and will require you to make some special configurations in the system. A sales organization, attached to a *Company Code*, is further divided into *distribution channel* and *divisions* in SD. A division typically represents a product line, and is assigned to a material in the material master.

42.   Outline the functions supported by 'Material Master.

The **Material Master** is the central master record catering to various business functions in *Logistics*. The data stored in this master support a variety of business functions and operations like:

- Production Planning

- MRP
- Procurement
- Invoice Verification
- Inventory Management
- Product costing
- Sales and Distribution
- Quality Management

The data are stored, within a material master, at different organizational levels. The **general data** is valid for all the Company Codes at the Client level. The purchasing information is valid at the plant level. The **sales information** is valid at the sales organization / distribution channel. Lastly, when **Warehouse Management** is activated, the data are maintained at the warehouse number / storage type level.

43. Explain why a 'Material Master' is divided into 'Views'.

Since the information in a material master needs to be maintained by a number of users across several modules, SAP has structured the master into a number of **Views** for facilitating easier access and updating of data. The views include:

- Basic Data
- Classification
- Sales
- Purchasing
- Purchase Order text
- Accounting
- Foreign Trade
- Work Scheduling
- Forecasting
- Storage
- Costing
- Plant / Storage Location stock
- MRP

44. What is the content of 'Accounting View' in a 'Materia Master'?

The most important information maintained on the **Accounting View** of a material master is the **valuation class** which needs to be assigned to individual materials. The valuation class, in-turn, helps in determining the relevant GL accounts for posting the valuation-relevant transactions like GR, GI etc.

You will also be maintaining the **price control indicator** on the accounting view, which enables determining how the stock of a material is to be valued (at **Standard price (S)** or **Moving average price (V)**).

45. Why do you need 'Material Type' in MM?

One of the ways to group materials is by **Material Type** (the other being by 'Industry Sector'). This grouping helps in the determination of what information or data is to be made available at the material master level for a particular material.

The material type (for example *FERT, HAWA, HALB, ROH* and so on) is used to control:

- Which are all the *Views* that can be maintained on the master record
- Which *Fields* are mandatory, optional or for 'display only' in the material master
- What kind of *Procurement* is allowed for that material (internal or external or both)
- How to *Number* (Internal / External) and what *Number Range* is allowed
- Whether *Quantity* and/or *Value* updating should be done in a particular *Valuation Area*
- Which *GL Accounts* will be posted to (via the *Valuation Class*) during goods movement
- What should be the default *Item Category Group* (S&D)
- What should be the default *Price Control Indicator* (S or V) and
- Whether the default Price Control Indicator is changeable during material master maintenance

46.   Explain 'Price Control Indicator'.

The **Price Control Indicator** is used by SAP to determine how a material will be valuated, by default. The indicator can be set to:

- Standard Price (**S**) or
- Moving Average Price (**V**)

When you set the indicator to '**S**', then the system carries out all the ***inventory postings*** at the standard price. The ***variances*** - due to a different price of a material in goods movement or invoice receipts - if any, are all posted to ***price difference accounts***. As a result, the standard price remains the same, unless it is changed intentionally by manual processing. This will be necessary only when the difference between the standard and moving average prices becomes very large. (While updating the price difference accounts, however, the system also updates the moving average price with these variances, so that you get a chance to adjust the standard price should the difference between the standard and moving average prices becomes very substantial).

Example:

- 1ˢᵗ April 2007
  - o Initial Stock   : 1000 units
  - o (Standard) Price / unit (A)   : $5
  - o Initial Stock Value (B)   : $5, 000
- 20ᵗʰ May 2007
  - o Goods Receipt   :1000 units
  - o GR Price / unit (A1)   : $6
  - o Stock A/c (Dr.) (C)   : $5, 000 (=1000 X $5)
  - o Price Difference A/c (Dr.)   : $1, 000 (=1000 X $1)

    The amount of $1,000 posted to the 'price difference' A/c represents the 'variance' reflecting the difference between the new price (A1) and the standard price (A)

  - o GR/IR A/c (Cr.)   : $6, 000 (= 1000 X $6)

    o   Stock Value, now (B1)   : $10,000 (= B+C) (i.e.. 2000 units @ $5)
- **29th May 2007**
  - o   Goods Issue   : 100 units
  - o   Price / unit (same as that of A)   : $5

On the other hand, when you set the indicator to '**V**' then all the goods receipts (GR) will be at the GR value. The system will then adjust the price in the material master by the GR price. However, if there is a difference between the moving average price of the material, and that of the goods movement / invoice receipt, then the price difference is moved to the stock account, and the price of the material in the material master adjusted accordingly.

Example:

- **1st April 2007**
  - o   Initial Stock   : 1000 units
  - o   (Moving Average) Price /unit (A) : $5
  - o   Initial Stock Value (B)   : $5, 000
- **20th May 2007**
  - o   Goods Receipt   : 1000 units
  - o   GR Price / unit (A1)   : $6
  - o   Stock A/c (Dr.) (C)   : $6, 000 (=1000 X $6)
  - o   GR/IR A/c (Cr.)   : $6, 000 (= 1000 X $6)
  - o   Stock Value, now (B1)   : $11,000 (= B+C) (= 2000 units @ $5.50)

       At this point, the price on the material master is adjusted upward from $5 (A) to $5.5 (A2) by the system automatically, to reflect the new stock value.
  - o   New Moving Average Price (A2)   : $5.50 (= B1 / 2000)
- **29th May 2007**
  - o   Goods Issue   : 100 units
  - o   Price / unit (A2)   : $5.50

47. Explain 'Prices Maintenance' for materials transferred from 'legacy' to SAP.

Before you transfer the initial inventory from a legacy system to SAP, you need to create the relevant master data for the materials.

If you are planning to maintain ***standard price*** for the materials, then you will create the material masters with 'S' as the *price control indictor* in SAP. With this control, when you enter the material inventory, then the system valuates this stock with the standard price defined. In case, you enter a new price then the system posts the price difference (between the standard price and the new price you entered) to a price difference account.

Similarly, if you are planning to maintain ***moving average price*** for the materials, then you will create the material masters with 'V' as the *Price Control Indictor* in SAP. With this control, when you enter the material inventory, then the system valuates this stock with the moving average price defined. In case, you enter a new price then the system adjusts the moving average price accordingly. If you enter only the quantity, and not any new price, the system continues to valuate the stock at the original moving average price, and the price of the material does not change.

48.   What is 'Material Status'?

The **Material Status** is 2-digit code enabling you to control the usability of material for various MM and PP applications. This status key also controls warehouse management, transfer order instructions, quality inspection instructions, how the system behaves when a *product cost estimate* is created and so on.

The material status can be maintained as (1) Plant-specific material status, (2) Cross-plant material status and (3) Distribution material status.

49.   What is 'EAN'?

EAN (International Article Number), equivalent of **UPC (Universal Product Code)** of the United States, is an international standard number for identifying a material which SAP allows you to assign (done in '*Eng./Design or Units of Measure*' screen) to the materials . The EAN is normally assigned to the manufacturer of a material. Made up of a prefix (to identify the country or company from where the material originates), article number and check digit (ensures correctness of an EAN number so that no incorrect entries are scanned or entered into the system).

50.   What are some of the 'Partner Functions' of a 'Vendor'?

Through the definition of **Partner Functions** in the Vendor Master, SAP helps to designate vendor for performing different roles. The partner role is designated by a two-digit code.

- **VN**   Vendor
- **PI**   Invoice Presented by
- **OA**   Ordering Address
- **GS**   Goods Supplier
- **AZ**   Payment Recipient

A **partner schema** (also known as **partner procedure**) is assigned to a **vendor account group.** The procedure specifies which partner roles are' allowed' / 'mandatory' / 'can be changed' for a vendor master with that account group. You may assign three different partner schemas to an account group, one for each level of purchasing data, i.e., one at the purchase organization level, one at the VSR level, and one at the plant level. This enables maintaining different partners at different organizational levels.

51.   What is a 'Batch' in the context of 'Batch Management'?

Representing a quantity of material with homogenous set of properties / characteristics produced during a particular cycle of manufacturing, a **Batch** is a sub-set of inventory quantity, which can not be reproduced again with the same properties. Batch is linked to the **classification system,** and you can use batch only when the classification system has been set up properly for the **batch management**.

The batch is unique for a single material, and is unique at the Client level as well. That is, you will be able to use a batch number only once in the Client regardless of the plant and material. The batch will be known only in the plant where it was created. The batch numbers can either be manually assigned or system generated.

52. What are all the possible values for 'Procurement Types'?

The possible values for **Procurement Types** are:
- No procurement
- External procurement
- In-house production
- Both procurement types

53. What are all 'pre-requisites' for a 'MRP Run'?

The following are the **Pre-requisites for a MRP Run**:
- MRP activated
- Valid MRP data for the material
- Valid MRP Type
- Valid Material Status

54. What is a 'MRP Area'?

A **MRP Area** is not an organizational structure, but a unit for which you can carry out **Consumption-based MRP**. The MRP area is used to carry out MRP for the components provided to a sub-contractor. There are three types of MRP area that you will come across:
- MRP Area for Storage Locations
- MRP Area for Sub-contracting Vendor Stock
- MRP Area for the Plant

55. What is a 'MRP List'?

A **MRP List** displays the results of the last *'planning run'*. Using a 'collective display' format, you will be able to display planning details for a number of materials for a given 'selection parameters'.

56. Explain 'Re-Order Point' procedure.

The **Re-Order Point** is the level of inventory which triggers material procurement. Once the inventory falls below this level, you need to create the **order proposal** either manually or automatically by the system.

In the case of **manual re-order point** procedure, you will define the re-order point and the **safety stock** in the material master. On the other hand, in **automatic re-order point** procedure, the system will calculate the re-order point and the safety stock based on the next period's consumption pattern.

57. Explain 'Inventory Management' sub-module.

The sub-module **Inventory Management** deals with the GR / GI of materials from / into the inventory. It also manages the transfer of materials from one storage location to another. As an important element of MM, this module is integrated with SD, PP, QM and PM modules.

58.   What do you mean by 'Goods Movement'?

The term '**Goods Movement**' represents an event causing a change in the stock, with the change being value or status, stock type or quantity. It also represents the physical movement of stock from one location to another. The goods movement is classified into:

- Receipt of goods / services
- Issue of materials
- Stock transfers.

59.   What happens during a 'Goods Receipt'?

The **Goods Receipt (GR)** results in an increase in the quantity / value of the stock in a plant / warehouse. The GR may be '*with / without reference to a Purchase Order*'. The GR leads to:

- A Material document
- An Accounting document (not always)
- GR Slip printing
- GL Account updation
  - o   Consumption Account
  - o   Stock Account
- Quantity updation
  - o   Stock quantity
  - o   Consumption statistics
  - o   Vendor Evaluation
- Other updation (if applicable)
  - o   Cost Centre
  - o   Project
- A Stock Transfer Order
- Purchase Order History updation

60.   Explain the 'accounting' side of GR.

When you post a GR with reference to a *purchase order*:

- *GR before Invoice Receipt:*
  - o   A posting will be made to the stock account (Stock value increases)
  - o   An Offsetting entry is made to the GR/IR Clearing account
    - ▪   Once the invoice is received, the GR/IR Clearing account is cleared
    - ▪   A posting is made to the A/P account for the vendor (Payables increases)
- *Invoice Receipt (IR) before the goods (GR)*
  - o   A posting is made to the A/P account for the vendor (Payables increases)
  - o   A posting is made to the GR/IR clearing account
    - ▪   Once the goods are received, the GR/IR Clearing account is cleared
    - ▪   A posting will be made to the stock account (Stock value increases)

When GR is for a consumable material, the initial posting will go to the 'consumption account' (expense account) instead of a 'stock account'. However, the offsetting entry will still go to the GR/IR 'clearing account'. The value of the posting to the stock account will depend on which type of 'price control' is being used.

61. What happens during a 'Goods Issue'?

The **Goods Issue (GI)** results in a reduction in the stock quantity / value. The GI can be (1) *Planned* (via sales order, production order, return delivery, delivery for internal usage etc) or (2) *Un-planned* (drawing a stock for a sample, scrapping etc).

The GI results in:

- Creation of a Material / Accounting document
- Updation of Reservation for the issue (if any)
- Updating of GL accounts
- Updation 'points of consumption' if applicable (cost centre, project, etc.)
- Updation of Stock quantity

62. Explain 'Stock Transfers'.

The physical movement of stock between locations is termed as the '**Stock Transfer**', which can be within a plant or between plants. The stock transfers can be carried out either in a single step or in two steps. The stock transfer may be from a:

- Company to Company
- Plant to Plant
- Storage Location to Storage Location

If there is a logical change in the stock type / status, then this kind of 'transfer' is called as the '*transfer posting*'. The transfer posting may be from a:

- Product to Product
- Quality Inspection to Unrestricted Use
- Consignment Store to Storage Location

63. What is a 'Stock Type'?

Used in the determination of available stock of a material, the **Stock Type** is nothing but the sub-division of the inventory at a *storage location* based on the usage of that inventory. In SAP, there are many kinds of stock type:

- *Un-restricted (use) stock* (the physical stock that is always available at a plant / storage location)
- *Restricted (use) stock*
- *Quality inspection stock* (not counted for un-restricted usage and may be made as available for MRP)
- *Stock-in transfer*
- *Blocked stock* (not to be counted as un-restricted stock and is not available for MRP)

Besides all the above, which are all known as *valuated stock,* you will also come across with one more type called, '*GR blocked stock*' which is a *non-valuated stock*.

The **GR-blocked stock** denotes all the stock accepted 'conditionally' from the vendors. This stock is not to be counted as available for 'un-restricted usage'. You will be using the **Movement Type 103** for the GR-blocked stock as against **Movement Type 101** which is used for a normal GR.

64.   Explain 'Return Delivery'.

You will use the '**Return Delivery**' when you return the goods to the supplier (vendor), for reasons like damaged packaging etc. Note that the '**reason for return**' is mandatory as this will help you, later on, to analyze the problems with a vendor. The system uses the **Movement Type 122**, and will create a **return delivery slip** which will accompany the goods being returned.

In case the 'return' is from a 'GR-blocked stock', then you need to use a different **Movement Type: 104**.

65.   What are all the various types of 'Physical Inventory'?

The following are the different types of **Physical Inventory** in SAP MM:

- **Periodic inventory** (All the stocks are physically counted on a 'key date' (balance sheet date), and all the stock movements will be blocked during physical counting)
- **Cycle counting** (Physical counting is done at periodical intervals)
- **Sampling** (Randomly selected stocks are counted physically, and the system uses this information to 'estimate' stock value on a given date)
- **Continuous** (Stocks are tracked continuously through out the fiscal year, with physical stock taking once a year, at least!)

66.   What is a 'Material Ledger'?

The **Material Ledger** is nothing but a tool for inventory accounting that provides new methods for 'price control' for 'material valuation' (you can store the material inventory values in more than one currency). It makes it possible to keep the 'material price' constant over a period of time (say, over the life of a production order). The **moving average price** field is used to store a 'periodic price'. This periodic price would stay constant and would be the price used for valuation until you close the material ledger. At closing, the periodic price would be updated based on the actual value of invoice receipts received for that material during the period.

67.   Explain 'Split Valuation'? Why it is necessary?

The **Split Valuation** allows sub-stocks of the same material to be managed in different stock accounts. This allows the sub-stocks to be valuated separately, and every transaction is carried out at the sub-stock level. So, when processing a transaction, it is necessary to mention the sub-stock.

The 'split valuation' is necessary if the material has:

- Different Origins
- Various levels of Quality
- Various Statuses

It is also required in situation when you need to make a distinction between 'in-house produced materials' and 'materials procured externally', or if there is a distinction between 'different deliveries'.

68.   Explain the basic steps in 'Configuring Split Valuation'.

The five basic steps for **Configuring Split Valuation** are:

1.   Activate '*Split Valuation*'
2.   Define '*Global Valuation Types*'
     For each '*valuation type*' you need to specify: (a) whether '*external*' purchase orders are allowed, (b) whether production orders are allowed and (c) the account category reference
3.   Define '*Global Valuation Categories*'
     For each valuation category specify: (a) default '*valuation type*' to be used when purchase orders are created and whether this default can be changed, (b) default valuation type to be used when production orders are created and whether this default can be changed and (c) whether a '*valuation record*' should be created automatically when a GR is posted for a valuation type for which no record yet exists.
4.   Allocate '*Valuation Types*' to the '*Valuation Categories*'
5.   Define which of the '*Global Categories / Types*' apply to which '*Valuation Area*'

69.   Outline 'Stock Valuation Methods' for material revaluation.

There are three methods with which you can re-valuate your stock for your Balance Sheet purposes. Irrespective of the method you select, you will be able to valuate your stock either at the **Company Code** level or at the **Valuation Area** level:

1.   **LIFO (Last-In-First-Out)**: This method is on the assumption that the materials received last were the ones issued / consumed first. The valuation is based on the initial receipt.
2.   **FIFO (Firs-In-First-Out)**: Here the assumption is that the materials received first are the ones consumed / issued first. So, the valuation is based on the most recent receipt. The FIFO method can also be used in conjunction with the **lowest value method**: by this you can determine whether the system should make a comparison between the FIFO determined price and the **lowest value price**. You can also determine whether the FIFO price should be updated in the material master record.
3.   **Lowest Value Method**: The stocks are valued at their original price or the current market price which ever is lower. This is suitable when inventory needs to be valued to take into account material obsolescence, physical deterioration, or changes in price levels.

70.   How does the 'Automatic Account Assignment' work in MM?

1.   '*GL accounts*' are assigned to '*Transaction Keys*'(BSX, WRX, PRD, UMG, GBB etc)
2.   Transaction Keys identify which GL Accounts are to be debited or credited
3.   Transaction Keys are assigned to '*Value Strings*' (say,WA01)
4.   '*Movement Types*' (say, 901) are associated with a '*Value String*'

71.   Explain 'Automatic Account Assignment' configuration in MM.

There are four steps required to complete the '**Automatic Account Assignment**' configuration settings for MM:

1. Finalizing the '*valuation level*'
2. Activating '*valuation grouping code*' option. (For this you need to group *valuation areas* using valuation grouping codes)
3. Maintaining '*valuation classes*' and '*account category references*' and their linkage to '*material types*'.
4. Maintaining the '*GL accounts*' for each combination of *Chart of accounts, valuation grouping code, valuation class,* and *transaction key*.

You may use the '*automatic account determination wizard*' to complete the configuration settings, as the wizard guides you with a step-by-step approach.

72.   Explain the 'Transaction Keys' in MM.

Also known as '*process keys*', the **Transaction Keys** are pre-defined in the system to enable transaction postings in *Inventory Management* and *Accounting (Invoice Verification)*. For each of the *movement types* in MM, there is a *value string* which stores these possible transactions.

The pre-defined *transaction keys* are:

- **BSX** (used in Inventory Postings)
- **WRX** (used in GR/IR Clearing Postings)
- **PRD** (used to post Cost / Price differences)
- **UMB** (used to post Revenue / Expenses from re-valuation)
- **GBB** (offsetting entry in Stock postings)

BSX, WRX and **PRD** are examples of *transaction keys* that are relevant for a GR with reference to a *purchase order* for a material with *standard price* control. The Transaction Key **UMB** is used when the *standard price* has changed and the movement is posted to a previous period. Likewise, **GBB** is used to identify the GL account to post to as the offsetting entry to the stock account (when not referencing a *purchase order*) like miscellaneous goods receipts, goods issues for sales orders with no account assignment, and scrapping.

73.   How system determines the correct 'GL a/c' for a posting?

Imagine that you are posting a goods movement.

- Since the goods movement is from a *plant*, and the plant is assigned to a Company Code, the goods movement identifies the relevant Company Code.
- As the *Company Code* has already been assigned to the *Chart of accounts*, the system is able to identify the *GL accounts*.
- The plant also determines the *valuation area* (and the optional '*valuation grouping code*').
- Since each *movement type* is assigned to a '*value string*' which in turn is identified with a *transaction key*, the goods movement determines the correct *transaction key*.
- Since each of the *Transaction Keys* is associated with the relevant *GL accounts*, through the *value string*, the *movement type* now identifies the relevant GL Account, and the transaction is posted.

Production Planning (PP)

74. Explain how the PP module is organized in SAP.

The **PP** module is made up of the following *components*:

- **PP-BD** Basic Data
- **PP-SOP** Sales and Operations Planning
- **PP-MP** Master Planning
- **PP-CRP** Capacity (Requirements) Planning
- **PP-MRP** Material Requirements Planning
- **PP-SFC** Production Orders
- **PP-KAN** Kanban
- **PP-REM** Repetitive Manufacturing
- **PP-PI** Production Planning for Process Industries
- **PP-PDS** Plant Data Collection
- **PP-IS** Information Systems

75. Explain how 'PP' is 'integrated' with other modules.

PP is one of the modules in SAP R/3 which is complex as the functions cut across many modules. The following modules are tightly *integrated* with PP:

- **CO** Controlling
- **FI** Financial Accounting
- **MM** Materials Management
- **SD** Sales & Distribution
- **PS** Project Systems
- **PD** Personnel Planning & Development

76. What is a 'BOM'?

BOM (Bill of Material, is nothing but a structured list of components (with the object number, quantity and unit of measure) that go into making of a product or an assembly. Depending on the industry sector, they may also be called *recipes* or lists of ingredients. The structure of the product determines whether the bill of material is *simple* or very *complex*.

77. What are all the 'BOM Categories' supported by SAP?

The following are the various *Categories of BOM*:

- Equipment BOM
- Material BOM
- Sales Order BOM
- Document Structure
- Functional Location BOM

- WBS BOM

78.   What are all the 'Technical Types of BOM'?

There are two Technical Types of BOM supported in SAP:
- Variant BOM
- Material BOM

79.   Differentiate 'Variant BOM' from 'Multiple BOM'.

While a **Variant BOM** groups together several BOMs that describe **different** objects (for example, different models of a car) with a high proportion of identical parts, a **Multiple BOM** groups together several BOMs that describe **one** object (for example, a product) with different combinations of materials for different processing methods.

The Variant BOMs are supported for the following BOM categories:
- Material BOMs
- Document structures
- Equipment BOMs
- Functional location BOMs

Multiple BOMs are only supported for *Material BOMs*.

80.   Is it possible to convert 'Multiple BOM' into 'Variant BOM'?

No: You can only create a Variant BOM from a simple Material BOM. No multiple BOMs can exist for a material.

81.   What is a 'Work Centre' in PP?

A **Work Centre** in PP (*PP-BD-BOM*) is an organizational unit which may be a combination of machine or group of craftsmen, people, and production lines, wherein certain operations are carried out to produce some output. Each of the work centres is assigned to a cost centre. A work centre can be assigned to a work centre in SAP-HR which will enable assignment of employees, qualification etc.

82.   What is a 'Routing' in PP?

A **Routing** in PP (*PP-BD-RTG*) is used to define the sequence of operations (work steps) and resources required to perform certain operations in order to produce a material with or without reference to an Order. It is necessary to enter the standard values of planned time for the various operations need to be entered into the routing.

There two different types of routing:
- Routing
- Rate routing

(A similar concept exists in PS wherein you define a '***task list***' which is similar to the 'routing' in PP).

83. What are all the 'Sub-components' of Production Orders?

The following are the **Sub-components of Production Orders** (PP-SFC):
- Order Planning
- Order Execution
- Order Close

84. What is a 'Product Hierarchy'?

Used in pricing, a **Product Hierarchy** is an alphanumeric character string consisting a maximum of 18 characters. It thus defines the product and its composition.

Example:
A product hierarchy represented by '00050002000300040005'. The first four characters '0005' could indicate that the product is a car. The next four characters '0002' could indicate the plant in which the car is manufactured. The third set of characters could indicate the colour of the car. The next set may determine its engine capacity and so on. Thus, the product hierarchy helps in defining the product composition.

85. Define 'BOM Group'.

BOM Group is a collection of BOMs that lets you describe a product or a number of similar products. Value in the *BOM group* field uniquely identifies the BOM group. You can use the BOM group as an alternative way of accessing the BOM. A BOM group comprises either of all the alternatives of a multiple BOM or all the variants of a variant BOM.

When you create a BOM group, the system checks the special characters you use. Apart from the usual alphanumeric characters, you can use the following special characters: ' - ', ' / ', ' _ '. You cannot use blanks.

86. Define 'SOP' (Sales & Operations Planning).

Suitable for long / medium term planning, with an aim to streamline a company's **Sales and Operational Planning**, **SOP** is a forecasting tool enabling to setup sales, production and other supply chain targets based on existing, future or historical data. SOP is most suitable for planning finished goods, and not for material component planning.

The SOP plans are passed on to the **Demand Management (DEM)** in the form of independent requirements, which in turn is fed into **MPS (Master Production Scheduling)** and **MRP (Material Requirements Planning)**. The results of SOP can be passed on to *profitability analysis, cost centre accounting and activity based costing.*

SOP contains two application components namely (1) **Standard SOP (PP-SOP)** and (2) **Flexible Planning (LO-LIS-PLN)**. The Standard SOP comes pre-configured with the system. Flexible planning can be configured in a variety of ways.

87. What is known as 'Demand Management'?

Demand Management (PP-MP-DEM) helps in determining the requirement quantities and delivery dates for finished good assemblies. It uses the **planned independent requirements** and customer requirements (customer requirements come from sales orders). ***Planning strategies*** help in deciding the kind of demand program: if production is triggered by *sales orders*, then it is known as '***Make-to-Order***' production; if not then it is known as '***Make-to-Stock***' production.

88.   What is 'Capacity Planning'?

Capacity Planning aims at economic usage of resources. It is integrated with SD, PM, PS and CS. There are 2 components within capacity planning: (1) ***Capacity evaluation*** and (2) ***Capacity levelling***. Capacity planning supports (a) Short-term detailed planning, (2) Medium-term planning and (3) Long-term rough-cut planning.

89.   Explain 'MRP' (Material Requirements Planning).

MRP aims to guarantee ***material availability***: it is used to procure / produce the requirement quantities on-time (both for internal purposes and for sales and distribution). This involves monitoring of stocks and, in particular, the automatic creation of 'procurement proposals' for purchasing and production. PP-MRP assists and relieves *MRP Controllers* (who are responsible for all the activities from specifying when, what, type etc of the material requirements) in their area of responsibility. With the automatic planning run in MRP, it is possible to determine any shortages so as to create procurement elements. With the system generating messages for critical parts and unusual situations, you can rework the planning results in the specific area with problems.

The material requirements can be planned at ***plant level*** or for different MRP areas. With MRP at plant level, the system adds together stocks from all of the individual storage locations, with the exception of individual customer stock, to determine total plant stock. In the case of material requirements planning on an ***MRP area level,*** only the stocks from the storage locations or subcontractor assigned to the respective MRP areas are taken into account.

90.   What are all the three 'MRP Procedures'?

- Materials Requirements Planning **(MRP)**
- Master Production Scheduling **(MPS)**
- Consumption-based Planning

91.   What is 'MPS' (Master Production Scheduling)?

Executed as that of a MRP, **MPS** is nothing but a special form of MRP which aims to ***reduce storage costs*** and to ***increase planning stability.*** With MPS you can flag materials, which greatly influence company profits or which take up critical resources, as ***master schedule items*** and to check and plan them separately with a series of special tools.

92.   What is 'Consumption-based Planning'?

Using past consumption data, **Consumption-based Planning** aims at determining the future requirements. In the process, it makes use of ***material forecast*** or any other 'static' planning procedures. The 'net requirements' calculation is triggered when stock level falls below a ***reorder point***. The net requirements can also be calculated by ***forecast requirements*** from historical consumption pattern.

Miscellaneous

7

Miscellaneous

1. Explain 'Cash Management' in SAP.

The **Cash Management** sub-module takes care of the following; by integrating the bank related accounting with the respective sub-ledger accounting:

- Check Deposit
- Cash Position
- Cash Concentration
- Bank Statement
- Liquidity Forecast
- Cash Concentration
- Money Market

2. What is 'Cash (Management) Position'?

The **Cash Management Position** helps to reproduce the activities of bank accounts. With the input controls for preventing data duplication, parallel management of foreign currencies and with the required documentation for revision of all planning activities, you will be able to (a) view up-to-date activities in the bank accounts and (ii) forecast cash position or daily liquidity. The cash management position is set up using the ***groupings*** which determine the levels and accounts to be displayed.

The data required for this activity are supplied from (a) FI postings in cash management relevant GL accounts, (b) payment advices entered manually and (c) cash flow transactions transferred from *Treasury Management* module.

The data can be displayed by resorting to any of the following formats:

- Aggregated- either as account balance (K) or as individual values of inflow/outflow(D)
- For any data in the past, present or future
- In increments (days, weeks etc)

3. Explain 'Groupings' and 'Levels'.

The **Groupings** determines how to summarize the data, with various 'groups' and 'levels' defined. A ***Group*** is adding- up of various bank accounts, and contains a number of 'levels'.

A **Level**, thus, denotes the sources of data or account transactions. Below the levels are the *line items* which will be displayed using a 'list display'.

Cash Management: Grouping Structure								
Grouping	Ty.	Selection	CoCd	ChAc	Exclude	Sum. term	Summ. acct	SCOCD
BANK-IST	G	++			☐	**		
BANK-IST	G	0000113100			☐	DEUTSCHE		
BANK-IST	G	0000113150			☐	DEUTSCHE		
BANK-IST	G	0000113160			☐	DEUTSCHE		
BANK-IST	G	0000113200			☐	DRESDNER		
BANK-IST	G	0000113250			☐	DRESDNER		
BANK-IST	G	0000113260			☐	DRESDNER		
BANKEN	E	++			☐	**		
BANKEN	G	0000113100			☐	DEUTSCHE		
BANKEN	G	0000113101			☐	DEUTSCHE		
BANKEN	G	0000113102			☐	DEUTSCHE		
BANKEN	G	0000113103			☐	DEUTSCHE		
BANKEN	G	0000113104			☐	DEUTSCHE		
BANKEN	G	0000113105			☐	DEUTSCHE		
BANKEN	G	0000113106			☐	DEUTSCHE		
BANKEN	G	0000113108			☐	DEUTSCHE		
BANKEN	G	0000113150			☐	DEUTSCHE		
BANKEN	G	0000113160			☐	DEUTSCHE		
BANKEN	G	0000113200			☐	DRESDNER		

Figure 97: Grouping Structure in Cash Management

4. Explain 'Liquidity Forecast'.

The **Liquidity Forecast** helps to reproduce the activities in sub-ledger accounts by (a) linking to all the 'system resident' data like customer open items in a customer account, (b) receipts and disbursements form FI/SD/MM, and (c) maintaining items like reversal, document change, open item clearing etc automatically.

The liquidity forecast helps to identify the liquidity trends in the sub-ledger accounts based on the information on expected payment flows. The incoming and outgoing payments per open item, from FI-AR and FI-AP, form the basis for the liquidity forecast. You will be able to branch to FI-AR or AP information system from liquidity forecast.

5. How to set up the 'Cash Management' in SAP?

Under customizing, you need to define the **Cash Management Groups** and assign these groups to *planning levels*. In customer / vendor master records, you need to enter the *cash management groups* to enable the system to transfer data between customer/vendor accounts and liquidity forecast. The cash management groups help to differentiate customers/vendors based on certain characteristics like behaviour (whether the customer takes cash discount), risk (credit rating) etc.

6. Explain 'Bank Statement' in Cash Management.

Bank Statement (*manual or electronic*) functionality runs on the same principle of **Check Deposit Processing**. Note that it is not necessary that *Cash Management* needs to be active for bank statement processing.

During processing, customer payments (except checks) are first posted to *bank clearing account*;

then customer open items are cleared when balancing the bank clearing account. Similarly, vendor payments are posted to a bank clearing account for outgoing payments where the balancing is done from the entries made from the payment program. The other payments like bank charges, bank interest etc will be posted to the respective GL accounts and they will not go through the bank clearing accounts. In case of unidentified payment transactions, you will post them first to the bank clearing accounts; and 'clear' them when you have appropriate information.

7. What are the configurations for 'Bank Statement Processing'?

Before you make use of the ***Bank Statement Processing*** functionality in SAP, you need to have the following defined or configured in your system:

- Start Variant
- Search ID
- Processing Type
- Internal Bank Determination

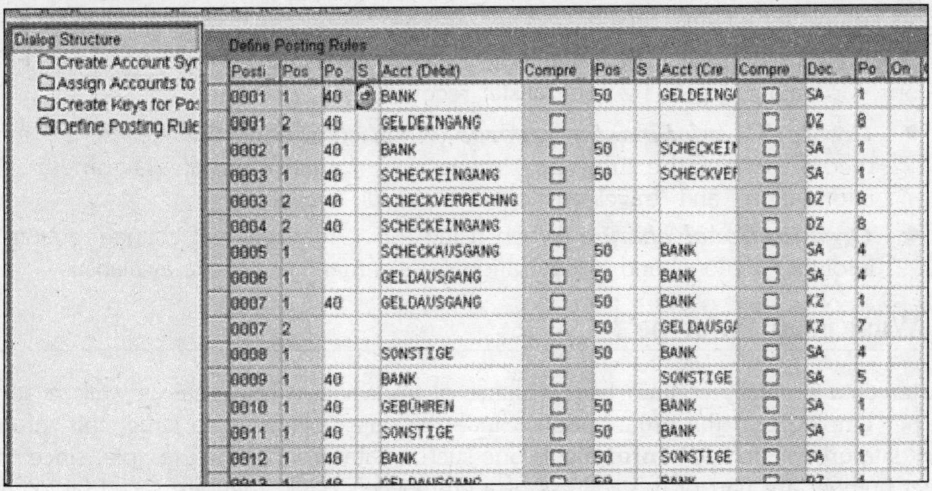

Posti	Pos	Po	S	Acct (Debit)	Compre	Pos	S	Acct (Cre	Compre	Doc.	Po	On
0001	1	40		BANK	☐	50		GELDEING/	☐	SA	1	
0001	2	40		GELDEINGANG	☐				☐	DZ	8	
0002	1	40		BANK	☐	50		SCHECKEI!	☐	SA	1	
0003	1	40		SCHECKEINGANG	☐	50		SCHECKVEF	☐	SA	1	
0003	2	40		SCHECKVERRECHNG	☐				☐	DZ	8	
0004	2	40		SCHECKEINGANG	☐				☐	DZ	8	
0005	1			SCHECKAUSGANG	☐	50		BANK	☐	SA	4	
0006	1			GELDAUSGANG	☐	50		BANK	☐	SA	4	
0007	1	40		GELDAUSGANG	☐	50		BANK	☐	KZ	1	
0007	2				☐	50		GELDAUSG/	☐	KZ	7	
0008	1			SONSTIGE	☐	50		BANK	☐	SA	4	
0009	1	40		BANK	☐			SONSTIGE	☐	SA	5	
0010	1	40		GEBÜHREN	☐	50		BANK	☐	SA	1	
0011	1	40		SONSTIGE	☐	50		BANK	☐	SA	1	
0012	1	40		BANK	☐	50		SONSTIGE	☐	SA	1	

Figure 98: Bank Statement Configuration

8. Differentiate 'Manual Check Deposit' from 'Electronic Check Deposit'.

The **Manual Check Deposit** function enables you to enter all 'checks' received by posting the entries in two steps: in GL and in sub-ledger accounts. It also helps to 'clear' customer invoices. You may also make use of additional functions for additional processing of checks thus entered.

The **Electronic Check Deposit**, in contrast to 'manual check deposit' function, enables you to process data even from an external data entry system provided the data is delivered in the SAP defined format. You will be able to enter check deposit details electronically so that you may complete and post individual data later with manual check deposit processing.

9. Explain 'Travel Management' in SAP.

The **Travel Management** sub-module of FI, FI-TR, helps you to plan travel and travel related activities (like calculating the trip costs, trip reimbursements etc) for the enterprise's human resources.

FI-TR transfers the travel expenses to the FI which in turn makes use of FI-AP to reimburse the employees. Employees are reimbursed for travel expenses using the 'payment program' (automatic /manual) in Financial Accounting. In order for the reimbursement process to work, a vendor master record has to be created for every employee who travels. Use **Transaction PRAA** to automatically create (through Bach Data input) vendor records for the employees.

If you are using SAP-HR, then you will be using **HR master data** to store employee's information; else you will create a **mini-master** record (scaled down version HR master) wherein you will be saving information like: personal information, address, bank details etc. Besides, you will also be defining (1) personal action, (2) travel privileges and (3) travel preferences.

10.   What is a 'Personal Action'?

A **Personnel Action** includes all **infotypes** that are processed as part of a personal procedure, such as hiring, organizational change, promotion, and so on. To ensure that no important information is forgotten, the relevant infotypes are made available for processing one after another. Each completed action is entered in the 'action' infotype, so that the 'actions' infotype has a log of all procedures completed for this person.

Personnel actions are normally completed in SAP-HR. If SAP-HR is not implemented, FI-TV offers two 'actions' for maintaining FI-TV mini-master records:

- **Create TV mini-master records** (When completing the 'Create TV mini-master record' action, the infotypes 'measures', 'organizational assignment', 'personal information', and 'travel privileges' are made available.)
- **Organizational change** (When using the 'Organizational change' action, only the infotypes 'actions' and 'organizational assignment' are made available)

11.   What is an 'Infotype'?

HR master data normally contain large volume of information (personal as well as employment related) per employee in the organization. Since the data volume is so large, this information is stored in data groups, in SAP. **Infotype** is one such a data group. (For example, since city, street, and street number are part of the address of a employee's bank, they are saved (along with other data) in the *Infotype Bank*).

IType	Infotype text
0000	Actions
0001	Organizational Assignment
0002	Personal Data
0003	Payroll Status
0004	Challenge
0005	Leave Entitlement
0006	Addresses
0007	Planned Working Time
0008	Basic Pay
0009	Bank Details
0010	Capital Formation
0011	External Transfers

Figure 99: Infotypes in SAP

12.   **Explain 'Travel Manager' in SAP.**

Travel Manager, in SAP, helps the employees to have an overview of travel and travel related items/objects (like travel requests, travel plans and travel reimbursements). He or she will be able to create:

A '***travel request***' notifying the company about his/her forthcoming business trip, based on the workflow configuration, moves to the *internal travel office* for further approval and processing.

The employee (or the designated travel agent of the company) makes use of the object **travel plan**, to plan the details of the **trip**. The system retrieves the **travel preferences** from the 'infotype' and helps in booking the means of travel.

The permitted **travel expenses** are configured in the system and are country specific. This configuration helps in **reimbursement processing** when the employee puts through the travel reimbursement claim to the internal travel office. After a trip is completed, the employee enters the travel expenses manually in the system or the same can be obtained from the travel plans and corrected later. Again, SAP provides the flexibility that the travel expenses can either be entered by the employees or by the travel office's representative.

For reimbursement settlement of the expenses, the system determines the total amount to be paid based on the travel plan, travel information, settlement rules and reimbursement records (for previous payments). The **settlement information** is sent to FI, where in the payment is made though FI-AP's payment program.

	Transaction Code
	TRIP

13.   **What is 'Value Pricer'?**

The **Value Pricer** tool, in SAP-HR, helps to compare the selected bookings (of a flight) and compares the price of the same with that of other carriers, for the same route(s) to arrive and recommend lowest cost fares for the travel plan.

14.   **What is 'Schedule Manager'?**

SAP's **Schedule Manager** helps you to organize, execute and monitor complex and repetitive business transactions (like, month end processing) from easy-to-use workspace, which resembles an all-in-one 'organizer' kind of utility containing:

- User notes window
- Task overview window
- Calendar window
- Daily overview window

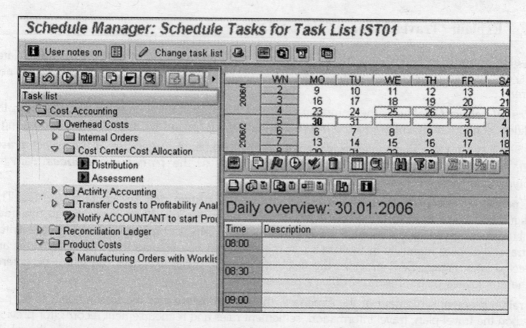

Figure 100: Schedule Manager

The **information window** provides with the details of what and how you can achieve the tasks by providing useful information with *hyperlinks* to processes and steps with in a process. This appears to the left of all other windows. Depending upon the requirement, this can be 'switched-on' or 'switched-off'.

The **task overview window** provides a complete 'drill-down' facility in a tree-structure of all tasks entered and monitored by you. The tasks are grouped into an upper level *task list*, which can be scheduled, released and monitored using the 'daily overview' window. Remember that, the tasks maintained in the task overview window needs to be properly scheduled / released for execution: the mere listing of tasks here will not start a transaction or a program or a report.

The **daily overview window** is similar to an appointment column of any organizer, with fully customizable time intervals (in increments of, say, 30 minutes, 45 minutes etc). Ideally, the tasks appearing in the *task list* in 'task overview' window, when scheduled / released, will appear here against the appropriate time slot. By selecting a task here, you can monitor the same using the 'monitor' icon or from the menu. A look at this daily overview window, at the beginning of a day, will remind you of the tasks scheduled for that day.

The **calendar window** is a calendar utility to help you organized better. However, this goes beyond the regular calendar by displaying, in different colours like *yellow / green*, a particular date indicating that the status of tasks scheduled for that day. A 'green' background indicates that every thing is OK, but a 'yellow' indicates that there are some warnings.

Transaction Code
SCMA

15. How you can use the 'Schedule Manager' in SAP?

The Schedule Manager has **three distinct functionalities** built in:

1. *Processes*

   This is the functionality which helps you to define the ***task list*** (also called as ***task group***) and the individual ***tasks*** (a task is essentially a *transaction* or a *program / report*), which are later on 'scheduled' / 'released' and 'monitored' using the special '***monitoring***' function available. Any number of task lists can be created and these lists are shown in a tree format for easy navigation. A task list may contain another task list or a ***chain of tasks*** within; and tasks are grouped into a task list.

   While defining the task itself, you can maintain who is the owner of the task, when this needs to be executed etc. The scheduling of tasks is also possible by simply dragging them into the appropriate time slots in the 'daily overview' window. You may also take the help of '***job wizard***' while scheduling. A task, by mere scheduling, is not started automatically unless the same is properly '***released***'. The tasks / task lists defined can be moved in the hierarchy up / down or deleted form a list. The tasks can also be documented using MS-Office Word or Excel etc.

2. *Scenarios*

   The *schedule manager* gives you ***three options*** for scheduling and monitoring:

   a. ***Start transaction / program / report online and schedule the jobs (tasks) in the scheduler:*** Here, you can create or select a new task list in the schedule, enter these in the 'daily overview' and monitor and control the tasks' execution in the 'monitor'.

   b. ***Start transaction / program / report online and schedule the jobs (tasks) / job chain (task chain):*** This is similar to (a) above except that you have the option of inserting a '***job chain***' defined in '***flow definition***' into the task list.

   c. ***Start transactions / reports online, schedule job or job chain, work-list:*** Here, you can also execute and monitor a complete work-list, involving several processing steps with all the step sequences. Besides scheduler, monitor, and flow definition, you can use the '***work-list monitor***', for monitoring the processing status.

3. *Help Functions*

   Schedule Manager supplements with useful functions like:

   - Runtime analysis
   - Working with variables
   - Releasing jobs

SAP Tables

8

SAP Tables

Financial Accounting (FI)

Sl. No.	Are you looking for:	Table
1	Account Assignment Templates for GLAccount items	KOMU
2	Account Master (Chart of Accounts)	SKA1
3	Accounting Correspondence Requests	BKORM
4	Accounting Data – A/R and A/P Information System	RFRR
5	Accounting Document Header	BKPF
6	Accounting Document Header (docs fromExternal Systems)	EBKP
7	Accounting Document Header	BKPF
8	Accounting Document Segment	BSEG
9	Accounting secondary index for customers	BSID
10	Accounting secondary index for customers - cleared items	BSAD
11	Accounting- Secondary Index for GL Accounts	BSIS
12	Accounting- Secondary Index for GL Accounts (Cleared Items)	BSAS
13	Accounting secondary index for vendors	BSIK
14	Accounting secondary index for vendors - cleared items	BSAK
15	Accounts Blocked by Dunning Selection	MAHN
16	Asset Accounting: Basic Functions	FI-A
17	Asset Class: Depreciation Area	ANKB
18	Asset classes- Description	ANKT
19	Asset Classes: Field Cont Dependent on Chart	ANKP
20	Asset Classes: General Data	ANKA
21	Asset Classes: Insurance Types	ANKV
22	Asset down payment settlement	ANEV
23	Asset Line Items	ANEP
24	Asset Master Record Segment	ANLA

25	Asset Master Record Segment	ANLX
26	Asset Master Record User Fields	ANLU
27	Asset Periodic Values	ANLP
28	Asset Texts	ANLT
29	Asset Type Text	ANAT
30	Asset Types	ANAR
31	Asset Value Fields	ANLC
32	Bank master record	BNKA
33	Business Partner Master (General Data)	BP000
34	Cash Management Line Items in PaymentRequests	FDZA
35	Create GL account with reference	TSAK
36	Credit Management : FI Status data	KNKK
37	Customer / Vendor Linking	KLPA
38	Customer master - general data	KNA1
39	Customer master - partner functions	KNVP
40	Customer master - sales data	KNVV
41	Customer master - sales request form	KNVD
42	Customer Master (Company Code)	KNB1
43	Customer Master Bank Details	KNBK
44	Customer Master Credit Management :Central Data	KNKA
45	Customer Master Credit Management :Control Area Data	KNKK
46	Customer Master Dunning Data	KNB5
47	Customer Master Special GL Transactions Figures	KNC3
48	Customer Master Transaction Figures	KNC1
49	Customer Payment History	KNB4
50	Depreciation Terms	ANLB
51	Document Header Asset Posting	ANEK
52	Document Header for Document Parking	VBKP
53	Document Header Supplement for Recurring Entry	BKDF
54	Document Type Texts	T003T
55	Dunning Data (Account Entries)	MHNK
56	Electronic Bank Statement Line Items	FEBEP
57	Financial Accounting 'Basis'	FBAS
58	GL Account Master (Chart of Accounts –Description)	SKAT
59	GL Account Master (Chart of Accounts –Key Word list)	SKAS
60	GL Account Master (Chart of Accounts)	SKA1
61	GL Account Master (Company Code)	SKB1
62	General Ledger Accounting: Basic	FI-G
63	General Ledger Accounting: Basic	FI-G
64	Global Settings for Payment Program for Payment Requests	F111
65	Index for Vendor Validation of DoubleDocuments	BSIP

66	Insurable Values (Year Dependent)	ANLW
67	Inter Company Posting Procedure	BVOR
68	Main Asset Number	ANLH
69	Management Records for the Dunning Program	MAHNV
70	Name of Transaction Type	AT10T
71	One-Time Account Data Document Segment	BSEC
72	Payment Medium File	PAYR
73	Payment Requests	PAYR
74	Pre-numbered Check	PCEC
75	Pricing Communication Header	KOMK
76	Run Date of a Program	FRUN
77	Secondary Index, Documents for Material	BSIM
78	Settings for GL Posting Reports	FIGL
79	Substitutions	GB92
80	Tax Code Names	T007S
81	TemSe - Administration Data	REGUT
82	Time Dependent Asset Allocations	ANLZ
83	Transaction Activity Category- Description	AT02T
84	Transaction Code for Menu TIMN	AT02A
85	Transaction type	AT10
86	Validation / Substitution User	GB03
87	Validation	GB93
88	Vendor Master (Company Code Section)	LFB1
89	Vendor Master (General Section)	LFA1
90	Vendor Master Bank Details	LFBK
91	Vendor master- dunning data	LFB5
92	Vendor Master Dunning Data	LFB5
93	Vendor master record: purchasing data	LFM2
94	Vendor master record: purchasing organization data	LFM1
95	Vendor Master Transaction Figures	LFC1

Controlling (CO)

Sl. No.	Are you looking for:	Table
1	Activity Type Master	CSLA
2	Actual Line Items for Reconciliation	COFIS
3	Assignment of Work Center to Cost Center	CRCO
4	Basic Settings for Versions	TKA09
5	Characteristic Values	AUSP
6	CO Object: Control Data for Activity Type	COKL
7	CO Object: Control Data for CostCentre	COKA
8	CO Object: Control Data for Primary Cost Element	COKP
9	CO Object: Control Data for Secondary Cost Element	COKS
10	CO Object: Control Data for Statistical Key Figure	COKR
11	CO Object: Document Header	COBK
12	CO Object: Line Items (by Fiscal	COEJ
13	CO Object: Line Items (by Period)	COEP
14	CO Object: Line Items for Activity Types	COEPL
15	CO Object: Line Items for Activity Type	COEJL
16	CO Object: Line Items for Prices	COEJT
17	CO Object: Line Items for Prices	COEPT
18	CO Object: Line Items for SKF	COEJR
19	CO Objects: Assignment	COSC
20	CO Period Locks	KAPS
21	CO Versions	TKVS
22	Controlling Areas	TKA01
23	Cost Center / Activity Type	CSSL
24	Cost Center / Cost Element	CSSK
25	Cost centre master data	CSKS
26	Cost centre texts	CSKT
27	Cost elements - data dependent on chart of accounts	CSKA
28	Cost elements - data dependent on controlling area	CSKB
29	Cost elements texts	CSKU
30	Dependent on Material and Receiver	A141
31	Dependent on Material Group	A143
32	Dependent on Material	A142
33	Distribution Rules Settlement Rule Order Settlement	COBRB
34	Document Header Controlling Object	BPBK
35	Document Header for Settlement	AUAK
36	Document Segment: Transactions	AUAV
37	EC-PCA: Actual Line Items	GLPCA

38	EC-PCA: Object Table for AccountAssignment Elements	GLPCO
39	EC-PCA: Plan Line Items	GLPCP
40	EC-PCA: Transaction Attributes	GLPCC
41	Line Item Annual Values Controlling Object	BPEJ
42	Line Item Period Values Controlling Object	BPEP
43	Line Item Total Values Controlling Object	BPEG
44	Object- Control Data for Cost Elements	COKA
45	Object- Cost Totals for External Postings	COSP
46	Object- Cost Totals for Internal Postings	COSS
47	Object Table for Reconciliation L	COFI01
48	Order Master Data	AUFK
49	PCA- Totals Table	GLPCT
50	Price per Company Code	A138
51	Price per Controlling Area	A136
52	Price per Cost Center	A132
53	Price per Country / Region	A137
54	Price per Profit Center	A139
55	Profit Center Master Data Table	CEPC
56	Profit Center Master Data Table	CEPC
57	Profit centre master data	CEPCT
58	Settlement Document: Distribution	AUAB
59	Settlement Document: Receiver Segment	AUAA
60	Settlement Rule for Order Settlement	COBRA
61	Settlement Rules per Depreciation	AUAI
62	Single Plan Items for Reconciliation	COFIP
63	Totals record - reconciliation ledger	COFIT
64	Totals Record for Annual Total Controlling Object	BPJA

Sales & Distribution (SD)

Sl. No.	Are you looking for:	Table
1	Billing Document Header	VBRK
2	Billing Document Item	VBRP
3	Condition for items	KNOP
4	Condition for transaction data	KNOV
5	Customer Master – Co. Code Data (payment method, recon. acct)	KNB1
6	Customer Master – Dunning info	KNB5
7	Customer Master Bank Data	KNBK
8	Customer Master Credit Control Area Data (credit limits)	KNKK
9	Customer Master Credit Mgmt.	KNKA
10	Customer Master Ship Data	KNVS
11	Customer Master Tax Indicator	KNVI
12	Customer Payment History	KNB4
13	Customer/Vendor Link	KLPA
14	Customers, General Data	KNA1
15	Delivery document - header data	VBAK
16	Delivery document - item data	VBAP
17	Delivery Document Header data	LIKP
18	Delivery due index	VEPVG
19	Delivery header data	LIKP
20	Delivery item data	LIPS
21	Document Flow	VBFA
22	Handling unit - header Table	VEKP
23	Header Status and Administrative Data	VBUK
24	Item Status	VBUP
25	Output type	KNVD
26	Packing - handling unit item (contents)	VEPO
27	Partner Function key	KNVP
28	Partners	VBPA
29	Sales Area Data (terms, order probability)	KNVV
30	Sales Document - Business Data	VBKD
31	Sales Document - Header Data	VBAK
32	Sales document - header status and administrative data	VBUK
33	Sales Document - Item Data	VBAP
34	Sales document - item status	VBUP
35	Sales document - partner	VBPA
36	Sales document - release order data	VBLB
37	Sales document - schedule line data	VBEP

38	Sales document flow	VBFA
39	Sales Document Schedule Line	VBEP
40	Sales Requirements: Individual Records	VBBE
41	Schedule line history	VBEH
42	SD document - delivery note header	VBLK
43	Shipping Unit Header	VEPO
44	Shipping Unit Item (Content)	VEKP

Materials Management (MM)

Sl. No.	Are you looking for:	Table
1	Account Assignment in Purchasing Document	EKKN
2	Document Header- Reservation	RKPF
3	Document Segment- Material	MSEG
4	General Material Data	MARA
5	Header- Material Document	MKPF
6	Header- Physical Inventory Document	IKPF
7	Help Texts for Movement Types	T157H
8	History per Purchasing Document	EKBE
9	Lists what views have not been created	MOFF
10	Material groups	T023
11	Material Consumption	MVER
12	Material Descriptions	MAKT
13	Material to BOM Link	MAST
14	Material Valuation	MBEW
15	Movement Type	T156
16	Number range intervals	NRIV
17	Physical Inventory Document Items	ISEG
18	Plant Data for Material	MARC
19	Plant/Material	A501
20	Purchase Requisition Account Assignment	EBKN
21	Purchase Requisition	EBAN
22	Purchasing Document Header	EKKO
23	Purchasing Document Item	EKPO
24	Purchasing Groups	T024
25	Purchasing Info Record- General Data	EINA
26	Purchasing Info Record- Purchasing Organization Data	EINE
27	Release Documentation	EKAB
28	Reservation/dependent requirements	RESB
29	Sales Data for materials	MVKE
30	Scheduling Agreement Schedule Lines	EKET
31	Storage Location Data for Material	MARD
32	Texts for Purchasing Document Types	T161T
33	Texts for Purchasing Document Types	T161T
34	Vendor Master (Company Code)	LFB1
35	Vendor Master (General section)	LFA1

Production Planning (PP)

Sl. No.	Are you looking for:	Table
1	BOM Explosion Structure	STPF
2	BOM Group to Material	MAST
3	BOM Header Details	STKO
4	BOM History Records	STZU
5	BOM Item Details	STPO
6	BOM Item Selection	STAS
7	BOM Sub Items (designators)	STPU
8	Capacity Header	KAKO
9	CAPP Sub-operations	PLPH
10	Characteristic Allocation to Class	KSML
11	Characteristic Detail	CABN
12	Characteristic Value Texts	CAWNT
13	Characteristic Values	AUSP
14	Characteristic Values	CAWN
15	Class Detail	KLAH
16	Component Allocation	PLMZ
17	Confirmation Pool	AFRV
18	Confirmations — Defaults for Collective Confirmation	AFRD
19	Confirmations — Goods Movements with Errors	AFFW
20	Confirmations — Header Info for Confirmation Pool	AFRH
21	Confirmations — Incorrect Cost Calculations	AFRC
22	Confirmations — Subsequently Posted Goods Movements	AFWI
23	Customer and priority	AENR
24	Hierarchy Header	CRHH
25	Hierarchy Structure	CRHS
26	Independent Requirements by Material	PBIM
27	Independent Requirements Data	PBED
28	Inspection Characteristics	PLMK
29	Intervals of Capacity	KAZY
30	LIS — Material Usage	S026
31	LIS — Reporting Point Statistics	S028
32	LIS — Run Schedule Quantities	S025
33	LIS — Stock/Requirements Analysis	S094
34	Maintenance Package Allocation	PLWP
35	Material Allocation to Class	KSSK
36	MRP Document Header Data	MDKP
37	MRP Firming Dates	MDFD

38	MRP Table Structure (no data)	MDTB
39	Order Batch Print Requests	AFBP
40	Order Completion Confirmations	AFRU
41	Order Header	AFKO
42	Order Item Detail	AFPO
43	Order Operations Detail	AFVC
44	Order PRT Assignment	AFFH
45	Order Sequence Details	AFFL
46	Planned Orders	PLAF
47	Planning File Entries	MDVM
48	Planning Scenario (Long-term Planning)	PLSC
49	PRT Allocation	PLFH
50	Relationships - Standard Network	PLAB
51	Reporting Point Document Logs	CEZP
52	Reporting Points - Periodic Totals	CPZP
53	Reservations/Dependent Requirements	RESB
54	Revision Numbers	AEOI
55	Routing Header Details	PLKO
56	Routing Link to Material	MAPL
57	Routing Operation Details	PLPO
58	RS Header Master Data	SAFK
59	Task List - Selection of Operations	PLAS
60	Workcenter Capacity Allocation	CRCA
61	Workcenter Cost Center Assignment	CRCO
62	Workcenter Header Data	CRHD
63	Workcenter Text	CRTX

SAP Transaction Codes

2. If you know part or more part of the Transaction Code, you may look...

enter the Transaction Code, then...

with a signal...

function tab and click on...

9

SAP Transaction Codes

Below are some of the important Transaction Codes (T-Codes), listed module-wise for your easy reference. The notable feature of these lists is the way these Transaction Codes have been arranged here: it is not an alphabetical list because such a list may not serve your purpose when you do not know the Transaction Code but are looking for with some description in your mind. The Transaction Codes are arranged based on their functionality or usage or task so that it becomes easier for any one to search. Look for key words in the 2nd column of the Table ('**are you looking for**'), and then look at the corresponding Transaction Code under '**T-Code**' column.

All the Transaction Codes are stored in the system in Tables **TSTC** & **TSTCT**.

It will not be practical to list all the Transaction Codes of SAP and is not required as well. As you get to know, you will learn to look for Transaction Codes by going through the **Transaction Code SE93**. Should you want to know some Transaction Codes which are not listed in the following pages, use the *Transaction Code SE93* for finding the same. Here is a short tutorial on how to look for the Transaction Codes in the system:

	Transaction Code
	SE93

1. Enter '**Maintain Transaction**' transaction by Transaction Code SE93:

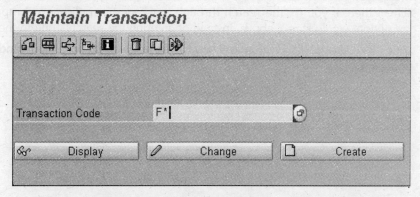

Figure 101: Maintain Transaction - Initial Screen

2. If you know some information of the Transaction Codes you are looking for, you may enter the same in the 'Transaction Code' field. For example, assume that you are trying to list all the Transaction Codes starting with 'F'. Then enter 'F*' as indicated in the Figure 101 and click on [⊙] button. The system will now bring out the list as indicated in Figure 102:

Transaction Code	Short text
F-01	Enter Sample Document
F-02	Enter G/L Account Posting
F-03	Clear G/L Account
F-04	Post with Clearing
F-05	Post Foreign Currency Valuatio
F-06	Post Incoming Payments
F-07	Post Outgoing Payments
F-18	Payment with Printout
F-19	Reverse Statistical Posting
F-20	Reverse Bill Liability
F-21	Enter Transfer Posting
F-22	Enter Customer Invoice
F-23	Return Bill of Exchange Pmt Re
F-25	Reverse Check/Bill of Exch.
F-26	Incoming Payments Fast Entry
F-27	Enter Customer Credit Memo
F-28	Post Incoming Payments

Repository Info System: Transactions Find (200 Hits)

Figure 102: List of Transactions starting with 'F'

3. In case you have no clue as to the Transaction Codes you are searching for, you may still get there if you try the search through 'package or application components, short description' etc. In step-2 above, instead of entering the search string in the 'Transaction Code' field, click on [⊙] button and you will be taken to the following 'Find Transaction' selection screen:

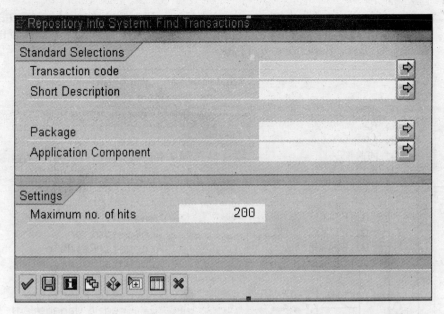

Figure 103: Standard Selection Screen to find Transactions

4. Maintain any of the known information under 'Standard Selections'. Assume that you are planning to search by 'Application Component': then click on the <img> button to the right of the '*Application Component*' field. Now the system takes you to the '***Select Application Component***' pop-up screen:

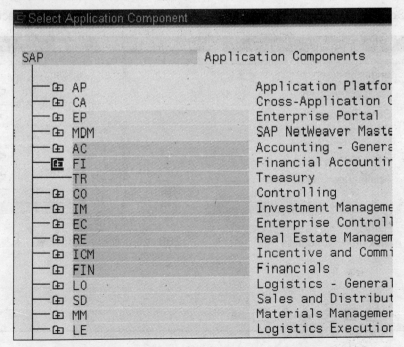

Figure 104: Select 'Application Component'

5. Expand the '*Application Components*' tree to reach the 'specific functionality' or 'component' you are looking for. Suppose that you are looking for Transaction Codes relating to '*Basic Functions*' in FI-AR:

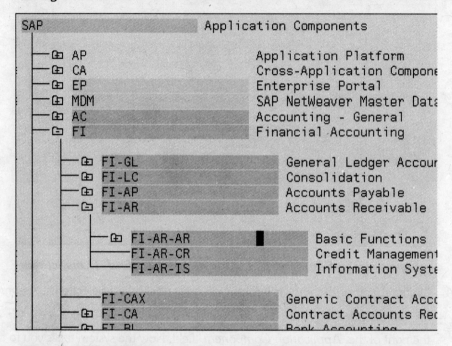

Figure 105: Selection of the specific Application Component

6. Double-click on 'FI-AR-AR', and you are taken back to the initial selection screen:

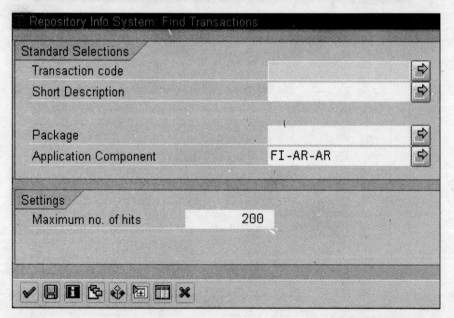

Figure 106: Standard Selection with FI-AR-AR under 'Application Component'

7. Press ✔, and the system will now bring the list of Transaction Codes of all 'Basic Functions' under FI-AR:

Transaction Code	Short text
F-60	Maintain Table: Posting Periods
F-62	Maintain Table: Exchange Rates
FBBA	Display Acct Determination Config.
FBBP	Maintain Acct Determination Config.
FBKA	Display Accounting Configuration
FBKF	FBKP/Carry Out Function (Internal)
FBKP	Maintain Accounting Configuration
FBMA	Display Dunning Procedure
FBMP	Maintain Dunning Procedure
FBTA	Display Text Determin.Configuration
FBTP	Maintain Text Determin.Configuratio
FSK2	Maintain Sample Rules
FSK2_OLD	Maintain Sample Rules
FTXA	Display Tax Code
FTXP	Maintain Tax Code
OB72	C FI Maintain Table T0010
OB73	C FI Maintain Table T031
OB74	C FI Maintain Table TF123
OB75	Cust.Pmnt Program: Available Amnts
OB76	C FI Maintain Table T045E
OB77	C FI Maintain Table T048/T048T
OB78	C FI Maintain Table T048B
OB79	C FI Maintain Table T048I
OB80	C FI Maintain Table T043K
OB81	C FI Maintain Table T056A

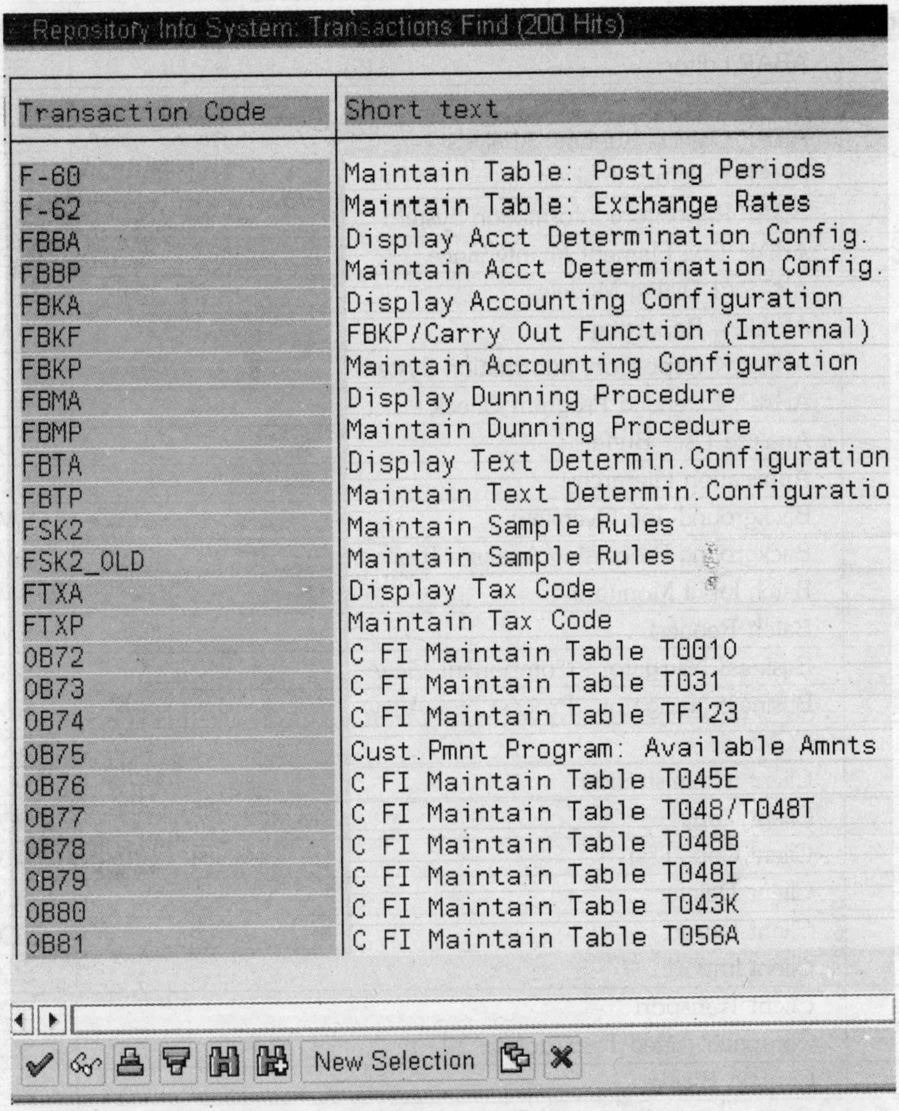

Repository Info System: Transactions Find (200 Hits)

New Selection

Figure 107: Transaction Codes of Basic Functions under FI-AR

Basis & ABAP

Sl. No.	Are you looking for:	T-Code
1	ABAP Editor	SE38
2	ABAP Function Modules	SE37
3	ABAP Objects Runtime Analysis	SE30
4	ABAP Program analysis	AL21
5	ABAP Repository Information System	SE86
6	ABAP Text Element Maintenance	SE32
7	ABAP/4 Dialog Modules	SE35
8	ABAP/4 Reporting	SA38
9	ABAP/4 Repository Information System	SE85
10	ABAP: Extended Program Check	SLIN
11	Analyze User Buffer	SU56
12	Application Hierarchy	SE81
13	Background Job Overview	SM37
14	Background Processing Analysis Tool	SM65
15	Batch Input Monitoring	SM35
16	Batch Request	SM36
17	Business Navigator - Component View	SB01
18	Business Navigator - Process Flow View	SB02
19	CCMS	SRZL
20	Client administration	SCC4
21	Client Copy	SCC0
22	Client Copy Log	SCC3
23	Client Delete	SCC5
24	Client Export	SCC8
25	Client Import	SCC6
26	Client Transport	SCC2
27	Computer Aided Test Tool (CATT)	SCAT
28	Context Builder	SE33
29	Convert Data Dictionary Tables on Database Level	SE14
30	Current Customizing	SPRM
31	Customer Enhancement Simulation	SE94
32	Customer Measurement	USMM
33	Customizing	SPRO
34	Customizing Organizer	SE10
35	Data Dictionary Display	SE12
36	Data Dictionary Maintenance	SE11
37	Data Modeler	SD11

38	Data Transfer Workbench	SXDA
39	Development Class Overview	OY08
40	Development Coordination Info System	SE88
41	Display and Delete Locks	SM12
42	Display Output Requests	SP02
43	Display Own Jobs	SMX
44	Display SAP Directories	AL11
45	Display Table Content	SE16
46	Display users	SU01D
47	Download to Early Watch	AL10
48	Dynamic menu	SMEN
49	Early-Watch Report	AL07
50	Enhancements	CMOD
51	Environment Analyzer	SE02
52	Execute Logical Commands	SM49
53	Generate Enterprise IMG	SCPF
54	Generate Table Display	SE17
55	Generate Table View	SE54
56	Global User Manager	SUMM
57	Installation Check	SM28
58	Integrated User Maintenance	SUPF
59	Job administration	SM68
60	Job analysis	SM39
61	Job scheduling	SM67
62	LAN Check with Ping	OS01
63	Language Import Utility	SMLI
64	List for Session Manager	SU54
65	List of SAP Servers	SM51
66	Local Client Copy	SCCL
67	Lock Transactions	SM01
68	Logical databases	SE36
69	Logon to Online Service System (OSS)	OSS1
70	Maintain Area Menu	SE43
71	Maintain Authorization Profiles	SU02
72	Maintain Authorizations	SU03
73	Maintain Internet Users	SU05
74	Maintain Logon Group	SMLG
75	Maintain Messages	SE91
76	Maintain Organization Levels	SUPO
77	Maintain Own User Parameters	SU52
78	Maintain PC Work Directory	SO21

79	Maintain Technical Settings (Tables)	SE13
80	Maintain Transaction Codes	SE93
81	Maintain Trees in Information System	SE89
82	Maintain User	SU01
83	Maintain User Parameter	SU2
84	Mass Changes to User Master	SU10
85	Mass Changes to User Master Records	SU12
86	Menu Painter	SE41
87	Modification Browser	SE95
88	Monitor Current Workload	AL05
89	Number Range Objects	SNRO
90	Object Navigator	SE80
91	OLE Applications	SOLE
92	Performance Monitoring	STUN
93	Performance, SAP Statistics, Workload	ST03
94	Performance: Upload/Download	AL06
95	Queue Maintenance Transaction	SM38
96	Quick-Viewer	SQVI
97	R/3 Documentation	SE61
98	R/3 Repository Information System	SE84
99	Record Batch Input	SHDB
100	Remote Client Copy	SCC9
101	Reporting: Change Tree Structure	SERP
102	Repository Browser	SEU
103	Repository Info System	SE15
104	Repository Info System	SUIM
105	SAP Alert Monitor	AL01
106	SAP Enhancement Management	SMOD
107	SAP Query: Language comparison	SQ07
108	SAP Query: Maintain Functional Area	SQ02
109	SAP Query: Maintain Queries	SQ01
110	SAP Query: Maintain User Groups	SQ03
111	SAP Web Repository	SMW0
112	SAPoffice: Inbox Overview	SOY5
113	SAPoffice: Outbox	SO02
114	SAPoffice: Private Folders	SO03
115	SAPoffice: Shared Folders	SO04
116	SAPoffice: User Master	SO12
117	SAPscript Font Maintenance (revised)	SE73
118	SAPscript Form	SE71
119	SAPscript Format Conversion	SE74

120	SAPscript Settings	SE75
121	SAPscript Styles	SE72
122	SAPscript Translation Styles	SE77
123	SAPscript: Form Translation	SE76
124	SAPscript: Graphics administration	SE78
125	SAPscript: Standard Texts	SO10
126	Screen Painter	SE51
127	Split-screen Editor: Program Compare	SE39
128	Spool and Relate Area	SP00
129	Spool Control	SP01
130	Spool Management	SPAD
131	SQL Trace	ST05
132	Start Report Immediately	SC38
133	System Administration Assistant	SSAA
134	System log	SM21
135	System Log Analysis	SM23
136	System Messages	SM02
137	System Trace	ST01
138	Table history	OY18
139	Table maintenance	SM31
140	Transport and Correction System	SE01
141	Transport Management System	STMS
142	Transport System Status Display	SE07
143	Transport Utilities	SE03
144	Update Program Administration	SM14
145	User Overview	SM04
146	Users Logged On	AL08
147	View / Table Comparison	SCMP
148	View-cluster Maintenance Call	SM34
149	Web Object Administration	SIAC1
150	Work Process Overview	SM50
151	Workbench Organizer (Initial Screen)	SE09
152	Workflow Definition	SWDC

Financial Accounting (FI): Customizing

Sl. No.	Are you looking for:	T-Code
1	Activate Functional Area Substitution	OBBZ
2	Activate Validations	OB28
3	Allocate a Company Code to Sample Account Rule Type	OB67
4	Assign Chart of Depreciation to Company Code	OAOB
5	Assign Country to Tax Calculation Procedure	OBBG
6	Assign Employee Groups to Credit Representative Groups	OB51
7	Assign GL Accounts to Reason Codes	OBXL
8	Assign Posting Keys to Document Types	OBU1
9	Assign Reference Interest Rates to Interest Indicators	OB81
10	Assign Tax Codes for Non-Taxable Transactions	OBCL
11	Assign Treasury Transaction Types to House Banks	OT55
12	Assign Users to Tolerance Groups	OB57
13	Automatic Account Assignment for Interest Calculation	OBV1
14	Automatic Account Assignment, Cross-Company Code	OBYA
15	Automatic Account Assignment, MM	OBYC
16	Automatic Postings Documentation	OBL1
17	Bank chain determination	FIBB
18	Cash Management Implementation Tool	FDFD
19	Configuration: Maintain Display Format	FAKP
20	Configuration: Show Display Format	FAKA
21	Configure Days in Arrears Calculation	OB39
22	Configure the Central TR-CM System	FF$X
23	Copy Chart of Accounts	OBY7
24	Copy Chart of Depreciation	EC08
25	Copy Company Code	EC01
26	Copy GL Accounts from Chart of Accounts to the Company Code	OBY2
27	Copy Vendor master Records Creation Program	FK15
28	Copy Vendor master Records Upload Program	FK16
29	Define Treasury Groupings	OT17
30	Define Additional Local Currencies	OB22
31	Define Asset Classes	OAOA
32	Define Base Method	OAYO
33	Define Cash Discount Accounts	OBXI
34	Define Cash Management Account Names	OT16
35	Define Check Lots	FCHI
36	Define Company Code (Create / Check / Delete)	OX02
37	Define Company Code Global Parameters	OBY6

38	Define Countries	OY01
39	Define Credit Control Areas	OB45
40	Define Credit Representative Groups	OB02
41	Define Credit Risk Categories	OB01
42	Define Currency Translation Ratios	GCRF
43	Define Customer Account Groups	OBD2
44	Define Customer Tolerance Groups	OBA3
45	Define Data Transfer Rules for Sample Accounts	FSK2
46	Define Depreciation Key	AFAMA
47	Define Document Types	OBA7
48	Define Financial Statement Versions	OB58
49	Define GL Account Groups	OBD4
50	Define GL Number Ranges	FBN1
51	Define House Banks	FI12
52	Define Line item Layouts	O7Z3
53	Define Lockbox Accounts	OB10
54	Define Number Range for Payment Request	F8BM
55	Define Number Ranges for Depreciation Postings	FBN1
56	Define Number Ranges for Master Classes	AS08
57	Define Number Ranges of Vendor Account Groups	OBAS
58	Define Number Ranges for Vendor Account Groups	XKN1
59	Define Posting Keys	OB41
60	Define Posting Period Variant	OBBO
61	Define Posting Rules for Electronic Bank Statement	OT57
62	Define Reason Codes	OBBE
63	Define Reference Interest Rates	OBAC
64	Define Screen Layouts for Asset Depreciation Areas	AO21
65	Define Sort Variants	O757
66	Define Source Symbols, for Treasury	OYOS
67	Define Special Fields	OBVU
68	Define Specify Intervals And Posting Rules	OAYR
69	Define Tax Accounts	OB40
70	Define Tax Codes for Non-Taxable Transactions	OBCL
71	Define Tax codes for Sales/Purchases	FTXP
72	Define Tax Jurisdiction Codes	OBCP
73	Define Tolerance Groups	OBA4
74	Define Vendor Account Groups	OBD3
75	Define Void Reason Codes for Checks	FCHV
76	Define Sample Account Rules	OB15
77	Depreciation Keys	OAYO
78	Determine Depreciation Areas in Asset Classes	OAYZ

79	Define Planning Groups for Treasury	OT13
80	Display Accounting Configuration	FBKA
81	Document Change Rules	OB32
82	Fast Entry Screens	O7E6
83	FI Configuration Menu (instead of IMG)	ORFB
84	Field Status Variants	OBC4
85	Integration with GL	AO90
86	Interest Indicator (Arrears Interest) for Int. Calculation Program	OB82
87	Internal Number Range for Payment Orders	FBN2
88	Loans Customizing	FDCU
89	Maintain Accounting Configuration	FBKF
90	Maintain Accounting Configuration	FBKP
91	Maintain Bank Chains for Account Carry-over	FIBTU
92	Maintain Bank Chains for House Banks	FIBHU
93	Maintain Bank Chains for Partner	FBIPU
94	Maintain Bank Chains for Partner	FIBPU
95	Maintain Business Area	OX03
96	Maintain Client Dependent User Exits	GCX2
97	Maintain Currency Translation Type	FDIC
98	Maintain Currency Translation Type	FGIC
99	Maintain Currency Translation Type	FKIC
100	Maintain Dunning Procedure	FBMP
101	Maintain Fiscal Year Variant	OB29
102	Maintain Functional Areas	OKBD
103	Maintain Key Figures	FDIK
104	Maintain Lockbox Control Parameters	OBAY
105	Maintain Lockbox Posting Data	OBAX
106	Maintain Payment Program Configuration	FBZP
107	Maintain Substitutions	GGB1
108	Maintain Text Determination Configuration	FBTP
109	Maintain Validations	GGB0
110	Map Internal Reason Codes to External Reason Codes	OBCS
111	Real Estate Implementation Guide	FEUI
112	Retained Earnings Variant	OB53
113	Scenarios for Bank Chain Determination	FIBC
114	Specify Round Up Net Book Valuation	OAYO
115	Structure for Tax Jurisdiction Codes	OBCO
116	Transaction Types for Electronic Bank Statement	OBBY
117	Transport Chart of Accounts	OBY9
118	Treasury Planning Levels	OT14

Financial Accounting (FI): Transactions

Sl. No.	Are you looking for:	T-Code
1	A/P: Account Balances	F.42
2	A/P: Account List	F.40
3	A/P: Balance Interest Calculation	F.44
4	A/P: Evaluate Info System	F.46
5	A/P: Open Items	F.41
6	A/R Summary	FCV1
7	A/R Dunning Run	F150
8	A/R: Account Balances	F.23
9	A/R: Account List	F.20
10	A/R: Balance Interest Calculation	F.26
11	A/R: Evaluate Info System	F.30
12	A/R: Interest for Days Overdue	F.24
13	A/R: Open Item Sorted List	F.22
14	A/R: Open Items	F.21
15	A/R: Periodic Account Statements	F.27
16	Accounting Editing Options	FB00
17	Accounts Detailed Listing from OI Account Accum. Audit Trail	F.5C
18	Accumulated Classic Audit Trail: Create Extract (RFKLET01)	F.59
19	Accumulated Details from Historical Accum. Balance Audit Trail	F.5A
20	Accumulated OI Audit Trail: Create Extract(RFKLET01)	F.5B
21	Acquisition from Purchase with Vendor	F-90
22	Advance Tax Return	F.12
23	Archive Bank Master Data	F041
24	Archive Customer	F043
25	Archive Transaction Figures	F046
26	Archiving Bank Data Storage	F66A
27	Archiving Banks	F61A
28	Archiving Check Data	FCHA
29	Archiving GL Accounts	F53A
30	Archiving Payment Request	F8BO
31	ArchivingVendors	F044
32	Asset Acquisition to Clearing Account	F-91
33	Asset Depreciation Run	AFAB
34	Asset Explorer	AW01
35	Asset Master Creation	AS01
36	Asset Retirement from Sale With Customer	F-92
37	Asset Scrapping	ABAVN

38	Asset Transfer	ABUMN
39	Asset, Create Sub-Asset	AS11
40	Automatic Clearing:ABAP/4 Report	F.13
41	Balance Sheet- ABAP/4 Report	F.01
42	Balance Sheet Adjustment: ABAP/4 Reporting	F101
43	Balance Sheet/P&L with Inflation	FJA3
44	Bill of Exchange List	F.25
45	Bill of Exchange Payment	F-36
46	Bill of Exchange Payment Request Dunning	F.70
47	Bill of Exchange Payment-Header Data	F-40
48	Bill of Exchange Presentation - International	FBWE
49	Block Customer (Accounting)	FD05
50	Block Vendor (Accounting)	FK05
51	Cash Concentration	FF73
52	Cash Journal Document Number Range	FBCJC1
53	Cash Journal	FBCJ
54	Cash Management and Forecast - Initial Screen	FF72
55	Cash Management Position / Liquidity Forecast	FF70
56	Cash Management Summary Records	FF-3
57	Cash Position	FF71
58	Change Bank	FI02
59	Change Check / Payment Allocation	FCHT
60	Change Check Information/Cash Check	FCH6
61	Change Credit Limits	FD24
62	Change Current Number Range Number	FI07
63	Change Customer (Accounting Data)	FD02
64	Change Customer Credit Management	FD32
65	Change Customer Line Items	FBL6
66	Change Document	FB02
67	Change GL Account Line Items	FBL4
68	Change Intercompany Document	FBU2
69	Change Last Adjustment Dates	FJA2
70	Change Line Items-Customer / Vendor / Asset / GL	FB09
71	Change Parked Document (Header)	FBV4
72	Change Parked Document	FBV2
73	Change Payment Advice	FBE2
74	Change Pricing Report	F/LB
75	Change Recurring Entry	FBD2
76	Change ReportSettings for Transaction Figures	FDI2
77	Change Report: Settings	FGI2
78	Change Report: Settings	FKI2

79	Change Sample Document	FBM2
80	Change Vendor (Accounting Data)	FK02
81	Change Vendor (Accounting Data)	FK04
82	Change Vendor Line Items	FBL2
83	Check Extract - Creation	FCHX
84	Check if Documents can be Archived	FB99
85	Check Register	FCHN
86	Check Retrieval	FCHB
87	Check Tracing Initial Menu	FCHK
88	Clear Customer Down Payment	F-39
89	Clear Customer: Header Data	F-32
90	Clear GL Account: Header Data	F-03
91	Clear Vendor Down Payment	F-54
92	Clear Vendor: Header Data	F-44
93	Confirm Customer Individually (Accounting)	FD08
94	Confirm Customer List (Accounting)	FD09
95	Confirm Vendor Individually (Accounting)	FK08
96	Confirm Vendor List (Accounting)	FK09
97	Correspondence: Delete Requests	F.63
98	Correspondence: Maintain Requests	F.64
99	Correspondence: Print Interest Documents	F.62
100	Correspondence: Print Letters (Customer)	F.65
101	Correspondence: Print Letters (Vendor)	F.66
102	Correspondence: Print Requests	F.61
103	Create Bank	FI01
104	Create Check Information	FCH5
105	Create Customer (Accounting)	FD01
106	Create Payment Advice	FBE1
107	Create Payment Runs Automatically	F8BU
108	Create Planning Memo Record	FF63
109	Create Reference for Check	FCHU
110	Create Vendor (Accounting Area Data)	FK01
111	Credit Management - Mass Change	F.34
112	Credit Management - Mass Change	FD37
113	Credit Management - Master Data List	FDK43
114	Credit Management - Missing Data	F.32
115	Credit Management - Overview	F.31
116	Credit Master Sheet	F.35
117	Customer Account Analysis	FD11
118	Customer Account Balance	FD10
119	Customer Balance Confirmation: ABAP/4 Report	F.17

120	Customer Balance Display	FD10N
121	Customer Balance: Display with Worklist	FD10NA
122	Customer Changes (Accounting)	FD04
123	Customer Down Payment Request	F-37
124	Customer Interest on Arrears: Post (w/ Open Items)	F.2B
125	Customer Interest on Arrears: Post (w/o Open Items)	F.2A
126	Customer Interest on Arrears: Post (w/o postings)	F.2C
127	Customer Line Items	FBL5N
128	Customer Noted Item	F-49
129	Customer/Vendor Statistics	F.1A
130	Customers Drilldown Reports: Background Processing	FDIB
131	Customers: FI-SD Master Data Comparison	F.2D
132	Customers: Report Selection	F.99
133	Customers: Reset Credit Limit	F.28
134	Data Extract for FI Transfer	FC11
135	Delete A/R Summary	FCV2
136	Delete Cashing/Extract Data	FCHG
137	Delete Manual Checks	FCHF
138	Delete Payment Advice	FBE6
139	Delete Payment Run Check Information	FCHD
140	Delete Recurring Document	F.56
141	Delete Voided Checks	FCHE
142	Display Account Determination Configuration	FBBA
143	Display Bank Chains for House Banks	FIBHS
144	Display Bank Chains for Partners	FIBPS
145	Display Bank Changes	FI04
146	Display Bank	FI03
147	Display Check Information	FCH1
148	Display Customer (Accounting Data)	FD03
149	Display Customer Credit Management	FD33
150	Display Customer Line Items	FBL5
151	Display Document	FB03
152	Display Document/Payment Usage	FB03Z
153	Display Dunning Procedure	FBMA
154	Display Electronic Bank Statement	FF.6
155	Display FI Amount Groups	F8+2
156	Display FI Main Role Definition	F8+0
157	Display GL Account Line Items	FBL3
158	Display House Banks/Bank Accounts	FI13
159	Display Intercompany Document	FBU3
160	Display of Payment Requests	F8BS

161	Display Parked Document	FBV3
162	Display Payment Advice	FBE3
163	Display Payment Document Checks	FCH2
164	Display Payment Program Configuration	FBZA
165	Display Payment Requests	F8BT
166	Display Payment Run	FBZ8
167	Display Pricing Report	F/LC
168	Display Recurring Entry Changes	FBD4
169	Display Recurring Entry	FBD3
170	Display Sample Document Changes	FBM4
171	Display Sample Document	FBM3
172	Display Text Determination Configuration	FBTA
173	Display Vendor (Accounting Data)	FK03
174	Display Vendor Line Items	FBL1
175	Display/Edit Payment Proposal	FBZ0
176	Document Archiving	F045
177	Document Changes of Parked Documents	FBV5
178	Document Changes	FB04
179	Down Payment Request	F-47
180	Download Documents	FBF4
181	Enter Accrual/Deferral Document	FBS1
182	Enter Bill of Exchange Payment Request	FBW1
183	Enter Customer Credit Memo	F-27
184	Enter Customer Invoice	F-22
185	Enter GL Account Posting	F-02
186	Enter Incoming Credit Memos	FB65
187	Enter Incoming Invoices	FB60
188	Enter Noted Item	FB31
189	Enter Outgoing Credit Memos	FB75
190	Enter Outgoing Invoices	FB70
191	Enter Payment Request	FBP1
192	Enter Recurring Entry	FBD1
193	Enter Sample Document	F-01
194	Enter Statistical Posting: Header Data	F-38
195	Enter Transfer Posting: Header Data	F-21
196	Enter Vendor Credit Memo	F-41
197	Enter Vendor Invoice	F-43
198	Exchange RatesTable Maintenance	F-62
199	F111 Customizing	F8BZ
200	Failed Customer Payments	FBZG
201	FI Account Assignment Model Management	FKMT

202	FI Display Structure	FINA
203	FI Easy Access - Banks	FBME
204	FI Easy Access - Customers	FDMN
205	FI Easy Access - Vendors	FKMN
206	FI Information System	F000
207	FI Initial Consolidation Menu	FCMN
208	FI Valuation Run	F107
209	Financial Statements Comparison	FC10
210	Financial Transactions	FBF2
211	Foreign Currency Valuation: Open Items	F.05
212	GL Account Assignment Manual	F.53
213	GL Account Balance Interest Calculation	F.52
214	GL Account Balances	F.08
215	GL Account Cashed Checks	FF.3
216	GL Account Interest Scale	FF_1
217	GL Account Line Items	FBL3N
218	GL Account List	F.09
219	GL Accounts Archiving	F042
220	GL Account Posting: Single Screen Transaction	FB50
221	GL Advance Report on Tax on Sales/Purchases with Jurisdiction	F.5I
222	GL Balance Carried Forward	F.07
223	GL Balance Sheet Adjustment Log	F.5F
224	GL Chart of Accounts	F.10
225	GL Compact Journal	F.02
226	GL Create Foreign Trade Report	F.04
227	GL Delete Sample Documents	F.57
228	GL Drilldown Reports: Background Processing	FGIB
229	GL General Ledger from Document File	F.11
230	GL GR/IR Clearing	F.19
231	GL Open Items	F.51
232	GL Post Balance Sheet Adjustment	F.5E
233	GL Profitability Segment Adjustment	F.50
234	GL Report Selection	F.97
235	GL Structured Account Balances	F.54
236	GL Update Balance Sheet Adjustment	F.5D
237	Generate Multicash Format	FEBC
238	Generate Payment Request from Advices	FF.D
239	Import Electronic Bank Statement	FF.5
240	Import Electronic Check Deposit List	FFB4
241	Import Forms from Client 000	FDIR
242	Import Lockbox File	FLB2

243	Import Reports from Client 000	FDIQ
244	Incoming Payments Fast Entry	F-26
245	Invoice/Credit Fast Entry	FB10
246	Maintain Bill of Exchange Liability	F.93
247	Manual Bank Statement	FF67
248	Manual Check Deposit Transaction	FF68
249	Mark Bank for Deletion	FI06
250	Mark Customer for Deletion (Accounting)	FD06
251	Mark Vendor for Deletion (Accounting)	FK06
252	Mass Reversal of Documents	F.80
253	Online Cashed Checks	FCHR
254	Open Item Balance Audit Trail: from Document File	F.58
255	Outstanding Bills of Exchange	FF-2
256	Parameters for Automatic Payment	F110
257	Parameters for Payment of Request	F111
258	Park Customer Credit Memo	F-67
259	Park Customer Invoice	F-64
260	Park Document	FBV1
261	Park Vendor Credit Memo	F-66
262	Park Vendor Invoice	F-63
263	Payment Advice Comparison	FF.7
264	Payment Advice Journal	FF-8
265	Payment Card Evaluations	FCCR
266	Payment Cards: Settlement	FCC1
267	Payment Request	F-59
268	Payment with Printout	F-18
269	Post Bill of Exchange Usage	F-33
270	Post Collection	F-34
271	Post Customer Down Payment	F-29
272	Post Document	FB01
273	Post Electronic Bank Statement	FEBP
274	Post Electronic Check Deposit List	FFB5
275	Post Foreign Currency Valuation	F-05
276	Post Forfaiting	F-35
277	Post Held Document	FB11
278	Post Incoming Payments	F-06
279	Post Lockbox Data	FLBP
280	Post Outgoing Payments	F-07
281	Post Parked Document	FBV0
282	Post Payment Orders	FF.9
283	Post Tax Payable	FB41

284	Post Vendor Down Payment	F-48
285	Post with Clearing	F-04
286	Post with Reference Document	FBR1
287	Posting Period Table Maintenance	F-60
288	Preliminary Posting	F-65
289	Print Check For Payment Document	FBZ5
290	Print Payment Orders	FF.8
291	Realize Recurring Entry	FBD5
292	Reconciliation between Affiliated Companies	F.2E
293	Recurring Entries: ABAP/4 Report	F.14
294	Reject Parked Document	FBV6
295	Release for Payments	FB13
296	Renumber Checks	FCH4
297	Report Painter	FGRP
298	Report Painter: Change Form-Customer	FDI5
299	Report Painter: Change Form-GL	FGI5
300	Report Painter: Change Form-Vendor	FKI5
301	Report Writer Menu	FGRW
302	Reprint Check	FCH7
303	Request from Correspondence	FB12
304	Reset Cleared Items (Payment Cards)	FBRC
305	Reset Cleared Items	FBRA
306	Reset Cleared Items: Payment Requests	F8BW
307	Returned Bills of Exchange Payable	FBWD
308	Reversal of Bank-to-Bank Transfers	F8BV
309	Reverse Bill Liability	F-20
310	Reverse Check Payment	FCH8
311	Reverse Check/Bill of Exchange	F-25
312	Reverse Cross-Company Code Document	FBU8
313	Reverse Document	FB08
314	Reverse Posting for Accrued /Deferred Documents	F.81
315	Reverse Statistical Posting	F-19
316	SAP Office: Short Message-Create and Send	F00
317	Special Purpose Ledger Menu	FGM0
318	Vendor Account Balance	FK10
319	Vendor Balance Confirmation: ABAP/4 Report	F.18
320	Vendor Balance Display	FK10N
321	Vendor Cashed Checks	FF.4
322	Vendor Check/Bill of Exchange	FBW6
323	Vendor Down Payment Request	FBA6
324	Vendor Interest on Arrears: Post (w/ Open Items)	F.4B

325	Vendor Interest on Arrears: Post (w/o Open Items)	F.4A
326	Vendor Interest on Arrears: Post (w/o postings)	F.4C
327	Vendor Line Items	FBL1N
328	Vendor Noted Item	F-57
329	Vendors Drilldown Reports: Background Processing	FKIB
330	Vendors: Calculate Interest on Arrears	F.47
331	Vendors: FI-MM Master Data Comparison	F.48
332	Vendors: Report Selection	F.98
333	Void Checks	FCH3
334	Void Issued Check	FCH9
335	Wire Authorization	FFW1

Material Management (MM)

Sl. No.	Are you looking for:	T-Code
1	ABC Analysis for Cycle Counting	MIBC
2	Allow Postings to Previous Period	MMRV
3	Analysis of Order Values	E81N
4	Archive / Delete Material	MM71
5	Archive Info Records	E17
6	Archive Purchase Requisitions	E97
7	Archive Purchasing Documents	E98
8	Archive Rebate Arrangements	EBR
9	Archived Purchase Requisitions	E5R
10	Archived Purchasing Documents	E82
11	Assign and Process Requisitions	E57
12	Assign Source to Purchase Requisition	E56
13	Assign User to User Group	EU0
14	Automatic Generation of POs	ME59
15	Buyer's Negotiation Sheet for Material	E1Y
16	Buyer's Negotiation Sheet for Vendor	E1X
17	Change Contract	E32K
18	Change Inventory Count	MI05
19	Change Material	MM02
20	Change Outline Agreement	E32
21	Change Physical Inventory Document	MI02
22	Change Purchase Order	E22N
23	Change Purchase Requisition	ME52N
24	Change Purchasing Info Record	E12
25	Change Reservation	MB22
26	Change Scheduling Agreement	E32L
27	Change Vendor (Purchasing)	MK02
28	Changes to Vendor Evaluation	E6A
29	Close Period	MMPV
30	Collective Release of Purchase Order	EW5
31	Conditions for Incoterms	EKI
32	Conditions for Invoicing Party	EKJ
33	Count/Difference	MI08
34	Create Conditions (Purchasing)	EK1
35	Create Contract	E31K
36	Create Material	MM01
37	Create Non-Stock Material	MMN1

38	Create Non-Valuated Material	MMU1
39	Create Operating Supplies	MMI1
40	Create Outline Agreement	E31
41	Create Physical Inventory Document	MI01
42	Create Purchase Order	E21N
43	Create Purchase Requisition	ME51N
44	Create Purchasing Info Record	E11
45	Create Quotation	E47
46	Create Request For Quotation	E41
47	Create Requirement Request	EW1
48	Create Reservation	MB21
49	Create Scheduling Agreement	E31L
50	Create Source List	E01
51	Create Vendor (Purchasing)	MK01
52	Currency Change: Contracts	EKRE
53	Delivery Addresses	EAN
54	Display Conditions (Purchasing)	EK3
55	Display Material	MM03
56	Display Material Archive	MM72
57	Display Material	IH09
58	Display Purchase Order	E23N
59	Display Purchase Requisition	ME53N
60	Display Purchasing Info Record	E13
61	Display Quotation	E48
62	Display Vendor Evaluation for Material	E6B
63	Display Vendor Evaluation	E62
64	Enter Inventory Count	MI04
65	Enter Storage Locations	MMSC
66	Evaluation Comparison	E64
67	Evaluation Lists	E65
68	Flag for deletion, immediately	MM06
69	Flag Purchasing Info Record for Deletion	E15
70	Goods Receipt - For PO Known	MB01
71	Goods Receipt - PO Unknown	MB0A
72	Goods Receipt Forecast	E2V
73	Info Records Per Material Group	E1W
74	Info Records per Material	E1M
75	Info Records Per Vendor	E1L
76	List of Customer Rebate Arrangements	ER5
77	List of Vendor Rebate Arrangements	EB5
78	Maintain Outline Agreement Supplement	E34

79	Maintain Quota Arrangement	EQ1
80	Maintain Vendor Evaluation	E61
81	Market Price	EKH
82	Mass Change of Purchase Orders	EMAS
83	Material List	MM60
84	Message Output: Purchase Orders	E9F
85	Message Output: RFQs	E9A
86	Other Goods Receipts	MB1C
87	Physical Inventory Document Recount	MI11
88	PO Change	ME22
89	PO Create - Vendor Known	ME21
90	PO Create - Vendor Unknown	ME25
91	Price Change: Contract	EDL
92	Price Change: Scheduling Agreements	EKL
93	Price Comparison List	E49
94	Procurement Transaction	EW0
95	Purchase Order Price History	E1P
96	Purchase Order	EPO
97	Purchase Orders by Account Assignment	E2K
98	Purchase Orders by Material Group	E2C
99	Purchase Orders by Material	E2M
100	Purchase Orders by PO Number	E2N
101	Purchase Orders by Vendor	E2L
102	Purchase Orders for Project	E2J
103	Purchase Orders for Supplying Plant	E2W
104	Quotation Price History	E1E
105	Release Contract	E35K
106	Release Outline Agreement	E35
107	Release purchase order	E29N
108	Release Purchase Requisition	ME54
109	Release RFQ	E45
110	Release Scheduling Agreement	E35L
111	Reservations by Account Assignment	MB25
112	Reservations by Material	MB24
113	RFQs by Material Group	E4C
114	RFQs by Material	E4M
115	RFQs by Vendor	E4L
116	Source List for Material	E0M
117	Stock Overview	MMBE
118	Transfer Posting	MB1B
119	Vendors Without Evaluation	E6C
120	Web based PO	EWP

Sales & Distribution (SD)

Sl. No.	Are you looking for:	T-Code
1	Access sequence	V/07
2	Assigning Sales Area to Sales Documents Type	OVAZ
3	Billing Due List	VF04
4	Billing Menu	VF00
5	Block Customer (Sales)	VD05
6	Blocked SD Documents	VKM1
7	Cancel Billing document	VF11
8	Cancel Goods Issue	VL09
9	Change Billing Document	VF02
10	Change Billing Document	VF02
11	Change Condition	VK12
12	Change Contract	VA42
13	Change Customer	VD02
14	Change Customer (Sales)	VD02
15	Change Customer Price	V-51
16	Change Material Price	V-43
17	Change Price List	V-47
18	Change Sales Order	VA02
19	Change Shipment	VT02N
20	Create Billing Document	VF01
21	Create Business Partner	V+23
22	Create Condition	VK11
23	Create Consignee (Sales)	V-06
24	Create Contract	VA41
25	Create Customer	V-09
26	Create Customer	XD01
27	Create Customer (Sales)	VD01
28	Create Customer Hierarchy Nodes	V-12
29	Create Inquiry	VA11
30	Create Invoice Party (Sales)	V-04
31	Create One-Time Customer (Sales)	V-07
32	Create Ordering Party (Sales)	V-03
33	Create Outbound Delivery with reference to Sales Order	VL01
34	Create Payer (Centrally)	V-08
35	Create Payer (Sales)	V-05
36	Create Quotation	VA21
37	Create Rebate Agreement	VBO1

38	Create Sales Order	V-01
39	Create Sales Order	VA01
40	Create Scheduling Agreement	VA31
41	Customer Account Changes	VD04
42	Customer Hierarchy Maintenance	VDH1
43	Define delivery types	OVLK
44	Define Sales Documents Type (Header)	VOV8
45	Delivery due list	VL04
46	Display Customer	VD03
47	Display Customer	XD03
48	Display Order	VA03
49	Flag for Deletion Customer	VD06
50	List of blocked SD documents	VKM1
51	List of Deliveries	VKM5
52	List of Outbound Deliveries for Goods Issue	VL06G
53	List of Outbound Deliveries for Picking	VL06P
54	List of Sales Documents	VKM3
55	List of Sales Orders	VA05
56	Maintain Pricing Procedure	V/08
57	Mark Customer For Deletion	VD06
58	Master data Menu	VS00
59	Material Determination	VD52
60	Modify Customer	XD02
61	Order Reasons	OVAU
62	Output for Shipments	VT70
63	Periodic Billing	V.07
64	Pricing Process Determination	V/06
65	Release Orders for Billing	V.23
66	Released SD Documents	VKM2
67	Sales Menu	VA00
68	Sales Support	VC00
69	Shipping Menu	VL00
70	Transportation	VT00

Production Planning (PP)

Sl. No.	Are you looking for:	T-Code
1	Change BOM	CS02
2	Change Order	CO02
3	Change planned order	MD12
4	Change planning calendar	MD26
5	Change production lot	MDL2
6	Change Standard Routing	CA02
7	Change Work Centre	CR02
8	Collective access of planning result	MD46
9	Collective availability check	MDVP
10	Collective Conversion of Planned order	CO41
11	Convert planned order into PR	MDUM
12	Cost Centre Assignment	CR06
13	Crate Standard Routing	CA01
14	Create Bill of Material (BOM)	CS01
15	Create Order for Project	CO10
16	Create Order for Sales Order	CO08
17	Create Order with Material	C001
18	Create Order without Material	C007
19	Create planning calendar	MD25
20	Create Planning Type	MC8A
21	Create Product Group	MC84
22	Create production lot	MDL1
23	Create Work Centre	CR01
24	Delete Task List with Archiving	CA99
25	Delete Task List without Archiving	CA98
26	Display BOM	CS03
27	Display BOM explosion number	MDSA
28	Display Order	CO03
29	Display planning calendar	MD27
30	Display production lot	MDL3
31	Display Standard Routing	CA03
32	Display Work Centre	CR03
33	Edit BOM explosion number	MDSP
34	Explode BOM by date	OPPP
35	Factory Calendar	OP43
36	Individual access of planned order	MD13
37	Interactive single-item planning	MD43

38	MRP list	MD05
39	MRP List Collective Display	MS06
40	MRP List Material	MS05
41	Multi-level BOM	CS11
42	Multi-level project planning	MD51
43	Multi-level, make-to-order planning	MD50
44	Order - Create With Material	CO01
45	Order progress	CO46
46	Order report	MD4C
47	Planning result	MD45
48	Planning Run On Line	MS01
49	Print MRP list	MDLD
50	Print MRP List	MSLD
51	Replace Work Centre	CR85
52	Shift Sequence	OP4A
53	Single Item - Multi Level	MS02
54	Single Item - Sales Order	MS50
55	Single Item - Single Level	MS03
56	Single Item Planning, Project	MS51
57	Single-item, multi-level planning	MD02
58	Single-item, single-level planning	MD03
59	Stock/Requirement List Collective Display	MS07
60	Stock/requirements list	MD04
61	Stock/Requirements List	MS04
62	Transfer Materials to Demand Management	MC90
63	Transfer to ABC	KSOP
64	Transfer to Cost Centre	KSPP
65	Where used, Work Centre	CA80
66	Work Centre Hierarchy	CR08
67	Work Centre List	CR05
68	Work Centre Reporting	CA80

SAP Terminology

10

SAP Terminology

ABAP/4: A 4-GL language, *Advanced Business Application Programming* or ABAP/4 is SAP's programming language.

ABAP Editor: The program editor in SAP which helps you to create / test / change ABAP programs and the associated program / screen elements.

ABAP Query: A programming tool which enables you to create reports without any ABAP programming skill or knowledge. Based on the *WYSWYG* (What-You-See-is-What-You-Get) principle, ABAP Query enables you to select the fields from Tables and arranging them on a report-layout. You may create simple reports (*Basic List*) or the more advanced ones (*Statistic or Ranked List*).

ABC Classification: Helps in grouping your vendor or materials or inventory or any other object so as to stratify into three categories, A, B and C. A is the most important and C is the least important in the group. ABC classification enables you to have effective management and monitoring based on laid out criteria.

AcceleratedSAP (ASAP): SAP's well renowned and path-breaking methodology to optimally implement SAP, both new as well as the upgrades, with a well-laid out '*Implementation Road Map*'. ASAP comes bundled with '*Accelerators*' that enable you to cut-down the implementation time substantially. It also comes delivered with tools like '*Implementation Assistant*' '*Q & A Database*' etc that aid in the implementation.

Accelerator: Used in ASAP implementation methodology, '*Accelerators*' are a collection of templates, '*how-to*' guides, and examples to enable easier and faster project implementations.

Access Sequence: Used in GL, CO, SD and other modules, *Access Sequence* relates to a set of steps, in a pre-defined order, accessing the *Condition Tables* searching for *Condition Records* for performing calculations for arriving at, for example, the tax, discount etc.

Account: A repository holding transaction figures within an accounting unit like Company Code.

Account Allocation: Used in *Asset Accounting* (*FI-AA*), these reconciliation accounts help in posting the business transactions automatically to *FI-GL*.

Account Assignment: A specification which tells the system which account needs to be posted to during a business transaction.

Account Assignment Category: In *MM*, this is an identifier which specifies which account assignment details that are required for an item (for example, cost center or account number). In *CO, Account Assignment Categories* determine the *Settlement Receivers* like G/L account, Cost Centre, Internal Order etc.

Account Assignment Group (of the Customer): The identifier in *Customer Master* record of the Payer that groups certain Customers (Domestic Customers, Foreign Customers etc) for 'Account Assignment' purposes. For example, revenue from Domestic Customers would be posted to a Domestic Revenue *GL Account*, whereas revenue from foreign customers would be posted to a Foreign Revenue GL Account.

Account Assignment Group (of the Material): The identifier in Material Master Record that groups certain Materials for 'Account Assignment' purposes.

Account-based Profitability Analysis: One of the two types (the other being *Period Based Profitability Analysis*) of *Profitability Analysis*, which reconciles the cost and revenue data stored in the accounts, between FI and CO.

Account Category Reference: A combination of *Valuation Classes*.

Account Determination: SAP's automatic system function to determine which accounts need to posted / updated with the amounts during any posting transaction in the systems. In CO, this relates to determination of adjustment accounts for reconciliation postings between FI and CO, either manually or though automatic substitutions.

Account Determination Procedure: Assigned to a *Billing Document Type*, this procedure determines Revenue *Account Assignment* in the Sales Documents.

Account Determination Type: A key which determines the *Access Sequence* and other conditions for *Revenue Account Determination* in the *Sales Document*.

Accounting Document: This is the document that records the value changes arising out of accounting transaction postings. The accounting document contains one or more line items; you may have up to 999 line items in a single accounting document.

Account Group (FI): Specifies which fields are relevant to a master record and defines the *Number Range* from which numbers are selected for the master record. There are *GL Account Groups, Vendor Account Groups, and Customer Account Groups* etc which need to be defined in the system. An Account Group needs to be assigned to each of the master records.

Account ID: Refers to a unique freely definable five-character code assigned to a Bank Account.

Account Key: A field that is assigned to Condition Types in the Pricing Procedure that enables the user to define GL Accounts like revenue, discounts or taxes.

Account Modification: This will allow the system to post to accounts that are different from the standard account assignment.

Account Modification Code: A code which is used to further sub-divide a Transaction / Event Key / Process Key which is assigned to a Movement Type.

Account Receivable Summary (A/R Summary): A collection of all credit-related information from the FI-AR that is used for credit checks during Sales Order Processing (SOP) in the SD. If you have centralized FI system and decentralized SD, then A/R summary can be useful to reduce the number of times data is accessed from the databases.

Account Symbol: A key, in FI-GL, which groups accounts from different *Charts of Accounts*.

Account Symbols are used in *Account Determination* in the *Accrual Engine*.

Account Type: Refers to an alphanumeric key that identifies the type of account like D = Customer, K = Vendor etc. This along with the account number helps you to identify a particular account.

Accounts Payable sub-module (FI-AP): An integral part of the Purchasing system, this is used to record and administer the accounting data for all vendors.

Accounts Receivable sub-module (FI-AR): An integral part of the Sales system, this is used in recording and administering the accounting for all the customers.

Accrual: The accrual concept helps to distribute expenses / revenues / profit / loss to the correct accounting periods based on the origin of the amounts.

Accrual Calculation: A method used in CO, to evenly spread out irregularly occurring costs by distributing them to correct periods. This helps to even-out the irregular fluctuations in business expenses occurrence.

Accrual Engine: A tool enabling calculation and posting of accrued costs automatically.

Accrual Order: An *Internal Order* in CO, used in monitoring the period-based accrual between the expenses posted in FI and accrual costs (like bonus paid to employees) debited in CO.

Acquisition and Production Costs (APC): APC will be the upper limit for valuation of an asset in the Balance Sheet. For all External Acquisitions, the APC is equal to all expenses of acquisition of the asset plus the incidental expenses like commissions, freight charges minus deductions to the purchase price like rebates, discounts etc. In the case of 'In-house Acquisitions', the APC will be equal to all production costs and a portion of administrative expenses which can be associated with that asset.

Acquisition Year: The Fiscal Year in which the acquisition of the asset takes place.

Activity Type: The classifier in CO, used to classify the type of activity (like the machine hours) performed in a Cost Centre.

Activity Type Category: An indicator determining how an Activity Type is allocated (like direct allocation, indirect activity allocation etc).

Activity Type Group: A grouping of similar Activity Types.

Activity Type Planning: A tool, in Cost Centre Accounting, to plan the various Activities (along with their price, their capacity etc) to be produced in a Cost Centre.

Actual Costs: The costs which are actually incurred. In CO-PC, actual costs represent the total debits made to a cost object.

Actual Cost Entry: This refers to transferring of primary costs from FI to CO. The transfer of primary costs occurs on a real-time basis via the *primary cost element*.

Additional Account Assignment: The extra items (like payment terms, cost object, payment method etc) entered in a *line item*, in addition to the account number, amount and posting key.

Additional Ledger: A ledger defined for the purpose of evaluation / reporting purposes, this will contain values and quantities at company or Company Code level.

Ad-hoc Estimate: A cost estimate (in *Easy Cost Planning* in CO-PC) which does not need an object to be created in the system.

Adjustment Method: Refers to adjusting, individual line items on an account or the balance on the account for *inflation*.

Agreement: A Contract defined in the system, in SD, with a Customer.

Allocated Actual Costs: Relates to the credit of *Cost Centres* (and business processes) from activity allocations and/or orders from Goods Receipts (*GR*) and *Settlements*.

Allocation Category: An indicator, in *Activity Based Costing (ABC)*, determining how activity quantities are planned / allocated. There are four allocation categories provided by SAP (like manual entry-manual allocation, manual entry-no allocation, manual entry-indirect allocation and indirect determination-indirect allocation).

Allocation Cost Element: A Cost Element used in *Activity Allocation* in CO.

Allocation Cycle: Consists of *Header Data* (valid for all Segments in a Cycle) and one or more *Segments*, with summarized rules and settings enabling allocation. The Segments within a cycle can be processed *iteratively* (one segment waits for the results of another) or *non-iteratively* (all the segments are processed independently) or *cumulatively* (to take care of variations in receiver *Tracing Factors* or sender amounts).

Alternate BOM: One of the *Bills of Materials* (BOM) in a *BOM Group*.

Archiving: This is the process of reading, removing and saving data - which is no longer required in the system - to an *Archive* file. This helps in reducing the system load as the database is removed of unwanted data. Once the data is 'archived', the same can then be 'Marked for Deletion', then *Delete*d later on.

Area Menu: Grouping of *Menus* containing a set of functions for performing a particular task in a Company Code.

Assessment: A method of internal cost allocation from a sender cost centre to receiver cost centre / cost objects through an as *Assessment Cost Element*. The basis of such an assessment will be on user-defined keys like *Statistical Key Figures* (SKF). It is possible to transfer a portion or the whole of the costs of the sender cost centre to the receivers.

Asset Accounting (FI-AA): One of the sub-modules of *Financial Accounting*, FI-AA is actually a sub-ledger to take care of all business activities associated with Fixed Asset Accounting.

Asset Acquisition: Relates to acquiring *Fixed Assets*, through external means like purchasing or through in-house production. It also deals with *Subsequent Acquisitions* (to an already capitalized asset) and *Post Capitalization* (in a period after actual acquisition).

Asset Class: A classification of fixed assets from business and legal point of view. The asset class holds the control parameters and default values for depreciation calculation and other master data. Each asset master record should be assigned to one asset class. The most common asset classes include buildings, machinery etc. Some of the *Special Asset Classes* are *Low-Values Assets, Technical Assets, Assets under Construction (AuC)* etc.

Asset Class Catalog: A list of all asset classes of an enterprise. The asset class catalog is valid at the Client level, though you will be able to maintain certain data (like the *Depreciation Key*) down at the *Chart of Depreciation* level.

Asset Catalog: A list of fixed assets according to branch-specific technical criteria.

Asset Component: This is nothing but a *Sub-Asset* forming a part of a *Complex Asset*. The asset components are, then, denoted by *Asset Sub-Numbers* of a *Main Asset Number*.

Asset Explorer: A versatile tool displaying all transactions of an asset in terms of its values: it displays both planned and posted values of the assets and their depreciation.

Asset History Sheet: A report displaying the history of an asset from the point of its initial capitalization or acquisition, displaying acquisitions, transfers, retirements and accumulated depreciation.

Asset Portfolio: The total value of all the fixed assets used permanently in an enterprise, and the value is shown as the balance sheet item.

Asset Sub-Number: A unique number which, in combination with the *Asset Main Number* identifies a *Complex Asset*. It is possible that you use sub-numbering for identifying the various components of complex asset or the subsequent acquisitions can be numbered as sub-numbers. Each sub-number will have its own asset master record.

Asset Transfer: Refers to the transfer of asset(s) from one Company Code to another of the same group company.

Asset Type: The classification of fixed assets in a company's balance sheet is known as the Asset Type which is nothing but a definition of some of the features of an Asset Class. Some of the examples of asset types include movable assets, lands, buildings, low-value assets etc.

Asset under Construction (AuC): AuC is a fixed asset which is being constructed or completed. These kinds of assets are shown as a separate balance sheet item and are typically managed using one of the 'special asset classes'. The investment on these assets can be managed in the form of *internal orders* or *projects*.

Asset Year-end Closing: This refers to the cut-off date after the end of a fiscal year. You will be using the asset year-end closing programs which will check posting of asset values to GL, depreciation postings and adherence of rules for *NBV (Net Book Value)*.

Assets Goods Receipt: The acquisition of new assets through MM module which is integrated with FI.

Automatic Postings: The postings, represented by separate line items that are done automatically by the system during some transactions like tax (output / input), exchange rate differences, cash discount etc.

Availability Check: Whenever there is a goods movement in MM, the system runs an 'automatic stock check' that prevents the physical inventory balances of those stock categories from becoming negative. However, the same refers to a procedure in PP which will ensure that there are enough components available for planned / production orders.

Average Rate: This is the exchange rate used for settlement of foreign exchange transactions, and is the arithmetic mean between the *bank buying rate* and *bank selling rate*.

Backflush: Refers to non-manual but automatic posting of some components of the production order at the time of *order completion confirmation.*

Background Processing: The automatic execution of ABAP programs, with fixed settings, in the background. There will be no *dialog processing* once the background job is scheduled.

Backorder: The *Sales Order* whose items can not be confirmed due to non-availability or shortage of materials.

Balance: The difference between the debit and credit sides of an account or document. The balance can be a credit balance (when the credits are more than the debits) or debit balance (when debits are more than the credits). You will not be able to post an accounting document if the balance is not zero.

Balance Audit Trail: A record of all transactions posted to an account during a specified accounting period. From the trail, it will be possible to understand how the balance has changed over a period from the opening balance to the closing balance.

Balance Carryforward: The accounting balances are carried forward from one year to another. All the balances on the asset side are carried forward to the respective accounts in the *Balance Sheet*, and the balance (profit or loss) of the *Profit & Loss accounts* will be carried forward to the *Retained Earnings account*(s) of the next year.

Balance Check: The system does a balance check of every accounting document before posting, to ensure that the credit side is equal to the debit side resulting in a zero balance. Else, the system issues warning / error messages so as to correct the line items. The system will not post the document if the balance is non-zero.

Balance Confirmation: A method by which you want the customers or vendors to confirm the correctness of balance as per your book of accounts irrespective of the fact whether this balances are the same or different from their book of accounts.

Balance Notification: A method by which you notify your customer or vendor of the balances as per your books, and you expect a reply only when there is a discrepancy between your books and their books.

Balance Request: A request made to your customers or vendors asking for balance of accounts as per their book of accounts.

Balance Sheet Adjustment: This relates to the retrospective assignment of receivables / payables / taxes to *Business Areas* and/ *Profit Centres* when this assignment was not done earlier while posting the original documents. This is accomplished at a specified cut-off date during closing operations. This may also relate to the preparations - like (a) valuation & adjustment of AR/AP posted in foreign currencies, (b) AR/AP adjustment postings with a changed reconciliation account, (c) adjustment of customers (with credit balance) and vendors (with debit balance) and (d) break-down & adjustment posting of AR/AP according to the remaining terms - before creating a balance sheet.

Balance Sheet Indicator: An indicator, in the GL accounts master record, to denote whether an account is managed as a balance sheet item or otherwise (P&L item).

Bank Buying Rate: A rate at which a bank buys foreign exchange (and securities etc).

Bank Chain: A chain specifying the banks through which the payments are made.

Bank Key: An identifier uniformly identifying the bank in the system, this may be same as that of the *Bank Number*.

Bank Master Data: The information – like name of the bank, country related details, address etc – relating to a bank stored centrally in the system.

Bank Number: A number used to identify a bank in the system. This may be the same as that of the *Bank Key*.

Bank Selling Rate: A rate at which a bank sells foreign exchange (and securities etc).

Bank Statement Time Period: The frequency (period, key date, next due date, day of the week etc) in which a bank statement may be prepared.

Bank Transfer: Transfer of funds from one bank account to another.

BAPI Explorer: A tool, integrated in the programming environment, used in *BAPI* development. The tool enables to look at all the BAPIs available in the *Business Object Repository*. Use the Transaction Code BAPI to get into the explorer.

Base Condition Type: A key, in CO, differentiating the *Direct Costs* to which *overhead* like material or labour costs are applied.

Base Depreciation Area: The depreciation area from which the system takes the values for revaluation of an asset for inflation.

Base Object Costing: A tool – in COPC - enabling manual input of items, in the form of *Unit Cost Estimates*, for planning of prices. This may be used as the basis for planning *cost estimates without quantity structure*, *CO production orders* etc.

Base Unit of Measure: A unit (of measure) in which the stock of a material is maintained.

Base Value: This is the value used as the basis for calculating depreciation in FI-AA.

Base Year: This is the fiscal year in which the data was first created for material valuation (*FIFO / LIFO*) in MM.

Baseline: In ASAP methodology, this is the base configuration agreed upon for further development and configuration. This is also referred to as *Baseline Configuration*, which typically covers 80% of the scope.

Baseline Date for Payment: The date from which the *Terms of Payment* will apply. This date is used by the system in (a) calculating the eligible cash discount and (b) determining the due date for payment of an invoice.

Baseline Configuration: See Baseline.

Basic List: In CO, this refers to a list containing the information like (a) number of objects processed in the processing step, (b) the criteria used to select the objects and (c) status as to whether an object has been successfully processed or not. In ABAP, a 'basic list' refers to the *List Level* 0, wherein a program's output statements are written by default. In a drill-down reports, the *List Level* changes to the next increment when you move away from the basic list.

Bill of Exchange List: A journal listing all the bills of exchange received.

Bill of Exchange Payment Request: A request made to a customer to pay his debts by a bill of exchange. The system posts these requests as *Noted Item*. This kind of payment request is common in countries like Spain, Italy etc.

Bill of Exchange Receivable: A bill of exchange from the creditor's (drawer) view point.

Bill of Exchange Usage: The practice of presenting a bill of exchange to a third party for getting payment by way of refinance. This presentation may be for collection or discounting etc.

Bill of Lading: A documentary proof, issued by the sender of goods, accompanying the shipped goods containing the details of the shipped goods and its condition.

Bill of Material (BOM): A structured list of items or components required to make a product or an object. The components are called as *BOM Items*.

Bill of Material (BOM) Category: SAP helps to maintain and manage BOMs for different objects. Some of the BOM Categories include: material BOM, equipment BOM, sales order BOM etc. In order to provide product variants for production alternatives, the system provides (a) *Variant BOM* and (b) *Multiple BOM*.

Bill of Material (BOM) Component: Also known as *BOM Item*, this refers to a part of a BOM.

Bill of Material (BOM) Item: Also known as *BOM Component*, this is a part of a BOM. Many such items grouped together form the BOM.

Billing Block: The 'billing block' is used to prevent automatic release of billing documents from SD to FI. However, the blocked billing documents may be released manually.

Billing Category: This is the summary of 'billing document types' in SD. An example of a billing category is *Down Payment Request*.

Billing Date: This relates to the date on which the billing is carried out, on the vendor side, and passed on to FI.

Billing Document: Refers to a general term used in SD to denote invoice, proforma invoice, credit / debit notes etc. Each billing document is made up of a header and one or more line items.

Billing Engine: Refers to a tool in SAP which is used for facilitating the process of billing / invoicing. The engine is capable of producing invoices with items from different business transactions.

Billing Plan: In SD, a 'billing plan' refers to a schedule specifying when a specific amount or a percentage will be billed.

Billing Request: Refers to a document, in SD, mentioning the various items of 'billable expenses'. The billing request can be created for sales orders, customer requests etc.

Billing Status: This is the *'document status'*, in SD, as to whether a document has been fully billed or partially billed or relevant for billing.

Bill-to-Party: This refers to a company or a person who will be billed for a delivery. The *bill-to-party* need not be the same as that of the *Payer* or *Sold-to-Party*.

Block Indicator: In FI-AA, this refers to an indicator used to 'block' an asset from acquisition postings.

Blocked Stock: This refers to valuated stock owned by a company, which can not be classified as 'unrestricted' and is not available for normal usage. When making the 'availability check', the system does not take this stock into account, and is regarded as 'not available'.

Blocking Reason: This refers to a key used in SD, for blocking the documents from further processing. There are different keys assigned with different reasons for (a) blocking the delivery – like credit limit, political reasons etc, and (b) blocking the billing – like price missing, calculation missing etc.

Blueprint Generator: In ASAP, the 'blueprint generator' generates a MS-Word document with inputs from 'Q & A database' and 'CI templates'. The *Business Blueprint* consists of the scenarios and process arranged in a logical way to help in the implementation. This is considered to be the

'*Bible*' for the implementation.

Bonded Stock: This refers to the stock or merchandise stored in a *Bonded Warehouse* or admitted into a customs territory or area without paying any customs duty, on the condition that the same would be used for exports or in production of goods for exports, and is not available for sales or use locally.

Book Depreciation: This refers to the valuation of fixed assets, for *Balance Sheet* purposes, based on certain laws relating to financial and accounting transactions. In SAP, the book depreciation is always denoted by *Depreciation Area* 01.

Book Inventory: The stock inventory, in the current period, as per the accounting books. It is necessary to correct the differences, if any, between the actual inventory and the book inventory, and is typically carried at the year closing.

Boolean: Developed in 19th Century by an English mathematician by name, *George Boole*, this is used to represent the logical combinatorial system of representing symbolic relationships using *AND, OR* and *NOT* operators in computer operations. (Example: If A=X, then X is 'true' only when A is 'true').

Boolean Operator: The words *AND, OR* and *NOT* are termed as Boolean Operators. When they are combined in a logical statement, the result is 'true' only when all the individual arguments are 'true'. (Example: If a search query 'xANDy' is true only when both 'x' and 'y' are true).

Branch Account: This refers to the account used to relate the head office with that of the branch offices of a customer or vendor. Each branch account is linked to a head office. When processing receivables or payables for the branch accounts, the transactions are posted to the *Head Office Account*. This is useful in cases of centralized procurements or centralized payments.

Breakpoint: Used in ABAP programming, 'breakpoints' help to interrupt a program at a particular point for analysis and debugging. The breakpoints may be *Dynamic Breakpoints, Static Breakpoints, Event Breakpoints, Keyword Breakpoints* or *Watchpoints*.

Budgeted Balance Sheet: A balance sheet, on a key date, derived from the partial plans of sales plan, production schedule, investment plan, financial budget etc.

Business Application Programming Interface (BAPI): A programming interface facilitating external access to data and processes in SAP. Defined in a repository called *BOR (Business Object Repository)*, BAPIs offer an *Object-Oriented* view of business components in the SAP system, and are implemented and stored as *RFC*-enabled *Function Modules* in the *Function Builder* of the *ABAP Workbench*. A *BAPI Explorer* is used in managing the BAPIs.

Business Area: In FI, this internal organizational unit represents a separate operational responsibility. Separate business area financial statements (both *Balance Sheet* and *P& L* statement) can be created for internal reporting purposes.

Business Area Consolidation: This refers to the grouping based on consolidation Units, with each consolidation unit representing one Company Code and one *Consolidated Business Area*. This helps in bringing out consolidated financial statements for a 'business area' with the internal relationships between its consolidation units removed.

Business Blueprint: This refers to the 2nd phase of in the *ASAP Roadmap*. The deliverable of this phase results in the *Business Blueprint Document* detailing the business processes, scenarios, objects etc identified during the business requirement gathering workshops with the user community. (Refer Blueprint Generator). This 'Bible' helps you to define the '*Baseline Scope*' and also the '*Project Schedule*'.

Business Blueprint Document: This is the main deliverable of the 2nd phase, *Blueprint*, in ASAP methodology of SAP implementation. (Refer Business Blueprint).

Business Configuration Set: Popularly known as *BC set*, these templates contain the configuration settings for customizing SAP for an industry or a corporate group.

Business Explorer: A component of SAP *Business Information Warehouse*, business explorer provides for flexible reporting and analysis tools for strategic analysis to support the decision-making process in enterprises.

Business Impact Map: A tool in ASAP, helping in prioritisation of risk assessment that summarizes the perceived impacts of risks on the business at the division or unit level.

Business Intelligence Cockpit: A web-based control panel with the content from *Business Intelligence (BI)* for providing an overview of all relevant business data to the management, the same way one looks at a news paper. For details, there are hyperlinks, drop-down boxes and push-buttons. As '*i-views*', business intelligence cockpits are integrated with the Enterprise Portal.

Business Partner: This refers to a *legal* or *natural person* (or a group of natural or legal persons) having business interest. The concept of business partner does not refer to an organizational unit in SAP.

Business Process: In CO-ABC, a business process refers to a series of activities involving various departments and consuming costs from a number of cost centres.

Business Process Master List (BPML): In ASAP, this refers to an Excel Spreadsheet listing of SAP business processes / transactions corresponding to the project scope documented in the *Business Blueprint*. The BPML helps in configuring /testing the system in an iterative manner.

Business Process Owner: This refers to the person responsible for creating or generating the Business Blueprint for one or more business processes.

Business Process Procedure (BPP): A MS-Word template, used in ASAP, BPP defines the procedures which correspond to the transactions listed in the *Business Process Master List*. Done in the *Realization Phase* of *ASAP Roadmap*, there will be one BPP for one transaction in the BPML.

Business Scenario: This refers to an application component (like CRM) which uses certain functions of CO to analyse costs and revenues, and to determine the technical settings between the application and CO. (Example: *CRM Sales*)

Business Scenario Questionnaire: Refers to the structured and open-ended questions in *Q & A Database* in ASAP, which enables requirement gathering on business processes or scenario.

Business Segment: This refers to the clearly demarcated sub-activity of a Company relating to the production of a product / service.

Business Workplace: This refers to SAP's equivalent of a desktop which an user can use to process work items, manage and store documents, send and receive mails or messages, and distribute process information across his/her workgroup or among the entire company.

Business XML (bXML): This is SAP's version of the popular XML, used in the transmission of BAPIs with a *BizTalk* envelope and for the transmission of *RFMs*.

Calculation Base: This refers to a collection of *Cost Elements* to which costs will be applied. The customizing can be done to apply the costs either to a single cost element or a group of cost elements. The cost element(s) will be assigned to the calculation base.

Calculation Method: A part of the *Depreciation Key*, the calculation method is used in setting up the parameters for the program which calculates the depreciation. SAP comes delivered with a number of calculation methods like *Base Method, Period Control Method, Declining Balance Method* etc. Except the base method, all other calculation methods are *Chart of Depreciation*-dependent.

Calculation Procedure (for Tax on Sales / Purchases): This is a set of rules defining how to calculate tax on sales and purchases.

Calendar for Invoice Dates: In SD, this refers to a calendar based on which the customers are billed on certain dates. During invoicing the system proposes these dates from this calendar, but the user can over-ride the same.

Cancellation Document: In SD, a cancellation document can be generated to cancel a billing document. When such a document is created, the system copies the data from the billing document to this document and an offsetting entry is posted to FI to square the transaction.

Cancellation Procedure: A set of rules, in SD, used to determine the cancellation date.

Capacity: In CO, this represents the maximum possible output of a cost centre and activity that is technically possible in given time period. In PP, this refers to the maximum capacity of a work centre.

Capacity Levelling: This relates to the exercise of streamlining the work load at various work centres by looking at the over-loads and under-loads.

Capacity Requirement: This is the required output capacity to fulfil the *Work Orders* (production or maintenance orders) and *Planned Orders* during a given time frame.

Capacity Requirements Planning: A tool used, in PP, to determine the available and required capacities. This tool also helps in *Capacity Levelling*.

Capitalization: A procedure used in FI-AA to post the fixed asset values.

Capitalization Method: This is the method specifying the basis for capitalization. A typical basis is the *APC (Acquisition and Production Costs)* for all the newly acquired fixed assets.

Capitalization of AuC: This relates to the accounting procedure used in acquiring an in-house produced asset. The APC collected under AuC will be transferred to another asset, as an AuC is shown under a different balance sheet item. SAP allows transferring the entire costs (*Summary Transfer*), or the same can be transferred on a line-item basis (*Line Item Settlement*).

Capitalized Costs: In CO-PC, this refers to the difference between the actual and calculated costs of an order, calculated using *RA (Results Analysis)*. The system calculates the capitalized costs only when the actual costs exceed the calculated costs: else this difference is shown as the '*realized loss*'.

Capitalized Profit: In CO-PC, this is nothing but the difference between the revenue generatable inventory and the capitalized costs, and is arrived at using *RA (Results Analysis)*.

CAPP Element: This is a method or formula or even a process used in PP to arrive at the *Standard Values*.

Cash Concentration: Refers to a process by which the balances of various bank accounts are transferred to a single header account (*Target Account*) without reducing the balance of any given account below a certain minimum. The closing balance at the target account is now available / used for various financial investments.

Cash Discount: A monetary reward for making payments within a certain period of time.

Cash Discount Base Amount: The portion of the invoiced amount, on which the system calculates the cash discount. This base can also be the entire invoice amount.

Cash Discount Terms: The terms under which cash discount is offered. The *Terms of Payment* definition in SAP provides for 3 different cash discount terms. (Example: 5% cash discount for payment within 10 days, 3% for payment between 10 and 30 days, and due 'net' (no discount) between 30 and 45 days)

Cash Journal: Showing the cash balance at any time (by adding the cash receipts and deducting the cash expenses, from the day's opening cash balance), the cash journal is a compact journal used to record the cash transactions in a double-entry format. Forming a basis for entries in GL, cash journal is also termed as '*Cash GL account*'.

Cash Journal Document: This document contains the business transactions (of a Company Code) in a cash journal, showing the changes in values over a period of time.

Cash Journal Posting: The postings in a cash journal are made up of (1) posting in the cash journal and (2) transferring the cash journal postings to GL. When transferred to the GL, the system creates a follow-on accounting document.

Cash Management Position: Also known as *Cash Position,* this refers to the short-term activity in the bank accounts displaying (1) cash management relevant FI postings to GL and (2) memo records (like payment advice notes) entered for planning purposes.

Cashed Checks: These are all the checks (Cheques) that have been paid by a bank. Banks generate data medium (DME file) which can be used to create postings in SAP.

CCMS: *Computing Centre Management System* or CCMS helps in monitoring & administering SAP system landscapes through a set of tools. CCMS monitors various systems across the landscape, determines & displays statistics on system performance and manages the system by starting / stopping SAP instances, background processing, printing, configuration, database administration etc.

Certificate of Origin: It is an official document declaring the name of the country where in the imported goods have been manufactured.

Change & Transport Organizer: A tool in BC-CTS (*Change & Transport System*) for managing development projects in *ABAP Workbench* and in *Customizing*, and for preparing and managing transporting of objects across SAP systems.

Change Management: In ASAP, this refers to the way the project manages the changes in *Scope, Time, Cost* and *Resources*. This may also refer, in general terms, to handling of SAP objects from one environment to another.

Change Manager: One of the user-roles defined in *SAP Solution Manager's* scenario, the person assigned with the role is responsible for accepting or rejecting a *Change Request* in change management.

Characteristic: In *BW*, this refers to one of the *InfoObject* like a Company Code, fiscal year, region, product etc. The characteristics provide classification possibilities for dataset, and the values are always some discreet names. In *FI*, this relates to the smallest unit in 'e-accounting': these characteristics enable valuation by user-defined categories. But it is mandatory that the standard characteristics like fiscal year variant, currency type, accounting community etc are defined in variant along with the user-defined characteristics. In *CO*, a characteristic refers to a selection criteria like cost centre, cost element, activity type etc. In *CO-PA*, this refers to the criteria used to analyze the sales /profit plan and the operating results. In *EC-CS* (consolidation), this refers to a classification (like the consolidation unit, financial statement item, fiscal year etc) for structuring data.

Chart Engine: An interpreter in the *Internet Graphics Server (IGS),* this is used to generate business graphics and is compatible with Win32 / UNIX /Linux environments. The chart engine is used only in the browser environment and is not compatible with *GUI (Graphical User Interface).*

Chart of Accounts: This is a list of *GL accounts* used in one or more Company Codes for recording the accounting values. For each GL account, the Chart of Account contains the account number, account name and other technical details. A Chart of Account must be assigned to each of the Company Codes and this chart is known as the *Operative Chart of Accounts.* The Company Code may also be assigned to *Country-specific Chart of Accounts* if there is a legal requirement to that effect. Besides these two, there is another Chart of Account called the *Group Chart of Accounts* which is required for consolidation purposes.

Chart of Accounts List: A list of all charts of accounts that can be used in a Client.

Chart of Depreciation: A list of *Depreciation Areas* along with the rules for evaluation of fixed assets that is valid in a country or economic area. Each Company Code needs to be assigned to one chart of depreciation, and more than one Company Code can work with the same chart of depreciation.

Check Lot: The summarization of all incoming checks originating from a single source is called as the 'check lot'. This may also refer to a collection of checks that need to be processed together. All the items of a 'check lot' will have the same 'currency key' and 'value lot' in the *Payment Lot Header* which prevents a different specification at the line item level.

Check Number Lot: The *Number Range* reserved for check number assignment is known as the check number lot.

Check Table: Also known as *Foreign-Key Table*, this is nothing but a Table containing the *Foreign Keys*. If there are two Tables Customer Master (with Customer-id as the *Primary Key*) and Customer Transactions (with Customer-ID as the secondary or *Foreign Key*), when there is a customer transaction the 'customer master' Table is checked to ensure that the customer (Customer-Id) exists in that Table. So, the customer master Table is called as the *Check Table* for the foreign key (Customer-Id) in 'customer transaction' Table. SAP uses the contents of check Table to populate the F4 'drop-down' help.

Check/Bill of Exchange: A financial arrangement that helps the buyer to borrow money in the short term. The buyer uses a check for payment and requests the vendor to draw a bill of exchange on him, at the same time. The buyer then accepts the bill of exchange and discounts the same with his bank thereby getting the required amount. On the due date of the bill of exchange, the bank presents the bill to the buyer who then retires it by making the payment to the bank.

Checkpoint: In ABAP, this refers to the *Breakpoint.* In Logistics, this relates to a physical location on the perimeter wherein all incoming or outgoing traffic (human as well as the transports) are checked-in / out.

Classification of FS Items: This relates a list financial statement items containing all the GL account master records and cost elements, ordered according to accounting principles.

Clean-out Order: In PP, this refers to the order, at the end of a production campaign, meant for preparing the line of production.

Clean-out Recipe: In PP, this refers to the recipe containing the labour / time / material / activity requirements to clean-out a vessel at the end of a production campaign.

Clearing: This refers to a process which results in one or more 'Open Items', in FI, being termed as *paid* or *cleared* or *squared-off*. (Example: An open sales invoice can be 'cleared' by an incoming payment of a matching amount)

Clearing Account: This is a temporary account (also called as *Auxiliary Accounts*) which are cleared from time to time. SAP uses these accounts when there is (1) a time-lag in accounting transactions as in the case of GR/IR clearing, (2) a distribution of tasks among various organizational units as in bank clearing, (3) a need to clarify certain transactions but that will not happen immediately when a transaction is posted.

Clearing Document: This refers to a document generated automatically during clearing. The system, upon *Zero Clearing* or when the *Automatic Clearing Program* is run, generates the document header automatically. The clearing document will not have line items, but there will be a note to indicate that this is a clearing document.

Clearing Procedure: There are two types of clearing procedures available in SAP: '*Account Clearing*' and '*Posting with Clearing*'. Account Clearing enables to clear open items in one currency only, and is used in situation where there is no need for making additional postings to clear the items. In case of open items in more than one currency, 'Posting with Clearing' helps to clear the open items as posting and clearing are possible in one step.

Clearing Transaction: This refers to the 'accounting transaction' triggering the clearing process of open items in FI. (Example: *Incoming payments*)

Clearing Value: In MM, this relates to the sum of the amounts posted to GR/IR Clearing Account when invoices are entered against a business transaction.

Client: This is the self-contained and top-most technical / commercial / organizational unit in SAP, with separate master data and own set of Tables.

Client Copy: The functionality in *Basis administration* that enables copying a Client (*Source Client*), with its entire customizing environment, to a *Target Client*, either in the same SAP system or different SAP system.

Client-Server Architecture: A system group comprising of *Servers* (at the *back-end* which typically store the information or data) and *Clients* (at the *front-end* which typically request service from the servers) connected in a network.

Client-specific Customizing: A task or transaction relating to a single self-contained unit is known as Client-specific customizing. The settings in *Client-specific Tables* are valid only in the Client that is accessed during the log-on, and these settings do not affect other Clients on the system landscape.

Closing Date: This is the last date determining the *period-end*.

Closing Operations: This refers to the execution of a series of steps towards (1) *day-end closing*, (2) *month-end closing* and (3) *year-end closing*.

Cluster Table: The data from several different Tables can be stored together in a *Table Cluster*. Tables assigned to a *Table Cluster* are referred to as *Cluster Tables*. A Cluster Table should be used exclusively for storing internal control information (screen sequences, program parameters, temporary data, and continuous texts such as documentation). The records of all Cluster Tables with the same key are stored under one key in the assigned Table Cluster. The values of the key fields are stored in the corresponding key fields of the Table Cluster. Data of commercial relevance is usually stored in *Transparent Tables*. A Cluster Table, thus, exists only in the *ABAP Dictionary* and not in the database.

CO interface: This program interfaces primarily with FI and also with various other application components like SD, MM, PP, IM etc determining the programs that need to be accessed.

CO Production Order: An *Internal Order* representing a Production Order, in CO-PC, from cost accounting view point.

Collaborative Business Map: Also known as *C-Map*, this *collaborative business map* is a graphical depiction of inter and intra-company business processes, offering several views (business view, interaction view etc) about the business partners involved in the business process, the business benefits etc

Collection: Refers to the collection of FI-AR in general, but bill of exchange in particular, that is already due.

Collection Procedure: This refers to the procedure for *automatic payment settlement* by way of check, bank transfer etc.

Collective Credit Memo: This is a credit memo with a difference that this single credit memo refers to a number of *Purchase Orders*.

Collective Document: Similar to a BOM, this collective document – in PP - contains a structure referencing to a document info record containing both document and text items.

Collective Invoice: In SD, a collective invoice is nothing but a billing document for all the deliveries to a customer, created at the end of a specified period.

Collective Invoice Account: This refers to a special *Contract Account* in FI, where in various line items belonging to different contract accounts are clubbed so as to apply the same *Dunning / Payment Procedure* for all the line items.

Collective Order: In PP, this refers to the linked *Planned / Production Orders* of several production levels.

Commitment: In *FI*, this refers to certain commitments / liabilities like the outstanding orders, open purchase orders, bill liability etc. In *CO,* the commitment refers to the contractual or scheduled commitments - in CO production orders, internal orders, maintenance orders, production orders, sales orders, networks, cost centres etc - that has not yet been passed on to FI but will result in actual expenditure in the future.

Common Area: In ABAP runtime environment, a common area is an *Interface Work Area* of a calling program and an external sub-routine.

Company: A Company – in SAP - refers to the smallest organizational unit for which individual financial statements can be drawn according to the legal / commercial requirements. A company may contain more than one *Company Code,* with all these Company Codes using the same *Operative Chart of Accounts* and the same *Fiscal Year Variant* though they all can use different *Currencies.*

Company Code: This is the smallest organizational unit in FI with self-contained accounts enabling drawing up of financial statements as per the legal / commercial requirements of the country wherein the Company Code is operating. Each Company Code is assigned to an *Operative Chart of Accounts*, and the same chart of accounts can be used by more than one Company Code. One or more Company Codes - with the same operational chart of accounts and the same *Fiscal Year Variant* - constitute a *Company*. Similar to the chart of accounts, a Company Code needs to be assigned to a *Chart of Depreciation* for enabling fixed assets accounting; more than one Company Code can work with a single chart of depreciation though one Company Code can not work with more than one chart of depreciation.

Company ID: This is a user-definable unique 6-digit identifier, used in FI-LC (Legal Consolidation), for denoting a Company.

Company Pair: Representing a pair of Companies having some sender-receiver relationship, this concept is used in FI-LC.

Complex Asset: An asset (with an *Asset Main Number)* made up of several components, each represented by an *Asset Sub-Number*, is termed as a complex asset in FI-AA.

Computer Aided Test Tool (CATT): A tool in SAP for combining and automating business processes as repeatable test procedures to (a) process transactions / transaction chains, (b) check transaction results, (c) to check system messages and (d) generate data. CATT, as a tool for transferring master data, is more suited for data transfer when setting up the system initially if the data load is small.

Concept Check Tool: One of the tools in ASAP, this helps in quality checks - during the first two phases of the implementation road map - on project preparation, configuration settings and technical infrastructure, thereby alerting on potential configuration conflicts or performance issues well in advance.

Condition: In Logistics, a condition determines how the price – net or gross – will be calculated by the system.

Condition Basis: This is the condition type which forms the basis for calculation of taxes or discounts or surcharges.

Condition Category: This refers to a classification of condition according to certain criteria which helps in certain analysis. (Example: discounts, packaging costs, surcharges, output taxes, delivery costs etc)

Condition Record: This contains specific output values – like the product price or a special discount etc – for a given input value (like customer, product etc) and is valid for a specific period of time. (Example: A special discount for a particular customer for a specific period of time)

Condition Table: This is a Table containing price information, in SD, on a master data type, and *Condition Records* are created in the relevant Condition Table. This Table determines the fields combinations that a 'condition record' should be made up of.

Condition Type: In SD, SAP uses condition types to differentiate between the prices in the system as separate condition types are created for price, discount surcharge etc. (Example: discount as a fixed percentage of the price of a product) Each condition type will have its own *Access Sequence, Condition Tables* and *Condition Records*. In CO, there are two condition types namely, (1) *Base Condition Type* and (2) *Overhead Condition Type*. The overhead condition types define the percentage of overhead to be applied to the base condition type. The base condition type specifies the object (like cost element) on which the overhead will be calculated.

Configurable Material: A configurable material is one which can have different variants, and represented by a *Super BOM* containing all components required for producing the variants of the material. It will also have a *Super Task List* for performing all the operations required for producing the variants. An example of a configurable material is a television which can have different screen sizes, cabinet colours etc.

Configuration Assistant: The 'configuration assistant' is used in *Smart Implementations* for configuring *Ready-to-Run R/3 (RRR)* or *SAP ERP* packages. The assistant supports distribution of individual software components to different servers thereby simplifying the integration of the components on a system landscape.

Configuration Case: Used in ASAP, a 'configuration case' represents a business flow with the corresponding inputs, criteria and conditions. The configuration cases are used to configure and fine tune configuration settings.

Configuration Cycle: ASAP comes with four pre-defined 'configuration cycles' aiming at development of configuration and test plans on a fast track. Each of these cycles represent a milestone so as to move to the next level of configuration, and there will always be an overlap from one cycle to another.

Confirmation: In LO (logistics), 'confirmation' refers to a part in order monitoring so as to distinguish between *partial* and *final confirmations*. A final confirmation, in SAP, determines at which work centre the operation was carried out, who carried out the operation, what was the yield including the scrap quantity etc.

Confirming Bank: Also known as the *Advising Bank*, this bank in exporter's country will guarantee the payment of L/C (Letter of Credit) when documents are presented to the bank are correct and presented as detailed in the L/C.

Conhecimento: The name of a freight invoice in Brazil.

ConnTrans: A program, in mobile sales in SAP, allowing you to synchronize data between a mobile Client and its server.

Consignment: This is a type of business wherein the vendor (supplier) maintains his stock of materials at a customer's (buyer) site or warehouse, even though the ownership of the materials lies with the vendor. The buyer is billed only for the portion of the materials used by him and the vendor is notified periodically of the withdrawals from the stock. Such a stock is known as *Consignment Stock*, and the stocked material is known as the *Consignment Material*.

Consignment Order: This relates to the request from the ultimate purchaser to the consignment vendor (external supplier maintaining his stock with the purchaser / customer / company) to replenish the consignment stock.

Consolidated Balance Sheet: This contains all the translated balance sheets pertaining to the individual entities in the consolidation.

Consolidation: Also called as *Legal Consolidation* (FI-LC), this refers to grouping together of financial operating results, according to the *Entity Theory*, of different companies within the corporate group to show the results as if from a single legal entity. This is achieved by (a) consolidation of investments, (b) elimination of payables and receivables, (c) elimination of intercompany profit or loss, (d) elimination of investment income, (e) elimination of revenues / expenses and (f) possible re-classification.

Consumption Cost Element: The cost element corresponds to the inventory change account in the income statement.

Consumption-based Planning: Under MRP in PP, the 'consumption based planning' is divided into (a) re-order point planning, (b) forecast-based planning and (c) rhythmic planning. This kind of planning takes into account the stock requirements as well as the past consumption values for the planning exercise.

Contextual Customizing: This refers to the settings used in several systems as, for example, in a *Global ASAP implementation*. With the *Cross-Client System Viewer*, the configuration settings across multiple systems can be viewed, compared and changed. The setting up of *Currency Table* is a classic example of contextual customizing.

Contract Account: Managed on an 'open-item basis' within contract accounts receivable / payable, a contract account is one wherein the posting data for contracts or contract items are processed in such a way that the same collection or payment agreements apply to all such contracts or contract items.

Control Totals: This refers to the totals to check whether the amounts of posted documents were entered correctly. The system can be set-up in such a way that the 'control totals' are updated when the posting is done in the system.

Controlling (CO): Focused on internal management for informed decision making, CO is nothing but *managerial accounting*. The CO module is, thus, primarily oriented towards managing and reporting cost/revenue. As in with any other module, this module also has (a) configuration set-up and (b) application functionality. The module is oriented towards the internal users, and helps the management by providing reports on cost centres, profit centres, contribution margins & profitability etc.

Controlling Area: A *Controlling Area* is the central organizational structure in Controlling (CO), and is used in *cost accounting*. The controlling area, as in the case of Company Code, is a self contained cost accounting entity for internal reporting purposes. The controlling area is assigned to the Company Code, so as to ensure that the necessary transactions, posted in FI, are transferred to controlling for *cost accounting* processing. A *Company Code* needs to be attached to a controlling area (*1: 1 relationship*); more than one Company Codes can work with the same controlling area (*1: n assignment*). A *Chart of Accounts* can be assigned to more than one controlling area. And, one or more controlling areas can defined under an *Operating Concern*. At the *Client* level, there can be one ore more controlling areas.

Controlling Area Currency: This is the currency in which the cost accounting transactions are performed: it will be the same, by default, as that of the Company Code currency if there is a 1:1 relationship between Company Code and the Controlling Area. It can also be different, if the relationship is '1' controlling area: 'n' Company Codes (*cross-Company Code controlling*).

Corporate Finance Management (CFM): A component of FI, this is meant for analyzing and optimizing business processes in the *Finance Area* of a company. CFM helps in managing in-house cash, market / credit risk / portfolio analysis etc.

Correspondence: This, in FI, refers to all the printed correspondence – like dunning notices, payment notifications, order confirmations etc - of a company.

Cost Base: This, in CO-PC, refers to the quantity on which the costs of a product are based.

Cost Centre: One of the cost objects in controlling, a 'cost centre' represents the location for cost occurrence or collection. The cost centres can be defined based on 'functional requirements' or 'allocation criteria' or 'responsibility for internal management' or just as physical locations.

Cost Centre Group: A collection of a number of cost centres, grouped according to certain criteria.

Cost Centre Hierarchy: A hierarchical arrangement of cost centres as nodes based on certain criteria. There needs to be at least one such hierarchy in a controlling area known as *Standard Hierarchy*. You may also have any number of *Alternate Hierarchies*.

Cost Component: This refers to a grouping of cost elements representing material costs, activity costs etc according to various requirements like material valuation, profitability analysis etc.

Cost Component Group: A condensed view of a group of cost components, in CO-PC, this definition of cost component group is done in customizing. This grouping is different from that of the cost component group used in *Report Writer Reports* - which is a copy of Cost Component Structure - which can contain a maximum of 40 cost components.

Cost Component Split: Refers to the breakdown of costs into 'cost components' – materials, processes and activity types - for providing cost information for accounting purposes. In SAP, there are two types of cost component splits namely (1) primary cost component split and (2) cost component split for *COGM (Cost of Goods Manufactured.* In CO-PC and CO-PA, the split may include material, internal activities, external activities, overhead and others. In *Overhead Cost Controlling (CO-OM)*, a split may comprise of raw materials, labour, energy etc.

Cost Component Split for COGM: This splits the cost of materials into various cost component items, and is used to create the *Standard Price* for a material. This split provides the necessary cost information to CO-PA with *COGM* or *COGS (Cost of Goods Sold)*. Unlike *Primary Cost Component Split,* here the internal activities are shown as secondary cost elements.

Cost Component Structure: This structure, in CO-PC, groups the cost elements into various 'cost components' to show the activity price of an activity type, to arrive at the cost of a process and to calculate the planned cost of a product.

Cost Component View: This is nothing but how the 'material cost estimates' are structured according to the various requirements within the system. It is necessary to define, for each cost component, which portion of its costs is displayed in the cost component view. Some of the cost component views defined in the system include COGS, COGM, sales and administrative costs, physical inventory (commercial / tax) etc.

Cost Element: Comprising of primary and secondary cost elements, a cost element represents a cost carrier either from FI to CO (*Primary Cost Element*) or within CO (*Secondary Cost Element*).

Cost Element Controlling: A component with in CO, 'cost element accounting' represents collection and monitoring of costs in CO.

Cost Element Category: The categorization of cost elements, into material cost elements, settlement cost elements etc, according to their usage in CO.

Cost Element Group: The grouping of cost elements of the same type so as to help in reporting or processing more than one cost element in a single business transaction.

Cost Object: The objects in CO, identified / assigned with costs like production orders, process orders, sales order items, product cost collectors etc. The cost objects decide the nature of postings as to (a) real postings or (b) statistical postings. The objects which are identified only with *statistical postings* are not termed as cost objects (example: profit centres).

Cost Object Controlling: A component within CO-PC, 'cost object controlling' deals with assigning of costs incurred in a company to various activity units of the company for comparing the actual against planned costs, actual and target costs. This controlling component supplies cost data to FI, CO-PA, EC-PCA, actual costing / material costing etc.

Cost of Sales Accounting: A kind of profit and loss statement, showing how the sales revenues match the costs or expenses, representing the economic outflow of various resources of the entity.

Cost Rollup: In CO-PC, this represents the process of allocating / rolling-up of the costs (in material costing) incurred at the lower level of production to the highest level. The costs are rolled-up by cost component. (Example: the direct labour costs in 'assembly' are rolled-up into the COGM as internal labour costs instead of material costs).

Costed Multi-level BOM: Nothing but the itemization of a costed quantity structure, in CO-PC, 'costed multi-level BOM' is the hierarchical overview of all items of a costed material (BOM) according to the material's costed quantity and structure (Routing).

Costing Method: This refers to the method of creating a *Cost Estimate* in CO-PC. The cost estimate may be of *Product Costing, Unit Costing, Multi-level Costing* or *Easy Cost Planning*. Normally, either *Product Costing* or *Unit Costing* is selected when a sales document is costed.

Costing Run: Refers to a process used in CO-PC, for costing a number of materials at the same time. In the case of *Product Cost Planning*, the costing runs (identified by a user-defined name and date) are used to cost materials based on planning data. In contrast, the *Actual Costing / Material Ledger* costing runs (identified by a user-defined name and a period) relate to the costing of materials with the actual data.

Costing Sheet: Used in *CO-OM-OPA (Overhead Orders) / CO-PC* for calculating overhead, in CO-PA for calculating anticipated values and in *CO-OM (Overhead Cost Controlling)* for calculating resource prices, a 'costing sheet' helps to determine how the system calculates various costs. Typically a costing sheet consists of (a) base lines on which the overhead is calculated, (b) calculation lines containing the percentage rates to be applied to the base line(s) and (c) totals lines representing the sum of the base and the calculation lines.

Costing Variant: Refers to variant, in CO-PC, containing all the control parameters for costing like how cost estimates are executed, how costing items are valuated etc. In the case of, for example, *Material Costing*, the variant determines the purpose of the cost estimate, prices for valuating the quantity structure and overheads, applicable dates for actual cost estimates, how BOMs and routings are selected etc.

Country Program: Refers to the program used to make country-specific customizing settings of objects and parameters in SAP. The program takes into account the legal / commercial requirements of the country in question.

Country Template: Relates to a series of customizing settings (with certain master data) supplied by SAP, along with the standard system, to take care of the legal / commercial requirements like depreciation, charts of accounts, taxation etc of a particular county. The *Country Installation Program* is used to install the country templates.

Country Version: A 'country version' relates to the standard SAP functionalities localized for a specific country so as to cover that country's legal and (most of) business requirements. A country version thus contains (1) *Generic SAP* functionalities, (2) *Country-specific* functions which are additional to the generic ones and (3) *Country Template*. As the standard system contains all the country versions (40 in numbers), any number of country versions can run, concurrently, from a single system.

Country-specific Standard Settings: These are all the SAP settings corresponding to the legal / business requirements of a specific country; SAP comes delivered with the settings relating to *Germany* as the standard country-specific settings. The *Country Program* is executed to activate and generate any other country-specific standard settings.

C-Project: A type of project in *SAP Change Manager* as a part of *Solution Manager's Change Request Management* scenario.

Credit Group: One of the control parameters in credit administration in SD, 'credit group' enables that all the business transactions assigned to a particular credit group are treated equally in a credit check routine.

Credit Memo: This refers to a transaction in FI which will bring down the account balance of AR. A credit memo, in SD, is created if the delivered goods turn out to be defective or when there is a mistake in pricing that has resulted in charging a higher price than what was actually agreed upon. This credit memo document, then, will reduce the *Bill-to-Party*'s liability to the vendor (seller).

Credit Memo Request: Before actually making out a credit memo for a customer, to compensate for higher-than-normal price charged or to pass-on a discount which was not put through when the sales was done, the system allows to create a 'credit memo request'. Once this request is approved, then a credit memo is created. The usage is known as *Complaints Processing* in SD.

Cross Application: Known as *CA*, 'cross-application' in SAP refers to an object accessing or 'talking' with many other data objects – Tables or processes or entities –relating to more than one business component / application. (Example: workflow).

Cross-Client: This relates to all the Clients. A setting made in one Client will affect all the Clients. (Example: Exchange rate Table maintenance). The *Cross-Client Customizing* enables logging-on to any of the Clients and making changes that will then be valid in all Clients. The tools like *Cross-System Viewer, Transfer Assistant* etc are used in 'cross-Client customizing'.

Cross-Company Code Posting: A single transaction affecting more than one Company Code is called as 'cross-Company Code porting'. (Example: centralized payments for procurement). The system creates a document for each of the companies involved in the cross-Company Code postings. A *Cross-Company Code Document Number* is used to denote all the documents generated during a single cross-Company Code posting.

Cumulative Activity Price: An activity price which increases by successive additions or accumulation of costs is termed as 'cumulative activity price'.

Currency Type: This is nothing but the currency key to identify the role for a currency like *Local Currency, Group Currency, Hard Currency, Index Currency* and *Global Company Currency*. In addition to the local currency, it is possible to have two more currencies as the *Parallel Currencies*.

Customer: A *Business Partner*, in SD.

Customer Credit Memo: This will be the basis for processing 'credit memo'.

Customer Enhancements: Also known as *Customer Exits*, these are all nothing but the *User-Exits*. These 'empty modification modules' help in putting additional or custom logic to meet the specific requirements of customers. Customer exits are created using the Transaction Code *SMOD*, then selecting the required enhancement by putting through the Transaction Code *CMOD*. All these exits are safeguarded in the future releases of the SAP software.

Customer Group: The grouping of customers for pricing or credit limits or for some statistical purposes. (Example: *DEBI*).

Customizing: This is the overall implementation procedure for setting up SAP system(s) at a customer place, aiming to customize the standard SAP functionality to industry / customer specific business requirements, enhance the standard functionalities and to complete the deployment of the SAP system in time on a cost-effective way. The Transaction Code *SPRO* leads to the initial *Customizing Menu*.

Customizing Cross-System Tools: See Cross-Client.

Customizing Data: Used in customizing, these are 'system settings' data stored in Tables of delivery class *C, G* and *E*. The 'customizing data' also relate to *Project and IMG Documentation*.

Customizing Object: This refers to a set of Customizing Tables / Views that are maintained or transported together. These objects are defined and managed in the *Customizing Object Directory* (Transaction Code *SOBJ*. They are classified as *Standard Objects* (views, Tables etc), *Non-standard Objects* (like transactions, logical transport objects etc) and *Other Objects*. During customizing, typically one moves from customizing initial screen (Transaction Code SPRO) to the customizing maintenance transaction to make new settings or change the existing settings.

Cut-Over: in ASAP, 'cut-over' relates to the transfer of data from the *Quality (Assurance) System / Legacy System*(s) to the *Production System*. A *Cut-Over Plan* details the activities to be carried out during this phase of the implementation.

Cycle: In CO, a 'cycle' represents the rules for cost allocation which are in-turn defined in *Segments*. Thus, one ore more segments constitute a cycle. The rules (relating to the sender / receiver in the segments) are processed iteratively when a cycle is processed.

Cycle Type: This represents the usage of a 'cycle' like distribution, assessment, periodic reposting, indirect activity allocation etc.

Data Archiving: Data archiving relates to the removal of old data – not required any more for the day-to-day operations – from the active database(s) and storing the same in *Archive* files. This helps in reducing the load on the active system(s). If required, the archived data can still be retrieved and accessed.

Data Archiving Process: The *Archiving Process* include (a) reading the data to be removed and writing the same to archive file(s), (b) storing the archive files in a file system or specialized storages and (c) reading the archive files and *'Deleting'* the data which have been *'Marked for Deletion'*.

Data Browser: The data browser is used to display the Table entries, Table fields and texts. The browser enables you to move from the Table to the corresponding 'Check Tables'.

Data Extraction Tool: A tool that enables extraction of 'live' data from a SAP system, and helps in storing the same in a text format.

Data Merge Tool: This tool enables to merge the data extracts created by *DART (Data Archiving Retention Tool)*.

Data Modeler: This enables creation of data models and mapping the same to the *ABAP Dictionary*. All the data models created using 'data modeler' will conform to *SERM (Structured Entity Relationship Model)* in SAP.

Data Monitor: In FI-LC, the 'data monitor' helps to manage the transfer of individual financial statement data into the consolidation system.

Data Rebuild Tool: This tool helps in re-building the data extract done earlier using the 'data extraction tool'. This exercise may be required if there is a time lag between the initial data extraction and usage, and there has been configuration change in between. The tool uses the same data from the initial extract, but rebuilds the same applying the new configuration parameters, if any.

Data Retention Tool: The tool, also called as *DART (Data Archiving Retention Tool)*, helps in extracting and retaining data from SAP systems to meet the legal data retention requirements. Also helping in reporting, the tool extracts the data and stores the same in *'sequential'* files. It also provides tools for viewing the retained data.

Data Transfer Workbench: This is the central tool in SAP for carrying out data transfer to the SAP system(s). Supporting various business objects (like customer / vendor master data), it employs various methods / technologies like *Batch Data Input, Direct Input, BAPIs* etc. Besides this tool, SAP also provides another tool called *LSMW (Legacy system Migration Workbench)*.

Day-end Closing: The checking, at the end of the day, to ascertain whether all the business transactions have been processed correctly in the system.

Dead Stock: Representing the minimum stock level over a period of time, 'dead stock' is a key figure in *Inventory Controlling* for identifying materials with inefficient stock level, for elimination of surplus stocks etc. A higher dead stock is a pointer that the 'safety level' has been set too high.

Debit Memo: Exactly opposite to the 'credit memo', a *Debit Memo* results in an increase in liability of the *Bill-to-Party*, to the vendor or his service agent. This may arise from a situation where a customer has been priced lower than what it should have been or has been provided with more discount than he was otherwise eligible.

Debit Memo Request: Used in *Complaint Processing* in SD, this is opposite but similar to *Credit Memo Request*. The 'debit memo request' is a sales document like a *Standard Order*. Once a debit memo request has been created and approved, then 'debit memo' can be processed in the system

Debit Position: This refers to a receivable posting (A/R) in FI.

Deep Structure: A structure, in ABAP, containing at least one *Deep Component*.

Deep Table: An Internal Table, in ABAP, having one or more *Deep Row Types*.

Default Project: In SAP Customizing, a default project refers to the *Project IMG* which is set as the 'default' so as to have direct access, rather than accessing the same through a 'Display List'.

Deficit Order: This relates to an order in CO-PC wherein the planned costs are more than the planned revenue. The system uses *Results Analysis* calculation to earmark some reserves for such orders.

Definitive Run: An update operation in FI aiming at adjusting GL or asset or material for inflation. The update uses a *Definitive Inflation Index*.

Delete Program: This refers to the program used to delete the data from database after archiving. The deletion is possible only when the record is 'marked for deletion'.

Deletion Flag: Also known as the *Deletion Indicator*, this is an identifier which, when set, enables the *Delete Program* to delete the data from the database.

Delivery Schedule Split: This relates to a function in SD triggering creation of the *Planning Delivery Schedule:* a supplier splits the *Forecast Schedule* lines into *Planning Delivery Schedule* lines for usage in planning and shipping.

Delta Balance Sheet Account: This refers to a FI account in CO-PC, to which the difference between the ending inventory valuation from periodic actual costing and cumulation is posted, with the offsetting entry posted to a re-valuation account.

Delta Customizing: This relates to the IMG activities that are required to be carried out - to make use of new functions in existing business applications – when there is a 'system or release upgrade'. All these IMG activities are collected in a *Project View*. The upgrade needs to be completed before attempting the delta customizing IMG activities.

Delta Posting: This relates to the posting to a delta balance sheet account. Refer *Delta Balance Sheet Account*.

Delta Version: In *Activity Based Costing*, a 'delta version' relates to an additional *Statistical Version* which is based on a *Reference Version*. A delta version enables additional allocations on selected transactions. However, as this is only of statistical significance, no process costs are updated in CO-PA, CO-PC etc. The delta version itself can be a 'reference version' referencing another version.

Demand Planning: In *APO (Advanced Planner and Optimizer)*, this refers to the component enabling forecasting market demand for a company's products so as to produce a demand plan.

Dependency Planning: This is nothing but a type of manual planning in which the primary costs / revenues are calculated as the product of *Activity* quantity or as the quantity of *Statistical Key Figure* and a *Factor* defined by a user.

Dependent Depreciation Area: In FI-AA, this relates to the 'depreciation area' that adopts its values from another depreciation area in the charts of depreciation, with the 'take-over logic' defined there.

Dependent Order: An order – in SCM or APO or PP - that has a relationship or a pegging to another order that needs to be considered in a detailed scheduling.

Depreciation: This is the reduction in the book value of a fixed asset due to its usage over a period of time. The depreciation can be calculated manually (*Unplanned depreciation*) or automatically (*Planned and Special depreciations*) in SAP system.

Depreciation Area: This refers to an area indicating the valuation of a fixed asset. The depreciation areas can be *Book Depreciation (01), Depreciation as per Income Tax Act (15) Cost Accounting Depreciation (20) etc*. Along with these 'real' depreciation areas, SAP allows to define '*Derived Depreciation Areas*' wherein the values are derived (calculated) from two are more 'real' areas.

Depreciation Base: The asset value which is considered as the base for calculating depreciation. The depreciation base may be the *APC (Acquisition & Production Costs), Net Book Value (NBV)* or *the Replacement Value*.

Depreciation below Zero: The depreciation continued even after reaching zero value of the asset, resulting in *Negative Book Value*, is known as 'depreciation below zero'. This is controlled by a key which indicates whether a particular asset is continued to be depreciated even after reaching zero book value. The concept is useful for calculating the *Imputed Costs* on an asset, after the planned life of the asset.

Depreciation Forecast: This is the projected depreciation, calculated either manually or by the system, of assets during a fiscal year. All the transactions occurring in these assets result in adjustment of the forecast already created.

Depreciation Key: The 'depreciation key', used in calculation of depreciation values, contains all the control parameters including the depreciation methods, for each of the depreciation areas, for automatic calculation of depreciation and interest.

Depreciation Method: The method of depreciating an asset - *Straight Line Depreciation, Sum-of-Year-Digits, Declining Balance* etc - is known as the 'depreciation method'.

Depreciation Period: The periodicity with which depreciation is calculated is referred to as the 'depreciation period', which normally corresponds to the *Posting Periods* in FI. SAP allows depreciating using *Half-Periods* as well.

Depreciation Trace: A system trace of different hierarchical steps in carrying out the depreciation. This is useful to pin-point the errors occurring during a calculation.

Depreciation Type: The classification of depreciation based on certain criteria, is known as the 'deprecation type'. SAP supports various depreciation types like (a) *Ordinary Depreciation*, (b) *Special Depreciation*, (d) *Un-planned Depreciation* and (e) *Depreciation for Write-off Reserves*.

Detail Management: A tool helping in the creation / editing of organizational units, and their assignments / relationships, in SAP.

Detailed Planning: Using exact data and time, a 'detailed planning' in CO-PP is based on 'routing' for short-term planning of individual capacities / people.

Determination Procedure: This refers to a structure, in SD's *Condition Technique*, outlining the order in which the system is expected to execute the *Calculation / Processing Steps* while determining the prices or discounts etc.

Development List: In ASAP, this is a development list referring to a MS-Excel spread sheet as a report from *Q & A Database*, containing all the structure elements (like reports, interfaces, data transfers etc) of the implementation scope corresponding to *BASIS* area of SAP. The list, generated during the *Realization Phase*, helps in managing the *Functional and Technical Specification* relating to all these elements, in a more structured way.

Development Review: This, in ASAP, helps to review the design and implementation of custom developments to ensure that they adhere to the established standards in design and development.

Diagram Explorer: Refers to a built-in tool of *'Q & A Database'* enabling to view the contents (and also the assignments among the organizational units, input/output relationships etc) of *R/3 Reference Structure.*

Direct Access: Refers to a method relating to the *Read-Only* access of the archived data.

Direct Capitalization: Refers to the acquisition of an asset wherein the costs are directly posted to the asset, instead of posting the same to an AuC or Order etc.

Direct Input: One of the methods of data transfer, 'direct input' is an alternative to Batch Input. The direct input method results in faster data upload with the SAP function modules doing the consistency checks (instead of screens doing checks as in the 'batch input' method).

Direct Payer: The customer who is also the payer, in SD, is known as the 'direct payer'.

Direct Quote: A currency value expressed in terms of local currency per unit of a foreign currency is known as the direct quote or *Direct Quotation* or *Price Notation.* (Example: 1 USD (Foreign currency) = 41 INR (Local currency).

Discounting: Refers to a practice of presenting 'bills of exchange' to a bank - before the due date - for getting the payment for the same. The bank deducts discount (nothing but the interest for the period between the due date and bill presentment date) and a commission before making the payment to the presenter.

Distribution: A business transaction, in CO, referring to the allocation of *Primary Costs.*

Distribution Channel: Refers to a channel –like retail, wholesale, direct sales etc – through which products / services sold reach the end customers. One or more distribution channels are assigned to a *Sales Organization.*

Distribution Rule: Forming a part of a *Settlement Rule*, this 'distribution rule' defines (a) settlement receiver, (b) settlement type – periodical or total, (c) settlement share (total or proportional) and (d) validity period for the distribution rule, for a settlement sender.

Division: Refers to an organization unit, in SD, that is responsible for the sales / profits from a saleable material or service. For each of this division, you may define and maintain customer-specific parameters like terms of payment, pricing etc. The division may come under one or more *Distribution Channels.*

Document: A proof of a business transaction, a document in FI may be a (a) original document – invoices, bank statements etc or (b) data processing document – accounting documents, sample documents, recurring entry documents etc. A document – like Sales document, Billing document, Shipping document etc - in SD relates to a printed record of business transaction.

Document Date: Refers to a date on which the original document – like the invoice in FI, Shipping document in SD etc – is created.

Document Extract: In MM, this refers to a program that transfers the valuation information from documents in SAP to the Tables for FIFO / LIFO valuation.

Document Flow: This represents the sequence of documents in a business transaction. (Example: A document flow in SD may represent *Quotation > Sales Order > Delivery > Invoice*).

Document Header: The portion of a document the details of which applies to all the line items in a document is known as the 'document header'. (Example: Document Date, Document Type, Document Number, Company Code etc).

Document ID: Refers to a unique description assigned to an 'archived' document.

Document Number: A number identifying a document in a Company Code in a fiscal year is known as the 'document number'. SAP provides the capability to assign *Internal* or *External Number Ranges* to documents used in the business transactions.

Document Principle: Refers to the basic principle in SAP transaction processing representing that postings are always stored in a document form.

Document Type: The 'document type' helps to classify a business / accounting transaction within the system, and is used to control the entire transaction determining the account types a particular document type can post to. For example, the accounting document type *'AB'* allows you to post to all the accounts, where as type *'DZ'* allows you to post only to the customer payments. Every document type is assigned to a 'document number range'.

Down Payment: A portion of the full price paid at the time of purchase or delivery with the option to pay the balance later. The down payments are shown separately in the balance sheet: *Down Payments Made* are shown as part of fixed / current assets, and *Down Payments Received* are shown as a part of Payables). In FI-AA, down payments relate to the payments made for an AuC.

Down Payment Request: Refers to a request made that a down payment be made at certain point of time. Down payment requests – identified by a *Special GL Indicator* called 'F'' - are *Noted Items* as they do not update any GL transaction figures, and are never shown in the financial statements. They are also termed as *Memo Entries* as they serve to keep track of such obligations.

Due Date for Net Payment: This refers to the due date for payment with no discount being eligible on that transaction. This is the farthest date for payment in a *Terms of Payment*.

Dunning: This relates to the reminding of business partners about their payments which are due. The system 'duns' the *Open Items* from business partner accounts. Dunning is administered through a *Dunning Program*.

Dunning Amount: This corresponds to the total of all the due items outstanding to be dunned, for a *Dunning Group*.

Dunning Area: Refers to an organizational unit for which the 'dunning' is carried out. It is optional, and is required only if dunning is not done at Company Code level. The dunning area can correspond to a *Sales Division, Sales Organization* etc.

Dunning Block Indicator: An indicator, defined with a *Dunning Block Reason* that helps to block certain accounts or line items from being dunned.

Dunning Key: Refers to a key that is used to identify the *Dunning Level* that needs to be used during a particular 'dunning run' for a particular account or item.

Dunning Level: This indicates how often dunning is carried out, for an account or an open item. Once dunned, the system automatically updates the dunning level information so that the correct level is selected when the dunning is done the next time.

Dunning Procedure: Refers to the specifications of how the customers / vendors are dunned during a *Dunning Run*. The dunning procedure defines the *Dunning Levels*, controls the *Dunning Intervals*, determines the transactions to be dunned, determines the interest to be applied etc.

Dunning Recipient: The business partner, who will receive the dunning notices, is known as the dunning recipient. This recipient need not be the customer.

Dynamic Credit Check: During the 'dynamic credit check', the system will ignore all orders beyond the *Credit Horizon Date*. The dynamic credit check is split into 2 parts (a) *Static Limit* and (b) *Dynamic Limit* – nothing but the *Open Order Value*. The sum total of Static and Dynamic limits should not exceed the *Credit Limit* established for the customer.

Early Watch Service: A remote diagnostic service provided by SAP to identify and resolve bottlenecks and issues in a new SAP implementation or in an existing production system.

Easy Cost Planning: Refers to a way of planning costs - based on *Costing Models* - quickly and easily for cost objects like internal orders, WBS elements, internal service requests etc.

ECC Number: Refers to the number assigned by tax authorities of India, to legal / natural persons for each of the registered premises like factory, warehouse, dealer centre, etc.

EDI: *EDI (Electronic Data Interchange)* refers to the cross-company exchange of business transactions data, in predefined electronic format, among domestic / international business partners having a number of hardware, software and communication infrastructures.

EDI Inbound Processing: This relates to the processing of incoming EDI data into the SAP system: the incoming data is first converted to SAP's standard format *IDoc* (by an EDI sub-system) before transferring the same into SAP. Upon transfer, SAP evaluates the incoming system and converts the same into appropriate business transaction, for example, *Purchase Orders*.

EDI Outbound Processing: The business application transaction data, like *Purchase Order*, is first converted into a SAP standard *IDoc (Intermediate Document)* by the EDI sub-system which transmits the same to an external system in a standard EDI format.

EDIFACT: Refers to an international, branch-independent EDI standard known as *Electronic Data Interchange for Administration, Commerce and Trade*.

Edited Table: A formatted display of fields in a Table enabling clear Table display for easy data entry and editing is known as an 'Edited Table' in ABAP Dictionary.

EBPP: *Electronic Bill Presentment and Payment* (EBPP) refers to the conversion of bills of exchanges into an electronic format which then can be linked to (a payment service) a bank.

Elimination Entries: These – like the elimination entries for payables & receivables, revenue & expenses, inventory profit & loss etc - together with other consolidation entries aid in transferring the individual summarized financial statements into 'consolidated financial statements', in FI-LC.

Elimination Difference: The difference arising out of eliminating inter-company payables and receivables, revenues and expenses etc is known as the 'elimination difference' which can arise because of exchange rate or other differences.

ELSTER: Refers to the electronic tax return, in Germany, and describes a procedure according to which companies in Germany must send their tax data to the tax offices.

End-to-End Scenario: In ASAP, this relates to a complete business flow cutting across various functional modules or components to complete the entire cycle of operation.

End-user Documentation: Refers to the company-specific documents prepared, in ASAP, for training the end-user community in the implemented SAP functionalities. These documents often serve as the 'reference' for the business procedures and the policies for the company people. *Business Process Procedure* (BPP) document prepared earlier would be the ideal starting point for preparing the 'end-user documentation'.

Engineering Change Management (ECM): Refers to an application component in *Logistics* that allows objects to be changed with history or with certain conditions (parameters). SAP allows changing the object types – like BOM, Task List, Documents, Materials etc – with a 'change number'.

Enterprise Controlling: An application component in SAP focused on *EC-CS (Enterprise Controlling-Consolidation)* and *EC - PCA (Enterprise Controlling – Profit Centre Accounting)*.

Enterprise Data Model: Refers to a semantic data model showing the entities and their relationships, in SAP.

Enterprise Information System (EIS): Refers to the information infrastructure of an ERP system.

Enterprise Intelligence (EI): This refers to, in *CRM*, the collection of *AI (Artificial Intelligence)* tools like *Intelligence Agent* and *Knowledge Management Tools* like *SDB (Solution Database)*. SAP's EI is very powerful in allowing the company to dynamically gather, organize and analyse comprehensive information for effective customer interactions.

Enterprise Model: Refers to the sub-set of *'SAP Reference Model'* or *'Industry Model'* for depicting the SAP functions required in a company.

Enterprise Organization: A logical representation of various organizational units – Company Code, Controlling Area, Cost Centre, Cost Centre Groups, Profit Centre, Profit Centre Groups, HR Organizational Units etc - indicating their relationships.

Enterprise Portal: A portal application from SAP allowing a company to integrate application, services and information on a browser-based user interface, is called as the 'enterprise portal'.

Enterprise Structure: Refers to the hierarchical depiction of various organizational units defined for company. This structure may be of a (1) *Logical Structure* – like the plant, cost centre, sales area, channel, purchasing organization etc and (2) *Social Structure* – like departments, divisions, HR units etc.

Environment Health & Safety (EHS): The application component within SAP to take care of the health and safety at the workplace besides taking care of the environment is called as EHS. The application addresses product safety, dangerous goods movement, waste management, occupational health hazards etc.

EOG Order: In PP, this refers to an order created using extended order generation. To facilitate bottom-up propagation of characteristics of a product, the EOG order contains only one operation so as to split the product.

Equal Distribution: This refers to a situation in which, independent of the order quantities, the system distributes equally the available stock to all the orders.

Equipment BOM: This is nothing but the list describing the structure of equipment and the spares for maintaining that equipment.

Equivalence Numbers: The weighing factor, in CO-CCA, used to distribute the planned costs - that are not planned by activities – to the individual activities of a cost centre.

Escape Sequence: Relates to the printer-specific operations / commands to control print operations.

Estimated Cost to Complete: Relates to the total costs expected, for a project when it is completed based on costs that have already been incurred on that project and based on the information of *Cost to Complete*.

Euro Workbench: A tool enabling planning, monitoring and executing Euro conversion related activities during the *Dual Phase* of the currency.

Eurojapan: Refers to the blended code pages, in ABAP, containing scripts of German, English, French, Italian, Danish, Dutch, Finnish, Norwegian, Portuguese, Spanish, Swedish and Japanese.

Evaluation Criteria: In MM, this refers to the criteria used in evaluation of vendors. The evaluation criteria will be stored on an *Evaluation Record* containing header and line items.

Evaluation Group: this is one of the fields in an asset master record that can be used for classifying the fixed assets. The evaluation groups can be used in reporting as well as accessing individual assets belonging to an evaluation group.

Evaluation Structure: The structure on which the data analysis for *LIS (Logistics Information System)* is based on is known as the 'evaluation structure' and is made up of (1) *Characteristics* (sales organization, purchasing organization etc) and (2) *Key Figures* (invoice value, sales volume etc).

Exception Handling: Refers to process that is triggered when there are errors in exception situations in IDoc processing, and these errors occur in the application or interface IDoc layer.

Exchange Rate: The rate at which one currency is exchanged for the other.

Exchange Rate Category: The key that identifies and stores exchange rates in the system is known as the exchange rate category; the category is used to store multiple rates for different purposes on the same date in the system.

Exchange Rate Difference: Refers to the difference in the valuation when a currency is translated using two different exchange rates.

Exchange Rate Type: Indicating the type of exchange rate in the system, this refers to buying rate, selling rate, average rate etc.

Exchange Rate Variance: In PP, this refers to the variance occurring because of changes in the price of the objects due to the fluctuations in exchange rates.

Excise Document: The system document used in excise transactions in SAP. The excise document may be an excise invoice, sub-contracting challans or ARE documents (ARE-1, 2 etc).

Excise Invoice: In a country like India, an 'excise invoice refers' to business document which is issued when excisable goods are sold to a customer (or moved to another plant) from the manufacturing plant.

Execution Service: Refers to the process triggered by cost planning with *Easy Cost Planning*, in controlling in SAP. The service may trigger purchase requisitions, purchase orders, reservations, GI etc.

Executive Menu: The compilation of various menus – mostly of non-customizing menus - under *EIS (Executive Information System)*.

Export Ledger: Refers to an additional ledger in *FI-SL (Special Purpose Ledger)* when the data is to be sent from a local system to a central system. This export ledger stores all the data that have been sent to the central ledger; if data are to be sent more than once, only the incremental changes, over the last export, are sent to the central system.

Extendable IMG Activity: This is nothing but a customizing activity that includes a *CMOD* exit or any other user-exit.

Extendable Material: Refers to a material that has some data which are yet to be maintained by other user departments.

External Processing: Refers to the operations of one company performed at another company.

Extract: In FI-SL, this is nothing but the extracted data for reporting.

Fact Sheet: In CRM, this refers to consolidated but concise information relating to a business partner. The information comes from a variety of sources like master data, statistical information, reports etc.

Fact Table: In BW, this refers to the central Table of an *InfoCube Star Schema*, containing all Key figures.

Factory Calendar: The 'factory calendar', defined on the basis of a *Public Calendar*, contains sequentially numbered working days. The validity period of a factory calendar has to be within the validity period of the public calendar.

FERT Generator: Refers to the functional enhancement, in SD, of *Variant Configuration* enabling production of storable finished good with their own master records from a *Configurable Material* instead of *Material Variants*.

Fictitious Cash flow: This refers to a part of a real transaction but there is no actual physical cash flow involved. Since it is not a physical flow, it is not included in any of the *NPV (Net Present Value)* calculations but needs to be included in any of the *Gap* analysis.

FIFO: Referring to First-In-First-out, this encompasses both FIFO *Withdrawal Method* and *FIFO Valuation Procedure*. The assumption here is that the first withdrawn material from the inventory was the one received first into the stock.

Final Backflush: In a *Repetitive Manufacturing* in PP, as a background job the system performs final confirmation with a 'final backflush', wherein the BOM is exploded, goods movements are posted, planned orders are reduced, and finally the costs & statistics are updated.

Final Configuration: The result of an iterative configuration process, starting with the *Baseline Configuration* based on *Business Blueprint* and expanding through the configuration cycles to reach the final solution ready for delivery.

Final Cost Centre: The bottom-most cost centre which does not have any sub-ordinate cost centres below it.

Final Costing: In CO-PC, this refers to the cost estimate of an activity based on the actual costs incurred for that activity. Besides determining and monitoring the costs, final costing enables comparing Actual Costs with the Target Costs.

Final Preparation: Representing the *Phase-4* of the *ASAP Implementation Roadmap*, 'final preparation' provides the structure and framework for complete *Final Testing, User Training,* and *Cut-Over Preparation (*data and system) for making the system 'live'.

Financial Document: Refers to a document used in *Documentary Payments* in *Foreign Trade*.

Financial Statement Imbalance: Refers to a situation wherein a transaction is posted to both the profit & loss account(s) and balance sheet accounts. SAP calculates the imbalance, in EC-CS, and posts the relevant adjustments automatically.

Financial Statement Version (FSV): This is the hierarchical arrangement of GL accounts based on certain (statutory) requirements. SAP comes delivered with country-specific versions, which can be copied and modified.

Finish-Finish Relationship: In PS (Project Systems), this refers to a relationship where a new activity can not start unless the predecessor one is finished.

Firm Zone: In *MM Purchasing*, this refers to the delivery schedule time frame within which all the schedule lines are construed as binding and confirmed. If there is firm zone of, say, 30 days, then all the schedule lines with the delivery dates not more than 30 calendar days from the current date are considered as firm and the orders are known as *Fully Binding Orders* or *Purchase Commitments*.

First Consolidation: In FI-LC / EC-CS, this refers to the activity which brings-in an organization for the first time into the consolidated financial statements as a subsidiary.

First Customer Shipment: Refers to the initial delivery of SAP software to a limited number of customers, to test and validate (not meant for any productive purpose) a technical upgrade of the software or the implementation itself.

First Productive Customer Programme: Refers to a service program for customers who want to 'go-live' with the *Controlled Availability (CA)* release. The customers with 'CA Release' need to get a prior approval form SAP before 'going-live'.

First Teach: Refers to a course conducted for the SAP customers for the first time. This course material will undergo changes based on the feedback from the 'first teach' sessions.

Fiscal Year: This is nothing but the period – normally made up of 12 months – for which a company draws up their financial statements and values their inventory. The fiscal year can be a *Calendar Year* or *Non-Calendar Year*. The fiscal year need not necessarily have 12 months (periods); in cases if the fiscal year is less than 12 periods, then it is known as *Shortened Fiscal Year*.

Fiscal Year Variant: One of the important configuration elements in FI, a 'fiscal year variant' helps in defining the relationship between the calendar and fiscal years, specifying the number of *Posting Periods* and *Special Periods* required in a fiscal year. There can be a maximum of 12 posting periods and 4 special periods in a GL accounting; however, the special periods can go as high as 365 in case of *Special Purpose Ledgers*. In EC-CS, when the consolidation elements use different fiscal year variants, it becomes important to convert these periods before transferring the financial data for consolidation.

FIX Value: This refers to the field value of a *Business Configuration Set (BC Set)* which is set as 'fixed' so that the value can not be modified in the target system during customizing.

Fixed Asset Balance Sheet Account: As against the *Accumulated Depreciation Account* wherein only the depreciation values are posted, 'fixed asset balance sheet accounts' are the GL accounts to which the *Acquisition and Production Costs (APC)* of fixed assets are posted to.

Fixed Depreciation: This relates to the portion of the depreciation that is not affected by the usage while calculating the depreciation. SAP enables to configure an asset to be depreciated both as 'fixed' and 'variable'. The *Multiple-Shift* factor is applied on the variable portion to calculate depreciation which varies with the usage.

Fixed-Cost Variance: This is nothing but the difference between the planned and actually allocated fixed costs, and is calculated only in the case of *Overhead Cost Controlling*.

Flexible General Ledger: An enhancement to the normal GL accounting, 'flexible GL' incorporates *SAP Dimensions* (profit centre, cost centre etc) and also the *Customer Dimensions* (region etc). The flexible GL, requiring only a minor configuration as against the *Special Ledgers*, enables year-end closing in both *Period Accounting* and *Cost of Sales Accounting*.

Flexible Upload: This is used in EC-CS to upload data from a front-end non-SAP system to SAP system, for initial and additional financial data upload.

Flow Logic Editor: Offering some of the functionalities of *ABAP Editor*, this is used in *Screen Painter* for entering the 'screen flow logic'.

FM Area: One of the organizational units in SAP, *Financial Management (FM)* areas helps in carrying out funds management.

Foreign Currency Valuation: Refers to the determination of the value of current assets / liabilities posted in a foreign currency, at a *Key Date*.

Form Painter: One of the ABAP tools. *Form Painter* helps in designing *SAPscript Forms* using either the (1) *Graphical Form Painter* or (2) *Alphanumeric Form Painter*.

Format Tree: Refers to the *DME* file format defined by an external organization like a bank.

Forward Scheduling: In PP, this refers to the scheduling the operations of an order forward, starting from the planned date. The 'forward scheduling' helps in arriving at the scheduled start / end dates.

FPC: *FPC* refers to the *First Productive Customer*, who participates in *CA (Controlled Availability)* releases of SAP software.

Framework Order: Having an extended validity period instead of a fixed delivery date, this *Purchase Order* is used to procure external material or resources, for accelerating the procurement process. The *Order Type 'FO'* is assigned to a framework order.

Free-of-Charge Delivery: In SD, this is a type of sales document used to deliver free samples to customers.

Front-end Statistics: In CCMS, this refers to the workload statistics, containing the volume of data sent / received along with the front-end time, of individual presentation servers.

FS Chart of Accounts: The chart of accounts used in EC-CS to record values and value streams in group accounting to generate consolidated financial statements, is known as the 'FS chart of accounts'.

Function Builder: The 'function builder' in ABAP, containing *Function Library*, enables creation, testing and documenting 'function modules'.

Functional Area: An organization structure based on *Cost of Sales Accounting*, functional area helps in classifying the expenses of an organization by functions like administration, sales & distribution, production, marketing etc. In CO, all the cost objects need to be assigned to a functional area.

Functional Specification: In ASAP, *Q & A Database* is used to collect the requirements, from a technical point of view, for enhancements, interfaces, reports etc, and the document which documents these requirements is called as the *Functional Specification*.

Functionality Releases: The upgrade version of the existing release of SAP software, - usually to correct major software errors like *Prioity-1 problems* - for introducing new or improved business process (es). All the functional releases are released as *Hot Packages*.

Future Standard Cost Estimate: Nothing but a 'material cost estimate' for the next period, the 'future standard cost estimate' helps in establishing the future standard price.

GL Account: Representing the account items in a *Chart of Accounts*, these accounts record the value movements in a Company Code. The transaction values are recorded per *Posting Period* in the GL accounts, the totals of which are used in reporting.

GL Account Document: An accounting document used to record the transactions in *General Ledger* for a Company Code, this contains a minimum of two line items whose balance is always zero.

GL Account Master Record: Besides the account number, name of the account etc, a 'GL master record' also contains control parameters on how data is entered into a GL account. The record also contains parameters controlling creation of the master records.

GL Increase Account: In *SBO (SAP Business One)*, this account is an *Offsetting Account* used for recording negative differences arising out of inventory valuation.

GA Release: Referring to the *General Availability (GA) Release*, unlike a *CA Release* which can not be used in a productive system without SAP's prior approval, this can be used by customers even in 'live' systems without any restrictions. *Support Packages* are provided by SAP for the GA releases aiming to correct software errors.

Gain Posting: Refers to posting of gains, being the difference between the revenue realised during sale of an asset and its *Net Book Value (NBV)*.

Gantt Chart: An outcome of *PMBOK (PM Body of Knowledge)*, this refers to the graphical representation of schedule related information, as bars with the activity or task name, task duration etc, in 'project planning'.

General Cost Object: Refers to an independent cost object, in CO-PC, that can be used in a variety of operations like planning and collection of costs.

General Download: Refers to the downloading of master data – exchange rates, versions, dimensions, FS chart of accounts etc – from a consolidation system to a front-end personal computer for data entry using MS-Access.

General Recipe: In PP-PI (Process Industries), this refers to a general description of a production process, outlining the products, components, resources, processes required, which is plant and site-independent.

General Storage Area: In *LE-WM (Warehouse Management)*, this area refers to a form of storage organization wherein only one *Storage Bin* is defined for each of the storage locations, and the *Quants* stored in this area is of mixed storage.

Generic Business Tools: These tools, in SAP, refer to the various functions used by the developers as well as end-users, to send e-mails, used to start, schedule and stop certain operations, organizing appointments etc.

Geocoder: A tool available to convert an address into *GEO-Coordinates* – longitude and latitude of that location - is called as the Geocoder.

Global Company Currency: With SAP allowing the use of more than one currency in accounting, this 'global company currency' refers to the currency used for an internal *Trading Partner*.

Global Implementation Program: Referring to the overall activities, in ASAP, to be performed for implementing SAP for an entire corporate group, this implementation program is made up of (1) *Global Activities* and (2) *Local Activities*. The local units are defined, and assigned to a global reference system based on the *Global Template*.

Global Ledger: In *FI-SL (Special Purpose Ledger)*, this 'global ledger' contains data of Company Codes assigned to Companies. Because of this assignment, when an account is posted in the Company Code, it is posted to the local ledger of the Company Code and also in the global ledger.

Global Program Core Team: The team (comprising of employees of management team, user departments and IT departments) is freed from other routine operations but engaged in the ASAP *Global Implementation Program*. This team will stay through the entire duration of the program from template design, development to rollout activities.

Global Reference System: The SAP system installed at the corporate headquarters of a company, containing global templates and shared data, serving as the common and reference source of configuration for rolling-out the implementation to other smaller downstream units, is known as the global reference system.

Global Release: This refers to the global roll-out projects using the global reference system.

Global Rollback Process: A process by which the system settings / configurations or the results of multiple local systems are rolled back into the global templates of a global reference system.

Global Rollout: This refers to a process by which the global template is installed in a local environment with modification suited to the local situation, leading to a local production system.

Global Standards: The agreed-upon criteria to be used in all the local SAP system are known as the 'global standards'.

Global Template: A collection of global requirements - *Models, IMG Projects, Customizing, Documentation, Data and Tests, System Topology and Transports, Customer Developments* etc - for subsequent roll-out to the global subsidiaries during SAP implementation.

Global Template Version: Refers to a template version created by maintaining an existing template. The template version so created will be rolled-out globally.

Go-Live: A part of the final phase (5th) in *ASAP Roadmap* wherein the SAP system is declared 'productive' or 'live' marking the end of the implementation and signalling that the system is now ready for commercial or business use.

Go-Live & Support: The 5th and final phase of *ASAP Roadmap* signalling the move from pre-production to 'production' environment. The implementation team sets up a *Help Desk* to provide 'post-go-live support' for users and to optimise system performance.

Goods Clearing Account: In *SBO (SAP Business One)*, this is an offsetting account used to park the open amounts arising out of closure of purchase documents.

Goods Transit: Relating to the goods that have been shipped to the customer, these can be taken into account in the calculation of *Results Analysis*, which can be capitalized in the balance sheet.

Goods Movement: Refers to the logical or physical movement of materials resulting in changed stock levels for that material.

Goods Receipt (GR): Referring to the physical inward movement of materials / goods, the GR can be against a purchase order, can be with reference to a production order or even without any reference at all.

Goods Receipt (GR)-based Invoice Verification: An invoice verification procedure enabling assignment of incoming invoices and deliveries to purchase order item, is known as the 'GR based invoice verification'. When defined for an order item, this enables entering an invoice with reference to a *GR Document* or *Delivery Note Number* for that item, at the time of GR. As a result, the system generates separate invoice for each GR. The system further enables validating the price and invoice accuracy at the item level.

Goods Receipt (GR) Blocked Stock: Not to be confused with the *General (non-GR specific) Blocked Stock,* 'GR blocked' stock refers to the stock received from a vendor which has been conditionally accepted but not yet regarded as the part of the inventory.

Graphical Screen Painter: One of the two lay-out editors in *Screen Painter*, this graphical mode supports *Drag & Drop* functionality for faster developments. Refer *Form Painter* also.

Group BOM: Created in the design phase before assigned to one or more plant for production, a group BOM is valid across the entire company and is not assigned to a specific plant.

Group Condition: In SD, this refers to a condition that can be used to determine the scale value of one or more items in a document wherein the system groups these items using the *Condition Key* for the appropriate *Condition Record*.

Group Costing: In CO-PC, this is nothing but the costing function calculating the value added for multiple profit centres across Company Codes, with the 'cost component split' generated for various partners like plant, profit centre, Company Code, business area etc.

Group Currency: In FI-LC, this refers to the currency used in the consolidated financial statements. When individual entitities are consolidated, the individual financial statements in the *Local / Transaction Currency* are translated into the group currency.

Group Reference System: Refer Global Reference System.

Group Template: Refer Global Template.

Group Template IMG: Refers to a *Project IMG*, denoting the scope outlined in a *Global Template* used for local roll-outs.

Group Valuation: Referring to the valuation of fixed assets of subsidiaries for consolidation into total fixed assets for the entire group concern, the 'group valuation' can be carried out separately in local currency as well as in the reporting currency for various depreciation areas.

Handheld Customizing: Refers to the customizing settings necessary for running SAP CRM handheld devices.

Hand-over Workshop: Refers to a two-day practical training at the customer site, this workshop aims at preparing the administrator, for *Ready-to-Run R/3 (RRR) System*, to carryout the various tasks.

Hard Currency: Refers to the country-specific second currency used in accounting, when there is a high rate of inflation in a country.

Heap: This is the memory area reserved by the system to store the data generated during the 'runtime' of a program.

Hierarchy: Consisting of nodes at various levels, a hierarchy helps to arrange the CO objects like cost centres, orders, WBS etc. All the nodes other than the end-nodes are used only for summarizing purposes.

Hierarchy Structure: In Customizing, hierarchy structure refers to a Table of *Hypertext* links which can be used for carrying out customizing or for accessing documentation.

House Bank: Refers to the designated bank through which the internal transactions of a Company Code are processed.

HR Master Data: Refers to the master data – personnel number, name, bank details etc - of employees that remain almost permanent in the system.

HTML Business Editor: A tool for editing HTML templates in '*SAP@Web Studio*', the editor helps in design, maintenance and testing of HTML templates and flow files.

IC Elimination: Refers to the 'inter-company elimination', in FI-LC, of payables / receivables, revenues / expenses and profit / loss. Refer *Elimination Entries* also.

ICMS: Referring to a percentage-included tax, this is a VAT levied at the circulation of goods and services in Brazil. ICMS is known as *Imposto sobre Circulação de Mercadorias e Serviços in Portugese.*

ICO Number: This is number used to identify a company in countries like Czech Republic and Slovak.

IDES: Internet Demo and Evaluation System, IDES contains several companies with sample business processes typical to the countries wherein these sample companies are situated. IDES is valuable for demos, training and presentations.

IDoc: ALE (Application Link Enabling) uses IDocs – the Intermediate Document – as the standard interface for exchanging data between R/3, R/2 or non-SAP system. Typically, an IDoc is created when message types (the format for the data for a specific business process) and methods are distributed.

IDoc Interface: Refers to the Formats (IDoc Types) and Methods (port definitions) for EDI between SAP and partner systems (another R/3 or R/2 or non-SAP system).

IDoc Type: This is nothing but the format of an IDoc for transferring business related information as 'Logical Messages'. A 'single IDoc type' can transfer more than one kind of message

IEPSL: A special type of tax, levied in Mexico, on goods like tobacco products, alcoholic drinks etc, this is typically calculated before charging VAT.

IMG Activity: The lowest node in an IMG Structure which is either (1) an *Executable Transaction* for object maintenance or assignments with related documentation or (2) an *Organizational Activity* used only for documentation.

IMG Info System: Helping in comparing (1) IMG activities between *SAP Reference IMG* and *Project IMG*, (2) IMG activities of Project IMG and its *Views,* and (3) repeatedly used IMG objects, 'IMG Info System' is a tool for checking the scope of IMG activities in *Customizing.*

IMG Note: Refers to a document describing the customizing settings for an *IMG Activity*, with reasoning for such a customizing setting.

IMG Structure: Made up of *Structure Nodes* and *IMG Activities*, the IMG Structure is hierarchical definition at the application level, and is a subset of *SAP Reference IMG.*

IMG Structure Attribute: As a part of the IMG Structure, each of the IMG Activities has attributes like *Enhancement, Critical Function, Country Assignment, ASAP Roadmap Assignment, Business Application Component Assignment* etc.

Immediate Write-off: A method of depreciation in FI-AA, to write-off the entire value of *Low Value Assets* as depreciation (100% depreciation) in the year / period of acquisition.

Implementation: Refers to the process of installing and configuring SAP system at a customer location using any of the implementation methodologies like *ASAP. See AcceleratedSAP* and *Solution Manager.*

Implementation Assistant: An important tool in ASAP methodology, the 'implementation assistant' provides access to *ASAP Roadmap, Question & Answer (Q&A) Database, Knowledge Corner, Concept Check Tool* and *Business Process Procedures*, for faster and effective SAP implementations.

Implementation Book: A tool for configuring the business applications in a SAP system, as required by the customer-Client, the 'implementation book' is structured in hypertext. For each of the applications, the book describes (1) the various steps involved in the implementation, (2) SAP's standard settings, and lists (3) the configuration activities that can be opened interactively.

Implementation Guide: Popularly called as *IMG*, the 'implementation guide' outlines all the steps required to configure / customize SAP application to meet the specific requirements of a customer. Arranged in a tree-like structure with the IMG activities at the bottom most nodes, the guide is a hierarchal structure of different application components. The IMG comes with the SAP supplied standard or default settings along with the relevant documentation. The *SAP Reference IMG* is the starting point from which one can derive the *Enterprise IMG* and various *Project IMGs*.

Implementation Project: A project outlining and carrying out the various business, organizational and technical tasks for enabling the required business processes or functions in SAP to become 'productive' on a declared date, is called as an 'implementation project'. There will be project team(s) comprising of the users / representatives from the customer, and from a SAP implementation partner(s) carrying out the project activities according to a plan and *ASAP Roadmap* to achieve the phase-wise deliverables.

Implementation Strategy: SAP recommends three types of 'implementation strategy' for implementing SAP for a customer requirement: (1) *Big-bang Approach* wherein all the applications 'go-live' on a single date, (2) *Phased Approach* in which the required applications or business processes are covered initially, and the rest of the application components implemented in a phased manner and (3) *Organization-wise Implementation* covering departments, plants etc.

Import Check: In *BC-CTS (Correction and Transport System),* the system carries out an 'import check' on the target system, during the export procedure, to determine whether all the objects of a transport request will be transported to the target system. In case of any protected objects in the target system, the import will be blocked.

Import Queue: Refers to the all the transport request, in BC-CTS, waiting to be transported.

Imputed Interest: In FI-AA, this refers to the 'opportunity cost' of capital tied-up in a fixed asset, which would otherwise have been economically deployed for earning some interest / revenue. SAP provides for taking into account this imputed interest for cost accounting purposes.

Inbound Delivery: The process starts with the vendor staging the goods at his/her shipping point and ends when the goods are received and GR posted by the customer. The inbound delivery document is generated with reference to a Purchase Order / Shipping Notification / Customer Return. The term inbound delivery is often used, interchangeably, to represent the materials as well as the delivery documents.

Inbound Error: The error resulting from an incoming IDoc from an external system, when the incoming IDoc is processed further in a SAP system.

ICM: *Incentive and Commission Management* is the solution for processing and managing all kinds of variable remuneration for employees and partners.

INCLUDE: Refers to grouped fields, according to some criteria or characteristics, inserted into a Table or structure, in ABAP.

INCLUDE Program: An ABAP program, within another ABAP program written using an *INCLUDE* statement. The INCLUDE program is not generated separately.

Incoming Invoice: Covering both the Invoices and Credit Memo in SAP, the incoming invoice is essentially a statement, from the invoicing party, with the details of amount due from the previous purchase transactions.

Indirect Activity Allocation: A method of periodic allocation, 'indirect activity allocation' is useful when it is difficult to enter the activity consumed by the receiver. The total activity quantity is distributed form the sender to receiver from the receiver's perspective.

Indirect Method: A way of calculating the *Cash Flow*, in FI-GL, wherein the items not related to the cash flow are subtracted from the *Income Statement* to arrive at the cash flow.

Indirect Quotation: Also known as *Volume Notation,* in an indirect quotation the currency value is expressed in terms of foreign currency per unit of local currency. Example: 1 INR (Local Currency) = 0.02439 USD (Foreign Currency).

Individual Picking: In Logistics Execution (LE), 'individual picking' relates to picking of an individual 'unit' of a material, and is the opposite of '*Complete Picking*' which is nothing but picking from one *Pick Area* independent of picking units.

Individual Purchase Order: When a vendor finds that the goods ordered by a customer are not available with his/her location, the same is ordered to one or more of his suppliers through individual purchase orders. The goods thus arrive at the vendor locations are managed as *Sales Order Stock*; the goods are delivered to the customer and invoiced.

Individual Value Adjustment: The devaluation of a customer's receivables, because of impossibility of collecting the overdue from the customer, is termed as 'individual value adjustment'. This is nothing but writing-off of an overdue A/R.

Individual Model: In ASAP, this relates to the model configuration in 'SAP Reference Model' to reflect a specific industry like aviation.

Inflation Adjustment Account: A GL account used to post the adjustments in transaction due to inflation, this account is usually posted on the balance sheet side with an offsetting posting on the profit & loss side. The adjustment results either in a gain or loss. Example: in the case of fixed assets, inflation adjustment will lead to either unrealised gain or loss.

Inflation Keys: These keys are defined in the customizing, and assigned to the relevant GL accounts which instruct the system on how to make the 'inflation adjustment'.

InfoCube: In 'Business Information Warehouse', an 'infocube' represents a self contained dataset made up of Relational Tables created as per *Star Schema*. The dataset can be queried using '*BEx Query*'.

Information Flow Model: Refers to the graphical representation of cross-application business activities in the system.

Infotype: Representing a group of data clubbed together according to a specific subject matter, Infotypes are normally used in *Personnel Management (PA)* in HR. Identified by a 4-digit key, *Infotypes* are nothing but the exact replicas mirroring the logical set of data records.

Initial Cost Split: A 'cost component split' for raw materials, the 'initial cost split' contains separate cost components like purchase price, freight charges etc.

INN: A tax number issued to both the legal and non-legal persons, in Russia.

Input Quantity Variance: Caused by the difference between the actual and planned quantities of activities consumed, 'input quantity variance' is the difference between the actual and target costs.

Input Tax: A tax on purchases, 'input tax' is charged by the vendor while supplying the goods and services. The deductible portion of the input tax can be claimed from the respective tax authorities by submitting a claim.

Inspection Stock: In QM, this relates to a stock reserved for inspection, and is not released for regular usage.

Installation Number: The 10-digit number printed on '*Request Fax License Key*' form, made available from SAP, when an *Installation Package* is delivered to a customer.

Insurance Type: In FI-AA, the insurance type is a setting used to control how an asset is insured, say, at the current market value or at its new value (as if purchased new).

Intercompany Billing: Refers to the process for invoicing the sales when the creation of sales order and the delivery happens from organizations in two different Company Codes of the same enterprise. That is, the Company Code where the sales is created is different than that of the Company Code from which the delivery is done.

Intercompany Clearing Account: An account to clear reconciliation entries between CO and FI in the case of 'cross-Company Code allocations'.

Interest Base Amount: Refers to the total of all line items in a business transaction on which the interest is calculated by the system.

Interest Key: A key connected to the *Interest Calculation Rule*, the interest key controls how interest is calculated by the system.

Interest on Arrears: Refers to the interest paid to the creditors when the payable is not paid within the net due date.

Interim Account: In FI, this refers to a GL account wherein all the incoming payments are posted if there is a problem in determining the correct contract account.

Intermediate Customer: Refers to the customer in between the final customer and the reseller / distributor in the *DRM (Distributor – Reseller – Management)* supply chain.

Internal Activity Allocation: Refers to allocating the valuated costs from sender cost centres to the receiver cost centres. The activity produced at the sender cost centre is multiplied by the activity price, and the resulting cost is allocated to the receiver cost centre by debiting the receiver and crediting the sender.

Internal Calculation Key: A part of the *Depreciation Key,* the 'internal calculation key' contains the parameters for controlling the depreciation calculation program.

Internal Order: An object, in CO, to monitor, collect and settle costs (some time, revenues also) is called as an 'internal order'. The internal orders can be of (1) *Overhead Orders*, (2) *Investment Orders*, (3) *Accrual Orders* and (4) *Orders with Revenues*.

Internal Trading Partner: The Company having a trading relationship with another Company in the same corporate group is called as the 'internal trading partner'.

Intracompany Transfer: In FI-AA, this refers to the transfer of values from one asset to another necessitated by situations like changed asset location, re-building of an asset etc leading to changes (say, in Asset Class) in an asset master record.

Inventory Adjustment Posting: Refers to the correction postings necessitated by the fact that there is a discrepancy between the actual and book inventory.

Inversion Posting: Refers to posting of same values to the objects in CO, but with the inverted sign of '+' or '-'.

Invoice Deficit: In MM, this refers to the difference when the invoiced quantity is lesser than the GR quantity.

Invoice Split: Refers to the creation of multiple billing documents from a single reference document (like sales order). The *Invoice Split* Function, in MM, is used for this purpose.

Invoice Verification: Refers to a process in which the invoice from the vendor is entered into the system and compared with the purchase order and GR, checking from the angle of content, price or quantity.

Invoice with PO Reference: Refers to the invoice entered into the SAP system, with reference to an existing PO in the local or back-end system.

Invoice without PO Reference: Refers to the invoice entered into the SAP system, without any reference to a PO in the system. This would be necessitated when there is an invoice in paper format, forcing some one to create the invoice manually in the system.

J J

Journal: A listing of all transaction entries in a period is known as journal in FI.

Journal Entry: Refers to a single line of entry in a journal.

Jurisdiction Code: A code denoting a 'tax jurisdiction' to where the goods and services are actually delivered. The jurisdiction code is used along with the tax code in calculating sales tax in cases where mutli-level taxation is in effect.

Kagami: Refers to the section in an invoice (both monthly and total) with the summary detailing total amount billed, total amount paid, total amount due, amount carried forward etc.

Kanban: An integrated JIT (Just-In-Time) production process, 'Kanban' refers to the replenishment or production of a material which will not be triggered until the production process actually requires the material. *Kan* meaning 'Card' and *Ban* denoting 'Signal', Kanban translates into signalling the need for a material through a card. Workstations located along the production line will produce or deliver materials just needed, and this is done when they receive the 'Kan' along with an empty container; they then produce or deliver material or components just to fill up the containers so that there is no need for storage.

Kanban Card: An integral part in Kanban production process, the *Kanban Card* is used to indicate the consumption of materials or components and also notify the required items which will then be produced or delivered by the workstations along the production line, eliminating the need for storage.

Kernel: Responsible for memory, process and task management, this is the central part of an *Operating System*, and is loaded first when the system is started.

Key Figure: Refers to a quantifiable yardstick for measuring business or technical or personal performance. Example: Sales per employee, sales per division, actual costs in current fiscal year etc. In BW, this just refers to a value or a quantity. Example: Sales revenue, fixed costs etc.

Key Figure Category: In CO-OM-CCA, this refers to an indicator to determine whether the values for a *SKF (Statistical Key Figure)* need to be interpreted as *Fixed Value (Key Figure Category 1)* which will remain the same across periods or as *Totals (Key Figure Category 2)* which will be valid only for that particular period.

Key Performance Indicator (KPI): Expressing abstract supply chain objectives in financial or physical units for effective comparison, KPI in *Supply Chain Cockpit* is used to evaluate the performance of supply chain. In Cross Application components, KPI indicates abstract company objectives in financial or physical units to evaluate the company's performance.

Knowledge Corner: One of the enabling tools in ASAP, the 'knowledge corner' contains a variety of documents (Links to *SAP Online Documentation*, *MS-PowerPoint* presentations, *Made Easy Guidebooks* etc) for facilitating various tasks during a SAP implementation especially in the initial phases of requirements gathering, blueprinting and configuration.

Language Support Package: Refers to the package, in 'Online Correction Support', used to import languages.

LaunchPad: This is nothing but the left-hand side frame of the web-browser, of the standard *mySAP Workspace*, used to launch an application or access information from a menu-tree.

Layout: In FI-GL, this refers to the definition of a screen layout with the various tabs used to process the master data relating to a GL master record.

Layout Editor: In ABAP, this refers either to the graphical or alphanumeric layout editor of the *Screen Painter* for designing screens.

Lead Currency: Stored in the transactions, the 'lead currency' is the main currency for transactions influencing the determination of fair value.

Lead Time: In PP, this is the difference between the order start time and order end time at the 'order level', and is the difference between the start and end of an operation at the 'operation level'.

Lead Time Scheduling: A function in PP which is used in the calculation of production dates and creation of capacities in either of the two ways: (1) *Lead Time Scheduling using Routing* and (2) *Lead Time Scheduling using Material Master*.

Leading Company Code: When a number of Company Codes come together for forming an integrated company, one of the Company Codes is denoted as the 'leading Company Code' to handle all the communications with the tax authority. The leading Company Code will directly settle all the tax payables with the other Company Codes.

Lean WM: *Lean Warehouse Management* enables management of stock without storing the same in bins. The *Transfer Orders* are used as the *Pick Orders*. As a result, the stock quantity is viewed in *Inventory Management* and not in *Warehouse Management*.

Leasing Type: In FI-AA, this indicator controls how a leased asset is managed (*Operating or Capital Lease*) for book-keeping purposes.

License Key: Refers to the 24-character key supplied by SAP for installation of SAP. (In the case of Java-only installations of the SAP Web AS, the license key has more than 100 characters).

Likelihood to Churn: In SAP CRM, this refers to the probability of a customer discontinuing the business with a company.

Line Item: A part of an accounting document, a line item contains information like account number, debit / credit indicator, amount etc relating to that particular item.

Line Item Display: For the accounts which are managed on an *Open Item Basis*, then it is possible to display the line item from one or more accounts. Mandatory for A/R and A/P, for GL accounts this need to be maintained in the *GL Master Record*.

Lines Flip-Flop: One of the design elements for lines, this causes every alternate line to be displayed in colour.

Link Table: In Archiving, this refers to an administration Table wherein the reference between a business object and the corresponding archive document is created during a current operation.

Load Balancing: Refers to the distribution of server load among the various application servers. In SAP, this is achieved by the *Message Server* when users log into the system.

Loading Group: A key identifying the equipment required for loading, this could be a crane or forklift etc.

Local Currency: This is nothing but the 'Company Code currency' (or *Country Currency*) which is used to maintain the local ledgers in FI. In FI-LC, if the local currency differs from that of the *Group Currency*, then the same needs to be translated into the group currency.

Lock Entries: Comprising of the user, Client, time, Table etc, a lock entry can be displayed using the *Transaction Code SM12*.

Lockbox: Used mainly in USA, this process is used to collect the checks, sent in by the business partners, by a bank or lockbox provider so that the payee's account is credited immediately and the information sent to the payee through file transfer.

Logical Database: Maintained through a *Logical Database Builder*, a 'logical database' is a run-time only object, wherein a special ABAP program provides other ABAP programs with data from the nodes of hierarchical tree structure. Typically, a logical database is made up of a structure with nodes, a database program written in ABAP, and a *Standard Selection Screen*.

Logistics Payment Block: An indicator informing why an invoice document is blocked for payment. The payment block may be *A* (blocked due to reasons mentioned in the invoice), *S* (stochastic block), *M* (manual block at the header level) or *W* (blocked though invoice verification on the internet).

Logon Group: Referring to the grouping of instances in a SAP system, the groups are defined using the *Transaction Code SMLG*.

Long Text: Refers to a text in the software interface, with the length of the text being more than 45 characters.

Main Asset Number: Identified as the single unit for valuation, this refers to the unique number in FI-AA, representing a fixed asset in a Company Code.

Maintenance BOM: In PP, this is a list containing the structure of the technical object along with the spare parts assigned for a maintenance object.

Maintenance Order: In PM, this is a detailed planning aid, listing out the tasks to be performed on any of the order types like *Investment Order, Calibration Order* or *Refurbishment Order*.

Major Defect: Though not critical, a major defect is likely to result in a failure in performing a required function of a complex function or program.

Make-to-Order Production: Made up of both the *Sales Order* and *Engineer-to-Order*, 'make-to-order production' in CO-PC refers to the manufacture of a product for a specific customer.

Make-to-Stock Inventory: Refers to the products that were not produced against a specific *Sales Order* or *Project*.

Manual Cost Allocation: One of the methods of internal cost allocation in controlling, manual cost allocation is used to avoid making complex customizing settings for simple allocations. It is used to transfer the external data.

Manual MRP: In MM, 'manual MRP' refers to a process wherein the MRP controller creates the order proposals manually.

Mapping of SAP Services: Refers to assigning of logical SAP services like update, dialog, batch etc to physical host machines.

Mark-for Store: In SD, this refers to a store that is the final recipient of the goods shipped.

Mass Change: Instead changing one-by-one, this enables to change the attributes of a number of objects (say, asset master) in one-go.

Mass Document Change: A special report, in SD, enabling simultaneous changing of large number of sales documents.

Master Data Management (MDM): A component in SAP, which in turn contains other components like *SAP BW (Business Information Warehouse), SAP XI (Exchange Infrastructure), SAP EP (Enterprise Portal)* and *SAP CI (Content Integrator)*.

Master Recipe: In PP-PI, this refers to the enterprise specific production process, in a process industry, which can not be associated with any specific order. This is similar to *Make-to-Stock Inventory*.

Matchcode: Also known, now, as the *Search Code*, this is a key which enables to find out particular record in a database. Example: Finding out the customer number by inputting information contained in that record. Press F4 while the cursor is on a field with drop-down symbol to see the possible values.

Material BOM: Created with reference to a Material Master, a material BOM contains stock as well as non-stock items, document items and text items.

Material Cost Estimate: A tool in CO-PC, this helps in calculating the *COGS / COGM* for providing a basis for material valuation with the standard costs. The material cost estimates can be created manually in *Controlling* (*Cost Estimate without Quantity Structure*) or can be created automatically in *PP* (*Cost Estimate with Quantity Structure*).

Material Credit Memo: Referring to the planned return of materials during a manufacturing process, material credit memo are represented as 'minus' items in a BOM.

Material Determination: Refers to finding out a material master by inputting a user-definable key instead of a material number during sales creation. Example: EAN (European Article Number), customer specific material number etc.

Material Document: A document containing one ore more items of material movements that can be printed as a GR/GI slip to accompany physical movement of goods.

Material Ledger: Forming the basis for *Actual Costing*, 'material ledger' is a tool in CO-PC used to valuate the material inventory in multiple currencies using different valuation approaches.

Material Number: A number uniquely identifying a material in SAP, it is necessary that all the materials in the system should have a material master defined.

Material Overhead Costs: Referring to costs that can not be identified with individual materials, material overhead costs are some of the costs like procurement costs, storage costs (when multiple materials are stored in a single storage area) etc.

Material Price Determination: A process for material valuation – in CO-PC- using the *Material Ledger*, material price determination (a) valuates the inventory in multiple currencies in different valuation areas, (b) makes new valuations in multiple currencies / multiple valuation areas and (c) posts the differences arising from transactions to material stock accounts.

Material Stock: Managed at the plant or storage location level, 'material stock' is nothing but a part of current assets of a company.

Material Substitution: The automatic substitution of one material with another during creation of sales document is known as 'material substitution'.

Material Valuation: In MM, the 'material valuation' of a stock of material is based on the *Valuation Price, Valuation Class* and *Valuation Method (at Standard or Moving Average Price)*.

Material Variant: Refers to the product variant of a configurable material.

MDoc: Refers to the objects (*MIME - Multipurpose Internet Mail Extension* - files, folders, document headers, document versions) that are stored in *SAP Collaborative Room Document Management (SAP C-Room DM)*.

Menu Painter: A tool in ABAP which enables creation of *GUI (Graphical User Interface)* consisting of title and status (*Menu Bar with Menus, Standard Toolbar, Application Toolbar* and *Functions with Function Key settings*).

Mix Variance: In CO-PC, this refers to the variance resulting from the difference between the actual and planned product blends as a product can be manufactured using various manufacturing processes.

Mixed Costing: Refers to a costing methodology in which 'multiple cost estimates' are used to calculate the mixed price for a material that can be used to update the standard price.

Model Order: A template order, with default values, used to create orders in CO is known as the model order; a model order can not be posted to.

Module Pool: Containing screens and dialog modules, a 'module pool' is an ABAP program that can be run only through a Transaction Code.

Movement Type: An indicator for material movement like GR, GI etc, the 'movement types' enable the system to determine the pre-determined posting rules and account determination for correct financial and material accounting entries. Example: Movement type 101 is used in GR based on a purchase order, 201 GI to a cost centre etc.

MPX Interface: In PS, MPX interface is used for data exchange between PS and *MS-Project*.

MRP (Material Requirements planning): Aimed at guaranteeing material availability, MRP is the procedure which takes into account the dependent and independent requirements, during order creation proposal, for planning the future requirements for both internal and sales purposes.

MRP Area: 'MRP area' is an organizational unit, in PP, for which material requirements planning can be done independently. In APO, these MRP locations are transferred as 'locations'. There are 3 types of MRP areas namely (1) Plant MRP Area, (2) MRP Area for Storage Locations and (3) MRP Area for Sub-contractors.

Multidimensional Product Cost Controlling: This is nothing but the cost accounting both at the product and responsibility area levels.

Multilevel BOM: A BOM consisting of assemblies (which in turn consist of components / assemblies) and components is known as a 'multilevel BOM'.

Multilevel BOM for Sales Order Item: This is made up of 'single level Order BOMs' and 'single level Material BOMs'.

Multiple Account Assignments: Refers to the assignment of multiple GL accounts to a single purchase order item, so that the costs can be apportioned based on quantity or amount.

Multiple BOM: This is nothing but a grouping of several BOMs describing more than one alternative combination of materials for producing a single product. During a planning run, it needs to be mentioned which one of the alternatives is to be selected by the system.

Multiple Work Centre: In PP, this refers to several work centres in the production line, wherein the same work is done.

Multiple-shift Depreciation: Refers to the calculation of higher depreciation by applying the *Multiple-shift Factor* to the variable portion of the depreciation when an asset is subject to usage in multiple shifts. The fixed portion will continue to be depreciated normally.

Namespace: Beginning and ending with a delimiter '/' and consisting of up to a maximum of 10 characters, the 'namespace' in ABAP is an ID assigned exclusively by SAP allowing SAP customers / partners and SAP to develop SAP components using SAP applications without any naming conflicts which are otherwise common.

Native SQL: Refers to the database language allowing you to include database-specific statements in ABAP programs.

Negative Goodwill: A result of the consolidation of investments exercise, a 'negative goodwill' occurs when the purchase price of an acquired company is less than the fair value of its net assets. The negative goodwill is shown on the stake-holder's section of the balance sheet.

Negative Posting: Refers to a type of 'reversal posting' in FI that brings down the transaction figures in an account of GL / customer / vendor. During this, the transaction figures (following the reversal) receive the status they would have had without posting the reversed document and its reversal document.

Negative Stock: In MM, this refers to a situation in which there is some physical stock available but there has not been matching GR. As a result, if there is a GI then the stock becomes negative.

Net Actual Cost: Enabling to arrive at the *Total / Production Variances* by comparing the net actual costs with that of the *Target Costs*, the net actual cost is nothing but the difference between the *Actual Cost* and *WIP (Work-In-Progress) + Scrap*

Net Book Value (NBV): In FI-AA, this is nothing but the net value of a fixed asset which is equal to its acquisition value or original value minus the depreciation.

Net Price: Refers to the price charged to a vendor after taking into account all the *Discounts* and *Surcharges*.

Net Target Cost: Represented by the *Target Cost Version* 0, 1 and 3 in the standard system, 'net target cost' is used to calculate the variance in *Product Cost by Period (* nothing but the Target Cost minus the WIP at Target Cost minus Scrap Variance*) and by Order (* equivalent to Target Cost minus Scrap Variance*)*.

Net Value: In SD this refers to the *Gross Value* minus the *Discounts* plus the *Surcharges*.

Net Worth Tax: In FI-AA, this refers to the tax collected on a property which forms a part of a fixed asset.

Network: In PS, this refers to an object containing instructions on what tasks to be performed / executed, in what order and in what time.

New Visual Design: As against the *Classic Visual Design* of SAP GUI appearing in grey colour, this 'new visual design' uses colours in GUI.

Non-Calendar Fiscal Year: Unlike a *Calendar Fiscal Year* which corresponds to the *Calendar Year*, a 'non-calendar fiscal year' can have any of the calendar months as the starting month for that fiscal year. Example: July to June.

Non-Conformity Costs: These are all the costs, in QM, associated with the defects. The costs may be associated with rework, scrap, repeat inspections, guarantees etc.

Non-Critical Activity: In SAP *Customizing*, this refers to the attribute of an IMG activity, when non-completion of this step would not result in any negative consequence.

Non-Leading Ledger: In FI-GL, if there is *Parallel Accounting*, then one of the *Parallel Ledgers* need to be designated as the *Leading Ledger*. All other parallel ledgers, then, are known as 'non-leading ledgers'.

Non-Required Activity: In SAP Customizing, there are certain IMG tasks which are standard and do not require to be changed, normally, for customer-specific requirements, and these activities are known as 'non-required activities' and the system can be made to 'go-live' without customizing any of these activities.

Non-Standard Object: Refers to an object, in SAP Customizing, that has not been created using the Transaction Code SE54. All the 'non-standard objects' need to be maintained manually in the system.

Non-Stock Item: This refers to a material as one of the BOM components, but there is no stock for that material. Example: PR (Purchase Requisition).

Non-Valuated Stock: Refers to the stock maintained in a company, only on a 'quantity basis' with out any valuation. To make use of such a stock, it is necessary that this is first transferred to '*Valuated Stock*'.

Nota Fiscal: Refers to a legal document, in Brazil, accompanying goods delivery. This document is used both as *Invoice* and *Delivery Note*. In its plural form this is known as '*Notas Fiscais*'.

Note Assistant: Refers to the functionality that will enable to load, apply and implement 'SAP Notes' in a SAP system.

Note Log: Downloaded along with the 'SAP Note download', this log will help in monitoring the various steps involved in implementing a SAP Note.

Note Type: SAP enables definition of various 'Note Types' according the content of these notes, in a project implementation. Some of note types are: Design, Minutes of Meeting, Issues, Project Standards etc. A Notes Editor (MS-Word or SAPscript) is used to enter the information.

Noted Item: Refers to a special item in FI, which when posted does not affect the account balance. It is just a document used as 'reminder'. Example: *Down Payment Request*.

Notification: A data record used to inform *PM (Plant Maintenance), QM (Quality Maintenance)* or *CS (Customer Service)* about some occurrence or event is known as the 'notification'. There are many *Notification Categories* like: *Maintenance Notification, Service Notification* etc.

Novation: The transfer of some or all POs / Contracts from one vendor to another, necessitated due to buy-out or merger of companies.

Number Assignment: Refers to the assigning of numbers to various business objects (documents, organizational elements etc) in SAP. The number assignment can be (1) *Internal* or (2) *External*.

Number Format: Refers to the settings for displaying numbers in a report. The settings include (1) *Decimal Places* (how many decimal places to be displayed) and (2) *Scaling Factor* (display in hundreds, thousands etc).

Number Range: Refers to a range of numbers that can be assigned to the similar business objects like *Master Records, Documents,* and *Materials* etc. Example: External Business Partners - Number Range 01 – Number Range Interval 100,000 – 199 999 – External Assignment.

Number Range Group: This refers to the combination of one or more *Number Range Objects* and one or more *Number Range Intervals*.

Number Range Interval: Refers to an interval of consecutive numbers (or alphanumeric characters) in a *Number Range*. There can be more than one 'number range interval' within a single number range.

Number Range Object: An object containing all the information that is required for assigning a 'number range' to a business object is known as the number range object. Belonging to one business object, a single number range object can have multiple *Number Ranges*.

Object Category: In Basis (*CTS-Change and Transport System*), the 'object category' refers to an area to which a maintenance and transport object is to be assigned. The categories may be of: *CUST* (used for Client-specific customizing objects), *SYST* (system related customizing objects), *CUSY* (Client-independent customizing objects) and *APPL* (application objects).

Object Currency: The currency defined in the master record for a controlling object like cost centre, order etc. While creating an object, the *Controlling Area Currency* is defaulted as the object currency but the same can be changed.

Object Navigator: Displaying all the objects (relating to a particular Object Category) in a tree-like structure, the 'object navigator' is a tool to process the objects centrally.

Object Type: In CO, this refers to the type of account assignment object like cost centre, profitability segment, internal order etc.

Off-Balance Sheet Transactions: These are all some of the transactions, like *Warranties*, *Guarantees* etc, that do not appear on the balance sheet but shown separately as 'Notes' to the Balance Sheet.

Offsetting Entry: In double-entry system of book keeping / accounting, this is the second entry offsetting the first entry so that the balance is always 'zero'.

One-System Landscape: Refers to a SAP system landscape with only one *'Production'* system.

One-Time Account: Refers to an account in FI, which records the transactions relating to a group of customers / vendors with whom the company conducts the business once or very rarely. These accounts require a special master record, and some of the details like address, bank etc are not updated in this master, but entered in the transaction document itself.

One-Time Customer / Vendor: Represented by a special master record for a collection of such customers / vendors, this customer / vendor is one with whom business is done very rarely or only once.

On-Order Stock: This is nothing but the sum of all *Open Purchase Order* quantities for a material.

Open Purchase Order (PO) Quantity: Refers to the PO quantity which has not yet been delivered. This becomes zero, when the PO quantity or more has been delivered. The open PO quantity is calculated by subtracting the *Delivered Quantity* from the *Ordered Quantity*.

Operating Concern: Having one or more Controlling Areas, an operating concern represents – in CO-PA - the sales market in a structured way by defining market segments as *Profitability Segments*, for analysing the profitability.

Operation: Referring to an activity in a work plan or work order, in logistics, an operation can be of production, inspection etc.

Operation Scrap: Entered in the *Routing* or *BOM*, this refers to the material(s) processed in an operation which failed to meet the quality requirements.

Order Hierarchy: Refers to the summarization of order values, level-by-level with the levels being the *Characteristics* (controlling area, business area etc). A *Total* is calculated for each of the levels. The value totalled may include planned cost, actual cost, target cost etc.

Order List: An overview of status of a Sales Order, the 'order list' is useful with detailed information on the content, processing status of the order, delivery scheduling etc.

Order Settlement: Referring to partial or complete crediting of an order, 'order settlement' results in debiting the accrued costs to one or more allocation receivers (like cost centre) in FI or CO.

Order Split: In PP, this refers to splitting of an original order (called as the Parent Order) into one or more orders (called as *Child Orders*).

Order Type: Being Client-Specific, the 'order type' contains all the information required to manage an order. The order type may include *Production Order, Maintenance Order, Marketing Order* etc. A single order type can be used in multiple Controlling Areas of a single Client.

Orders with Revenue: Settled to *Profitability Segments* at the end of a period, these orders are used (1) replace the CO functions of SD sales orders if SD is not implemented in an organization, and (2) obtain revenue-to-cost information if billing is automated.

Ordering Costs: These are all the costs incurred on each of the PO or Production Order, over and above the PO cost or 'cost of production', regardless of the lot size of the order. The ordering costs are directly proportional to the number of orders placed.

Ordinary Depreciation: Accounting for the normal wear and tear of usage, 'ordinary depreciation' is nothing but the *Planned Depreciation* which reduces the *APC* of a fixed asset over its normal *Economic Life* through a *Depreciation Method*.

Organization Model: Refers to the mapping of *Logical Enterprise Structure* of an organization structure to SAP *Organization Elements*.

Organizational Change Management (OCM): Refers to the systematic management changes in an organization with the implementation of SAP. In *ASAP,* an OCM plan is prepared to handle the changes, at every phase of the project, with recommendations for mitigating risks arising out of the proposed changes.

Organizational Structure List (OSL): Consisting of all the organizational elements arising out of the scope in Q&A database, corresponding to SAP organizational units that need to be configured during the *Realization Phase*, OSL helps to define the structure and configuration of SAP organizational elements.

Original Document: A document in FI that will prove that a posting is correct.

Outbound Delivery: In Logistics, this is nothing but the operation that starts with *Picking* of goods and ending with *Shipping*. An 'outbound delivery document' is created during the process of (1) goods shipped to a customer, (2) goods returned to a vendor and (3) *Stock Transfer Orders*. The entire operation results in a decrease in the stock quantity of that material or product.

Output Tax: An opposite of *Input Tax*, this is levied on the customers.

Overhead Cost Controlling: A part of the Controlling (CO) that is used to monitor overhead costs in an organization to provide strategic decisions to the enterprise to manage these costs.

Overhead Cost Order: One of the *Internal Order* types, this kind of orders are used to monitor or collect overhead costs for a specific periods, irrespective of the cost centre structure or business processes of an organization, and settled at the period end to cost centres, WBS elements, profitability segments or other internal orders.

Overhead Costing: The most common way of costing the cost objects in *Cost Object Controlling,* this type of costing first assigns all the *Direct Costs* (from *Cost Element Controlling*) to the relevant *Cost Objects*, then pro-rated overhead costs are applied to the objects in proportion to their direct costs.

Overhead Key: In CO-PC, this is used to calculate the percentage overhead rate for specific materials or orders.

Overhead Rate: Lump-sum or percentage or quantity-based one, this is the rate at which overhead is allocated to the direct costs to be charged on the cost objects with the proportion of the overhead costs belonging to them.

Overhead Structure: Used in *Cost Centre Accounting* to Accrual Costs, this structure defines how the overhead is calculated and posted. A typical structure consists of a (1) *Base Row* on which the overhead rate is applied, (2) *Calculation Row* contains the *Overhead Rate* which needs to be applied on the base row and (3) *Total Row* is the sum of the base and overhead amounts.

P & L Statement Account Type: Refers to the key which is used to define the *Retained Earnings* account.

PA Transfer Structure: Use to settle Orders to assign direct postings to *Profitability Segments* from FI / CO or allocated activities in CO, the 'PA transfer structure' is used to assigns costs / revenues from other applications. The costs/ revenues are assigned to the *Quantity & Value Fields* in *Profitability Analysis*.

Package Builder: One of the Workbench tools in ABAP, the 'package builder' is used to define the hierarchy of packages, the interfaces for user packages and create user access for use of services from other packages.

Packaging List: Not requiring a specific format, a 'packaging list' consists of goods and packaging.

Park: Refers to a function that enables 'parking' of an accounting document by saving the data in the database. A 'parked document' can later on be changed, deleted, saved or posted.

Parked Invoice Document: The system uses the '*Park Incoming Invoice*' function to 'park' a vendor's invoice in MM. The 'parking' becomes necessary when there is some information missing, or when the balance is not zero or when the invoice processing done by several people. However, it is necessary that the information like document number, vendor, invoicing party and account assignment needs to be entered before parking an invoice.

Partial Clearing: Refers to the clearing in FI in which the *Open Items* are not cleared in full.

Partial Confirmation: In PP, this refers to the confirmation of an operation which is still being processed, and not yet completed.

Partial Delivery: Refers to the receipt of goods which is less than the ordered quantity.

Partial Settlement: This is the payment towards partial settlement of an outstanding invoice.

Partner Determination: The process of the system determining the 'partner' (*Sold-to-Party, Ship-to-Party, Bill-to-Part, Payer* etc) during 'sales order' creation is known as the 'partner determination'.

Partner Function: In SD, this refers to the rights and responsibilities of each of the partners in a business transaction, and the function relate to 'Sold-to-Party' and 'Ship-to-Party'.

Payer: In SD, this refers to the person or entity paying the bill on behalf of *Bill-to-Party*.

Payment Block Indicator: Entered in a customer / vendor master record or in the line item of a document, the 'payment block indicator' is a key used to block an account or a line item from being paid. The *Payment Block Reasons* are defined in the system and assigned to the payment block indicators.

Payment History Analysis: Refers to the history of customer payments. The analysis provides information on payment frequency, instances of customers crossing the due date, cash discount offered to the customers etc.

Payment Lot: Created either manually or automatically, the 'payment lot' refers to the grouping of payments, incoming / outgoing, that are combined for processing together.

Payment Medium Format: Refers to the format in which the payment information is created for processing by the banks. The formats include (1) *International Formats* like *MT100, IDoc* etc, (2) *Document-based Formats* like *Bank Transfer Forms*, (3) *Non Document-based Formats* like *DME, EDI* etc., and (4) *Country Specific Formats* like *ACH*.

Payment Medium Workbench: Refers to the tool offered by SAP for creating 'payment medium files' based on customized settings and the generic file formats explained in Payment Medium Format.

Payment Method: Refers to methods like *Check, Cash* or *Bank Transfer* specifying how the payment is made from / to the SAP system.

Payment Program: Refers to the program which controls the payment processing in SAP. The program results in *Payment Documents* and *Payment Media*, and enables posting of the payment transactions processed during the *Payment Run*.

Payment Tolerance: This refers to the *Payment Rules* for handling payment differences: what can be the maximum difference allowed between the invoice and actual payment made, how to account for the *Residual Items* etc. This also takes are of the process to handle '*Payment Difference*', if any.

Payroll Account: The most important document on wages and salaries, the 'payroll account' is updated every time the payroll is run. The payroll account contains all the cumulated payroll information besides the personal information of all the personnel.

Pegged Order: This is used to determine which assemblies, planned or customer independent requirements are not covered if delivery or production is delayed or incomplete.

Period Accounting: In contrast to the *Cost of Sales Accounting*, the 'period accounting' takes into account all the costs incurred in a particular time frame irrespective of the fact whether the matching revenue has been earned or not.

Period Closing Program: A program, in Logistics, used to ensure that data are properly updated in the correct period and, goods movements are posted properly in the respective period.

Period Control: A part of the *Internal Calculation Key* in FI-AA, the 'period control' enables determination of start / end date of depreciation during asset acquisition or retirement. Allowing defining of individual period controls for various transaction types like acquisition, transfer or retirement, SAP comes delivered with many default period controls like Pro *Rata Temporis, Pro Rata at Mid-period, Fist Year Convention* etc.

Period Indicator: In PP, this refers to the key specifying for which time duration the consumption / forecast values should remain in the system.

Period Lock; In case of Internal Orders, this refers to the procedure which 'locks' the planned / actual transactions for a given combination of controlling area, fiscal year and version.

Period-End Closing: Refers to the periodic transactions performed at the end of a period, after the Primary Cost postings have been made. In CO-CCA, this refers to the periodic transactions like *Assessment, Distribution, Periodic Transfer Postings* and *Imputed Cost Calculation*. In the case of Cost Object Controlling, period-end closing encompasses calculation of (1) *Overheads*, (2) *WIP* and (3) *Variance*, and (4) *Settlement*.

Periodic Allocation: Refers how the costs collected on a cost centre is periodically allocated to other cost objects based on certain allocation basis.

Periodic Inventory: This is nothing but the period-end physical inventory of all the stocks of an organization.

Periodic Reposting: Aimed at correcting posting errors or discrepancies, 'periodic reposting' refers to an allocation method that uses *Cycle* and *Segments* to credit the allocation cost centres with the correct cost.

Personal Identification Number: This is nothing but the number used, in FI, to identify a natural person, in Korea. In SD, this may refer to the legitimate owner as the 'cardholder'.

Personal Ledger Account: Used in India, this refers to a bank account which collects all the excise duty payable from where the tax authorities deduct the appropriate excise duty for that organization.

Personnel Area: An organization element in HR, this is used in personnel administration, time management and payroll accounting.

Phantom Assembly: A logical grouping of materials, this 'phantom assembly' is used to describe a number of components with an idea to manage them as whole, by placing the components in a *Superior Assembly*.

Phase: Represents a major milestone, ASAP contains five phases: *Project Preparation*, *Business Blueprint, Realization, Final Preparation, Go-Live & Support*.

Picking: Refers to the process of grouping materials / products on the basis of sales orders, delivered etc picking is carried out as per the 'Transport Orders'.

Plan Version: In CO, this refers to a collection of functions. SAP enables planning in multiple versions, and the default version is *'000'* which is generated by the system when the *Controlling Area* is created for the first time. Only this version allows entering both planned and actual costs.

Planned Scrap: Resulting from a manufacturing of a product, the planned scrap may be (a) *Component-based* or (b) *Operation-based*. While the 'component-based scrap' is defined in the BOM, the 'operation-based scrap' is defined in the routing.

Planner Profile: A hierarchical definition of *Planning Layouts* and *Planning Area*. One or more 'planning layouts' are used per 'planning area'.

Planning Layout: Refers to the structure of data entry screen for planning, this 'planning layout' consists of a *Header* (Planning period, version etc), *Lead Columns* (Objects to be planned) and *Value Column* (the plan values).

Planning Period: Refers to the period for which a '*Cost Estimate*' will be valid.

Planning Profile: In Controlling, this refers to a functionality used to group the control parameters for planning / budgeting operations.

Planning Run: Divided into main work steps like (1) *Lot Size* calculation, (2) *Net Requirement* determination, (3) *Procurement Element / Type* determination and (4) Scheduling, the planning run refers to the execution of *Material Requirements Planning (MRP)* for all the materials / assemblies.

Planning Variant: In *Variant Configuration* in *Logistics*, a 'planning version' refers to the variant for planning the components of a '*Configurable Material*' which are critical or required frequently.

Planning Version: This is nothing but the planning data on '*SOP*' (Sales & Operations Planning), stored in different versions. Though there are multiple versions in the system, in PP, version '*A00*' is termed as the *Active Version*, and all other versions are *Inactive* in the standard system.

Plant: A plant in SAP is an organization element wherein materials or goods / services produced.

Plant-Specific Purchasing Organization: Refers to the 'purchasing organization' which is responsible for the procurement activities for a plant.

POH: '*Process on Help (POH)*' is an event triggered by *F1* for providing help information of an input field on the screen.

POS: *POS* or '*Point of Sale*' is a *Cash Point* from which merchandise is sold to a customer.

Pool Table: This is one of the Tables in a *Table Pool*. Due to structure restrictions of Table Pool, the name of the Pool Table (also called as *Pooled Table*) can not exceed 10 characters, and all the fields of a this Table should have *Character Data Type*. It is also to be noted that the total length of all the *Key Fields / Data Fields* of a Pool Table can not exceed the '*Varkey*' or '*Vardata*' field of the Table Pool.

Post Depreciation: The depreciation determined by the *Depreciation Key* or determined manually is posted in the system periodically. The *Depreciation Posting Run*, with all the necessary information for posting depreciation amounts to FI, creates a *Batch Input Session* which when processed creates the necessary postings.

Post to a Prior Period: When a transaction is entered with the posting date relating to a previous period, the system corrects the data for the current and previous periods.

Post-Capitalization: Refers to the correction of the value of assets in FI-AA, because the value of the asset was set too low previously as there was no capitalization in the past. The correction may also apply to the value of an asset which was considered as an expense earlier.

Posting: As a document entry, posting in FI relates to updating of one or more transaction ledgers in the system with the data from the document entered.

Posting Block: Refers to a key that when entered prevents an account from further postings. The 'posting block' may be set (1) *Centrally* affecting all the Company Codes or (2) *Locally* at the Company Code level affecting only a specific Company Code.

Posting Key: A 2-digit numeric key determining how the line items in a document are posted by controlling (1) posting side (credit or debit), (2) the account types to which a transaction can be posted and (3) screen layouts for data entry.

Posting Lock: In *Contract Management*, this refers to the locking of transactions due to business related reasons like bankruptcy, death of the natural person etc.

Posting Period: Derived from the 'Posting Date' of a document, the transaction figures are updated in the system, per 'posting period'. As a result, every transaction is associated with a posting period.

Posting Rule: In CO-PC, this refers to the rule determining which data from *RA (Results Analysis)* are transferred to FI-GL when the settlement takes place.

Posting Variant: Defined in customizing, a 'posting variant' is a system object which ensures that the asset revaluation, in FI-AA, is carried out at proper intervals.

Postponed Accounting System: Applicable only to *Belgium, Netherlands* and *Luxembourg*, this arises out of a situation wherein the transactions between 'business partners' are exempt from tax yet needs to be reported to the Tax Office. Under this system, the vendor shows a portion of the invoiced amount as both *Input Tax* and *Output Tax*.

POV: Triggered by *F4*, *Process on Value (POV)* request is to display the *Possible Entries* of an input field of a screen.

Power User: Refers to one or more users, identified during the SAP implementation, having an in-depth knowledge of the business processes, and who is/are known as the *Point of Reference* for all other users.

Pre-Allocated Stock: By-passing the normal storage route, a 'pre-allocated stock' is one which when received at the warehouse is sent immediately to the goods issue area for transfer to the appropriate location.

Pre-Configured Client (PCC): Consisting of frequently used customizing settings for a country, this Client comes loaded with country-specific chart of accounts, *UOM (Units of Measure)* etc so that the most of the basic processes in *FI/CO, SD* and *MM* does not require any further customizing and are operational from the day the Client is set-up.

Pre-Configured Material: Used as 'master data' in *Quotations* and *Sales Orders*, the 'pre-configured material' is a pre-set configuration of a product or material master item.

Pre-Configured System: A 'pre-configured SAP system' for a particular industry containing all the necessary structures, for that industry, with the default values and the corresponding knowledge for all these typical structures.

Preferred Storage Location: Refers to the first choice of a storage location, from which the materials are taken for fulfilling a delivery. Only when there are no materials at this preferred location, the system looks for other storage locations.

Preferred Vendors: Refers to the vendors proposed by the users, from an existing list, when the assigned / normal sources of supply failed to deliver the materials. The 'preferred vendors' need to go through the approval from the purchases before they become the 'supply sources'.

Preparation for Consolidation: In FI-LC, this refers to the preparations for enabling automatic transfer of data from application components like *FI, SD, MM* and *EC-PCA*, into the Consolidation System so as to maintain *Additional Account Assignments* like *Transaction Type, Trading Partner, Acquisition Year* etc.

PREPARE: Refers to the program, in SAP, that 'prepares' an existing system for an upgrade. Running in *Sequential Phases*, besides making *Preparatory Checks* automatically, this copies the *Tools* needed by the upgrade to the database, and also copies programs and data to the upgrade directory. Capable of resetting and repeating as often as required during the upgrade preparations, the tool helps to upgrade without pains.

Presentation Layer: Distributed across many *Presentation Servers*, the presentation layer (like *SAPGUI, Web Browser* etc) is nothing but the software level of the SAP system displaying the *User Interface*, which processes the user instructions and passes them to the *Application Layer*.

Presentation Server: A single site server of an ABAP based SAP system in which the *Presentation Layer* is realized either through the *SAPGUI* or *Web Browser*.

Pretty Printer: Used to optimize the layout of an *ABAP Program*, this is one of the functions of *ABAP Editor*.

Prevention Costs: These are all the costs associated with the preventive and corrective operations in QM.

Price Change Document: Refers to a GL document in MM, which records the changes in the valuation of the price of a material.

Price Control: Refers to the procedure of determining material valuation in MM, either at (1) *Standard Price* or (2) *Moving Average Price*.

Price Difference: In CO-PC, this is nothing but the difference between the *Valuation Price* and the price used for movement of a material with an external amount. When *Material Ledger* is active, this price difference is collected to the *Price Difference Accounts*, irrespective of the *Price Control Indicator* in the material master for that material.

Price Difference Account: In CO, this refers to the account which records the difference in prices for a material managed on *Standard Price*. The account is also used to record the difference between the *PO Price* and the *Selling Price*.

Price Group: Refers to the grouping of customers, like retail customers, wholesale customers etc., for the purpose of pricing.

Price Strategy: In CO-PC, this refers to the determination of how materials, production activities, external activities etc are valuated for a given costing type.

Price Table: In Controlling, this refers to a special 'Condition Table' used in resource planning

Price Type: Refers to a key to identify a price in BW; the 'price types' like *Standard Price, Moving Average Price (also called as Periodic Unit Price), Tax Price* and *Commercial Price* are used in SAP.

Pricing Procedure: Refers to the process of defining *Conditions* (or *Condition Records*) and the (*Access*) *Sequence* in which the system will read these condition records for determining the price. SAP comes delivered with *Material Price, Discount, Surcharge* etc. It is easier if the standard procedure is copied and changed for a specific requirement.

Price Reference Material: The *Material Master* record that is used by the system as a reference for determining the price is known as the 'price reference material'. When this reference is entered into a new material master, all those conditions applicable to the reference material will apply to this new material as well.

Pricing-Procedure Results Table: Refers to a Table that stores the results from the *Pricing Procedure*. The system stores this information at each step of the processing and is used internally for transferring the relevant information to the document that is being created.

Primary Cost Component Split: In CO-PC, this refers to an alternative way of grouping *COGM* showing the *Primary Costs* for internal activities. In the case of *Overhead Cost Controlling*, the 'primary cost component split' shows how the price of an *Activity Type* is made up of.

Primary Cost Element: Corresponding to GL accounts in FI, 'primary cost elements' originate outside CO. This also refers to the *Accrual Costs* that are used in CO purpose only.

Primary Product: In PP, this refers to the manufacturing of the primary product. Unlike the primary product, there will not be any independent order items created in the manufacturing of by-products and co-products.

Primary Table: In ABAP, this is nothing but the first Table introduced in an aggregated object consisting of many Tables, all of which are connected through the *Foreign Key*.

Print Output Program: Also known as *Printer Writer*, this program helps to maintain printer settings. The printer output program reads a *Spool File* from the *Print Queue* and sends the same to the printer for printing.

Prior Vendor: A manufacturer of a product, the 'prior vendor' is one-step behind in a *Supply Chain* from a 'source' from which a material is supplied.

Pro Forma Invoice: A quotation, with the details on product description, quantity to be supplied, price, payment terms, selling terms etc., from a buyer.

Pro Rata Temporis: In FI-AA, this is a *Period Control* used to calculate proportionate asset values by taking the 'first date' of the period as the starting date for depreciation calculation. In the case of retirements, full depreciation is calculated if the asset retirement falls in the first half-year; and no depreciation is calculated if the retirement is in the 2nd half of the period.

Product Configuration: In SD, this refers to the compilation of a *Product Variant* from several variants, with the values assigned to the underlying characteristics of the underlying standard product.

Product Costs by Order: In CO-PC, this is nothing but costing *of Products* by Orders (*Production or Process Orders*) as these orders are analyzed by period.

Product Costs by Period: Refers to the lot-based cost object controlling for periodic cost management at order / material levels.

Product Costs by Sales Order: Used in complex *Make-to-Order* situations, this refers to the costing of products by *Sales Orders*, wherein the planned / actual costs and revenues are calculated to a sales document item.

Product Cost Controlling: A component in CO, this is made up of (1) *Product Cost Planning* – with / without Quantity Structure, Simulation and Reference Costing, (2) *Cost Object Controlling* – Product Cost by Period / Order / Sales Order, and Costs for Intangible Goods / Services, (3) *Actual Costing / Material Ledger* and (4) *Product Cost Controlling Information System*.

Product Cost Planning: Includes the tools for planning costs and setting prices for materials (*Cost Estimate with / without Quantity Structure*) and for other objects of cost accounting (*Base Object Costing, Simulation Costing*), 'product cost planning' enables planning of costs before an order is commenced for manufacturing.

Product Costing: 'Product costing' calculates the *COGM* and the *COGS* per product unit. The products are costed automatically using the *BOMs* and *Routings* in PP.

Product Group: Refers to a collection of materials (or products) according to user-defined criteria. The group may contain products from other product groups (*Multi-Level Product Group*): in this case it is essential that the lower most group contains materials.

Product Hierarchy: In CO-PC, a 'product hierarchy' is made up of: *Plant > Product Group > Product > Order*. The system uses the hierarchy to analyze the costs at each level. However, in *Logistics* the hierarchy refers to an alphanumeric string that groups materials according to certain characteristics and is used for pricing / evaluation.

Product Life Cycle Management (PLM): *PLM* in SAP refers to a suite of solutions for digitally managing a company's product information, throughout the life cycle of a product by (1) *Life-Cycle Data Management*, (2) *Life-Cycle Collaboration*, (3) *Program and Project Management* and (4) *EHS (Environment Health and Safety)*.

Product Structure: Refers to a list of objects in SAP - like *Material Document, BOM* or *Change Number* – that are functionally related.

Production Cost Collector: Created separately for each version of a product or material, the production cost collector is a cost object used to collect costs in *Repetitive Manufacturing / Kanban Production*. The actual costs are collected from (1) *Final or Reporting Point Backflush*, (2) *Internal Activity Allocation*, (3) *Overhead Calcula*tion etc., and settled to the inventory at the end of a period. At period-end closing, 'production cost collectors' perform (a) *WIP Calculation*, (b) *Variance Calculation* and (c) *Settlement*.

Production Overhead: Refers to the costs incurred in a production process that can not be assigned to particular cost objects.

Production System: Also known as the *Delivery System* in *Global ASAP*, this is nothing but the system containing the business processes of an enterprise that is used to record the '*live*' or '*production*' data. The direct access to the production system for making changes in customization is restricted, and is done through the CTS from the *Quality Assurance System*.

Production Variance: This is calculated as the difference between the *Actual Costs* and the *Target Costs* (the target costs are calculated on the basis of the actual lot size delivered to the stock), based on the *Preliminary Cost Estimate* for an order.

Profile Generator: This is used to generate *Authorization Profiles* for *Role Maintenance*.

Profit and Loss Adjustment: Done on a key date, the adjustment relates to some of the account assignment objects like *Business Area, Profit Centre, Trading Partner Profit Centre / Business Area* etc.

Profit Centre Area: One of the structural elements in *Profit Centre Hierarchy*, the *Profit Centre Area* represents the lowest node in the structure to which *Profit Centers* can be assigned.

Profitability Analysis (CO-PA): Based on the *Cost of Sales Accounting* methodology, the 'profitability analysis' can be (a) *Costing Based* or (b) *Account Based*, in SAP.

Profitability Segment: Corresponding to an external *Market Segment*, this is an object in CO-PA to which costs and revenues are assigned. A part of the *Operating Concern*, the profitability segment is made up of *Characteristics* (System defined or user defined).

Program Type: In SAP there are several 'program types' like *Executable Program (ABAP Report), Include Program, Module Pool, Interface Pool, Class Pool, Function Group* etc.

Project: In CO, this refers to an object consisting of tasks within a specified *Controlling Area*, and is used to monitor schedule, resources, capacities, cost, revenues, and funds availability. In *ASAP*, this refers to the subset of *Enterprise Model* consisting of various implementation objects that are distributed into several *Project Areas*. (A *Project Area* is made up of implementation objects that are handled by a *Project Team*).

Project Charter: One of the key deliverables of *Phase-1 of ASAP*, the 'project charter' is a document prepared by the project manager which contains a clear definition of the project, its scope, objectives, implementation time line / schedule, implementation strategies, resources, roles & responsibilities etc. The charter prepared by the project manager forms the basis for further work on the project in terms of *Project Planning and Control*, and this needs to be ratified by the *Project Sponsor* or management. Each of the sub-projects within a major project needs to have separate project charters.

Project Documentation: Refers to the record of work on an implementation. In ASAP, this is made up of documentation of (a) *Target structure* / procedure based on Reference IMG, (b) *System settings* based on Customizing activities in the IMG and (c) *Day-to-day project administration* and management like the deliverables, minutes of meetings, status reports etc.

Project Estimator: A tool in ASAP, the 'project estimator' is used to determine the first-cut information on the project scope, time and cost relating to a proposed SAP implementation. Done very early, at the pre-sales phase, this tool contains several questions which when answered would provide the basic estimates.

Project IMG: Nothing but the sub-set of *Enterprise / SAP Reference IMG*, the 'project IMG' enables the implementing team to complete the customizing activities in a project in a structured way. The project IMG can be generated (a) manually from the *SAP Reference IMG*, (b) manually by selecting the *Application Components*, (c) from *Q & A Database* by assigning the various processes to the application components. Multiple *Project Views* can be defined for a project IMG, so as to limit the customizing activities to different groups of the implementing team according to their responsibility area.

Project Object: Refers to *Activities* or *Activity Elements* or *WBS (Work Breakdown Structure) Elements* or *Milestones* in SAP's Project Systems (PS).

Project Plan: In ASAP, this refers to a plan made up of (a) Budget Plan, (b) Resource *Plan* and (c) *Work Plan*.

Project Preparation: Refers to the 1st phase of ASAP, this involves definition of project goals / objectives, implementation scope, implementation strategy, project schedule, implementation sequence. The project team is also set-up during this phase.

Project Review: Focusing on monitoring project management in terms of deliverables and adherence to schedules, the 'project review' is recommended to be conducted at the end of each phase of

ASAP Roadmap. Aimed at identifying and resolving the issues for timely completion of project phases, the review is also expected to focus on *Critical Success Factors.*

Project Scope: Refers to the scope of the proposed implementation, this is the collection of structured items taken from *SAP Reference IMG* for meeting the exact functions of a specific enterprise. The scope is documented in the *BPML (Business Process Master List)*, transferred to *IMG* before the *Project IMG* is generated.

Project Standard: Aimed at removing unnecessary work, the 'project standard' refers to rules and procedures defined in ASAP for improving consistency and effective communication in a project. The standard needs to be developed for managing the scope, configuration, testing, issues, communication and documentation.

Project Systems: A component of SAP, *PS (Project Systems)* enables planning, executing and accounting projects as a part of the enterprise's business processes.

Project Type: Refers to a categorization of projects in PS, the 'project type' includes development projects, capital-intensive projects, customer projects etc.

Proportional Consolidation: One of the methods of consolidation in FI-LC, 'proportional consolidation' relates to the investments of joint-venture companies.

Prototype: Used to check the results of specific business processes, within the context of *Business Blueprint*, configured in a SAP system before going ahead with the full configuration.

Public Holiday Calendar: A combination of *Annual Calendar* and *Public Holidays* in a year, the 'public holiday calendar' can be customized to show holidays for various countries in a year.

Purchase Order (PO): A request / instruction from a *Purchasing Organization* to an external vendor (or a plant with in the company) to deliver a specified quantity of a material or to provide certain services at a certain point of time.

Purchase Order History: Refers to the deliveries effected or invoices received in respect of a PO item.

Purchase Requisition (PR): A request / instruction to Purchasing for procuring certain quantity of a material / service at a certain point of time, is known as PR.

Purchasing Group: Being the primary channel for dealing with certain vendors, the 'purchasing group' is nothing but a buyer (or group of buyers) who is internally responsible for procuring certain materials.

Purchasing Info Record: Refers to the source of information for procuring certain material from certain vendors.

Purchasing organization: One of the organizational structures in an enterprise, the 'purchasing organization' is entrusted with the procurement of materials and services from vendors form time to time. The purchasing organizations are assigned to the Company Code and plant(s). There are three scenarios for the purchasing organization structure: (1) *Enterprise-wide*: One purchasing organization fulfilling the requirements of all the Company Codes in a Client, (2) *Company-Specific*: One purchasing organization per Company Code, and (3) *Plant-Specific*: One purchasing organization per plant.

Putawy: This is nothing but the storage of goods in a *Storage Area* or *Storage Bin*, in SAP WM *(Warehouse Management)*.

Quality Assurance System: Refers to a SAP system, for final test, into which the customizing parameters along with the tested and stable development objects are transported at periodic intervals, from the *Development* or *Test System*. Any transport to the 'production system' is routed through this system only.

Quality Costs: The costs associated with the planning / assuring a product / service quality and inspection activities are known as the 'quality costs'. The quality costs are classified into (1) *Prevention Costs*, (2) *Appraisal Costs* and (3) *Non-Conformity Costs*.

Quant: Refers to the stock of a material in a *Storage Bin*. Created through warehouse movements, the quantity of a quant is increased when there is an addition to the stock.

Quantity Structure: Consisting of a *BOM* and *Routing*, the 'quantity structure' is the basis for calculating material cost estimates in CO-PC. In the case of *Process Manufacturing, Master Recipe* is used in the place of a BOM, and in the case of *Repetitive Manufacturing*, a *Rate Routing* is used instead of routing.

Quantity Structure Determination: Refers to the process for determining a valid quantity structure for costing, this determination can be through the settings in the quantity structure control or through the default values in the material master.

Quantity Variance: In MM, this is the difference between the *Planned (Budgeted or Target) Costs* and the *Actual Costs*, arising out of variations between the *Planned* and *Actual Quantity* of a material.

Query: Also known as *ABAP Query* or *SAP Query*, this relates to the creation of a report by users with no programming knowledge. These queries always relate to a *Functional Area*. To create a query the user needs to be assigned to a *User Group,* to which the functional area should be assigned. Refer *ABAP Query.*

Question and Answer Database: Popularly known as '*Q&A db*', this is one of the tools in ASAP which enables mapping of customer requirements to the various functionalities available in SAP system during an implementation. The database consists of (1) *SAP Reference Structure* for defining the scope of the project by selecting, re-arranging and adding structure items, (2) *Associated Items* - like questions, transactions, user roles etc that are assigned to the structure items – enabling to draw the *Business Blueprint*, (3) *Issue Management* for collecting / managing project issues, and (4) *Reporting Functions*.

Quick Sizer: One of the tools in ASAP, this helps in calculating the CPU, disk and memory requirements based on the estimated number of users. Providing an idea of the 'system size' to run the estimated work load on the SAP system, this tool is invaluable for initial planning and budgeting in an implementation.

Quick Viewer: Another tool for defining reports, without any programming skills, the quick viewer enables creating *WYSWYG* (*What-You-See- is-What-You-Get*) reports by using the *Drag & Drop* functionality or through the functions in the *Toolbars*.

R/3 Implementation Tools: These are all the tools that enable SAP implementations and support. The tools include: SAP *Reference Structure, IMG (Implementation Guide), Industry Models, Pre-Configured Clients* etc.

R/3 Repository: Referring to the central repository of ABAP/4 objects, the 'R/3 repository' contains objects like *Programs Objects, Function Group Objects, Business Engineering Objects, Dictionary Objects* etc

R3up: Refers to the central coordination program used in SAP system upgrades. Once started, this program controls the upgrade in sequential phases through tools like '*R3load*', '*tp*' and '*R3tran*'. R3up uses RFC to communicate to the SAP system. The pre-requisite to use R3up is that *PREPARE* modules should have been completed successfully. Refer PREPARE also.

Rate Routing: This is the routing used in *Repetitive Manufacturing* for planning production quantities or volume. Refer Routing also.

Rate-Based Planning: Refers to a part of the *Capacity Planning*, 'rate-based planning' makes use of *Rate Routing*.

Raw Material Cost Estimate: A cost estimate for raw material or a material component, the 'raw material cost estimate' uses the price data from the Purchasing Info Record or *Purchase Order*, to which the *Delivery Costs* (freight etc), *Additive Costs* and *Overhead Costs* are all added to arrive at the cost estimate.

Ready-to Run Implementation: This comprises of a complete concept for administration of the *mySAP.com (SAP ERP) Workplace*, as well as *Pre-Configured* Interfaces for integrating component systems. The configuration of the system landscape is performed using the *Workplace Configuration Assistant.*

Realignment: In CO-PA, this refers to the retrospective changes to the master data, updating the *Characteristics*, in such a way that the values already posted are also changed.

Realization: Referring to the 3rd phase in *ASAP Roadmap* in a SAP implementation, this phase enables implementation of the business processes / functions documented in the *Business Blueprint*, so as to set up the SAP system with the necessary customizing. During this phase, the implementing team also completes the *User Manual* and *Training Material*.

Rebate Settlement: In SD, this is nothing but the verification of all the volume rebate amounts relating to the business transactions within a validity period, for creation of the relevant *Credit Memos.*

Recipe: This is nothing but the instructions for a production process. There are two kinds of recipe: (1) *Manufacturing Recipes* - Master and Control Recipes and (2) *Non-Manufacturing Recipes* – Change-over, Set-up and Clean Recipes.

Reconciliation Account: Represents a GL account used to post automatically whenever there is a transaction in a sub-ledger account like *Customer, Vendor, Assets* etc. The 'reconciliation account' is set-up in such a way that a group of GL accounts (say, accounts representing overseas vendors) post to a single reconciliation account.

Reconciliation Ledger: Used to reconcile CO transaction data with the FI, this 'reconciliation ledger'

displays only the summarized values. This is also useful in providing an overview of all costs incurred.

Reconciliation Posting: Refers to the generation of some adjustment items in FI, whenever there is a cross-company or cross-business area or cross-functional area posting in CO.

Recurring Entry Document: 'Recurring entry documents' are set-up in FI to deal with the periodical postings of business transactions that happen regularly like payment of insurance premium, rent etc. The mere creation of a recurring document will not update the accounting figures in the system. The system will create the accounting documents based on the recurring entry document. The templates for creating recurring entry documents are known as *Recurring Entry Original Documents*.

Reference and Simulation Costing: Used as the building block for other cost estimates, this is the tool for planning costs and setting prices in the form of *Unit Cost Estimates*.

Reference Currency: Refers to the currency used in the exchange rate calculation for a particular *Currency Type*.

Reference Document: This document is used as a reference while posting FI accounting documents. The 'reference document' may be an *Accounting Document* or a *Sample Document*. In SD, this denotes to a document from which the data are copied to another document.

Reference Order: In CO, this refers to a postable order or non-postable order (also known as a *Model Order*) which can be copied while creating a new order.

Regenerative Planning: A planning run, in PP, wherein all the materials are included in the MRP run.

Region Code: Refers to the code used in SAP to denote a region both logically and geographically.

Register RG1: Used for excise purposes in India, this RG1 is used to record the movement of excisable finished goods from a factory to a store.

Register RG21A / 23C: Previously a statutory requirement, in India, to show the receipt of all excisable *raw materials* (RG21A) and *capital goods* (RG23C) separately, this is no longer the case. However, within SAP this distinction still remains.

Register RG23D: Used in India to record the goods issue / receipt as kept by the depots.

Regular Vendor: Not the opposite of one-time vendor, this refers to a vendor who supplies at the *Client* level (meeting the requirements of the entire corporate group).

Relationship: In PS, this refers to the start and end of activities in a Network. Used in Sequencing of activities, the relationship may be of: *SS (Start-to-Start), FS (Finish-to-Start), SF (Start-to-Finish) and FF (Finish-to-Finish)*.

Release: Referring to an activity in CO-PC, the release of a *Standard Cost Estimate* leads to writing the *Material Cost Estimate* into the material master, as the current *Planned / Standard Price* for that material. To be able to release a cost estimate, it is necessary that the same is 'marked' before the release.

Release Note: Refers to the information about the changed or deleted or new functionality or structure changes since the last release of the (SAP) software. The release note may be of: (1) *Functional Release Note* (information on changed / deleted / new functions in IMG in an area), (2) *Structure Release Note* (information on changes to an existing structure in an area) and (3) *Composite Release Note* (overview of all IMG structure changes in all application areas)

Release Procedure: Refers to the procedure followed in a company wherein the approved persons give the go-ahead for purchase of materials or services externally. The 'release procedure' is applicable to *PR (Purchase Requisitions)* and all external purchasing documents like *RFQ (Request* *for Quotation), PO (Purchase Orders), Scheduling Agreements and Service Sheets. Release Strategies* will be used for the release procedures.

Release Project: Refers to the list of customizing activities that need to be carried because of a new release, and this may be of *Delta Customizing* or *Upgrade Customizing* in SAP.

Release-Specific IMG: Refers to the *Project View* displaying all the IMG activities / documentation relating to a specific *Release Note*.

Relevancy to Costing: A tool in CO that is used in cost estimates with quantity structure to check (a) whether a *BOM* item is costed, (b) whether an operation in the *Routing* has been costed or (c) what portion of *Fixed / Variable Costs* is used in the costing.

Remaining Variance: This is nothing but the difference between the *Target Cost* and the costs that can not be attributed to any single variance.

Remote Function Call (RFC): In ABAP, this refers to the 'calling' of a remote system using either a *Function Module* (in case the remote system is also a SAP system) or special programmed functions (in the case of non-SAP remote systems). The RFC may be (a) *Synchronous*, (b) *Asynchronous* or (c) *Transactional*.

Remote Function Module: Nothing but RFC-enabled *Function Module* like BAPI.

Remote User: A user logging on to a SAP system by *RFC* from an external location.

RemoteCube: Refers to an 'Infocube' wherein the structure of the cube is defined in SAP BW, but the reporting data is read from an external sources using a BAPI.

Reorder Point: in PP, this refers to the threshold value of the available stock (plant stock plus the fixed scheduled / receipt) below which procurement proposals may be created.

Repair Order: This refers to an order, in SD, for recording the business processes for handling the faulty goods send in by the customers for repairing.

Replacement Value: In FI-AA, this refers to the current valuation of an asset (which can be different from that of the *APC*) due to price changes (due to inflation or technological advancements).

Report Group: In CO, this refers to the collection of report(s) using *Report Writer* or *Report Painter*.

Report Painter: Helps in creating user-defined reports from the SAP supplied reports; the 'report painter' is a tool with which the reports can be created quickly, from various applications, by using the *Graphical Report Structure*.

Report Tree: Refers to the hierarchical arrangement of reports / pre-generated lists (both SAP supplied and user-defined) in the form of nodes attached to a tree.

Report Writer: Enabling to report from multiple application areas, the 'report writer' is used to create specific and complex reports using functions like *Sets / Variables / Cells / Key Figures*. Unlike *Report Painter*, this tool supports (a) multidimensional column structures, (b) user-defined inactive row/column combinations, and (c) using cells in column formulae.

Reporting Currency: Used in FI-LC for the consolidated financial statements, this is nothing but the *Group Currency*.

Reposting: In CO, this refers to the posting of Primary Costs under the original cost element (or the Sender).The 'reposting' may be of (1) *Periodic Reposting* (on a real-time basis) or (2 *Transactional Reposting* (costs are initially collected in a Clearing Cost Centre, then reposted a the end of a period)

Rescheduling: Refers to the automatic processing of *Backorders* in SD. During this process, the system checks the availability again and creates new delivery date(s) if required.

Reserved Stock: This is nothing but all the stock that has been reserved for withdrawl from the stock.

Residual Item: Refers to the un-cleared difference of amount during 'clearing' of an *Open Item* in FI.

Resource-Usage Variance: In CO, this refers to the difference between the *Target Cost* and the *Actual Cost* due to the usage of a different input than the one originally planned to be used.

Results Analysis (RA): In CO-PC, RA refers to the periodic valuation of orders / projects so as to understand the relationship between the costs and the progress (towards completion) of an order.

Retail Ledger: Used in IS-Retail, this is used to collect data from FI, CO, HR and MM as a part of the analytical application, *Profit Centre Analytics Retail*.

Retirement: In FI-AA, this relates to the removal of an asset from an *Asset Portfolio*.

Returnable Packaging: Refers to packaging or transportation equipment that is supplied to a customer but needs to be returned to the supplier (vendor).

Revaluation: Helping to valuate the assets at their *Replacement Values*, in FI-AA, this refers to the adjustments made to an asset for compensating for inflation or for adopting market value principles.

Revaluation Area: Refers to the *Depreciation Area* for recording asset revaluations, in FI-AA. Revaluations need to be recorded separately (in a separate 'revaluation areas') so as to keep the revaluation separately from that of the APC.

Revenue Account Determination: In SD, this refers establishment of *Revenue Accounts* for posting prices / discounts / surcharges. SAP uses the *Conditions* to determine the correct revenue accounts during the transaction postings.

Reversal: In FI, this is nothing but posting of an identical accounting document but on the opposite side of the account so as to offset the original transaction. A *Reversal Document* is created during a reversal.

Reverse Business Engineer: A tool in ASAP, this helps the customer who is running a SAP system to look back, from the data from the production environment, to analyze how the system is performing. This helps in identifying the potential for improvements in the business processes. This tool is used in the 3rd phase of the *ValueSAP*.

Rework: In CO-PC, this is taken as a variance as this relates to the costs involved in correcting the defects after a product has been manufactured.

Risk Category: In SD, this is used to group customers according to certain perceived credit risks associated with these customers.

Risk Matrix: In ASAP, this is used to plot the risks identified in a project, against the risk's influence on the project. The risks may be categorized as high, medium or low and presented in the matrix.

Roadmap: In ASAP, this refers to the framework for implementation or upgrade or continuous improvement of SAP application deployment using well defined 'stage gates' or 'mile-stones' or 'phases' which are characterized by well defined deliverables and clear documentation aided by tools and techniques, accelerators etc. The roadmap is made up of five phases: *(1) Project Preparation, (2) Business Blueprint, (3) Realization, (4) Final Preparation and (5) Go-Live & Support.*

Rollout Roadmap: In ASAP, this refers to the modified or localized roadmap for setting up the SAP system locally, and may be linked to a central system (for master data, for example).

Routing: In PP, this refers to the sequence of operations in a production process. A *Routing Group* can be used to group routings with various lot sizes. Refer Rate Routing also.

Run-Time Analysis: This is used to measure the performance of programs, transactions etc with an idea to identify the bottlenecks in the programming statements in terms of un-necessary use of 'select' loops or function modules, database accesses etc.

Run-Time Error: Documented in the system as *Short Dump*, this results from a program with errors which can not be handled during the program execution. When the 'short dump' is created, the system performs a *Database Rollback* as well.

Safety Stock: In PP / APO, this refers to the minimum stock that is always available to meet any unexpected high demand. Though not used in production (PP), this may be considered for production (in APO) should there be a delay expected in delivery.

Safety Time: In PP, this refers to the number of days the existing stock in the warehouse will meet the material requirements without any further material receipt.

Sales & Operations Planning (SOP): Supporting high-level and complex planning hierarchies, 'SOP' is a forecasting and planning tool used in setting targets for sales, production and supply chains based on historical / current / estimated data. Capable of both the *Top-Down and Bottom-Up planning*, this can be used for both *(1) Standard SOP and (2) Flexible SOP*.

Sales Activity: Refers to recording of the activities (sales call / telephone call / sales letter) involved in interacting with a customer or a prospective customer.

Sales Area: Refers to the combination of *Sales Organization, Distribution Channel and Division*. The 'sales area' can be used for reporting purposes. A *Sales Office* is assigned to a 'sales area'.

Sales Deduction Account: Refers to an account to which the sales discount / surcharges are posted.

Sales District: Refers to a geographical area (district or region) to which customers are assigned so as to generate certain sales statistics.

Sales Document: Consisting of a header and one or more document items, there are various types of sales documents like *Inquiry, Quotation, Sales Order, Outline Agreements (Contracts and Scheduling Agreements) and Complaints (Returns, Credit / Debit Memo Requests)*.

Sales Document Category: Made up of several *Sales Document Types*, 'sales document category' controls how the system proposes the right sales document. (The sales document category *'Sales Order'* includes Sales Document Types like *Standard Order (OR), Cash Sales (BV), Rush Order (SO)* etc).

Sales Document Type: Refers to the control indicator for processing the sales documents defined in the system according to the type of a business transaction. Some of the pre-defined 'sales document types' include *Inquiry (IN), Quotation (QT) and Sales Orders (OR)*.

Sales Group: Refers to an organizational group that is responsible for sales activities. The staff of a *Sales Office* may be formed into sales groups. Several *Sales Persons* can be assigned to a *Sales Group*.

Sales Office: Assigned to a *Sales Area*, this is nothing but the organizational unit in a geographical area of a Sales organization.

Sales Order: Received by the *Sales Area* that is responsible for fulfilling the order, a 'sales order' represents the request from a customer for delivery of goods / services at a specified time at the specified price.

Sales Order Costing: The method of costing the items in a *Sales Order* is known as 'sales order costing' in CO-PC.

Sales Order Stock: Refers to the stock that is retained in the warehouse for fulfilling a specific sales order.

Sales Organization: This is nothing but the top-most organizational unit that is responsible for selling / distributing the products / services. One or more *Distribution Channels* are attached to a 'sales organization'.

Sales Plan: The starting point for demand management, a sales plan consists of specification of sales in terms of quantities to be sold in a future period.

Sales Unit: Refers to the unit of measure in which an item is sold. It is possible to define several sales units for a single material as the system is capable of referring to the base unit of measure.

Sample Account: Refers to a master record that enables defining default values for Company Code-specific data in GL account master records. To make use of sample accounts, it is necessary that *Data Transfer Rules* are defined properly to control how the values are transferred from the sample accounts.

Sample Document: One of the *Reference Documents*, the 'sample document' is used to create default entries while creating an accounting document. The figures in the sample document will not update account balances, but the accounting document created with reference to a sample document will update the transaction figures.

Sample Organizational Unit: Refers to the country-independent organizational units configured in the default SAP system, which can be used to create new units by copying the same. Appropriate *Country Templates* needs to be applied to the copied units so as to localize them for the country in question. All the sample organizational units are numbered as '0001' in the standard system.

Sandbox Client: A copy of the *SAP Reference Client*, the 'sandbox Client' is a *Development Client* used by the entire implementation team to experiment with the customizing and testing.

SAP Add-on Installation Tool: Refers to a tool for installing / upgrading 'add-ons' directly from SAP system.

SAP Assistant: A PC tool used to access *BAPI, RFC* or *IDoc* Meta data from outside the SAP system.

SAP Best Practice: Refers to a SAP product that is nothing but industry-specific *ASAP* version and a *Pre-Configured System* that is ready to meet 80% of that industry's business requirements. Aimed at reducing implementation costs considerably, the 'SAP best practices' speed up the implementation.

SAP Business Connector: A middleware enabling bi-directional synchronous / asynchronous communication between SAP and SAP / non-SAP applications, this makes all SAP functions that are available via *BAPI / IDoc* accessible to business partners over the Internet as *XML*-based service.

SAP Business (Information) Warehouse: A core component of *SAP NetWeaver*, SAP BW provides data warehousing functions, with a business intelligence platform replete with a suit of business intelligence tools.

SAP Business Workflow: Aimed at cutting the lead time and cost of business processes to improve quality and efficiency, this workflow is nothing but an application component consisting of tools and technologies for automated control and editing of cross-application business processes.

SAP Collaborative Room: Provides users with a user-specific, context-sensitive and authorizations-based view on their projects. It integrates several communication services (such as poll, discussions, and conferencing tools), a document service and system services (such as user management) with business services (such as shopping cart, contract, and decision support).

SAP Easy Access: This is the initial menu displayed by the system when a user logs on to an ABAP-driven SAP system. This may be (1) *SAP Menu* or (2) *User Menu*. Users can add their favourite Transactions to the SAP Easy Access Menu.

SAP Going-Live Check: A remote service, done pro-actively, by SAP to analyze the SAP system on the verge of 'going-live', to determine the readiness for starting the production. The check consists of five *Service Sessions*: (1) *Project Session* – part of the project Preparation phase, the focus is on the planned implementation methodology, (2) *Project Feasibility Session* – done during the 2nd phase of the project implementation, the focus is to find out the feasibility of identified business process, and is done after the completion of the *Business Blueprinting*, (3) *Analysis Session* – focusing on hardware sizing this is typically done eight weeks before 'going-live', (4) *Optimization Session* – focus is on optimizing the application components and business processes configured in the system and (5) *Verification Session* – done around four weeks before 'going-live' this is focused on system behaviour, especially the system response time.

SAP GUI: Refers to the SAP system component on the *Presentation Server*, representing the SAP-specific GUI of the ABAP based *Application Server* applications.

SAP Maps: A comprehensive approach of implementing SAP, this analytical tool in SAP is helpful in developing and implementing tailor made SAP implementations by making use of (1) *SAP Solution Maps*, (2) *SAP Business Technology Map* and (3) *SAP Service Map*.

SAP Query: Refer ABAP Query / Query.

SAP Reference IMG: A complete implementation guide consisting of all the IMG activities arranged by application components.

SAP Smart Forms: A tool used to create forms in SAP; the 'smart forms' combine the print program component and the form component which were separate previously.

SAPNet: Also available to SAP partners / customers, this is the intranet portal of SAP that provides a role-based and personal interface using a Web browser as GUI. Employees can personalize SAPNet to their individual needs and can use SAPNet as personal inbox and central access point to Employee Self-Service and procurement.

SAPPHIRE: SAP conference that takes place several times a year, in various parts of the world where the customers and partners share SAP success stores / show-cause SAP developments or enhancements.

SAPscript: A text editor used in SAP for managing texts, besides creating SAP forms.

Schedule Line: Refers to the division of a sales item into various schedule lines according to quantity and delivery time.

Schedule Manager: Refers to a tool that is used to automate and simplify the definition, scheduling and execution of tasks / operations which are all run periodically (like period-end closing).

Scheduling: Referring to the calculation of 'start' and 'finish' dates of orders (or operations in an order), scheduling in PP is used in *Material Requirements Planning, Capacity Planning and Networks*. The scheduling may be of (a) *Forward Scheduling*, (b) *Backward Scheduling* and (3) *Current Date Scheduling*.

Scheduling Agreement: In MM, this refers to the *Outline Agreement* for procuring materials at pre-determined dates over a certain period in future.

Scheduling Type: In PM, this refers to an indicator controlling the calculation of due date for maintenance. The standard SAP system comes delivered with 'scheduling types' like *New Start, Manual Call, Scheduled* etc.

Scope: In ASAP, this refers to the business process boundaries identified for the SAP implementation. Around 80% of the scope is covered during the *Business Blueprint* phase of *ASAP Roadmap*.

Scrap: In QM, this refers to the non-conforming product that will not meet the quality requirements even after re-work, and the same can not be used for any other purpose. In MM, this refers just to the percentage of material that does not meet the quality standards.

Scrap Variance: This is nothing but the value of unplanned scrap occurring in the production process. The unplanned scrap is equal to the difference between the target scrap quantity and actual scrap quantity.

Scrapping: Refers to a posting in MM which results from intentional / unintentional destruction of material as the materials have deteriorated in quality or have become obsolete because of being in the storage for long.

Screen Painter: A tool for creating *Dialog Transaction Screens* in ABAP, the 'screen painter' is made up of a *Text Editor* for defining the *Flow Logic* underlying the *Form*, and a *Graphical Layout Editor* for designing the *Screen Layout*. The 'layout editor' can be run in (a) *Graphical Mode* or (b) *Alphanumeric Mode*.

Screen Variant: This is nothing but an object determining the input fields that will be displayed on a data entry screen.

Secondary Cost Element: Used in CO, the 'secondary cost elements' help in allocating costs for internal activities. Unlike *Primary Cost Elements*, these secondary cost elements do not have corresponding GL accounts in FI.

Secondary Index: In addition to the *Primary Index* created on the *Primary Key Fields* of a *Table*, it is possible to create additional indexes for the same Table, and these additional indexes are called as the 'secondary index'.

Segment: In FI, this refers to the division (*Business Segment* or *Geographical Segment*) of a company for which *Financial Statements* can be created for external reporting. It is possible to derive the segment during transaction postings, as segment is entered into the master record of a Profit Centre. In CO-PA, this is nothing but the combinational of *Characteristics*. See *Cycle* also.

Sender Cost Centre: This is nothing but the *Cost Centre* that provides *Activities* and / costs to other *Cost Objects*.

Sequence: In PP, this refers to the sequence of operations in a 'Routing'. The sequence may be *Standard* or *Alternative* or *Parallel*.

Service Part: This is a 'material' used in performing a repair in a service.

Service Report: Refers to the summarized findings from a *SAP Service* like *SAP Going-Live Check, SAP Early Watch Session* etc

Service Session: Refers to one of the several remote analyses done through *SAP Service*. For example: *SAP Going-Live Check* has five 'service sessions', with each of the sessions having specific objectives and detailed action lists to be performed. The service sessions are carried out using the computer-based *Service Session Workbench* that is an integral part of the *SAP Solution Manager*.

Session: In SAP, this refers to a connection between two logical units. When the connection is broken, the session 'expires'. SAP uses *Session Manager* (a graphical navigation interface used to manage one or more *SAP R/3 Systems* and several *Clients)* to manage the sessions.

Set: In FI-SL, a 'set' refers to specific or group of values assigned to a specific object. SAP's default sets include: *Basic Sets, Key-Figure Sets* and *Single / Multi-Dimension Sets*.

Settlement: In CO, this refers to the partial / full allocation of costs from one cost object (*Settlement Senders*) to another (*Settlement Receiver*). *Settlement Cost Elements* are used to in such settlements. All such settlements result in *Settlement Documents*.

Settlement Order: In PM, this is nothing but an order to which costs of a *Maintenance Order* can be settled.

Settlement Rule: Refers to the *Distribution Rule* that determines which portion of the *Settlement Sender*'s cost is settled to the *Settlement Reciver*(s).

Settlement Type: SAP comes delivered with several settlement types, used in CO, like *PER (periodic settlement), FUL (full settlement), AUC (capitalization of AuC), PRE (preliminary settlement) and LIS (line item settlement for AuC)*

Setup Order: Refers to a type of *Order* in PP, which is used in the initial stages of production to setup and prepare the line for production. In the case of PP-PI, this is known as *Setup Recipe*.

Shipping Document: In LE, this refers to the document for a shipping transaction. There are several shipping documents – like *Delivery, Grouped Delivery* etc - available in the standard system.

Shipping Notification: Containing the details like anticipated delivery date, quantity, material details etc, the 'shipping notification' is sent by the vendor to the recipient for intimating the details of the shipment. The notification can be by *EDI* or fax or any other media.

Ship-To Party: May not necessarily be the *Sold-to-Party* or *Bill-to-Party*, or even the *Payer*, the 'ship-to-party' is one who will receive the shipment from the vendor.

Short Dump: An error message created and saved when a program execution is terminated due to a *Run-Time Error*. Refer *Run-Time Error* also.

Shortened Fiscal Year: Used when there is change or shift from one *Fiscal Year* (say Jan-Dec) to another (say, Jul-Jun), the 'shortened fiscal year' is set-up in the system to cover the period from the end of the old fiscal year to the start of the new fiscal year (say, Jan to Jun).

Shutdown: In FI-AA, this refers to the temporary removal of a fixed asset from service, and is achieved by activating the indicator in the asset master record so that no depreciation is calculated by the system for this period.

Silk Road: In ABAP, this refers to one of the blended Code-pages containing Japanese, English and Greek scripts.

Silo Stock: Refers to the stock containing one material or one batch of a material stored in a silo. The 'silo stock', in PP, can be stored in different types of containers.

Simulation: In FI, this is a step used in 'creating' a transaction but before actually posting a document so as to ensure that the debits are equal to the credits. When simulated, the system brings up the data which helps in correcting the entries before actually posting the transaction. 'Simulation' does not update the database.

Simulation Costing: In CO, this is used to cost the changed single / multi-level assemblies within a structure of a product so as to have an understanding cost implication of 'what if' there is a change in the assembly.

Simultaneous Costing: In CO-PC, this is nothing but the process of assigning the actual costs incurred, till date, to a cost object.

Single Material: In LE, this refers to the storage of a single material in a single bin location. Once defined as 'single storage, the system will allow to store only one bin quantity for that bin location.

Single Sign-On: Refers to a mechanism which obviates the need for signing-on to multiple systems;

a 'single log-in' is sufficient to access any number of systems brought under this setup for an authorized user.

Single-Level BOM: Refers to a 'BOM' made up of direct components of an 'assembly'. This can also contain an assembly as a component, but the assembly is not exploded any further.

Slow Moving Item: Refers to an inventory item that has not been moved out for a long time.

Smart Implementation: Referring to the comprehensive technical solution for implementing *mySAP.com (SAP ERP)* components easily and quickly, the 'smart implementation' has many advantages like (1) *Easy Configuration and Automatic Installation* (using *Configuration Assistant*), (2) *Pre-Configured Software* components (Web server, ITS instances etc), (3) *Easy Integration* into a system landscape, (4) *SAP Best Practices* etc.

SOAP: *Simple Object Access Protocol.*

Software Development Manager: Refers to a tool in SAP, for delivering non-SAP ABAP developments.

Sold-To-Party: Refers to the person or company placing an Order for goods / services. Though this party can perform the functions of *Bill-to-Party, Payer* etc, it is not necessary that 'sold-to-party' should be the same as that of *Bill-to-Party,* or *Payer,* or *Ship-to-Party.*

Solution Review: In ASAP, this refers to the review of the application design and the business process parameters considered for implementation in a SAP system, and the review can be scheduled as early as the 2nd Phase.

Source Document: In FI, this refers to the original document from which one or more accounting documents are generated. The system assigns a unique number to the 'source document', which is saved in the corresponding accounting document(s) for easy tracing back and forth.

Source List: Refers to the list of sources for a material, with details like when a source will be able to supply that material.

Special Asset for Gain / Loss Posting: Not an actual fixed asset, in FI-AA, this refers to an asset master record created with the sole purpose of collecting gain / loss arising out of asset retirements.

Special GL Account: Refers to a *Reconciliation Account* for recording special business transactions like *Guarantees, Down Payments,* and *Bill of Exchanges* in the sub-ledger, this special GL account should not be balanced with the A/R and A/P. An indicator, called *Special GL Indicator,* is used by the SAP system to identify a special GL transaction.

Special Period: Refers to the last regular *Posting Period* that has been divided into one or more (not exceeding four) posting periods for enabling closing operations.

Special Purpose Ledger (FI-SL): A customer-defined ledger used for reporting purposes, the 'special purpose ledger' can be used either as a *GL* or as a *Sub-Ledger* with the necessary account assignments like account, region, business area etc.

Special Stock: In MM, this refers to some of the stock materials, like *Consignment Stock,* that needs to be stocked separately because of reasons like ownership, location etc. MM uses *Special Stock Indicators* (E-Sales Order Stock, Q-Project Stock, W-Consignment Stock with Customer etc) to denote such stocks separately from other stocks.

Split Revaluation of Depreciation: Mandatory in some of the countries, this is necessary to adjust the revaluated depreciation for the inflation. The current month's revaluated depreciation is to be debited to the *Depreciation Expense Account* and credited to the *Accumulated Depreciation Account.* The revaluated accumulated depreciation needs to be treated separately: debited to

Inflation Gain / Loss Account and credited to *Accumulated Depreciation Account*.

Split Valuation: In MM, it is possible to valuate differently, the different stocks of a single material using 'split valuation'. This is required in case a portion of the stock is procured internally, and the rest procured externally. SAP allows different 'account assignments' for these two different stocks, of the same material, and valuate them at different prices.

Splitscreen Editor: In ABAP, it is possible to display / edit two different programs, even if they belong to two different systems, side by side on the same screen using 'split screen editor'.

Spool Request: In SAP, this refers to the document sent to the *Printer* or *Archiving*. The 'spool request' contains the data relating to *Print List* of the current program.

Spread: Also known as the *Exchange Rate Spread* or *Exchange Spread*, this refers to the difference between the *Spot Rate* and the *Buy /Offer Rate*.

SSO Administration Wizard: A system tool in SAP that will enable configuration of logon tickets for *Single Sign-On (SSO)*.

Staging: In SAP BW, this is nothing but the process of preparing the data in a *Data Warehouse*.

Staging Area: In SD, this refers to an intermediate storage area in a warehouse, located near the doors. The 'staging area' is used for GR or GI before the goods are 'received' or 'issued'.

Standard BOM: Used internally for *Plant Maintenance* and *Standard Networks*, the components of a 'standard BOM' represent frequently occurring structures that are not object-dependent.

Standard Cost: Refers to a cost that will remain stable over a long period of time. Based on an activity unit, the 'standard cost' of material can remain stable at least for a year.

Standard Cost Estimate: The most important costing type in material costing, in CO-PC, the 'standard cost estimate' is typically created for each of the materials at the beginning of an year (or season) and is expected to remain unchanged for that year / season. These estimates form the basis for *Profit Planning / Product Costing* with focus of determining the variances.

Standard Hierarchy: In *Cost Centre Accounting*, this refers to a tree-like structure consisting of all the *Cost Centres* of a *Controlling Area*. Assigned to the lowest nodes in the tree, the cost centres may be grouped into *Cost Centre Categories* and represented in the hierarchy just above the end nodes. The name of the top-most node of the 'standard hierarchy' needs to be mentioned when the controlling area is defined. In the case of *Activity Based Costing*, the same structure holds well except that instead of Cost Centre, it is the *Business Process* that is assigned to the end nodes of the tree.

Standard Layout: In FI-SL, the 'standard layout' provides the default values (that can be changed) for the parameters for the reports. The layout parameters include row / column total parameters, row / column text parameters, general parameters like page length / width etc.

Standard Material Type: Defined in a standard SAP system, the 'standard material type' includes *Raw Materials* and *Semi-Finished* products.

Standard Price: In MM, this refers to the constant price of valuating a material irrespective of the goods movements and invoices.

Statistic: In ABAP, this refers to the one of the three types of *ABAP Query*. Refer *ABAP Query / SAP Query / Query* also.

Statistical Key Figure (SKF): Refers to the statistical values describing the cost objects (cost centre, order, profit centres etc) in controlling. SKF is used as the basis for allocating costs, when it is difficult to apportion the common costs. A number of SKFs can be grouped into a *Statistical Key Figure Group* for processing these SKFs in a single step.

Statistical Order: Not an 'Order' in the strict sense, 'statistical orders' are used in controlling only for informational purposes as it is not possible to settle the costs of a statistical order.

Statistical Posting: Refers to the transactions (say, *Down Payment Request*) in *Special GL Accounts* with the offsetting entries posted automatically to a clearing account defined.

Steering Committee: In ASAP, this refers to the decision making body which provides the direction during implementation.

Stock Determination: Using *Stock Determination Rule* and *Stock Determination Group*, the 'stock determination' is a process to determine the stock from which a material is withdrawn (for stock removal or staging operations or order fulfilment).

Stock-in-Transfer: The material that has been taken out of the stock, but has not yet arrived at the point of receipt. The 'stock-in-transfer' material is considered as part of the valuated stock but is not available for 'unrestricted usage'. The essential difference between the *Stock-in-Transfer* and *Stock-in-Transit* is that while the former denotes transfer postings (excluding movements arising out of *Stock Transfer Orders*) within *Inventory Management*, the later arises because of *Stock Transfer Order*.

Stock-in-Transit: Refers to the material withdrawn from storage at the issuing plant based on a *Stock Transport Order*, but has not reached the receiving plant. This also forms a part of the valuated stock but is not available for 'unrestricted usage'. The essential difference between the *Stock-in-Transfer* and *Stock-in-Transit* is that while the former denotes transfer postings (excluding movements arising out of *Stock Transfer Orders*) within *Inventory Management*, the later arises because of *Stock Transfer Order*.

Storage Area: In LE, this refers to a logical or physical area based on the storage type.

Storage Bin: Often referred to as a *Slot*, this is the smallest storage space in a warehouse. The address of a 'storage bin' is determined based on *Coordinates*. Example: Coordinate 04-05-03 represents the bin at level 3, under stack 5 at row 4.

Storage Location: In LO, this represents an organization unit differentiating storage of various stocks of a material in a *Plant*. One or more 'storage locations' are assigned to a single plant.

Storage Type: In WM, this is nothing but physical or logical division of a warehouse for carrying out certain functions. The 'storage type' may be of GR area, GI area, Picking area and so on.

Straight-Line Depreciation: Refers to the method of depreciating a fixed asset, evenly throughout its economic life, so as to ensure that the *Book Value* of the asset becomes zero at the end of this period. Refer *Depreciation Method* also.

Stress Test: In ASAP, this refers to testing the entire SAP environment which has just been deployed to test all the components to ensure that it performs to the pre-determined levels. Involving cooperation from *Users, Basis / Application Consultants*, the test aims at pushing the system to its peak capacity so as to make the system reliable and fast enough for the production usage.

Structure Modeler: Using MS-Visio, it is possible to display the SAP enterprise organizational structure in a graphical way using this modeler in ASAP.

Sub-Contracting: A form of outsourcing, 'sub-contracting' in MM refers to the processing of materials (supplied by a customer), by an external supplier.

Subledger Accounting: In FI, this refers to managing the accounts of vendors, customers, and assets at the subsidiary ledger level. SAP uses *Reconciliation Accounts* in GL while managing the sub-ledgers.

Substitution: Refers to automatically substituting the values as they are entered into the SAP system, based on certain Boolean logic.

Supply Chain: Refers to the sequence of operations / centres through which the supplies move from one supplier to the ultimate customer or point of usage.

Supply Chain Cockpit: One of the planning applications of the *Advanced Planner and Optimizer (APO)*, the *Supply Chain Cockpit (SCC)* is a graphical instrument panel for modelling, navigating and controlling the supply chain. It acts as a top planning layer through which the user can oversee other planning areas within an enterprise including demand, manufacturing, distribution and transportation.

Support Package: Compiled periodically and made available at *SAP Market Place*, the support package refers to the corrections for serious software errors of SAP software. SAP provides a tool called *Support Package Manager* for importing the support packages into the SAP system.

Support Release: Represents the SAP software release, together with all the *SAP Support Packages* till a certain point of time. SAP recommends using this 'support releases' as it may take a long time to import all the support packages for an earlier release.

Surcharge: In FI, this refers to an additional tax levied, in India, over and above the *Withholding Tax*.

SWIFT Code: Used for faster and automated bank payment settlements, this *Society for Worldwide Inter-bank Financial Transactions (SWIFT)* Code refers to the code assigned to individual banks.

System Administration Assistant: SAP's online tool for simple administration of SAP system(s).

Table Category: In ABAP, this refers to how a Table is implemented physically. The 'Table categories' include (1) *Transparent Database Tables*, (2) *Pooled Table* (Table data stored in Table Pool) and (3) *Cluster Table* (Table data stored in Table Cluster).

Table Cluster: This is nothing but the database Table containing the data from several logical *Cluster Tables*.

Table Pool: This is nothing but the database Table containing the data from several logical *Pooled Tables*.

TAN: In FI, this refers to the *Tax Account Deduction Number* used in India, which is issued to all legal entities and natural persons for deducting *Withholding Tax*. If a company has more than one legal entitities, then there will be more than one TAN.

Target Costs: In CO-PC this refers to the costs expected to be incurred when certain quantity is produced. The target costs are used to find out the variances, to valuate WIP and to valuate the unplanned scrap.

Target Quantity: In SD, this refers to the total quantity of a material a customer agrees to buy from a vendor.

Target = Actual Activity Allocation: An allocation technique in controlling wherein actual quantities to be allocated are not entered directly but calculated by the system based on the planned activity input of the receivers.

Task: In *ASAP Roadmap*, a 'task' is at the lowest level, containing instructions to be followed by a project team member. A number of tasks represent an *Activity*. A task can also denote an essential element in the *Transport System*: in this case a user can use a task to lock or unlock cross-Client objects for specific processing.

Tax Category: In SD, this refers to the 'categorization' used by the system to apply the 'country-specific taxation' during pricing.

Tax Code: Refers to the 2-digit code enabling the system to use certain specifications (like *Tax Rate, Tax Type – Input or Output Tax, Calculation Method – Percentage Included or Percentage Separate*) for tax determination.

Tax Depreciation: In FI-AA, this is calculated to meet the special tax regulations, and is normally more than the *Book Depreciation*. The difference is shown as a special entry on the liability side of the balance sheet.

TDS Return: In FI, this is a statement showing the income *Tax Deducted at Source (TDS)* in India. The statement, showing the details of TDS deposited in a bank, is to be filed with the tax department.

Tear Down: Refers to the process, in PP, wherein a work centre is restored to its normal state after a production process.

Technical Review: In ASAP, this refers to an analysis of the technical implementation components and operational procedures such as security, backup, performance management, printing and desktop operations. Typically, it is performed during the *Business Blueprint* phase.

Technical Specification: In ASAP, this refers to the technical requirements for developing *enhancement / interfaces / reports / conversions / forms* etc for fulfilling the requirements outlined in a *Functional Specification*.

Test Case: A procedure to test an object in SAP, this is a description for either manual testing or automated testing using CATT. Refer CATT also.

Test Catalog: Denotes one or more *Test Cases* in *Hypertext* format with some supplementary information or link to supplementary documents.

Test Plan: Represents a set of *Test Cases* used at a particular time for a particular purpose, and is based on one or more *Test Catalogs*.

Test Procedure: In ASAP, this refers to the procedure outlining how to set up, test and evaluate a particular *Test Case*.

Test Workbench: A tool in SAP for managing the *Test Cases in Test Catalogs*.

Third-Party Order Processing: Refers to a type of external procurement in which a PO is issued to a vendor with the instruction to supply the ordered materials to (or perform the services for) a third party.

Third-Party Purchase Order: Refers to a PO which is issued to a vendor with the instruction to supply the ordered materials to (or perform the services for) a third party.

TODO: A software *Quality Assurance* program that allows developers to find formal errors in their programs. It also provides an overview of the status of the checks they have carried out. The TODO, running regularly in the *Consolidation System*, monitors *ABAP code, Usability, Messages and IMG structures*. Results from this check are then transported back to the *Development Systems*, and the monthly status reports in QM are based on these results. Use the Transaction Code *TODO*.

Total Variance: In CO-PC, this is nothing but the difference between the *Target Costs* calculated in the *Standard Cost Estimate* for a material and the *Actual Costs*. This can also be represented by the difference between the debit and credit for an order.

Tracing Factor: In CO, this is a 'user-defined key' for calculating cost / quantity assignments in periodic allocation.

Trading Partner: In FI-LC, this refers to a legally independent entity belonging to the same group of companies.

Transaction Code: Entered in the Command Field, in a SAP transaction screen, the 'transaction code' identifies a transaction in SAP. Made up of alphabets A to Z and numerals 0 to 9 a transaction code can contain a maximum of 20 characters including underscore (_), with the stipulation that it should begin only with a letter. Use Transaction *Code 93* to maintain / change / display transaction codes.

Transaction Figures: In FI, this refers to the sum of all postings made to an account, broken down into *Posting Period*-wise credits and debits.

Transaction Type: In FI-AA, this denotes various transactions like acquisitions, retirements, transfer etc. For example the transaction type 100 is used for 'external acquisition', 120 for 'goods receipt', 150 for 'acquisition from affiliated company' and so on. A 'transaction type' belongs to a *Transaction Type Group*.

Transparent Table: This is a database Table defined in *ABAP Dictionary* and created in the database.

Transport: In *CTS (Change & Transport System),* this refers to the movement of objects from one SAP system to the other. The components to be transported are listed in the *Transport Request*. Each transport undergoes a two-stage operation: (1) An *Export* process reads the objects or components to be transported from the *Source System* and stores the same in a data file at the *Operating System* level, and (2) An *Import* process reads this information from the data file and writes the same into the database of the *Target System*. Every 'transport process' is duly logged by the system for easy *Roll-backs*.

Transport Management System: A part of CTS, this refers to a set of tools provided by SAP for organizing, performing and monitoring *Transports* in SAP system.

Transport Request: In CTS, this refers to a document for copying corrections between different system types. It records released corrections. When the transport request is released, the transport is performed.

Troubleshooting Roadmap: Refers to a guide for 'quick diagnosis' of problems in the SAP System. It enables the administrator to localize the causes of standard problems and technical difficulties for taking appropriate action.

Unchecked Delivery: An 'unchecked delivery' can be converted to a delivery with a document status 'checked', which can be used for subsequent functions such as picking, packing or posting goods issue.

Uniform Valuation: Refers to valuating all the stocks of a material with the same *Valuation Criteria*.

Unit Costing: In CO-PC, this refers to a method of costing that does not use BOM or routings. It calculates planned costs for base planning objects. It also supports detailed cost planning for objects like orders, projects, cost objects, material cost estimates with quantity structure.

Unit of Measure (UOM): Denoting the size of a quantity of a material, the 'unit of measure' in SAP includes unit of issue, base unit of measure, unit of entry etc.

Unloading Point: In SD, this refers to the goods receiving point at the *Ship-to-Party's* location.

Unplanned Depreciation: Refers to the (permanent) reduction in an asset's value, due to the occurrence of unexpected events (like fire).

Usage Variance: In CO, this denotes the difference between the planned and actual costs arising out of higher usage of inputs / time that what was planned originally.

Use Tax: In FI-AP, this refers to the one-time tax levied on the usage of a personal property which is purchased in another state.

Useful Life: This is nothing but the economic life of an asset within which period the asset is depreciated fully. The 'useful life' – normally lower than that of the actual technical life - can be different in the individual depreciation areas.

Valuated Stock: Refers to the stock of a material owned by a firm that is part its current assets. The valuated stock of a material at a plant is the sum of *(1) Unrestricted-use stock, (2) Stock in quality inspection, and (3) Stock-in-Transfer.*

Valuation Area: In MM, this is an organizational unit in Logistics, subdividing an enterprise for the purpose of uniform and complete valuation of material stocks.

Valuation Class: Assigning materials to a group of GL accounts, the 'valuation class' determines the GL accounts that are updated as a result of a valuation-relevant transaction or event such as a goods movement. The valuation class makes it possible to (1) post the stock values of materials of the same material type to different GL accounts, and (2) post the stock values of materials of different material types to the same GL account.

Valuation Method: In FI, this refers to the method of foreign currency valuation as a part of closing process. In FI-AA, this refers to how an asset is valuated – through *Depreciation Key, Useful Life* etc – during its economic life.

Valuation Procedure: In MM, this refers to the option of valuating the materials according to different principles like LIFO, FIFO etc.

Valuation Strategy: In CO-PC, this refers to the strategy for the valuation of materials, internal activities, and external activities in costing. It depends on the *Costing Variant* and the *Valuation Variant*.

Valuation Type: In FI-AA, this refers to the criteria of valuating an asset in a *Depreciation Area*. In addition to APC, the asset can be valuated using special valuation types like *Revaluation, Interest, Special Depreciation, Investment Support* etc.

Valuation Variant: The 'valuation variant' controls how the materials and activities in the cost estimate are valuated, in CO-PC. While a *global valuation variant* is valid for all plants, a local valuation variant is valid only for a specific plant. The valuation variant specifies the parameters like (1) price in the material master (such as the *standard price*) or in the purchasing info record (such as the *net order price*) that is used to cost a material in the BOM, (2) planned or actual price that is used to valuate the internal activities, (3) version in Cost Center Accounting that is used to valuate internal activities, (4) *costing sheet* that is used to calculate overhead and (5) whether, and to what extent, a BOM item or an operation in the routing is relevant to costing. In *Cost Object Controlling*, the 'valuation variant' that can is used for the valuation of work-in-process at *Target Costs* and for the valuation of *Scrap Variances*.

Value Filed: In *Costing-based PA*, 'value fields' represent the highest level of detail for analyzing quantities, revenues, sales deductions, and costs for *Profitability Segments* in profitability analysis or *Contribution Margin Accounting*.

ValueSAP: In ASAP, this is a strategic initiative geared toward optimizing the benefits of SAP software over the entire life cycle. 'ValueSAP' provides a combination of methods, tools, services and programs that are used in a targeted manner in the phases '*Discovery & Evaluation*', '*Implementation*', and '*Continuous Business Improvement*' to maximize the ROI *(Return on Investment)*.

Variable Depreciation: In FI-AA, this refers to the calculation of depreciation proportional to the multiple-shift usage of an asset. Refer *Multiple-shift Depreciation* also.

Variance Category: In CO, this refers to the categorization of variances based on the nature of their cause. The variances on the *Input* side are categorized into scrap variance (CO-PC), resource usage variance, input price / quantity variance etc. On the *Output* side the 'variance category' includes output price / quantity variance, lot size variance, fixed cost variance (CO-PC), mixed price variance and so son.

Variance Variant: This is nothing but the parameter determining the variance categories that are calculated in the system.

Variant BOM: A non-configurable BOM, 'variant BOM' is a combination of a number of BOMs describing one or more products that have a number of identical components. Refer *Bill of Material (BOM) Category* also.

Variant Configuration: Refers to the description of complex products that are manufactured in many variants, for example, motor bikes. All variants are defined as one *Variant Product*, which has a *Super BOM*, containing all the components that can be used in the product, and a *Super Task List*, containing all the operations that can be used to manufacture the product. By assigning the 'variant product' to a class, the characteristics are assigned to the variant product. These characteristics are used to describe an individual variant. Object dependencies ensure that the correct components are selected from the *Super BOM* and the correct operations are selected from the *Super Task List*.

Vendor Account: A 'vendor account' contains transaction figures arising out of business transactions and these value movements are recorded as periodic totals in A/P subsidiary ledger. All the payables to the vendors are recorded simultaneously in a GL account by assigning a *Reconciliation Account* in the master record of the vendors.

Vendor Evaluation: In MM, this decision making functionality helps in the selection / control of *Sources of Supply*. The system assigns score to each of the main criteria (like price, quantity, delivery reliability etc) based on weightage given by the user for each of the criteria. The user will also decide the maximum attainable score against which the system generated score for a particular source or vendor is compared and evaluated.

Vendor Net Procedure: This procedure enables to post materials to the inventory at invoice price less the cash discounts eligible.

Vendor Quotation: Refers to an offer from a vendor to a *Purchasing Organization* to supply materials or perform certain services as per certain agreed upon terms and conditions.

Vendor-Managed Inventory: The vendor manages the materials of the customer-company's requirements, and is possible only when the vendor has access to customer's current stock and sales data, which may be made possible through EDI.

Version: In CO, this enables more than one planning (say optimistic plan data, pessimistic plan data etc) for the same object for the same fiscal year. The 'version' is nothing but the collection of fiscal-year dependent indicators like value date, methods of calculating actual activity prices, exchange rate type, copying allowed etc.

View: Refers to the fields from one or more Tables with a common interface. A view is created by business criteria, using the Transaction Code SE54 (same as that of General Table Maintenance).

View Cluster: This is nothing but the collection of several *Views*.

Virtual Account Number: This is dummy bank account number, in FI, issued by the *House Bank* to identify the payments from customers.

Virtual SAP System: Refers to a SAP system used as a place holder for another SAP system which has not yet been configured.

Volume-based Rebate: In MM, this denotes the period-end cumulative discount granted by a vendor to a customer, and is based on the volume of transaction the vendor had with that customer during that period.

Walkthrough: In ASAP, this refers to the *EPC (Event-driven Process Chain)* wherein the user is 'walked-through' the entire process, step-by-step, stopping at every function, process etc so as ensure that the user understands the process flow and the dependencies within EPC.

WBS Element: This is nothing but a task / partial task in the *Work Breakdown Structure* (WBS) in the hierarchical organization of a project.

Web Application Builder: This is a tool that enables development of web applications - both *ITS (Internet Transaction Server) based* and *BSP (Business Server Pages)* based - from *ABAP/4 Workbench*.

Web Reporting: This helps the users to access the business information in a SAP system through a *Web Browser*. Made possible by a special *WebRFC* to access the data from the SAP system, 'web reporting' also has the flexibility of interactive reporting as that of the traditional *ABAP/4 Reports*.

WIP Calculation: In CO-PC, this refers to the period-end procedure for calculating the *Work-In-Progress (WIP)* for both Production Orders and Process Orders. Once settled, WIP postings will be generated in FI.

Withholding Tax: A kind of tax (Income Tax, in India) which is normally deducted (at source) at the beginning of the value flow. The amount so deducted (withheld) is paid to the tax authority on behalf of the person who has been subjected to the tax. SAP supports both (1) *Classic Withholding Tax* and (2) *Extended Withholding Tax*. (The 'extended withholding tax' allows assigning of more than one *'withholding tax type'* to a *Business Partner,* and is used in countries like Argentina).

Work Centre: In LO, this refers to an organizational unit which defines where and when an operation needs to be performed. Each 'work centre' has an *Available Capacity*. The work centre can be machine, people, assembly line etc. The activities performed at the work centre (or by the work centre) are valuated by taking into account the activity price or charge rate. Several work centres with common characteristics are grouped to form *Work Centre Groups*.

Work Centre Hierarchy: A hierarchical arrangement of work centres at various levels; this is used in capacity planning to cumulate the available capacities or capacity requirements. It is also used to locate work centers.

Work Order: A generic term used to denote a task to be performed, the 'work order' may be of production order, process order, maintenance order, inspection order etc.

Work Package: Refers to the collection of several groups of activities to complete a major portion of a phase in *ASAP Roadmap*. More than one 'work packages' constitute a phase.

Work Plan: Refers to a subset of the *Project Pan,* a 'work plan' is made up of detailed set of *Phases, Work Packages, Activities* and *Tasks* from the *ASAP Roadmap*. Organized in a project management planning tool such as *Microsoft Project*, the work plan may result in a *Gantt Chart* to display timelines, dependencies, and resources.

Workbench Organizer: A part of the *Change & Transport Organizer (CTO)* within the *CTS (Change & Transport System)*, the 'workbench organizer' is a tool to manage - both centralized and de-centralized - development projects in *ABAP Workbench*.

Workflow Builder: A modelling tool in SAP for defining a 'workflow'.

Worklist: In LO, this represents the grouping of documents requiring follow-up action. From the *Worklist Overview*, it is possible to perform the follow-up action either for a single document or multiple documents.

Worklist Monitor: A tool in *Schedule Manager*, this is used to monitor and manage the 'worklists'.

WorkSpace: Refers to the right-hand side frame of the web browser in a *mySAP (SAP ERP) Workplace*. Called also as a *Push Area*, this browser frame is used for displaying the user-specific business applications.

WWI: Used in *EHS (Environment Health & Safety)*, this is a modified version of MS-Word that is called from a SAP system to edit a document template.

XBRL: Based on XML, XBRL (*eXtensible Business Reporting Language*) can be used by the enterprises to create, publish, analyse and compare information, with special emphasis to financial statements.

XRFC: Previously known as *RFC-XML*, this is the XML format for transmitting *RFC (Remote Function Call)*.

XSF: This is nothing but the XML for *SmartForms*.

XXL: Known as *eXtended eXport of Lists*, XXL is a tool available in SAP for downloading list objects like spreadsheets from SAP to PC environment.

XXL List Viewer: This tool presents SAP data in MS-Excel, taking into account the information supplied by SAP on the structure of the data. It makes available special functions in a separate menu and toolbar, and also limits Excel functions to guarantee the consistency of data supplied by SAP.

Year-end Closing: Refers to the closing of accounting, in FI, at the fiscal year's end so as to bring out the external statutory requirements like *Balance Sheet*, and *Profit & Loss Statement*.

Year-end Settlement: In CO, this refers to the settlement of *Investment Orders* that have not yet been closed. These orders are settled to *AuC (Assets under Construction)*, at the end of the fiscal year.

Yield: In CO-PC, this denotes the production that is not categorized as *Scrap*. According to PP, this is nothing but the production that meets the quality standards.

ZZ

Zero Clearing: In FI, this refers to the clearing of 'open items' in one or more accounts, which does not involve any clearing postings.

Zero Stock Check: Refers to a check / inventory procedure which checks when a storage bin becomes empty after a goods movement, whether the storage bin is really empty. This is to ensure accuracy of stock figures, and the result is communicated to the system during the confirmation of the *Transfer Order*.

List of Figures

Index

11

Index

A

ABAP List Viewer, 22
ABAP/4 Dictionary Elements, 23
ABAP/4 Program Types, 18
ABAP/4 Query, 22
ABC, 149
Accelerated SAP, 33
Access Sequence, 64
Account Assignment, 69, 74, 97
    Group, 97
    Model, 69
Account Category Reference, 200
Account Currency, 59
Account Determination, 96, 97
    Automatic, 96
    Material, 96
    Revenue, 96, 97
Account Group, 76, 79, 89
    Customer, 89
    Vendor, 89
Account ID, 94
Account Key, 63, 97
Account Type, 68
Accounting Document, 67
Accounts Payable (s), 45, 106
Accounts Receivable, 45
Accrued Costs, 170
Accumulated Depreciation, 132
Acquisition & Production Costs, 130, 132

Activity Based Costing, 149
Activity Dependent Costs, 162
Activity Independent Costs, 162
Activity Price Calculation, 166
Activity Price, 158, 166, 170
Activity Type, 158
Activity Type Group, 158
Actual Cost Entry, 167
ALE, 20
Allocation, 100, 154
Allocation Cost Element, 170
Allocation Price Variance, 167
Allocation Structure, 165
Allowed Payer, 91
Alternate Chart of Accounts, 52
Alternate Hierarchy, 157
Alternate Payee, 90
Alternate Payer, 90
ALV, 22
ALV Programming, 22
APC, 130, 132
Application Layer, 15
Application Link Enabling, 20
Archiving, 81, 128
ASAP, 33, 35
    BPML, 35
    Roadmap Phases, 33
    Roadmap, 33
Assessment in Secondary Cost Planning, 164
Assessment, 154, 158, 164, 165

B

C

D

Notes

+65 6875 1519   Agnes
+65 6323 1516

Kinkos
609 799 4568 Fax no

CIS00Z00 &
72SKXU9Y

→ Indira Dixit — 732-476-8745

Vidya 609-269-8364
      609-216-3952